CRIMES OF WRITING

BOOKS BY SUSAN STEWART

Theory

Nonsense: Aspects of Intertestuality in Folklore and Literature

*On Longing, Narratives of the Miniature, the Gigantic,
the Souvenir, the Collection*

Poetry

Yellow Stars and Ice

The Hive

CRIMES OF WRITING

Problems in the Containment of Representation

SUSAN STEWART

New York   Oxford
Oxford University Press
1991

Oxford University Press

Oxford   New York   Toronto
Delhi   Bombay   Calcutta   Madras   Karachi
Petaling Jaya   Singapore   Hong Kong   Tokyo
Nairobi   Dar es Salaam   Cape Town
Melbourne   Auckland

and associated companies in
Berlin   Ibaden

Library of Congress Cataloging-in-Publication Data
Stewart, Susan.
Crimes of writing:
problems in the containment of representation / Susan Stewart.
p.   cm.   Includes bibliographical references and index.
ISBN 0-19-506617-0
1. Literary forgeries and mystifications.
2. Mimesis in literature. 3. Law and literature.
4. Ut pictura poesis (Aesthetics)   I. Title.
PN171.F6S74   1991
098'.3—dc30   90-39822

1 2 3 4 5 6 7 8 9

Printed in the United States of America
on acid-free paper

For George McFadden

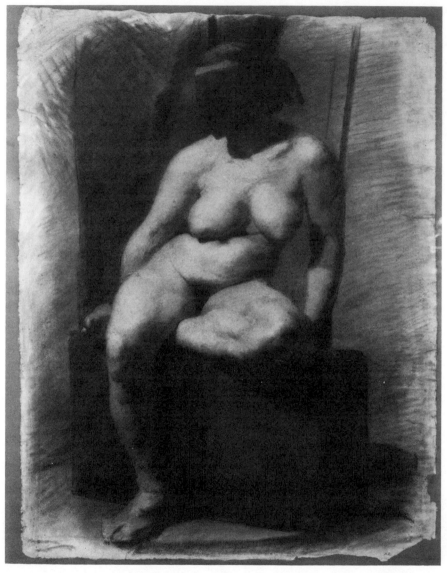

Thomas Eakins. *Nude Woman Seated Wearing a Mask* (1874–1876). (Courtesy of the Philadelphia Museum of Art; given by Mrs. Thomas Eakins and Miss Mary Adeline Williams.)

Preface

Several years ago, at the entrance to a large exhibit of Thomas Eakins's work at the Philadelphia Museum of Art, I saw for the first time the charcoal drawing on the facing page. According to Eakins's biographer and critic, Lloyd Goodrich, the drawing is one of a series of twenty-one sketches of nude models, men and women, done by the artist at an early stage in his career.[1] The museum now dates the series of drawings as from 1874 to 1876, which would mean that they were completed when Eakins taught evening life classes at the Philadelphia Sketch Club during those years.

Abstract, massive, characterized, as Goodrich notes, by plays of light and shadow and, at the same time, tremendous weight, this work nevertheless compels us to look at that bandage or obstruction that is precisely the site of nonlooking: the blindfold. Nude women models as a rule in Philadelphia—and even occasionally in as cosmopolitan a city as Paris, where Eakins had spent some time working and studying before his return to Philadelphia in 1870—were blindfolded. Such a blindfold protected the anonymity of the model and of course, as a consequence, protected the anonymity of all concerned. Yet the blindfold would also refuse the possibility of drawing a seeing being seen, and this is the quality of the drawing of most consequence for the project I have conducted here.[2]

This problem—the impossibility of a seeing that could see itself seeing, and consequently of a writing that could write itself writing— appears at the limit of representation; it *is* the limit that defines the very possibility of representation, the blank or blinded time/space that enables all representation to *take* time and space. As we shall see in the essays that follow, a fundamental detachment—of writing from context, of speaking from voice, of a proper name freed from its body in forgery, and of a body freed from its proper name in imposture and pornography—enables a simultaneous formalization and fragmentation of practices, now severed from their particular origins. Thus the art student who draws the seeing of an inability to see seeing, both masters an object of representation by abstracting it to form and mass[3] and accepts the limiting contingency of all representation as "standing for" and "standing in." We find here the transformation of a limit, then, into a kind of rule or standard. The student's practice, as a mastery of contingency, must continue to impose form and stasis, to inscribe where before there was only light, shadow, and motion. It is clear from the outset, then, that we cannot consider this mastery as a reduction, for to do so is simply to retrospectively impose a repleteness and totality on the object of the artist's practice that could only arise in compensation for that practice.

The introduction to this study will look further into the historical emergence of the concept of representation in late-seventeenth- and early-eighteenth-century writings on politics and aesthetics, but what immediately should engage us in the problematic of the Eakins drawing is an allusion that arose for me at the entrance to the exhibition: that is, the ways in which this drawing is an aesthetic, and secular, version of the figure of Justice as blindfolded. Of course, if Eakins had wanted to produce an allegorical figure of Justice, he would have done so. But in this work, as in his small masterpiece *William Rush Carving the Allegorical Figure of the Schuylkill River* (1876), he chose to depict the emergence of allegory in the historical particularity of drawing and painting as practices. Futhermore, the drawing poses for us the problem of distanciated intention, the absent intention characterizing all representations as artifacts surviving their makers. For the life of the form here supersedes the life of both maker and referent. It is insufficient to explain away the conditions of the drawing's appearance—the blindfold is not accounted for by historical convention, by a transhistorical thematic, or even by an evolutionary theory of artistic practice. It is a drawing of the nonreciprocity enabling all drawing. And in this it reminds us that the criminal "facing" punishment and the figure of Justice share the same blindfold, the same capacity for anonymity and abstraction. Thus their mutuality points to a complicity in the rule of law and the system of representation. The blindfolded agent is one who dreams of a transaction between positions without necessitating an origin or a consequence rooted in the particularity of those positions.

I have therefore taken from this drawing a method for the critique of the law and its relation to aesthetic representations. Inevitably, I have both aestheticized and secularized the law in doing so. But the project has been to investigate the particularity and contingency, and thus the interplay between philosophy and history, under which representation and its rule of law emerge.

The writing of these essays was greatly aided by a grant from the John Simon Guggenheim Foundation and by a grant-in-aid from Temple University. Throughout my research I have benefited from the services of the British Library, the Library Company of Philadelpia, the National Library of Scotland, the Edinburgh University Library, the Folklore Archives of the School of Scottish Studies at Edinburgh, and Temple University's Interlibrary Loan Departent. Barbara Tomasi of the Galleria D'Arte Moderna e Contemporanea di Roma graciously secured permission for the use of De Chirico's *Gli Archeologi*.

I also had the useful opportunity to read versions of these essays and listen to responses at the Summer Institute for Semiotic Studies, Università degli Studi, Urbino; the Institute for European and Comparative Studies, University of Florida; the University of Pennsylvania; Syracuse University; the Tudor and Stuart Club of Johns Hopkins University; the History of Consciousness Program at the University of California at Santa Cruz; the Tenth International Congress in Aesthetics, Montreal; and the American Folklore Society Meetings of October 1989.

Although I have acknowledged more specific debts in the notes to individual essays, I could not have completed this work without the help of my family, Daniel Halevy, Jacob Stewart-Halevy, and Sam Stewart-Halevy; my colleagues Magali Sarfatti-Larson, Alan Singer, and Susan Wells; my assistant during the completion of the manuscript, Elisabeth Joyce; and our college manuscript typist, Nadia Kravchenko. The curriculum preparation for the Temple Seminars in Art and Culture in Rome and the team teaching Alan Singer and I have conducted there for two years have been inestimably helpful to my thinking regarding issues of representation, writing, and artifactuality. The steady support of my editor, William P. Sisler, in this, our third project together, has been of much encouragement to me, as were the comments by the anonymous reader at Oxford University Press. I am also grateful for the careful attention this manuscript received from John Eastman, Irene Pavitt, and Clifford Browder.

Some of these essays have already been published: "Psalmanazar's Others" in *History of Anthropology*, George Stocking, editor; "Scandals of the Ballad" in *Representations*; "The Birth of Authenticity in the Progress of Anxiety: Fragments of an Eighteenth-Century Daydream" in *Critical Studies*; "Ceci Tuera Cela: Graffiti as Crime and Art" in *Life After Post-Modernism*, John Fekete, editor; "The Marquis de Meese" in *Critical Inquiry*; "Reverse Trompe l'Oeil\The Eruption of the Real" in *Public Culture*; and "Notes on Distressed Genres" in *The Journal of American Folklore*.

Philadelphia   S. S.
June 1990

Notes

1. Lloyd Goodrich, *Thomas Eakins* (Cambridge, Mass.: Harvard University Press, for the National Gallery of Art, 1982), pp. 10–11.

2. In *Realism, Writing, Disfiguration: On Thomas Eakins and Stephen Crane* (Chicago: University of Chicago Press, 1987), Michael Fried gives a remarkable and intriguing account of Eakins's relation to writing and Crane's relation to seeing. Although he does not discuss this particular drawing or series, his discussion of such issues as "facing" and "facing away" in pictorial scenes, and his description of Crane's description of upturned faces and corpses, are quite suggestive for the problem of the blindfolded model.

3. And here, of course, the fact that this must be the figure of a woman is a difference making all the difference in the articulation of a gendered system of making and objects of making. The tradition of Themis and Astraea/Virgo as figures of justice who weigh, judge, and distribute materials relating to an impious world that they have themselves fled or refused extends from antiquity to the conventions of this late-nineteenth-century drawing class. For a tenth- or eleventh-century example of the Virgo figure, see Jean Seznec, *The Survival of the Pagan Gods: The Mythological Tradition and Its Place in Renaissance Humanism and Art*, trans. Barbara F. Sessions (New York: Pantheon Books, 1953), p. 152.

Contents

CRIMES OF WRITING

Crimes of Writing

These essays concern themselves with the relations between subjectivity, authenticity, writing, speech, and the law. Because they
focus for the most part on specific cases of forgery, literary imposture,
pornography, and graffiti, I have gathered them under the title
"crimes of writing." But I have used this title for another reason as
well—to connote the ways in which such practices are in fact inversions or negations of cultural rules and so have opened a more
"properly" transgressive space for those aesthetic writings stretching
from Romanticism to the avant-garde. By establishing a realm of
prosecutable actions, laws regarding crimes of writing might be seen
to "spare" such aesthetic practices and at the same time to bracket,
and thereby trivialize, their intentions and consequences.

From the outset we should recognize that these "crimes of writing" are delineated by law because they quite specifically undermine
the status of the law itself; they point to the irreducible fact that
the law is written and hence to the consequent fact that the law is
subject to temporality and interpretation. Thus I attend to the ways
in which the law developed as a particularly idealized and transcendent form of writing. And I bring forward the obvious psychoanalytic
analogy here as well: the already written status of the law; the role
of the law in positioning subjectivity; the tragedy of one's entry into
the domain of the law as an enabling subjection; and the possibilities
of remedy offered by utterance as a form of modification and novelty.
I intend that such an analysis of "crimes of writing" provide at least
a partial history of the gestures made in establishing the grounds of

writing's relation to subjectivity and authenticity. Such an account would, as several of the essays demonstrate, often necessarily be a kind of hysterical writing—a writing moving not simply from position to position but between positions as well; a writing refusing, and incapable of, "an ordered account," and yet a writing that is in crucial ways symptomatic of history in that it continually asks questions regarding its place in history.

Thus these studies rest in several ways upon a catechresis in levels of analysis and a catechresis in temporality. First, I am willing to confuse the literal and the metaphorical here in order to suspend a number of "natural" assumptions about signification and authenticity. I have begun by assuming that notions of the law, even in disparate domains, have a common influence as well as a common etymology. And I have assumed that an account of the relations between speech, writing, subjectivity, and authority would have to work inductively from certain problems appearing in the history of those relations. Second, I have read two periods in relation to each other—the contemporary and the eighteenth century—not because of some particular "relevance" that each has for the other (a relevance that would necessarily and tautologically be implicated in some preexisting "moral")—but because both eighteenth-century and postmodern aesthetics are tied to transformations in the production of "literature." Within the eighteenth-century transformation of the literary marketplace—the decline of patronage, the rise of booksellers, the advent of mass literary production and copyright, the development of the concept of "intellectual property"—lies a central set of questions regarding the relations among speech and writing, authorship, authenticity, and audience. As Bertrand Bronson expressed in his essay "The Writer": "The gradual detachment, through print, of the writer from a present and familiar audience is one of the most far-reaching influences of modern times in our western civilization; and its special problems emerge with crucial insistence for the first time in the 18th century."[1] Thus the eighteenth-century concept of the writer was gradually transformed, as the context was transformed from the face-to-face domains of patronage and the court to new commercial scenes of printing and bookselling. By 1758 James Ralph in his work *The Case of Authors by Profession or Trade* complained:

Where all must pay, all ought to be paid. Notwithstanding which, Authors are still living, who have been as communicative of the Use of their Parts, as great Men ought to be of their Fortunes; and who on those Occasions neither receiv'd, nor expected to receive, any other Reward, than the inward Satisfaction arising from the Consciousness of having done a Service, and thereby discharg'd a Duty. But instead of standing on the Defensive only against the Petulancy or Bitterness of such generous Maligners, might not a writer of this Class, if any such could be found, who had not only Vouchers to produce of Abilities, but also of Services resulting to the Public, by a proper and seasonable Exertion of them, take upon him to shew, without any Breach of Modesty, That he has more to complain of than to answer for? The writer has three Provinces. To write for Booksellers. To write for the Stage. To write for a Faction in the Name of the Community.[2]

I attend particularly here to ways in which the field of eighteenth-century literary production, newly characterized by rapid and mechanical means of dissemination, was drawn to folkloric or oral forms as a model for immediacy, organicism, and tradition. The impossibility of this attraction—its unsuitability and the nostalgic distortions accompanying it—is what is of foremost interest to me, for that impossibility has at its core the impossibility of mastering temporality. It is not particularly difficult, in the style of Walter Benjamin's studies of the baroque, to allegorize this problematic of temporality into current postmodern conditions of the production of art and literature: the advent of a new, late-capitalist culture industry; the invention of a mass-market subjectivity of authorial "stardom" within a context of deepening anonymity; the rapid production, dissemination, and disappearance of cultural objects; and the crisis in authenticity arising from various phenomena characterized by simulacral and nostalgic thematics and form. The postmodern "problems" of rapidity and fragmentation might be seen as either an inheritance of or parallel to eighteenth-century cultural developments.

Yet to hold these "periods" against or up to each other is also to realize the persistence of certain enduring problems in the history of the philosophy of representation. At the outset, we recognize the place of representation—as opposed to similarity or description, for example—in both maintaining and cutting off its referent, its signified. For representation implies a type of substitution that undermines its own status as a purportedly transcendental gesture, figuring a referent that always exceeds and escapes the very aim of representation's function—a sufficient signification. In the examples I consider here, what might be called the worlds of life and talk can be represented only within conditions both valorizing those worlds and, as I argue in relation to oral genres, "killing them off." Thus while representation might be defined by its quality of being not "misrepresenting," there is a fundamental error (i.e., misrepresentation) in this very formulation. For the sufficiency of representation, its authority and its capacity for attribution and comprehension, will depend upon a necessary forgetting. And the liberation of representation into a domain of signification always opens onto a pattern or structure of absences—that which it is the task of the representation to bring forward as a "making present."

In this process we find, in fact, an important merging of aesthetic and political forms of representation; that is, whether the representative "freely" acts on a mandate from his or her constituency, or whether he or she is in fact portraying the wishes of the electorate, has its corollary in the operations of representational signifiers in the aesthetic realm. In the first, formalist case, the representation is both constitutive and endowed with powers of its own; in the second, historicist case, it appears as the vehicle, the effaced materiality, of a transcendent signified. If it is obvious that both these positions are idealizations—the first an ideal of absolutism, the second an ideal of transparency—it is equally obvious that they contaminate each other in the play of signification that must describe any account of representation. Furthermore, the representational relation between the spoken and the written is not simply a matter of a material transformation, but one that comes imbued with a certain positionedness—an ethic or a cultural matrix enabling writing as a mode of abstraction and typification. But we must emphasize that qualities such as abstraction and typification are part of a *thematic* of writing, not part of the conditions of writing's production, and that this thematic presents the oral as both overparticularized and indeterminate.

We find the endurance of a contradictory and ironic relation to time in such problems of representation. I am especially mindful in these essays of the paradox of temporal self-consciousness (the necessary experiences of mediation in time; awareness of discontinuity, disruption, interruption, intensity, and emptiness), leading to a consequent consciousness of what must be termed a kind of temporal loss. Enlightenment views of temporal progression and anachronism, as we have inherited them, both enable history and define the impossibility of experiencing it beyond the predicative and causal model presented by "history" itself. Here the eighteenth century and the recent twentieth share a key stylistic in *le mode rétro*, with its unhappy consciousness of time, its nostalgia, and its concomitant desire for animation. Obviously, we have arrived once more within a central problematic of representation, for such an animation will stubbornly remain an animation, as the brief survey of the idea of "distressed genres" here demonstrates. Anachronism prompts a representation of time that is necessarily a portrayal.

"Born originals," Edward Young asked in his 1759 essay "Conjectures on Original Composition," "how comes it to pass that we die copies?"[3] Young's comment, especially in its argument for originality and ultimately genius, appears at a pivotal moment, reflecting on the endurance of Renaissance and neoclassical views of imitation and anticipating the promulgation of originality in Romanticism. Yet it also illuminates a central problem in the relation of subjectivity to language—the surrendering of one's subjectivity to language, to an inheritance, in exchange for the articulation of self that inheritance can provide.

These essays examine the notions of authorship, authoring, authenticity, and authority within this history of exchanges between subjectivity and language. We might begin this consideration with two key glosses on the relation between authoring and authority: the first, chapter 16 of Hobbes's *Leviathan*, "Of Persons, Authors, and Things Personated"; the second, the more recent reflections of Michel Foucault's "What Is an Author?" Hobbes's chapter is concerned with a definition of person, and in this lies its radical use for us, since a person becomes, in the development of Hobbes's argument, a site of inferred action. Significantly, Hobbes's definition thus immediately necessitates a social ground and marks a bifurcation between originality and derivation:

> A person is he, whose words or actions are considered, either as his own, or as representing the words or actions of an other man, or of

any other thing to whom they are attributed, whether Truly or by
Fiction. . . . When they are considered as his own, then is he called
a *Naturall Person*: And when they are considered as representing the
words and actions of an other, then is he a *Feigned* or *Artificiall person*.[4]

Hence the second possibility: he who represents another—that is,
does not represent his own originality—is an actor, acting by the
authority of another, the author. Hobbes's discussion obviously is
an exercise in investigating the conditions of political authority and
what he calls, despite what is obviously a mechanistic system, "cov-
enants between man and man": significantly for the thematic of
Leviathan as a whole, this chapter ends rather abruptly with a final
distinction between those authors who own the actions of others
simply and those who own the actions of others conditionally.

We must also note that Hobbes does not at all assume a mutuality
of interests between the state and its subjects. As Durkheim outlined
in his study of the legal thinking of Montesquieu and Rousseau,
Rousseau contended that a law is expressed in terms of the general
will—for Rousseau a rather utopian conflation of the aims of the state
and the aims of individuals once the latter aims are purged of any
idiosyncrasy: "there is only a difference in viewpoint between the
body of the society and the mass of individuals." But in Hobbes,
by contrast,

> "the laws are made for Titus and Caius, and not for the body of the
> state" (*De Cive*, XII). The reason for this difference is that Hobbes
> assumed a clear line of demarcation between the sovereign authority
> and the multitude of subjects. The former, he held, was external to
> the latter and imposed its will upon each individual.[5]

Yet within this orderly account of separate, even binary, interests,
Hobbes also allows for a character who is of great importance to us
in the context of the laws of writing, and that is the person whose
words are in fact his own, yet are represented by him to be another's
"by fiction." Thus this person, the fraud or swindler, enjoys the
same congruity between speaking and invention as the "Naturall
Person," but must of necessity be a "Feigned or Artificiall person"
of a special type. This possibility, which is in essence the possibility
of a singular invention of the grounds of the social (which ironically
must be "uncovered" by the social in a judgment exposing its

origins), is in fact the central gesture of those transgressions of the law that are crimes of writing.

Hobbes's contribution here is to define an author as a site of attribution. He thus creates the possibility of a system of authorship (implicit in the social recognition necessary for all authoring, whether original or feigned, and implicit as well in his allowance for authorship by guardians and by "inanimate things" such as the vehicles of governors, authorship, etc.). Hobbes's work thus severs individuality from originality, the natural person appearing as the special case.

Analogously, Foucault's essay asks: "How, under what conditions, and in what forms can something like a subject appear in the order of discourse? What place can it occupy in each type of discourse, what functions can it assume and by obeying what rules?"[6] Among other examples, he cites the reversal between authorial conventions of the Middle Ages, when literary texts were unattributed and scientific works attributed, and those of the seventeenth and eighteenth centuries, when literary works became attributed and scientific works unattributed. Obviously, what emerges here is a restriction of originality to the domain of imagination and a proliferation of a public domain of rationality. Yet Hobbes's essay, appearing at a key point in this transition of conventions of attribution, points us to the complexities underlying Foucault's speculations. If we begin with the relation between authority and writing practices rather than with an assumption of authorial originality, we arrive at a quite different sense of this history, a history of originality as a concept emergent in the decline of the absolutist state, in the advent of mechanical modes of literary production, and in the rise of social democracies. Before I turn to the issues arising from these developments, I want to survey this history and thus provide a background to such issues.

The most rudimentary sense of copyright, developed during the Middle Ages, placed the monopoly for multiple production of works in the hands of publishers. Copyists in the medieval university towns of Paris and Bologna, for example, by 1200 were subject to the monopolies of the guilds of stationers and booksellers. These monopoly rules, like the quasi patents of silk designs issued in Genoa and Venice, had to do with notions of the integrity of production and the producer's responsibility for that integrity. Thus although ideas, like designs, were intangible property, they were also thereby subject to possession. These concepts set the stage for the seventeenth-century development of the classic liberal principles of intellectual property as articulated in the writings of Locke and later Diderot. The idea that no one is so much the master of his goods as a man is the master of the products of the labor of his mind would emerge in a complex figuration regarding the nature of work, materiality and ownership, and, eventually, the relation of these concepts to mental labor and originality.[7]

At the time of the emergence of printing, there were in Paris and Orléans alone more than ten thousand copyists,[8] but for the early printers, as well as for such copyists, the idea of the personal ownership of words, or certainly personal ownership of the order of words, was not available. If printing therefore was the locus of ownership, it could also be made the locus of censorship, for throughout the fifteenth and sixteenth centuries extensive censorship centered on the activities of the press. The Star Chamber, England's special prerogative court, was established by the Tudors in 1487 to try crimes of treason and other "subjects too mighty to be dealt with in the common law courts."[9] Such subjects included the enforcing of economic regulations that often interfered with those property rights warranted by Parliament and the common-law courts, the regulation of printing, and the restriction of treasonable utterances. In 1556 the Stationers' Company was founded for the purpose of licensing printers and booksellers.[10] The point of such licensing, under the Statutes of Scandalum Magnatum, dating from the rule of Edward I (1272–1307) and continuing to 1887, was to protect peers of the realm, judges, and officers of the Crown from scandal. Such utterances were normally not actionable when spoken against a private person. Thus whereas the Stationers' Company from its inception regulated the commercial life of printing, it as well took on the function of regulating the contents of works—that is, the function of censorship. The charter of the company authorized the following conditions: only members of the company could print; the master and wardens of the company could search houses and businesses and seize anything printed contrary to statute or proclamation; and anyone printing without such authorization could be imprisoned for three months without trial and fined five pounds, half of which was to go to the Crown and half to the company.[11]

Aside from the express structural purpose of these institutions in protecting the absolutism of the Crown, they also had a theme: preventing the propagation of dissent. (Similarly, by 1566 the Edict of Moulins decreed that all books could be published only by permission of the French king.)[12] The Star Chamber Decree of 1586 helped concentrate the power of the Stationers' Company. Concentrating power in London was in the interests of both the company and the government, for the company could thereby monopolize commercial interests, and the government could keep a stronger hold on content. In 1637, by order of the Star Chamber, the number of authorized printers in London was reduced to twenty; brutal corporal punishment was delivered to those who printed illegally.[13] All foreign books had to be approved by the bishops; any reprinted books, regardless of previous license, had to be relicensed. Among books refused license were Luther's *Table Talk*, Foxe's *Book of Martyrs*, Bishop Jewell's *Works*, Bishop Bayly's *Practice of Piety*, and the Geneva Bible, with its antiauthoritarian marginal notes.[14]

The seminal Treason Act of 1351, known as the Statute of 25 Edward III, had limited treason to several definite classifications, among which were "the compassing" or imagining of the death of the king, the queen, or their eldest son and heir; the levying of war against the king; and the giving of aid and comfort to the king's enemies. But in the seventeenth century, "treason" acquired a specifically literary character. From the forged *Eikon Basilike* to John Lilburne's *England's New Chains Discovered*, a maelstrom of inflammatory pamphlets evoking shifting alliances surrounded the fall of Charles I. Thus we find that the Act of July 17, 1649, made a departure from this older conception of treason as overt action prompted by the traitorous imagination. The 1649 act declared treason to include the publishing, writing, printing, or declaring of sentiments against the Commonwealth. And in September 1649, a further act was published forbidding the publication of "any book or pamphlet, treatise, sheet or sheets of news" without a license, and imposing penalties for the writing, printing, selling, and purchasing of "scandalous and libellous" books.[15] Consequently, when in 1663 the printer John Twyn issued, but did not author, a book imagining the death of Charles II, he was hanged, cut down alive, his "privy members" were cut off, his entrails taken out, and with him "still living, burnt before his eyes."[16] Twyn's gruesome fate as well emphasizes for us the primacy of the role of the printer and bookseller over that of the author at this time. Before the development of concepts of original genius and intellectual property, all thoughts were potentially held in common, all thoughts were appropriable by readers, and it was those who disseminated ideas who reaped any rewards or punishments prompted by such ideas.

The historian of copyright law Augustine Birrell, in his *Seven Lectures on the Law and History of Copyright in Books*, explains that "in England censorship was always centralized and derived from the royal prerogative. In France there were as many censors as ecclesiastics, while Universities and Parliaments contributed as well."[17] Yet throughout the complex history of seventeenth-century restrictions on the press, a set of concomitant issues regarding freedoms of the press emerged, and these issues return us to the key notions of subjectivity, authorship, property, and originality addressed by Foucault. Throughout the seventeenth and eighteenth centuries in France and during the latter half of the eighteenth century in England, a debate arose as to whether authors were entitled to exclusive rights of multiplying copies of their books and, if so, whether this was by "property" or "privilege."[18] In France the question was framed as whether the rights of authors existed subject to royal patronage or whether they were an absolute right, a right of person. Hence even today in France, an author's writings are not simple property, but a *droit moral*, a projection of the self.[19] In England, the question was framed as whether the rights of authors were property rights under common law or statutory rights resulting from the prerogatives of the Crown or statute book.

The Star Chamber was abolished in 1641 by the Long Parliament, "foreasmuch as the reasons and motives inducing the reaction and continuance of that court do now cease, and the proceedings, censures and decrees of that Court have by experience been found to be an intolerable burden to the subjects and the means to introduce an arbitrary power and government."[20] In the consequent years, cheap newspapers and pamphlets proliferated. In 1645, for example, there were 722 English newspapers.[21] Yet throughout the period of the Commonwealth, Parliament attempted to regulate the offenses of writers and printers by establishing licensing rules and inspectors. We find Milton publishing his *Areopagitica* in protest of these rules in 1644 and serving as a licenser himself in 1651 and 1652. Censorship was fully restored by the 1649 acts granting Parliament control of the press; by 1655, Cromwell had banned all periodicals without official sanction.

As the case of John Twyn makes clear, the Restoration did not signal a lessening of control over the press. The Licensing Acts of 1662 to 1665 imposed rigid censorship and a number of provisions. All books and pamphlets had to be licensed and entered into the register books of the company of stationers. Law books were to be licensed by judges, history books by the secretary of state, heraldry books by the earl marshall, and all others by the archbishop of Canterbury or the bishop of London or, within Oxford and Cambridge, by the chancellors and vice-chancellors, provided such books did not deal with common law or affairs of state. Books could have no contents contrary to the Christian faith or against the state. No one else could print or imprint books that the Stationers' Company or any others held letters patent for, upon pain of loss or forfeiture of books. Every printer had to set his name and that of the author upon his book. The name of the Stationers' Company could not be forged or counterfeited. No "haberdashers, iron mongers, chandlers, shop-keepers or anyone else who hasn't been seven years an apprentice to a bookseller, printer or bookbinder" could sell any books. No press could be set up without notice to the stationers. Twenty master printers were named, each of whom could use one or more presses. A search of printing houses was authorized. Anything not licensed could be seized. A copy of every book printed had to be presented to the Common Hall of the Stationers' Company and sent to the Bodley Library.[22] Sir William Berkeley announced in a report to the Lords of Committee for the Colonies in 1671: "I thank God we have not free schools nor printing. . . . For learning has brought disobedience and heresy, and sects into the world; and printing has divulged them and libels against the government."[23] Thanks largely to the passionate arguments of John Locke, who prepared the case against them, the Licensing Acts expired in 1695. But at that time, Chief Justice Scroggs declared into the common law of criminal libel the government's right to license, announcing that "to print or publish any news, books, or pamphlets of news whatsoever is illegal."[24] Pamphleteers such as Daniel Defoe were imprisoned or pilloried; John Matthews was hanged for high treason in 1719 for having published a pamphlet in support of James III.

Nevertheless, the hold of censorship had been loosened by the turn of the century, the reign of the bookseller had begun, and the issuance of books and their consumption had become a more complex matter of rights and property-holding. The first English copyright act, "An Act for the Encouragement of Learning, by Vesting the Copies of Printed Books in the Authors or Purchasers of Such Copies, during the Times therein Mentioned," appeared in 1709. This statute protected the rights of authors to some degree, but its major focus was to prevent the London booksellers from maintaining a continuous hold on the most valuable old copyrights. Books were to be copyrighted for fourteen years, and if at the end of that term, the author was "still alive," the copyright could be extended for another fourteen years. By the end of the century, a number of important debates on the nature and extent of copyright, authorship, intellectual property, and the dissemination of letters had been conducted.

The two most important cases of the period were *Millar* v. *Taylor*, presented before the King's Bench in 1769 with Lord Mansfield directing the proceedings, and *Donaldson* v. *Beckett*, presented before the House of Lords in 1774. These cases brought forth a variety of issues that can be summarized as follows: Is the right to intellectual property held by an author? If so, does this right continue after the publication of a work? Are the rights declared by the 1709 Statute of Anne (the fourteen-year rule) adequate to such common-law rights regarding intellectual property? Can such common-law rights then supersede the Statute of Anne?

In *Millar* v. *Taylor*, Mansfield and the majority decided that such common-law rights did supersede the 1709 statute. Following classic liberal principles of intellectual property, Mansfield contended that an author's right should continue after publication as well as, obviously, before.

In *Donaldson* v. *Beckett* the tension between an author's rights and the "monopoly" posed by perpetual copyright became emphasized. The voting was mixed, with the judges supporting the author's common-law right controlling the first publication of the work and supporting as well the author's right as surviving publication. But the historical record is confusing as to whether the vote was 5 to 6 or 6 to 5 regarding perpetual copyright, and the final result was that the Lords voted in favor of the claims of the Scottish bookseller

Donaldson and the principle that copyright should be limited in time. Thus not only was copyright given a limited rule, but the authority of statutory law was upheld over the common-law rights of authors as "persons" creating original "works." If state interest and commercial interest were one in this regard, such a collusion had a long history in the role that the Stationers' Company had been willing to play in the censorship of works since its founding. The right of authors was merely a thread amid the complex relations between state interest, common-law rights to intellectual property, and commercial competition emerging throughout the eighteenth century.[25]

Although the legislation mandating the licensing of books was not overturned until 1765, by 1792 the freedom of the press had been placed under the protection of a jury.[26] The first American federal copyright statue had been passed in 1790, while in 1793, with revolutionary fervor, France had passed an International Copyright Act. In 1814 England established a copyright act protecting works for twenty-eight years, or longer if the author was still alive, and in 1838 passed its first International Copyright Act. The Convention of Berne in 1886 established an international set of copyright provisions subscribed to by a union of countries including Germany, Belgium, Spain, France, Great Britain, Haiti, Italy, Switzerland, and Tunisia.[27]

Thus the history of the emergence of copyright is a history of a set of relations between speech, the body, writing, and property transformed by the changing political status of these very terms. The subjection of speech to the demands of the absolutist state, and the rectification of crimes of speech by the suffering of the body, evolves into a new view of speech as intellectual property—a property whose dramatic separation from its site of production is best illustrated by the status of the debate regarding its ownership. But once writing is considered as property, it is severed from the provenance of its authorial location and hence freed from that bond at the very moment of its attachment; in fact, what happens is the textualization of the authorial location, the site of the author as a site of a textual system, a place of quotation already located within a system of quotation.

These essays therefore frequently return to the consequences of what might be termed a "naive materialism"—that is, the problem of the law's conception of property.[28] It is beyond the scope of this study to present any full-scale critique of the concept of property, but this limited focus on certain cruxes in the notion of literary or intellectual property might prove useful as a sketch for such a critique. For the outline of this notion is the indefinable aspect of the literary as that which escapes being, that which resists appropriation and genealogy. Hence both the law and literary criticism take on the tasks of restoring these qualities to that space of literature continually escaping them. This "property," which must transcend its materiality and, in order to be recognized, must by definition be shared, thus becomes surrounded by a discourse of genealogy, inheritance, derivation, production, and reception—a merger of the attributive systems for persons as well as the attributive systems for things. Furthermore, the oxymoron of "literary property" continually appears as the site in which the law works out all that it is *not* as a form of writing: the unlocalizable, the excess of the signifier, the nondeclarative in syntax. The idealized conditions of codification—authority, genealogy, precedence, application, specificity, and transcendence—are established as qualities of a literary realm that it becomes the task of the law—as writing that is *other*—to regulate.

In seventeenth-century France, authors argued that "in whose so every hands a manuscript might be found, it still remained the Author's property."[29] Hence, as we have noted, French law developed in the direction of considering writing as a projection of the author's being. In England and the United States, this problem was resolved by considering literary property, like chattels, as "personal property" rather than real property such as land or buildings.[30] The revolutionary idea that one has dominion over one's ideas is reflected in Locke's position on property: "yet every man has a property in his own person . . . the labor of his body, and the work of his hands, we may say, are properly his."[31] Locke's comment, in fact, reminds us of Bunyan's earlier reply in *Holy War* to attacks on his originality:

> Manner and matter too were all mine own,
> Nor was it unto any mortal known,
> Till I had done it. Nor did any then,
> By books, by wits, by tongues, or hand, or pen,
> Add five words to it, or write half a line:
> Therefore the whole, and every whit is mine.[32]

But what is "manner and matter"? As copyright law developed in the ensuing century, ideas, themes, subject matter, words in the dictionary, and objects of the senses such as sounds, colors, and shapes were not protected. Copyright resides in particulars both substantial (quantities) and material (qualities) and is dependent therefore not upon abstraction, but upon the rhetoric of an argument of similarity and a history of accessibility between textual practices.[33]

Furthermore, copyright shifts historically with changes in the notion of the law itself. What is the function of the law? What is the function of writing? Between the seventeenth and late eighteenth centuries, radical shifts in the answers to these questions are signals of changing perceptions of speech, writing, and individuality. Lyman Ray Patterson explains in his history of copyright: "Copyright was not a product of the common law. It was a product of censorship, guild monopoly, trade-regulation statutes, and misunderstanding."[34] Thus as copyright developed from printer's patent to the monopolies afforded by stationer's copyrights and thenceforward to statutory copyright and finally common-law copyright, founded upon the "natural rights" of authorship, it moved from a tangible quality of copies themselves to an intangible and abstract matter of expressive originality.

Here writing obviously splits into a set of contrasts at least as old as the *Phaedrus* between a transcendent writing, written on the soul (the language of truth), and a material writing (produced, willed, shaped by rhetoric and convention):

> But he who thinks that in the written word there is necessarily much which is not serious, and that neither poetry nor prose, spoken or written, are of any great value . . . and that only in principles of justice and goodness and nobility taught and communicated orally and written in the soul, which is the true way of writing, is there clearness and perfection and seriousness; and that such principles are like legitimate offspring . . . —this is the right sort of man.[35]

This discussion, we must remember, comes amid a general critique of the rhetorical pretensions of Lysias, and more directly follows from a discussion of the ways in which "in courts of law men literally care nothing about truth." Hence the rhetoric of testimony in courts of law depends upon a sense of probability related to "that which many think"—that is, a general social and logical sense rather than a particular historical one.

The history of the notion of copyright—because it establishes often contradictory ideas of speech, action, authorship, and property—gives us a vehicle for understanding the social process of negotiating authorial subjectivity, of establishing a boundary between the subjective and the social. All the differences and identities characterizing this boundary thus become an exercise for the establishment of social meaning and the grounds for an intersubjectivity underlying the articulation of individuality and originality. Yet we also see that the invention of the author and of his or her concomitant literary property is another aspect of the reification of the status of the law as regulator of language, for it is the law that decrees the rights, natural or otherwise, of the body and the claims that the body has upon what it produces. Perhaps nothing emphasizes this so much as the fact, from the very first copyright statutes, that the law continues to exercise its claims on writing once the author has died; it is the law that defines the nature of the "public domain"—that realm in which language acquires its most purely social character.

Furthermore, those very qualities of writing that distinguish it from the contexts of speech and face-to-face behavior—its "materiality," its relation to death, its anonymity, its capacity for deception as well as definition, its call for supplementarity and commentary—move it from the sphere of event to the sphere of property in which the law is the arbiter of its appropriation. In fact, at the same time that authorship is emerging as a concept of original genius, the law is undergoing a shift to an increasingly formal and ideal status. How can the law maintain a distance from its status as writing at the same time that it proclaims and delimits a domain of writing?

We see this process at work in two necessarily opposing directions. First, the law itself never addresses its own materiality; it is not subject to a historical account aside from a broadly evolutionary model in which the law becomes fuller, more elaborated, and more just. The law is not subject to claims of authorship and originality. And second, the law is not subject to a specific ontology. The law maintains thereby its status as event, but a special case of event. In speech-act parlance, the law has two modes: the verdicative and the exercitive. According to J. L. Austin, the verdicative involves the pronouncement of findings on the basis of evidence; the exercitive involves the announcement of rulings. As Austin explains, "an exercitive is the giving of a decision in favour of or against a certain course of action, or advocacy of it. It is a decision that something is to be so, as distinct from a judgement that it is so."[36]

We may speculate further that the felicity of the exercitive, the authority that must precede and accompany the legitimacy of its pronouncement, is the general condition on which the verdicative, as the more particular form, must rely. The fixity of the law, the rules of evidence, and all the structural and structuring capabilities of the law must be assumed, must be *in place*, before such pronouncements can take place—and specifically, before such pronouncements can acquire authority and the capability of amendation. This fixity is in fact only *emphasized* by the idea that the law is amended. Here we have a suggestive commentary on the notion of retraction: we cannot "go back on" what the law has said; the law is in this sense both metalinguistic and performative. In contrast, the law can require human agents to produce retractions designed to function as forms of erasure. Now, of course, this metaphysical status of the law is not in any philosophical or historical sense given or absolute—what seems natural, as law or right, is of course historical. As recent debates centering on essentialist interpretations of the American Constitution have emphasized, the law functions by eliding its historical and material conditions of production and reception.

This transcendence is what Wittgenstein described in his *Lectures and Conversations* as the "super-hardness of the Law":

> We say that people condemn a man to death and then we say the Law condemns him to death. "Although the Jury can pardon [acquit?] him, the Law can't." (This *may* mean the Law can't take bribes, etc.) The idea of something super-strict, something stricter than any Judge can be, super-rigidity.[37]

Wittgenstein here makes an analogy between the law and the laws of logic as "super-hard" systems, idealities having their own trajectories despite the circumstances of their particular appearance. He is here taking part in a debate regarding representation that extends at least as far back as Aristotle's *Rhetoric* (book 3, chapter 1): "we might in fairness to fight our case with no help beyond the bare facts: nothing, therefore, should matter except the truth of those facts. Still, as has been already said, other things affect the result considerably."[38] We might more readily conclude that "other things" always affect the result and that, indeed, results are determined by a process of retrospective attribution regarding such other things. The trajectory of "super-hardness" is a matter of consensus regarding structural or formal loci of power, a consensus necessarily subsuming the particularity of its own history in order to appear, if not natural, at least as a given. And so we should also attend to the subtle transformations of power implicit in Wittgenstein's account of the relation between the social uses of the law and its abstract standing as the "super-hard." The death sentence, like other sentences, is delivered by particular human agents acting in particular situations. Such agents deliver that sentence upon its object—the "criminal"—at the same time that they deliver their responsibility for their agency to the rule of law. The super-hardness of the rule of law is evidenced by its singular trajectory—the law does not waver, return, or even turn back. Thus the law is summoned, as any rule is summoned, when the example calls forth the occasion of its implementation. Thus just as the rule is a function of the example (and not the reverse), so is the law a function of a predication that needs to give up the burden of its context, of its situatedness or particularity.

The law is both schematic and efficient. It operates in the interests of an economy of social life and serves to reify that idea of economy, with its regulation of property, market, and citizen rights, within a notion of, as Roberto Unger has termed it, "ordered freedom." The abstraction of the law enables it to reach beyond itself at any given historical moment: the law is accommodating precisely by means of its refusal of the particular and the contested. In his introduction to his program for a critical legal studies, Unger eloquently summarizes this "formalist" notion of legal doctrine, a notion to which he is radically opposed:

> Legal doctrine or legal analysis is a conceptual practice that combines two characteristics: the willingness to work from the institutionally defined materials of a given collective tradition and the claim to speak authoritatively within this tradition, to elaborate it from within in a way that is meant, at least ultimately, to affect the application of state power. Doctrine can exist, according to the formalist view, because

of a contrast between the more determinate rationality of legal analysis and the less determinate rationality of ideological contests.[39]

Unger contends that only a revision of the underlying conditions in which legal rationality is emergent can provide the grounds for changing social practices:

> Modern legal doctrine . . . works in a social context in which society has increasingly been forced open to transformative conflict. It exists in a cultural context in which, to an unprecedented extent, society is understood to be made and imagined rather than merely given. To incorporate the final level of legal analysis in this new setting would be to transform legal doctrine into one more arena for continuing the fight over the right and possible forms of social life.[40]

We can argue that it is the function of legal doctrine regarding writing to establish a sphere of authorship, originality, and subjectivity—and to establish a space in the public domain within which, importantly, transgression, as well as modes of reification, can be contained. Thus the laws regarding writing seem to proceed with an exasperated gesture of accommodation, regulating a materiality of signification that, in theory as well as practice, does not exist. But this is a kind of bad-faith gesture, for it in fact strengthens that ground upon which the law stands—its transcendence, its capacity for regulating itself, for reifying the law by this deflection of our gaze from its situated quality. The law hovers. It exists in a distant space, is already written, and has written the present. The law is the form out of which the problematic of form and matter arises.

Here the advent of modern law and the rationality of subjectivity and legal authority—contract—rise in response to the model of absolute sovereignty. The law takes on the qualities of absolutism under an assumption of consent to the power of that law on the part of all "free men." For our purposes, the question becomes the ways in which the particularizations of literary form, the specification of a certain kind of literary textuality, come to acquire qualities—as a practice of writing—that the law will presumably not share. The law cannot share these qualities, for if it does, it loses its power to legislate as a metadiscourse. Of even more consequence, to share in these qualities would be to admit the literariness of the law. Thus the codification of copyright, the linking of the author to a singular and personal intellectual authority, the linking of writing to the author's body, and the legislation of writing as a commodity as well as an act of speech mark, it is true, an advent of "entitlement" that replicates other revolutionary entitlements of the eighteenth century. But as well, such developments protect the law within a domain of idealized and transcendent intersubjectivity, shielding it from critique as an ideological practice itself.[41]

Before we turn to particular instances of "crimes" of writing, we should consider, therefore, the ways in which writing in the eighteenth century takes on an appearance suited to its status as both commodity and property. Emerging literary modes such as description, compendium, fragment, and dialogue all emphasize the secondary or staged quality of literary discourse. In attempting to characterize an originality—the originality of antiquity, the Middle Ages, or peasant culture, for example—such writing always underscores both its own partiality (its necessarily metonymic relation to history) and its own secondariness. Consider the qualities of "Romantic genre" outlined by Philippe Lacoue-Labarthe and Jean-Luc Nancy in their study *The Literary Absolute*:

> the relative incompletion (the "essay"), or absence of discursive development (the "thought") of each of its pieces; the variety and mixture of objects that a single ensemble of pieces can treat; the unity of the ensemble, by contrast, constituted in a certain way outside the work, in the subject that is seen in it, or in the judgment that proffers its maxims in it.[42]

Lacoue-Labarthe and Nancy are interested in that boundary at which Romanticism and idealism both blur and distinguish themselves. For, as they explain, Romanticism always claims the impossibility of accommodating the Idea at the same time that it constantly strives toward it.[43] Now in those eighteenth- and twentieth-century forms considered here, there is a continual reinstatement of the "nature" of this blurring, since a striving *approximation* of an object and an integrity *as* an object become the two dominant characteristics of these literary modes. The result of these two characteristics, these two goals, is a development of a particular form of authorial subjectivity, responsible for an unbearable originality and for the development of a notion of literary system as a matter of intertextuality, allusion, notation, and reference. All the devices of textual connection here reify a textual singularity and mime the systematization of literary production. Thus I have intended the essays here on the concept of "distressed genres" to focus on the temporal emergence of literary forms and the nostalgia for authenticity and subjectivity inherent in this Romantic relation to time. The ballad scandals of the eighteenth century in particular show the ways in which the ballad is a paradigmatic case of the rise of the legislation of originality, authenticity, and authorship. These essays emphasize the development of literary scholarship as a kind of apparatus specializing in such legislation.

I have begun here with a study of literary forgery and imposture—that of the pseudonymous George Psalmanazar's fabricated *Description of Formosa*. Psalmanazar's case emphasizes the ways in which authenticity begins to become a quality of documents as well as of experience. Hence Psalmanazar's two devices of "going back on" his imposture: first, an attempt at justifying himself through writing (necessarily failing because of its status as "mere writing"), and second, his conversion to piety and a life of rectitude. Psalmanazar's story emphasizes the notion of conversion that appears throughout these studies as the law's remedy for crimes of writing. The conversions posed—that of the pornographer, the graffiti artist, the plagiarist—are re-forms not of writing, but of authorial subjectivity. The confession is the discourse of the conversion, but it must be supplemented by testimony—that textuality most concretely linked to orality and "firsthand" experience. The subject after conversion appears as the integrated and authentic offspring of a writing that the law has produced by command. Yet the integrity of this "offspring" is split by the very qualities it shares with writing. First, its authenticity reifies its original position; by turning back on itself, it confirms the position of that self it seeks to abandon, fixing it through the rhetoric of testimony. Second, it cannot sustain the originality of its own position as anything more than a position "fallen" from an original nature. Its identity becomes "what is no longer"—a product of transformation—just as a writing staged as speech becomes "a language that is no longer," a transformation that is neither here nor there. The converted subject and the converted language thus appear in abeyance. Such an abeyance must be framed, however, not as a transcendent one, but as one caught between the demands of a transcendent law and the particularities of a proper, singular history that cannot satisfy those demands. We can readily see how Augustine's moment of transformation, caught in book 10 between the narrative propulsion of the first part of the *Confessions* and the vague lyricism of the second, becomes the prototype of all such scenes of writing.

I have not devoted a separate study to plagiarism here,[44] but note that plagiarism of course arises as a problem at the same time that other issues of writing's authenticity come to the fore. Plagiarism, however, is a crime legislated in England and America by the community of scholarship and not by the more general law. Hence we might conclude that plagiarism's misrepresentation is deemed separable from that of forgery. Certainly, plagiarism is quite clearly connected to imposture, for the plagiarist poses as the originator of a discourse, making claims that the discourse bears a productive relation to his or her person. In fact, the etymology of *plagium* as the stealing of a slave from his or her master, a kind of kidnapping, emphasizes the contradiction in plagiarism's relation to bodies and goods.[45] But literary forgery and pirating involve claims of ownership and theft and hence are more readily covered by copyright law as a law of property. Although a forger, unlike a plagiarist, makes a claim for the authenticity of a document rather than for the authenticity of himself or herself as a site of production, a forger is in fact often caught because of the "unnatural" relations between himself or herself and the document. An early-twentieth-century handbook designed for lawyers investigating forgeries explains:

> Writing naturally unconscious and automatic follows the fixed grooves of habit, but as soon as attention is given to it, it necessarily becomes strained and unnatural. Self-consciousness of a familiar act always tends to produce unnaturalness, and as fraudulent writing is inevitably written with the attention fixed on the process of writing, this is one of the main reasons why it is not well-executed.[46]

Here we see that a quality of bodily action, that natural "grace" of habit in handwriting, is abstracted (quite literally as handwriting turns to the abstractions of the mechanical production of writing) to a quality of the author's person. One's writing should flow, according to this theory, as naturally from the originality and singularity of one's consciousness as a signature does from a pen.

Yet while the U.S. Supreme Court, echoing Locke, contends that the "foundation of all rights of this kind is the natural dominion

which everyone has over his ideas,"[47] there reappears here the contradiction implicit in the intangibility of literary property: the necessity of reorganizing the inherited nature of ideas, themes, subject
matter, words in the dictionary, and so on, and the difficulty of
attributing content and access. An ideal originality would result in
an incomprehensible idiolect; an ideal device of citation would be
a full (and necessarily impossible) history of the writer's subjectivity;
and an authentic writing, necessarily a sacred text, the metaphor of
metaphors, the mixture of mixtures, the word outside of time and
yet perfectly merged with it—necessarily, a kind of law. The essays
on the writing practices of the eighteenth century conclude here
with reflections on the psychoanalytic and philosophic implications
of such problems. The essay on anxiety and authenticity looks at
the relentless syntax of the daydream as the paradigm for imagining
originality and authenticity, and poses the work of the eighteenth-
century engraver Giovanni Battista Piranesi as a crucial examination
of the relations between interiority, temporality, and history.

The final essays of this volume explore the contemporary history
of graffiti and pornography as crimes of writing. Here I have considered graffiti as a crime of mode of production, as an attack on
property and the cultural system of display and exchange. The fu-
tility of graffiti as a critical practice is of considerable interest to me
here. For graffiti serves as a staging ground for conversion, and the
culture takes up this challenge, transforming the graffiti writer into
a criminal or an artist, and so transforming his or her writing into
either defacement or painting. Thus graffiti aggrandizes the very
culture of novelty and consumption it seeks to attack. It does not
create a "genuine" alternative to existing forms of artistic expression
and consumption, so much as it presents itself as a practice of novelty
and individuation quite analogous to such existing forms.

"The Marquis de Meese" analyzes pornography as a crime of
content, focusing upon the ways in which the reproduction and
dispersal of sublimation become the end of sublimation and hence
a threat to representation itself. *The 120 Days of Sodom* and the
attorney general's *Final Report* on pornography are compared as instances of the construction of a metadiscourse of pornography necessarily based upon their historical contexts of sexuality—libertinism
and simulacral forms of sexual imagination. This essay particularly
focuses upon the law's doomed attempt to desire a desireless con-

dition for itself. In the conclusion, "Coda: Reverse Trompe l'Oeil\The Eruption of the Real," I take up the broader problem of the eruption of alterity, particularly nature and death, in any system of representation posing as a surface of signs or metaphors. Representations of this eruption, from the Gothic novel to postmodern representations of the collision of sex, death, and technology, are examined as reinscriptions of the Symbolic.

Notes

1. Bertrand Bronson, "The Writer," in *Man Versus Society in 18th Century Britain,* ed. James L. Clifford (Cambridge: Cambridge University Press, 1968), p. 103. Other useful glosses on the period's transformations regarding literary production include A. S. Collins, *Authorship in the Days of Johnson: Being a Study of the Relations Between Author, Patron, Publisher and Public, 1726–1780* (1927; reprint, Clifton, N. J.: Augustus M. Kelley Publishers, 1973); Alvin Kernan, *Printing Technology, Letters and Samuel Johnson* (Princeton, N.J.: Princeton University Press, 1987); and Paul Korshin, "Types of Eighteenth Century Literary Patronage," *Eighteenth-Century Studies* 7 (1973–74): 453–73. In *The Age of Patronage: The Arts in England 1660–1750* (Ithaca, N.Y.: Cornell University Press, 1971), Michael Foss surveys the various scenes of the production of eighteenth-century art in general. His book is particularly helpful for examining the ways in which literature, especially because of its capacity to bear a satirical relation to the hand that fed it, was separated from the sphere of patronage more readily than painting and architecture—those arts still most tied to patronage today. Foss briefly relates the emergence of copyright for painters and engravers (the so-called Hogarth Act of 1735) to developments regarding literary copyright on pp. 180–81.

2. James Ralph, *The Case of Authors by Profession or Trade (1758) together with The Champion (1739–1740),* introduction by Philip Stevick (Gainesville, Fla.: Scholars' Facsimiles and Reprints, 1966), p. 19. Ralph discusses the "Hogarth Act" on pp. 61–62.

3. Edward Young, "Conjectures on Original Composition," in *A Letter to the Author of Sir Charles Grandison* (1759; reprint, Leeds: Scolar Press, 1966), p. 42. Martha Woodmansee ("The Genius and the Copyright: Economic and Legal Conditions of the Emergence of the Author," *Eighteenth Century Studies* 17 [1984]: 425–48) discusses Young's "conjectures" in relation to eighteenth-century German aesthetic theories of originality and genius. Young's distinctions between two modes of genius are crucial here, for he sets up a typology wherein original geniuses imitate Nature and correspond thereby to adult genius that "comes out of Nature's hand fully grown," whereas "imitations" imitate other authors and, as "infantine" geniuses, must be nursed and educated by a learning that can mislead or overwhelm its subject.

4. Thomas Hobbes, *Leviathan* (Buffalo, N.Y.: Prometheus Books, 1988), p. 83. See also Hanna Pitkin's discussion of this chapter of Hobbes in *The Concept of Representation* (Berkeley: University of California Press, 1972), pp. 14–37.

5. Emile Durkheim, *Montesquieu and Rousseau: Forerunners of Sociology,* trans.

Ralph Manheim, foreword by Henri Peyre (Ann Arbor: University of Michigan Press, 1965), p. 117.

6. Michel Foucault, "What Is an Author?" in *Textual Strategies*, ed. Josué Harari (Ithaca, N.Y.: Cornell University Press, 1979), pp. 141–60. In his recent study, *Forgers and Critics: Creativity and Duplicity in Western Scholarship* (Princeton, N.J.: Princeton University Press, 1990), Anthony Grafton implicitly argues against this approach, which claims a gradual evolution of the concept of authorship. Grafton writes that in contradistinction to the argument that "forgery flourishes in cultures and periods that lack a sense of individuality, especially where writing is concerned," forgery flourished in the Hellenistic age, "when a keen sense of literary individuality was accompanied by a keen desire to deceive" (pp. 36–37). Grafton concludes that "forgery is a sort of crime" (p. 37), and his book argues a common set of motives, from ambition to fancy, for forgeries from classical times to the "Hitler diaries." Grafton's formidable learning and wit distinguish his essay, but I think we cannot— as we remember the counter-example of Hellenistic individuality—overlook the historical transformations in the status of writing and authoring in their specificity. Forgery is a crime, but not a "natural" one. Another useful survey of literary forgeries is in Richard Altick, *The Scholar Adventurers* (New York: Macmillan, 1950), which provides accounts of John Payne Collier's forgeries and alterations of Elizabethan materials, Thomas J. Wise's invented "first edition" pamphlets of Romantic and Victorian writers, the forged letters and documents produced by the spurious "Major Byron" in the 1840s and 1850s, and the fake Scottish documents created by Alexander "Antique" Howland Smith at the end of the nineteenth century. A succinct description of William Lauder's attempt, in 1750, to accuse Milton of plagiarizing contemporary Latin poets—when, in fact, Lauder had "planted" lines from William Hog's Latin translation of *Paradise Lost* in their work—can be found in Ian Haywood, *The Making of History: A Study of the Literary Forgeries of James Macpherson and Thomas Chatterton in Relation to Eighteenth-Century Ideas of History and Fiction* (Rutherford, N.J.: Fairleigh Dickinson University Press, 1986), p. 195. In addition, Gilbert Bagnani ("On Fakes and Forgeries," *The Phoenix* 14 [1960]: 228–44) discusses problems in the attribution of antiquities and other objects. Haywood's later work, *Faking It: Art and the Politics of Forgery* (New York: St. Martin's Press, 1987), discusses some contemporary examples of forged artifacts. Unfortunately, the eighteenth-century material in this book is merely a repetition of the discussion in *The Making of History*. In art history scholarship, Otto Kurz's important study, *Fakes: A Handbook for Collectors and Students* (New York: Dover, 1967), has recently been augmented by a major show at the British Museum on art fakes and forgeries and its catalogue: Mark Jones, ed., *Fake? The Art of Deception* (Berkeley: University of California Press, 1990).

7. F. D. Prager, "The Early Growth and Influence of Intellectual Property," *Journal of the Patent Office Society* 34 (February 1952): 106–40, especially 126–34.

8. Augustine Birrell, *Seven Lectures on the Law and History of Copyright in Books* (London: Cassell, 1899), p. 47. The turn-of-the-century essayist and author of *Obiter Dicta* is himself the object of some criticism by Alice and Henry James. Alice writes in her diary of Birrell's "intellectual foppishness," adding: "I asked Harry one day if he felt it and he said, yes, and that the curious part of it was that it existed in his features in the same way; that after he said anything there was a movement of his nostrils and a smack of his lips immediately suggestive of self-applause" (*The Diary of Alice James*, ed. Leon Edel [New York: Dodd, Mead, 1964], p. 126).

9. Birrell, *Seven Lectures*, p. 58; Christopher Hill, *The Century of Revolution, 1603–1714* (London: Sphere, 1969), p. 35.

10. Birrell, *Seven Lectures*, pp. 47–55. See also Cyprian Blagden, *The Stationers' Company: A History, 1403–1959* (Cambridge, Mass.: Harvard University Press, 1960).

11. Frank Thayer, *Legal Control of the Press* (New York: Foundation Press, 1962). For discussion of the stationer's charter, see Blagden, *Stationers' Company*, p. 21.

12. George Haven Putnam, *The Question of Copyright* (New York: Putnam, 1891), p. 18.

13. Birrell, *Seven Lectures*, p. 58. See also Blagden, *Stationers' Company*, p. 33.

14. Hill, *Century of Revolution*, p. 92. A full discussion of the 1637 Decree Concerning Printing is in Blagden, *Stationers' Company*, pp. 118–21.

15. J. R. Tanner, *English Constitutional Conflicts of the Seventeenth Century, 1603–1685* (Cambridge: Cambridge University Press, 1962), p. 162. The American poet Susan Howe has recently completed a remarkable poem cycle on the *Eikon Basilike: A Bibliography of the King's Book or, Eikon Basilike* (Providence: Paradigm Press, 1989).

16. Thayer, *Legal Control*, p. 11.

17. Birrell, *Seven Lectures*, p. 53.

18. Ibid., p. 10.

19. Ibid., pp. 9–10; Richard Wincor, *Literary Property* (New York: Clarkson Potter, 1967), p. 10.

20. S. R. Gardiner, ed., *The Constitutional Documents of the Puritan Revolution*, 2nd ed. (Oxford: Clarendon Press, 1899), pp. 179–82.

21. Hill, *Century of Revolution*, pp. 154–55.

22. Birrell, *Seven Lectures*, p. 60.

23. Quoted in Thayer, *Legal Control*, p. 43.

24. Hill, *Century of Revolution*, p. 216; Thayer, *Legal Control*, p. 9.

25. F. D. Prager, "A History of Intellectual Property from 1545 to 1787," *Journal of the Patent Office Society* 26 (November 1944): 711–60; Lyman Ray Patterson, *Copyright in Historical Perspective* (Nashville, Tenn.: Vanderbilt University Press, 1968); Benjamin Kaplan, *An Unhurried View of Copyright* (New York: Columbia University Press, 1967); Gwyn Walters, "The Booksellers in 1759 and 1774: The Battle for Literary Property," *Library* 29 (1974): 287–311; Mark Rose, "The Author as Proprietor: *Donaldson* v. *Becket* [*sic*] and the Genealogy of Modern Authorship," *Representations* 23 (Summer 1988): 51–85. Walters's essay is particularly helpful as an outline of the struggle between London booksellers and provincial booksellers over literary property, and emphasizes the role of "pirated editions" in the copyright controversies.

26. Birrell, *Seven Lectures*, pp. 19–26; Thayer, *Legal Control*, p. 15.

27. Putnam, *Question of Copyright*, p. 18; Birrell, *Seven Lectures*, pp. 27–30.

28. In *An Introduction to the Philosophy of Law* (New Haven, Conn.: Yale University Press, 1961), Roscoe Pound gives an account of the evolution of this problem of property: "Upon the downfall of authority, seventeenth- and eighteenth-century jurists sought to put natural reason behind private property as behind all other institutions. When Kant had undermined this foundation the nineteenth-century philosophical jurists sought to deduce property from a fundamental metaphysical datum: the historical jurists sought to record the unfolding of the idea of private property in human experience, thus showing the universal idea; the utilitarian demonstrated private property by his fundamental tests and the positivist established its validity and necessity by observation of human institutions and their evolution" (pp. 113–14).

29. Birrell, *Seven Lectures*, pp. 14–15.

30. Alexander Lindey, *Plagiarism and Originality* (New York: Harper, 1952), pp. 96–97.

31. John Locke, *Two Treatises of Government*, ed. Peter Laslett (Cambridge: Cambridge University Press, 1960), Second Treatise, chapter 5, section 27, pp. 305–6.

32. John Bunyan, *Holy War* (Philadelphia: Presbyterian Board of Publication, 1803), p. xv.

33. Thayer, *Legal Control*, p. 609; Lindey, *Plagiarism and Originality*, pp. 4–8, 21. In the chapter "Defamation, Obscenity, and Copyright," Richard Posner (*Law and Literature: A Misunderstood Relation* [Cambridge, Mass.: Harvard University Press, 1988], pp. 319–52) briefly discusses the distinction between "idea" and "expression," wherein only the latter is protected by copyright law (p. 341). Posner's book is unreliable for any account of the emergence of concepts of authorship. Indeed, he assumes that the fixity of the law is given and that literature is, in contrast, subject to vagaries of interpretation. In "Don't Know Much About the Middle Ages: Posner on Law and Literature," Stanley Fish links Posner to the larger agenda of neoconservative legal formalism and its attempts to suppress (in Posner's case, according to Fish, by a pointed silence) awareness of the impact of literary theory and, analogously, of the Critical Legal Studies movement on current legal thought (*Doing What Comes Naturally: Chance, Rhetoric and the Practice of Theory in Literary and Legal Studies* [Durham, N.C.: Duke University Press, 1989], pp. 294–311).

34. Patterson, *Copyright in Historical Perspective*, p. 19.

35. Plato, *Phaedrus*, in *The Works of Plato*, trans. B. Jowett (New York: Tudor, n.d.), vol. 3, pp. 446–47.

36. J. L. Austin, *How to Do Things with Words*, ed. J. O. Urmson (New York: Oxford University Press, 1962), p. 154. The abstraction and fixity of the law as writing are also evidenced by the erasure of subjectivity and context in the conventions of legal drafting. See, for example, Reed Dickerson, *The Fundamentals of Legal Drafting* (Boston: Little, Brown, 1965), where the regulatory functions of public instruments and the dispositive functions of private instruments are merged as acts of writing: "the fact that dispositive provisions operate at specific times instead of having continuing force affects only minimally the way in which they are written" (p. 5).

37. Ludwig Wittgenstein, *Lectures and Conversations on Aesthetics, Psychology and Religious Belief*, ed. Cyril Barrett (Berkeley: University of California Press, 1972), pp. 15–16.

38. Aristotle, *Rhetoric*, in *The Basic Works of Aristotle*, ed. Richard McKeon, trans. W. D. Ross (New York: Random House, 1941), pp. 1435–36. The relation of this argument to others regarding ideal forms, including Husserl's concern with geometry, must find a resource in Aristotle's claim in this passage that "nobody uses fine language when teaching geometry" (p. 1436).

39. Roberto Mangabeira Unger, *The Critical Legal Studies Movement* (Cambridge, Mass.: Harvard University Press, 1983), p. 2. For an illuminating discussion of Unger's work as an exploration of the "antimony of theory and fact," see Stanley Fish, "Critical Legal Studies, Unger, and Milton," *Raritan* 7 (Fall 1988): 1–20, and "Critical Legal Studies (II), Roberto Unger's 'Transformative Politics,' " *Raritan* 7 (Winter 1988): 1–24 (both reprinted in Fish, *Doing What Comes Naturally*, pp. 395–435).

40. Unger, *Critical Legal Studies Movement*, p. 18.

41. Obviously, the law can be "changed" or "overturned"—and yet by completely

legal, not only by revolutionary, means. The law is not fixed in stone, but we see the sphere of legislation—the activity of making law—as this vehicle of ideological conflict and particularized interests. Thus once the law is "made," it is "proclaimed"; it "takes effect." Within this formulation, it moves only forward in its great disinterestedness.

42. Philippe Lacoue-Labarthe and Jean-Luc Nancy, *The Literary Absolute: The Theory of Literature in German Romanticism*, trans. Philip Barnard and Cheryl Lester (Albany: State University of New York Press, 1988), p. 40.

43. Ibid., p. 122.

44. See, however, Lindey, *Plagiarism and Originality*—a compilation of the history of plagiarism—as well as Daniel T. Ames, *Ames on Forgery: Its Detection and Illustration* (San Francisco: Bancroft-Whitney, 1899); Ralph D. Mawdsley, *Legal Aspects of Plagiarism* (Topeka, Kans.: National Organization on Legal Problems in Education, 1985); Peter Shaw, "Plagiary," *American Scholar* 51 (1982): 325–37; and Harold Ogden White, *Plagiarism and Imitation During the English Renaissance: A Study of Critical Distinctions* (Cambridge, Mass.: Harvard University Press, 1935). White explains that classical literary theories contended, for example, that "imitation is essential; fabrication is dangerous; subject matter is common property" (pp. 6–7). White also gives an account of Martial's coining of *plagiarus:* "Martial's protest at the piracies of which he had been the victim is probably the most famous in all literature, because in it he first used the word *plagiarus*, literally 'kidnapper,' for a literary thief. Someone had 'kidnapped' a few of Martial's poems by claiming them as his own; their rightful master addressed an epigram to a patron, appealing for justice" (p. 16). Thomas Mallon's recent work on plagiarism, *Stolen Words: Forays into the Origins and Ravages of Plagiarism* (New York: Ticknor and Fields, 1989), gives anecdotal accounts of cases of plagiarism from Laurence Sterne on. He concludes that both the desire to write and the desire to plagiarize stem from the ego's need to assert itself. Mallon assumes that *authorship* and *originality* are stable terms from the invention of the printing press to the present (p. 238). In this sense, although his book is both lively and witty, it suffers from the same lack of historical awareness as Posner's on the relations between law and literature. And its readily functionalist account, wherein all acts of plagiarism have to do with a common set of motives and ends, closes down the complexity of the problem. A far-ranging survey of issues regarding forgery and plagiarism appears in Giles Constable, "Forgery and Plagiarism in the Middle Ages," *Archiv für Diplomatik, Schriftgeschichte, Siegel-und Wappenkunde* 29 (1983): 1–41. Constable shows the changes in concepts of truth and intention from the Middle Ages forward and the transformations in the writer's role as scribe, compiler, commentator, and author. He concludes that the medieval writer did not see the contents of writing as an expression of personality or opinion, but as part of a total knowledge, a truth that was an inheritance of ancient learning. Therefore, "the term plagiarism should indeed probably be dropped in reference to the Middle Ages, since it expresses a concept of literary individualism and property that is distinctly modern" (pp. 38–39).

45. Lindey, *Plagiarism and Originality*, p. 95.

46. Albert S. Osborn, *Questioned Documents* (Rochester, N.Y.: Lawyer's Cooperative Publishing Co., 1916), p. 13.

47. Quoted in Lindey, *Plagiarism and Originality*, p. 97.

2

Psalmanazar's Others

The next pain in the balls was anthropology and the other
disciplines, such as psychiatry, that are connected with it, dis-
connected, then connected again, according to the latest discoveries. What I liked in anthropology was its inexhaustible
faculty of negation, its relentless definition of man, as though
he were no better than God, in terms of what he is not. But
my ideas on this subject were always horribly confused, for my
knowledge of men was scant and the meaning of being beyond
me.   Beckett, *Molloy* (1950)

Who speaks writing? This question must hover as the thematic of
the study with which I will begin—an account of the writings of the
eighteenth-century forger, impostor, and friend of Samuel Johnson,
"George Psalmanazar." We know no other name than this pseudonym, which he took from 2 Kings 17:3—"Shalmaneser," one of
a line of Assyrian kings by this name. From 1702 to 1708, Psalmanazar presented himself to British society as a Formosan pagan
converted to Christianity. Furthermore, he wrote a widely accepted
Historical and Geographical Description of his "native" country. The
aberration Psalmanazar poses in the description of otherness is an
aberration that is nonetheless typical of a period in which, as we
have seen, the claims of writing—the claims of authorship, originality, genius, and documentation—were in tremendous flux. In looking at the historical conditions of Psalmanazar's writing, we find a
problematic of artifice and authenticity that speaks particularly to
ethnography's current self-consciousness regarding its roots in rhetoric as well as its roots in ethnology. The historical evolution of
representational forms, and the emergence of the articulation of
social practices *as practices*, are bound up together in a dialectic that

31

defines the place of the speaking subject as it enables the description
of what is other to that subject.[1] If we have an opportunity here to
pursue "interdisciplinary" work beyond the "connections" and "dis-
connections" of Molloy's "latest discoveries," the point is not the
reduction of anthropological writing to the operation of literary
tropes, but an investigation of the historical emergence of a writing
so necessarily separated from its referent that a scholarship of documentation and verifiability, a science of universal social laws, and
conversely a cult of authorship, originality, and genius were necessary as cures for its instability.

Impostor, Forger, Ethnographer

Through a rich essay and diligent bibliography, Rodney Needham
has brought the curious case of George Psalmanazar to the attention
of contemporary anthropologists.[2] Psalmanazar's account of his Formosan origins presented to the British literary, religious, and schol-
arly communities an elaborate deception, thus concealing his true
identity—an identity, as we shall see, that can itself be gathered
only through his "confession" of his crime.

If we find in Psalmanazar an impostor who was also an ethnographer and a forger, we also find that each term of this triple identity
has a complementary and reciprocally canceling term. Like many
recent ethnographers, Psalmanazar wrote two tandem texts: the first,
an account of his travels and a description of a remote society; the
second, a personal memoir.[3] But unlike other ethnographers, Psalmanazar invented this society of a piece, and then invented a character for himself to accompany it (here, "going native" has its own
ironic reflexivity as a return to an origin one has oneself fabricated).
And since to do this was technically a crime, Psalmanazar later wrote
his final text as a form of repentance—that is, a repentance effected
by a particular rhetoric of conversion. Our terms must necessarily
slide here, for Psalmanazar "invented" a Formosa in toto, and the
exposed fictional nature of his purportedly real invention resulted
in the fictionalization of his own personal status—the "turn of fate"
awaiting all impostors. But if he was clearly a "liar," Psalmanazar
must also be referred to, even anachronistically, as an ethnographer,
for his project is a complete description of a culture—his Formosa—

its language, customs, religion, architecture, costumes, and social organization. As might be expected, the fabulous narrativity of his account of his own captivity and travels is separated in his ethnography from the present tense and indirect free style of his cultural descriptions. Yet this separation has the effect of foreclosing our questions regarding his "true story," as well as suggesting the infinite possibilities for detailing and describing all cultural forms, let alone invented ones.

There is little "external history" regarding the career of Psalmanazar. Contemporary accounts rely on the information provided in Psalmanazar's own work: *Memoirs of* ****, *Commonly Known by the Name of George Psalmanazar: A Reputed Native of Formosa. Written by himself, In order to be published after his Death.*[4] In a brief passage in her *Anecdotes*, Hester Piozzi (Mrs. Thrale) suggested that "his [Psalmanazar's] pious and patient endurance of a tedious illness confirmed the strong impression his merit made upon the mind of Mr. Johnson,"[5] while Boswell recorded a conversation in which Johnson said that he "sought after George Psalmanazar the most."[6] Sir John Hawkins quoted Johnson as saying how much he admired Psalmanazar's "piety and devotion at the close of his life," adding that Johnson said, "I should have as soon have thought of contradicting a bishop."[7] These reverential comments deserve particular attention, since they come from the figure most suffused with authenticity during the period; we should remember here, for example, Johnson's offended attitude toward the hoaxes of Chatterton and Macpherson.[8]

From Psalmanazar's *Memoirs*, we know that he was born somewhere between Avignon and Rome (he was said to have been from Languedoc and to have had a Gascon accent), that his parents were Roman Catholics, and that his father was from "an ancient but decayed" family. His parents were separated, his mother living in France and his father in Germany; his mother raised him. He successively attended a free school run by two Franciscan monks, a Jesuit college, a school taught by the rector of a small Dominican convent, and a university. He was fluent in Latin and possessed a general facility for languages. At sixteen he secured his first false passport, in which he had himself described as a young Irish theology student. Setting out for Rome, he decided instead to visit his father, five hundred miles away in Germany; but when his father was unable to support him, he set off again, this time through Germany and the Netherlands with a new forged passport in which he designated himself as a Japanese convert to Christianity. Soon, however, he modified this detail so that he appeared as a Japanese pagan. Living on raw flesh, roots, and herbs, he constructed a language with an alphabet and grammar, practiced an invented religion, and renamed himself "Psalmanazaar" (at some later point, he dropped one of the final *a*s). In this character he had many adventures: he was captured as a spy at Landau, was hired as a coffeehouse waiter at Aix-la-Chapelle, and enlisted in the army of the elector of Cologne. After a spell of poor health, he reenlisted in the duke of Mecklenburg's regiment, made up of Lutherans serving the Dutch.

In 1702 his regiment moved to Sluys, then under the governorship of Major General George Lauder. Here Psalmanazar's imposture was detected by the villainous William Innes, chaplain to the Scots regiment at Sluys. Threatening exposure of Psalmanazar's hoax, Innes suggested that they conduct a kind of publicity stunt where he would baptize the "heathen" Psalmanazar as a Protestant, thereby commending themselves to Henry Compton, bishop of London. Innes made several refinements in Psalmanazar's story, declaring that the heathen was from Formosa (less well known to Europeans than Japan) and that, when kidnapped from that country by Jesuits, he had resisted pressure to convert to Catholicism.

Bishop Compton was duly impressed, and at the end of 1703 Innes and Psalmanazar arrived in London. Psalmanazar presented the bishop with a Church of England catechism translated into "Formosan," and for the next four years Psalmanazar's imposture was a complete success. Although Father Fountenay, a Jesuit missionary to China, criticized him at a public meeting of the Royal Society, Psalmanazar successfully rebutted the accusations. In 1704, at the expense of Bishop Compton and his friends, he spent six months at Oxford, where he studied a variety of subjects and gave popular lectures on "Formosan" practices, including human sacrifice. That same year, at the age of twenty, he published *An Historical and Geographical Description of Formosa, An Island Subject to the Emperor of Japan.*

By 1707 Innes had abandoned him, taking an appointment as chaplain general to the English forces in Portugal—a reward for his conversion of Psalmanazar. After 1708 Psalmanazar's patrons drifted away, and he was generally ridiculed and led by poverty into a life of aimlessness and dissipation. He did, however, make one more attempt at imposture. In 1712 a man named Pattenden persuaded him to invent "a white sort of Japan" paint that Psalmanazar was to introduce as "white Formosa work" from his own country. When this venture failed, he became a tutor and then a clerk of a regiment in Lancashire involved in the suppression of the Jacobite rebellion. In 1717 he tried fan painting for a while and did some literary work for a London printer. In 1728, after a serious illness, he had a conversion experience. He denounced his past life and wrote his *Memoirs*, designed to be published after his death. In his remaining years, during which he regularly took opium for his "every other day ague," he studied Hebrew assiduously and wrote hackwork, including *A General History of Printing* and contributions to the multivolume *Universal History* compiled by George Sale and others. Psalmanazar lived this life in Ironmonger's Row until May 3, 1763, when he died at the age of approximately eighty-four, enjoying the general esteem noted in Johnson's recollections of his saintly character.

Psalmanazar and the Eighteenth-Century Crisis in Authenticity

Rodney Needham's reading of Psalmanazar's career focuses on the question of ethnographic verification and the "intrinsic difficulty of inventing a society." Providing a close reading of Psalmanazar's spatial symbolism, Needham shows how it maps onto a system of analogical classification that he has claimed appears in worldwide distribution.[9] Needham argues that the hoax was successful for a time because of a combination of Psalmanazar's personal qualities— secrecy, consistency, effrontery, and an air of sincerity—and concludes with a testimony to Psalmanazar's extraordinary character: "Given the opportunity, what a marvelous genuine ethnographer he could have been."[10]

Yet here I would like to reopen the case of Psalmanazar, for his writings can as well be seen in light of a larger eighteenth-century crisis in authenticity—a crisis that, far from being resolved by the later advent of a scientific enthnography, still pursues us in the irreducible conditions of ethnography as writing. It will be the point of this account of Psalmanazar's work to note that one is given such an "ethnographic" opportunity only within one's own particular moment in historical understanding. The crime of Psalmanazar should not be conceived as that of a failed ethnographer who, overly eager to make his reputation, traversed the boundaries of truth. Nor can we see Psalmanazar as simply one in a series of eighteenth-century literary fakirs. Rather, we find here a "crime" tied up with the problem of authenticity in the eighteenth century. If our current sense of the ethnographer's heroism often relates to our cultural valorization of marginality, the eighteenth-century sense of the ethnographer's value relates to a quite different set of qualities and circumstances: the persistence of cultural tradition in the face of an onslaught of technical innovations and a flood of evidence giving testimony of cultural relativism; the charm of novelty as long as it is strictly confined to its own sphere; the clash of religious differences as a clash of practices manifesting a more elusive system of belief; and the sense of culture as specimen rather than as system.

Furthermore, the specific conditions of Psalmanazar's ethnographic writing can be connected to the specific conditions of writing in general during this period. The background to Psalmanazar's hoax is a social scene in which the rise of new forms of literary production was resulting in a commodification of literary discourse. And this commodification of writing gradually demanded an authenticating apparatus, for to separate cultural productions from their contexts of origin was also to separate them from their grounds of intelligibility and closure.

During this period, older scenes of literary production—the patronage system, the court, the world of the coffeehouse, and subscriptions—gave way to those more entrepreneurial modes described in the previous chapter in James Ralph's *The Case of Authors*, particularly the emerging reign, in the first third of the century, of the booksellers.[11] Although we find Psalmanazar initially protected by Bishop Compton, throughout his career as writer he was subject to the pressures and demands of printers and to the need to generate income through the sale of his manuscripts and literary hackwork. Consider this account from Psalmanazar's *Memoirs* of writing his *Description*:

> And this I was left to hammer out of my own brain, without any other
> assistance than that of Varenius's description of Japan, which Dr.
> Innes put into my hands, to get what I could out of it. All this while,
> both he and the booksellers were so earnest for my dispatching it out
> of hand, whilst the town was hot in expectation of it, that I was
> scarcely allowed two months to write the whole.

Psalmanazar adds that "the person, who englished it from my Latin
likewise was hurried on by the booksellers."[12]

Psalmanazar arrived on the London literary scene at a moment
when the classical public sphere of letters was beginning to disin-
tegrate under pressures from private commercial interest, from the
dissemination of literacy, from the expansion of wealth and population, and from the rise of a professional writing. In genres ranging
from ballad imitations to the novel, with its new and abstracted
forms of publication, finding an immediate context for one's voice
was becoming problematic, and the relation of author to audience
increasingly one of speculation. In this gap between a context of
production and a context of reception, a certain slippage was inevitable—a slippage of the referent, and a corresponding necessity
of invention. How, then, was the writer to authenticate the grounds
of his or her authorial subjectivity outside the worlds of patronage
and literary community? The most obvious method was the generation of more discursiveness: the author must incorporate these
grounds by writing them. Here we find the problem of the constantly
self-inventing grounds of nostalgia, the already fallen status of a
desire for a point of origin that is "merely" the product of that desire
and not its originating cause. Here too we find the relentless discursiveness of a history that must constantly authenticate its own
foundations of intelligibility by the generation of more history, more
contexts. Thus we find the basis for, on the one hand, a "realistic"
fiction, based on the commonly held assumptions regarding the
immediacy of firsthand experience,[13] and, on the other, a grandiose
lie—that is, an often unattributed literature of imitation, conjecture,
and fantasy. During this period, the "responsibilities" of authorship
were undergoing a great upheaval: conventions of originality, genius,
authenticity, documentation, and even genre itself remained subjects of speculation and interest rather than of either natural "rights"
or formulated law.

Although the century began with an idealization of Augustan Rome, a more eclectic mix of historical styles emerged as it went forward: Greek classicism, medievalism, orientalism, and primitivism appealed in turn to eighteenth-century aesthetics. The concomitant taste for a literature of sensation and terror appeared as the logical consequence of such movements simply as forays into an otherness of time or space. As early as 1692, Sir William Temple had claimed in his essay "On Heroic Virtue" that certain parts of the world had been neglected by historians. He surveyed China, Peru, the Gothic north, and Islam as his examples. By the close of the century, each of these cultures had been culled for its moral, political, or artistic possibilities.[14]

But an intense desire to repeat history is doomed by its limitation as the production of history, the generation of more history whose irony and inauthenticity as a made product, a labor, rather than an imagined spontaneity, continually return to haunt the desire to simply be in time. Thus on the one hand, we find the author looking for an authentic role for himself or herself within an imagined feudal hierarchy; the minstrel, the poet/monk, and the bard appeared here as authorial roles grounded in patronage and its perhaps less mediated forms of production and reception. And on the other hand, authors invented a subjectivity marked by a tautological return from a foray into otherness.

These "unnatural" labors, these self-conscious forays into otherness, inevitably resulted in a series of humiliations and, eventually, scandals: humiliations such as the Wits' derisive reception of the imitative "epic" works of Richard Blackmore, Richard Glover, William Wilkie, James Ogden, and James Ogilvie early in the century, and scandals of imposture like James Macpherson's *Ossian* poems, Joseph Ritson's and Lady Wardlaw's ballad forgeries, and Thomas Chatterton's forgeries of the works of an imaginary medieval monk, Thomas Rowley, toward the middle and latter parts of the century.[15] These were all writers who attempted to invent an imaginary, and radically distant, context for their writings. It is one of the more elegant ironies of Psalmanazar's ethnography that he claimed that many cultural practices of the Formosans, including the calendar, were established by a prophet named, appropriately enough, Psalmanazar. We can thus begin to see Psalmanazar's writing, with

its self-invented grounds of authenticity, as a kind of typical aberration.

From the time that Chinese visitors had first appeared in Europe
at the close of the seventeenth century, their appearance produced
its own anamorphosis. In his *Memoirs and Observations* of 1699, the
Jesuit emissary and, later, travel writer Louis Le Comte wrote of
his encounter with a lady who assumed the role of a Chinese princess
swept to Europe by a series of shipwrecks and captivities. Le Comte
exposed her imposture when she audaciously attempted to "pass
off a wild ridiculous gibberish" as Chinese.[16] But even actual visitors
from China had little to do with the construction of the Orient in
the literary culture. During the eighteenth century's "Chinese
vogue," the cultural Other was an occasion for reflexivity in the form
of satire, the literary form that above all others assumes a natural
stance in its focus upon the critique of all artificiality.[17] But these
singular foreign visitors cast upon the shores of British literary culture
held up another kind of satirical mirror to the stranded authorial
subjectivity of the period. Without a context, without a tangible
social world, any "visitor" could be an impostor; any pauper a prince;
and any author a God, to put it positively, or a forger, to put it
negatively. Moreover, such visitors—prototypical ethnological "in-
formants"—had their corollary as items for collection and consumption in the literary "discoveries" of the period from among the lower
classes and their promotion by the aristocracy.[18] Here the literary
culture estranges itself from its own past as well as from the cultural
other in order to invent a myth of cultural origins.

Throughout the eighteenth century, a variety of individuals are
"set loose" from their moorings in a cultural context and are consequently aestheticized. The self-consciousness of this "natural"
artifice will eventually, we might conclude, find its release in the
transgressions and expressiveness of Romanticism, but earlier in the
period a variety of "cross-dressing" appears—tangential, surrepti-
tious, even coy in its deliberations of *le mode rétro*. Aristocrats and
bourgeois authors collaborated in the production of a "written folklore"; orientalism and feudalism were combined in an apotheosis of
spatial and temporal "otherness"; colonialism developed a market
based on the consumption of exotic and exoticized goods. And everywhere, as Henri Lefebvre has noted in a more contemporary context,

capitalism revealed its capacity for the reinscription of everything—
including history—as novelty:

> Capitalism has not only subordinated exterior and anterior sectors to
> itself, it has produced new sectors, transforming what pre-existed and
> completely overthrowing the corresponding institutions and organi-
> zations. The same is true of "art," knowledge, "leisure," urban and
> everyday reality. It is a vast process which, as usual, is wrapped in
> appearances and ideological masks. For example, capitalist produc-
> tion loots previous oeuvres and styles, changes them into objects of
> "cultural" production and consumption and thus recapitulates these
> styles in restituted and reconstituted form as "neo" this or that, elite
> fashions and high quality products.[19]

The production of knowledge does not take place in some transcendent context: in Psalmanazar's strange case, we see the gap
between subjectivity and otherness as the enabling possibility of
both understanding and, of course, its flip side, delusion. At a time
when the self-consciousness of ethnography as a form of writing has
reached a new and no less enlightened pitch, it would be wise to
remind ourselves of this shifting historical relation to a referent. The
anthropologist as impostor is involved in an ultimately tragic production of signifiers. And ironically, a collapse of writing into the
referent will suffer no less from the same end, a simple reversal,
should the tide turn to a predominance of an ever elusive "signified."

Analogy and Difference:
Psalmanazar's Cultural Reasoning

In his *Memoirs* Psalmanazar explains his decision to change his imposture as an itinerant Irish theology student to that of a native of
Japan:

> I recollected, that whilst I was learning humanity, rhetoric, and ge-
> ography with the Jesuits, I had heard them speak of the East-Indies,
> China, Japan, &c. and expatiate much in praise of those countries,
> and the ingenuity of the inhabitants. . . . I was rash enough to think
> that what I wanted of a right knowledge of them, I might make up
> by the strength of a pregnant invention, in which I flattered myself I
> might succeed the more easily, as I supposed they were as little known
> by the generality of Europeans, that they were only looked upon, in

the lump, to be Antipodes to them in almost every respect, as religion, manners, dress, &c.[20]

Thus it would be Psalmanazar's goal to differentiate the lump in line with these "antipodal" expectations. He eventually arrived at a perfect method for the generation of ethnographic information:

> Alas, for me, my fancy was but too fertile and ready for all such things, when I set about them, and when any question has been started on a sudden, about matters I was ever so unprepared for, I seldom found myself at a loss for a quick answer, which, if satisfactory, I stored up in my retentive memory.[21]

There is no supply of answers here without the demanding questions: the con man's rule, "give 'em what they want," became for Psalmanazar a way of structuring an imaginary social whole—its closure provided by the prior assumption of closure on the part of its audience. The content of that closure, its very remoteness, ensured by this isolated and figuratively "inverted" island, was on hand to help Psalmanazar even before he began, as was the fact that in England, as opposed to continental Europe, the Jesuit letter books, with their rich accounts of Asia, were neither circulated nor translated widely.[22]

Psalmanazar's presentation was convincing in part because of his complete invention of a "native" personality for himself. While attached to the duke of Mecklenburg's regiment in Holland, he watched the Lutheran and Calvinist services:

> But as for me, after listening awhile to them, I was commonly driven by my rashness and vanity to turn my back to them, and turning my face to the rising or setting sun, to make some awkward shew of worship, or praying to it, and was no less pleased to be taken notice of for so doing. This vain fit grew up to such a height, that I made me a little book with figures of the sun, moon, and stars, and such other imagery as my phrensy suggested to me, and filled the rest with a kind of gibberish prose and verse, written in my invented character, and which I muttered or chanted as often as the humour took me.[23]

As he left with Innes for England, he invented another ruse:

> I fell upon one of the most whimsical expedients that could come into a crazed brain, viz. that of living upon raw flesh, roots, and herbs; and it is surprising how soon I habituated myself to this new, and till

now, strange food, without receiving the least prejudice in my health; but I was blessed with a good constitution, and I took care to use a good deal of pepper, and other spices, for a concocter, whilst my vanity, and the people's surprize at my diet, served me for a relishing sauce.[24]

We can imagine the spectacle of Psalmanazar during this period: his "rude, cast off clothing," donated by Innes; his little book of the sun, moon, and stars; his diet of barbaric simplicity; and, not least of all, his prodigious classical learning. Here was a fusion of classicism and the exotic—and at the same time a complete negation of any ordinary presentness—which was to become the daydream of the more marginal developments of eighteenth-century literary culture.

What is the shape of Psalmanazar's *Historical and Geographical Description of Formosa?* How does he go about inventing a social totality? Two aspects of this ethnography immediately present themselves as paramount. First, there is the production of a system of differences—that is, an immediately apprehensible and hence comparable system of categories of the social: manners, gestures, means of transport, architecture, costumes, ritual, and so on. Such categories then internalize the situation of difference, as social rank enters into them in a pervasive and equally systematic way. And second, there is an internal consistency whose cumulative effect will be that of a rational necessity.

The *Description* begins, as might be expected, with etiology—an account of the relation of Formosa to other islands "in the remotest parts toward the East," especially Japan. Then there is a brief, dramatic account of how Formosa "preserved its form of government independent of a Foreign Prince until Meryaandanoo [a Chinese] first ravished Japan by villany, and then conquered Formosa by a trick." All this is designed to explain why Formosa is under the contemporary rule of a Japanese "superintendent King." The extensive account of the Emperor Meryaandanoo, like any myth, tells of the origins of cultural practices, legitimating them by appearance in a narrative rather than by some more abstract rationale. But we must not underestimate another function well served by this initial narrative—that of entertainment. For Psalmanazar's description was not simply a contribution to science, but a text designed for public consumption. Following this narrative introduction, the schematic contents of the *Description* are frequently alleviated by anecdotal passages and long interpolations on Formosan religion, with its obvious allegorical relation to Western religions and Psalmanazar's own situation. Psalmanazar's tasks were to balance authority and originality, and convention and idiosyncrasy, for a public clamoring for novelty—a novelty that should remain nonetheless familiar.

The *Description*'s outline of the social life of the Formosans clarifies the universality of a system of differences that must have been more than familiar to Psalmanazar's readers. Murderers, thieves, slanderers, robbers, traitors, adulterers, and other rebels against family and state meet appropriate, if often shockingly "barbarous," ends. The religion of the Formosans includes a sacred text, the *Jarhabandiond* ("The Election of the Land"); a revelation of "one supreme god"; a practice of child sacrifice; and a prophet named, in the "coincidence" noted above, Psalmanazar, or "the Author of Peace." It is Psalmanazar who orders the construction of a temple, who establishes the calendar as ten months (each named for a star), and who commands that every year the hearts of eighteen thousand young boys under the age of nine years should be sacrificed. But throughout the text, it is the Formosan religion that is most strongly delineated: festivals, fasting days, ceremonies; the procedures for sacrifices; the election of priests; the worship of the sun, moon, and stars; the postures of the body in adoring; the ceremonies observed on the birth of children; weddings; funerals; the state of souls after death; and the form of priestly garments—all are carefully described.

Following the establishment of the principles of religious order, there are chapters on manners, customs, and physical characteristics. Perhaps because by this time Psalmanazar was having difficulty explaining his complexion and overall facial appearance to missionaries who had been to the Orient, he describes "the men of Estates, but especially the Women, [as] very fair; for they during the hot season, live underground in places that are very cold." We are next given an outline of costume by gender and rank; a description of cities, houses, palaces, and castles; "those commodities they have, and some that they want"; weights and measures; superstitions; diseases; revenues of those in high places; "the Fruits of the Ground"; "Things which they Commonly Eat"; animals; the language; the shipping; money (figure 1); arms; musical instruments; education; the liberal and mechanical arts in Japan; "the splendid Retinue that

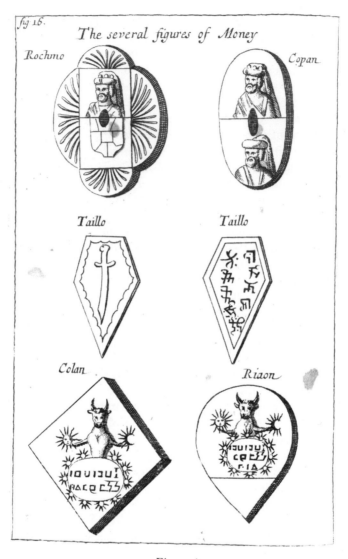

Figure 1
"The several figures of Money." From George Psalmanazar, *An Historical and Geographical Description of Formosa*, 2nd ed. (Courtesy of The Library Company of Philadelphia)

attends the Vice-Roy of Formosa when he goes to Wait Upon the
Emperor of Japan"; "the History of the Jesuits in Japan"; "the
History of the Dutch in Japan"; and "Of the new Devices of
the Jesuits for getting into Japan."

Yet the table of contents here does not do justice to the careful
blend of anecdote, detail, and evaluation making up Psalmanazar's
Description. Religious practice and its relation to belief are woven as
themes into nearly every part of his account. Psalmanazar carefully
balances what one needs to know and what he needs to tell, always
portraying details through a firsthand knowledge, but hedging his
judgments by claiming the limits of his experience as a member of
the culture, rather than a transcendent observer, and by reflecting on
his changed status as a convert away from the culture—a Christian.
The reader is thus constantly aware of a principle of differentiation
as the basis for culture—a principle whose structure is linked to the
West, but whose "Formosan" referents constantly emphasize a defining otherness. It is therefore not surprising that rank is the first
principle of Formosan social order: the king: the queen, the viceroy,
the viceroy's lady, the general, the general's lady, a gentleman, a
gentlewoman, a burger, a country bumpkin. These categories are
elaborated in the discussion of costume (figure 2), which itself becomes reduced in quantity as well as quality as one descends in
rank: "The Country People who dwell in Villages and Desert-places,
wear nothing but a Bears skin upon their shoulders, and a Plate to
cover their Privy-parts made of Brass or the shells of Fish, or the
bark of Trees."[25] In contrast, figures of the upper ranks are clothed
in silk, gold, silver, and precious stones. Thus rank is tied to proximity to nature, the upper ranks being linked to elaboration, re-
finement, and detail, and the lower ranks to simplicity and raw
materials.

As is evident from the paired categories, gender is elaborated as
another important principle of order. There are differentiated habits
for differentiated categories of women: infants, virgins, brides, married women, and widows. And finally, in a category close to his own
experience, Psalmanazar describes the military. Here rank is separated into the king's officers and guards; the viceroy's guards; the
soldiers guarding the city; the drummers and the ensigns. Psalmanazar's emphasis on costume, like his emphasis on architecture, is a
brilliant device for reifying appearances. Just as narrative forestalls

Figure 2
Formosan figures in costume. From George Psalmanazar, *An Historical and Geographical Description of Formosa*, 2nd ed. (Courtesy of The Library Company of Philadelphia)

the questions of founding principles, so does costume assign differences in rank to the realm of surfaces already given. Psalmanazar concludes his discussion of costume: "This is all I thought worthy to be remark'd as to their Apparel, which altho it may appear ridiculous to the Europeans, yet is there accounted very Beautiful and Splendid."[26]

In addition to the familiar categories of Western European rank—the aristocracy, the gentry, the peasantry, the clergy, and the military—we find the familiar literary categories of historical difference, categories that would have been well known to Psalmanazar's audience from traveler's accounts and other literary forms. The emphasis upon cremation rather than burial of the body (figure 3), the worship of the sun, moon, and stars, and the practice of animal

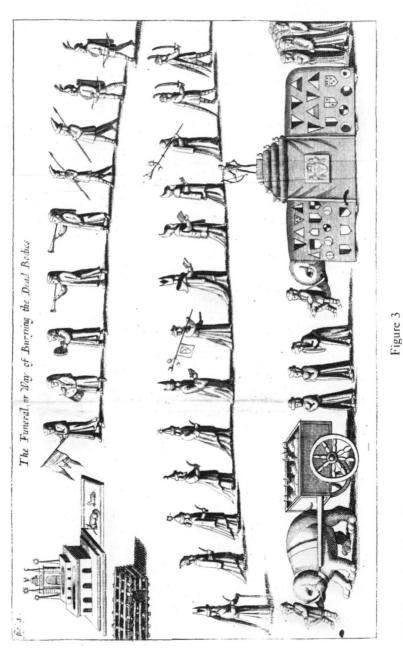

Figure 3

"The Funeral, or Way of Burning the Dead Bodies." From George Psalmanazar, *An Historical and Geographical Description of Formosa*, 2nd ed. (Courtesy of The Library Company of Philadelphia.)

sacrifice would all have echoed to Christian perceptions of paganism. Similarly, the practice of polygamy, and Psalmanazar's account of a husband's varying loyalties to his various wives, echoed the attack on Islam by medieval European writers who charged Muhammad with promiscuity for the practice of polygamy.[27] And Psalmanazar's repeated descriptions of the prostrate body, in his accounts of ceremony and ritual, would have reminded readers of the "humiliating" kowtow ceremonies that the Chinese had imposed on seventeenth-century Dutch traders.[28] Finally, the paradisiacal commodities of Psalmanazar's Formosa—gold, silver, and silk—provide a familiar background for Psalmanazer's fantastic narrative of greed and colonization. From Herodotus, Ctesias, and later writers, Europe had imagined the Orient as a land overflowing with precious stones and treasure.[29] Thus the strange is always allied to the familiar in this system of resonant allusions and "antipodal expectations." We are reminded of the tradition of "digging to China, where everything will be upside down," in passages such as these: "The Tree is like a Wall-nut Tree, but in this differs from all other Trees, that whereas their Fruit stands downward, the Fruit of this stands upright"; "Chilak is a kind of powder made like Coffee, but in this it differs from Coffee, that it may be drunk cold, whereas Coffee is always drunk hot."[30]

No detail affirms the difference of Psalmanazar's Formosa, its existence as irredeemably other, more than his account of the practice of child sacrifice. But as the imaginative limit of cultural difference, this practice, too, appears often in eighteenth-century literature. We are reminded, of course, of Swift's *Modest Proposal*, where in fact Psalmanazar is mentioned:

> the famous Sallmanaazar, a Native of the Island Formosa, who... told my friend, that in his Country when any young Person happened to be put to death, the Executioner sold the Carcass to Persons of Quality, as a prime Dainty, and that, in his Time, the Body of a plump Girl of fifteen, who was crucified for attempting to Poison the Emperor, was sold... in Joints from the Gibbet.[31]

In this shocking relation, we find in fact an entirely Western European daydream: the crucifixion and the transubstantiation of Christ mapped onto an allegory of total commodification, as well as the memory of a "barbaric" legal code aimed at the rectification of the body and only recently supplanted by a penal system designed to rectify the spirit.

But perhaps even more strikingly (because an echo and not, as in Swift's case, a precedent), we find here the sentiments of that foundation statement of the underlying principle of cultural variability, Locke's *Essay Concerning Human Understanding* (1690), and its dogmatic insistence on the impossibility of innate moral principles:

> Have there not been whole nations, and those of the most civilized people, amongst whom the exposing their children, and leaving them in the fields to perish by want or wild beasts has been the practice; as little condemned or scrupled as the begetting them? Do they not still, in some countries, put them into the same graves with their mothers, if they die in childbirth; or despatch them, if a pretended astrologer declares them to have unhappy stars? . . . There are places where they eat their own children. The Caribbees were wont to geld their children on purpose to fat and eat them. And Garcilasso de la Vega tells us of a people in Peru which were wont to fat and eat the children they got on their female captives, whom they kept as concubines for that purpose, and when they were past breeding, the mothers themselves were killed too and eaten.[32]

Locke goes on with his list of moral atrocities that nevertheless affirm the variable organization of human culture—cannibalism, infanticide, parricide, and the special case of cannibalism of one's own progeny. "Anthropophagi," or man-eating, had been part of the Western European mythology of the cultural Other from Homer on. Psalmanazar's account of Formosan sacrifice thus touched on several familiar notions, especially the linking of cannibalism, human sacrifice, and addiction to human flesh.[33] It is therefore not so surprising that the eccentric Psalmanazar himself came to be accused of cannibalistic deeds. In a sham advertisement in *The Spectator* for March 16, 1711, an opera is announced, *The Cruelty of Atreus*, to be performed at Haymarket, "the scene wherein Thyestes eats his own children is to be performed by the famous Mr. Psalmanazar, lately arrived from Formosa: The whole Supper being set to kettle-drums."[34] Later, such satire was recorded as fact. Needham notes the following passage from Boucher de la Richarderie's *Bibliothèque universelle des Voyages* (1808): "Psalmanazar himself, transported to London, had retained this depraved taste to such an extent that,

excited to eat the flesh of a woman who had been hanged, he did so
without repugnance."[35]

Psalmanazar had described the practice of child sacrifice with a
hyperbolic intensity that was likely to elicit such horrified responses,
but that also elicited disbelief. In the preface to the second edition
of the *Description*, he answers twenty-five objections, including a
number referring specifically to his account of sacrificial practices.
Thus the seventeenth—"Is it possible that any people can be so
barbarously superstitious as to sacrifice so many thousand children
every year?"—is rebutted by arguing that the Formosans lack the
blessing of revealed religion and by pointing to numerous instances
of such sacrifices in the Christian Bible. To the eighteenth objection,
that George Candidius, the early-seventeenth-century Dutch missionary to Formosa, did not mention this custom, Psalmanazar replies that Candidius—whose *Account of the Island of Formosa* was in
fact the major source for his own account—is a forger and that these
sacrifices are not as strange as Candidius's own mention that women
pregnant before their thirty-seventh year have their bellies stomped
until they miscarry. And to the nineteenth objection, that "the
sacrifice of 18,000 boys a year would soon depopulate the island,"
Psalmanazar offers four responses: this is what the law says, but
they never sacrifice that many; polygamy produces many children;
children are sacrificed at a very young age; and, finally, "just consider
how many Englishmen emigrate; there are now four times as many
women as men."

If the familiarity of hierarchy and the exoticism of cultural
practices form a rhetoric of analogy and difference, Psalmanazar
adds to this rhetoric an undercurrent of satire, continually mut-
tering comments against the priestly class in a clear attempt to
criticize all priests, particularly the Jesuits, who function as his
enemies in his account of his "kidnapping" and in his current
debates with missionaries such as Father Fountenay. This anti-
clerical subtext is evident, for example, in comments on priestly
greed:

> But after such a Beast dies of itself, or is offer'd in Sacrifice to our
> God, then they believe that the Soul which was in it, shall be trans-
> formed into a Star in Heaven, where it shall enjoy eternal happiness.
> But all this seems to me to be a fiction invented by our Priests,

because they reap great profit and advantage by it, for when anyone
dies, the Relations of the Deceased, are to pay them a great sum of
Money, more or less, according to their ability.[36]

The theme also appears in comments on priestly hypocrisy. In a
passage describing "a Notable story" regarding superstitions, Psalmanazar tells how a countryman exposed a hoax by a priest. Consequently, "the High Priest, or their Pope," condemned the priest
to perpetual imprisonment and the countryman to death "for not
yielding due Deference and Submission to the Priest; from whence
everyone may clearly perceive what Tyranny the Priests exercise
over the common people, who are not permitted to declare Publickly
any doubt they have even of those things they know to be false."[37]

Once again, we see Psalmanazar working to maintain a balance
between the novel and the comprehensible. Yet while idiosyncrasy
served the interests of a rhetoric of credibility here—the particular
detail, in this early phase of the realist tradition, lending authenticity
to the whole—only replicability could ensure the cohesion of such
facts. We find Psalmanazar, in his encounters with objections, scrambling to make analogies to the cultural practices of the Japanese as
the Formosans' landlords and closest neighbors, to the polygamy of
the Turks, and to the foodways of the Tartars. These are objections
of function, relying upon assumptions that a culture is interested in
its own perpetuation and that cultural practices have some purpose,
some material end. While Psalmanazar's British audience may have
been willing to believe that God would sacrifice his only son for the
life of humanity, common sense rebelled against the portrayal of a
widespread cultural practice of child sacrifice. Psalmanazar had to
at one and the same time manage a radical difference that would
ensure his own authority and a system of analogies that would make
his claims intelligible. Thus he often points to "aberrations" in
English culture—the beheading of Charles I before his own palace,
the emigration of the male population, the inadequacy of existing
English histories, even the "chalk scores" milkwomen use instead
of numbers. What "gets lost in translation here" is in fact the surplus
that ensures that "there is something there there," to paraphrase
Gertrude Stein. Consider Psalmanazar's answer to the twenty-fifth
objection in the second edition: "If he's really a Christian, why does
he talk about returning home, where he must renounce his religion

or be crucified?" Psalmanazar writes that he "can answer this in
private," a reserve thereby constituting "a reserve," a kind of treasure of the unsaid.

We must note here that rationality is not simply a matter of logic,
causality, or effect but also a matter of predictability and repetition.
As any spy knows, one's ability to reproduce the culture is what
gives integrity to the culture. But because of the obvious fact that
he has no referent, Psalmanazar can only produce a culture; he
cannot reproduce one. Thus we find a central, tragic scene in Psalmanazar's biography: his "fall from language," the exposure of his
forgery's singularity brought about by the equally cunning con man
William Innes.[38] At the onset of his imposture, Psalmanazar had
invented a Formosan alphabet (figure 4), including "names for the
letters" and a partial grammar.[39] During his service with the Scots
regiment at Sluys, Innes expressed interest in converting Psalmanazar, yet

> he was so far from believing me to be what I pretended, that he had
> some time before taken a most effectual way to convince himself of
> the contrary, beyond all possibility of doubting. His stratagem, if I
> may so call it, was to make me translate a passage in Cicero *de natura
> deorum*, of some length, into my (pretended) Formosan language, and
> give it to him in writing; and this I easily did, by means of that
> unhappy readiness I had at inventing of characters, languages, &c.
> But, after he had made me construe it, and desired me to write another
> version of it on another paper, his proposal, and the manner of his
> exacting it, threw me into such visible confusion, having had so little
> time to excogitate the first, and less to commit it to memory, that
> there were not above one half of the words in the second that were
> in the first. His desiring me to construe this likewise, confused me
> still more; especially when he showed me the palpable difference.[40]

Innes, far from being scandalized, was, as we know from Psalmanazar's consequent relation to him as the patron of his "imposture,"
pleased with Psalmanazar's "memory and readiness." As if to make
up for this exposure, Psalmanazar armed his chapter on the language
of the Formosans in his *Historical and Geographical Description* with
the catechisms he had given to Bishop Compton: translations of the
Lord's Prayer, the Apostles' Creed, and the Ten Commandments.

The *Description*, we must remember, is flanked by two conversions:
preceding the ethnographic description, Psalmanazar gave a detailed

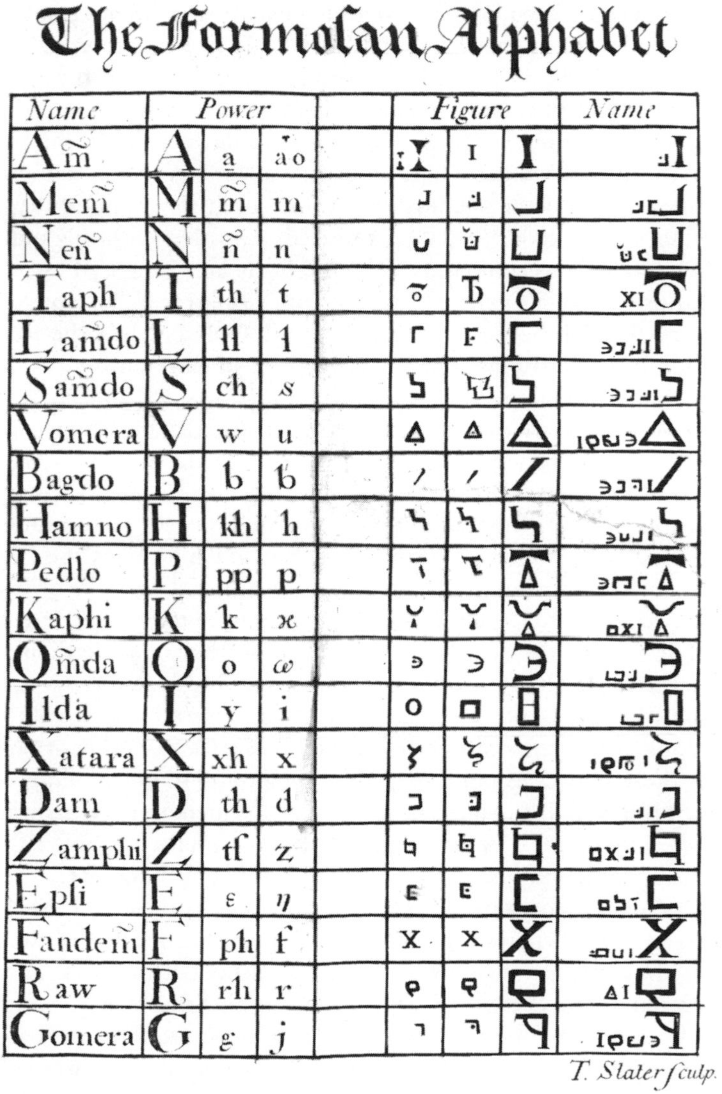

The Formosan Alphabet

Name	Power			Figure			Name
Am	A	a	ao		I	I	ꓩ
Mem	M	m̃	m		ꓘ	ꓘ	ꓴ
Nen	N	ñ	n		∪	ŭ	⊔	ŭᴄ⊔
Taph	T	th	t		ꝺ	Ƀ	O	xi O
Lamdo	L	ll	l		ᒥ	Ⅎ	ᒪ	ꝺꝺᴵᒪ
Samdo	S	ch	s		ᒯ	ꕥ	ꙅ	ꝺꝺᴵꙅ
Vomera	V	w	u		△	△	△	ıꝺꙅꝺ△
Bagdo	B	b	b		∕	∕	⟋	ꝺꝺᴵⱶ⟋
Hamno	H	kh	h		�	�	�5	ꝺᴜᴵ�5
Pedlo	P	pp	p		ꓔ	ꓕ	▲	ꝺꓵᴄ▲
Kaphi	K	k	x		ꙏ	ꙏ	Ꙑ	ꝺxı Ꙑ
Omda	O	o	ω		Ǝ	Ǝ	Ǝ	ꝆꙆᴶ Ǝ
Ilda	I	y	i		○	□	☐	Ꝇᴜᴄ☐
Xatara	X	xh	x		ꙡ	ꙅ	ꙟ	ıꝺꙟıꙟ
Dam	D	th	d		ꓩ	ꓩ	ꓩ	ꙅᴵᒪꓩ
Zamphi	Z	tf	z		ꓷ	ꓷ	ꓷ	ꝺxꙅᴵꓷ
Epfi	E	ε	η		E	E	Ꞓ	�ꞒꙅᴵꞒ
Fandem	F	ph	f		x	x	X	ꙅꝺᴜᴵX
Raw	R	rh	r		ꝑ	Ꝓ	Ꝗ	▵ıꝖ
Gomera	G	g	j		ꓶ	ꓶ	Ꝙ	ıꝺꙅꝘ

T. Slater ſculp.

Figure 4
"The Formosan Alphabet" from "George Psalmanazar," *An Historical and Geographical Description of Formosa*, Second Edition. (The Library Company of Philadelphia.)

and schematic account of his fictional conversion from paganism to Anglicanism. The issues here have multiple levels of reference. His rejection and even vilification of the Jesuits throughout the *Description* stemmed from their presence as the only extant "counterintelligence" regarding Formosa. His ingenious questioning of the tenets of faith referred directly to the questions occupying the more skeptical members of his readership. "How could the wonderful works pretended to be done by Christ and his Apostles [be] true and real Miracles, such as could only be wrought by an Almighty Power and not done by the Tricks of Jugglers and Conjurers?"[41] "How could one distinguish between Objects of Faith Only [such as the Roman belief in transubstantiation] and Objects of our senses?"[42] "How could one be certain, that what the Evangelists and Apostles assert is Truth; for they might impose upon us, and write things which never were performed?"[43] "How can one be sure that the Books we have of the New Testament are the same the Evangelists and the Apostles penn'd, and that in Succession of Time they have not been changed and altered?"[44] "If the sacrificing of Children by the Pagans seems so very unnatural, surely the Death and Passion of Christ shew much more Cruelty; it is harder therefore to believe, that God should require the Sacrifice of his only Son, than of some thousands of Infants."[45] Here once more Psalmanazar brilliantly "covered his tracks," making invisible a writing that referred only to its own making as writing, erasing the "source" of its assumption of power. For these questions point to a common ground of questioning; they are, after all, the issues raised against Psalmanazar by his critics. And as well, they point to the ingenuous quality of the cultural Other, whose very naiveté is evidence of his authenticity.

Psalmanazar provides sixteen plates. There is no record that I can discover as to whether he did these drawings himself, but the fact that they closely illustrate rather than embellish the text, and his mention in the *Memoirs* of his drawings in his little book of worship, lead me to conclude that Psalmanazar is most likely the artist. His text is full of specific and noncontradictory details: here was clearly a photographic imagination, if not a photographic "memory." Psalmanazar had truly drawn a world from his reading and his imagination. Thus the *Description* fulfilled an ultimate Enlightenment dream—the dream of animation where logical consistency can itself produce a referent, a world engendered by reason alone, unencum-

bered by history, materiality, or nature. Psalmanazar, we must assume, recognized the skill of this accomplishment. When in the
second preface he answers the objection that he is too young to have
such a knowledge of his culture, he counters:

> You do me more Honour than you are aware of, for then you must
> think that I forg'd the whole story out of my own Brain. . . . he must
> be a Man of prodigious parts who can invent the Description of a
> Country, contrive a Religion, frame Laws and Customs, make a Lan-
> guage, and Letters, etc. and these different from all other parts of
> the world; he must have also more than a humane memory that is
> always ready to vindicate so many feign'd particulars, and that without
> e'er so much as once contradicting himself.[46]

Here we find the ethnography's integrity, its closure as a systematic description, and its collapse, its dislocation as a kind of refusal
of common grounds of intelligibility. Psalmanazar's forgery could
not stand up to the pressures of its own claims by 1708: it "burst
at the seams," and he himself played a primary role in its collapse.
This is the vulnerability of all forgeries—their incapacity to carry
their appropriate contexts with them. Thus we can see forgery as
the antithesis of plagiarism, for while plagiarism's crime is an inappropriate repetition, forgery's crime is an inappropriate, and entirely invented, singularity. The forger is always already an impostor
by his or her attempt to escape the social grounds of subjectivity
and authorship. Psalmanazar's brilliant move was to forge an entire
social world and hence to provide such grounds sui generis. If this
was the dream of Enlightenment reason, it was also the dream of
Enlightenment authorship: to usher in whatever is necessary to make
the world, as a textual world, cohere.

The Figure of Conversion

If it was the discursiveness and materiality of his writing that enabled
Psalmanazar to accomplish his imposture, these very features were
to be remedied by his final conversion. The work of his later life
(after the fiasco of the "Japanning" paint, a final pun on the "covering" of the material grounds of his being) was designed as a kind
of crosshatching (to use an eighteenth-century writing practice as a

metaphor) of his earlier texts. Psalmanazar contributed anonymously to Bowen's *Complete System of Geography* of 1747, providing the entry on Formosa and using it as a forum to criticize the imposture of Psalmanazar and, strikingly, the account of Candidius, which deserved "as little credit as that of our pretended Formosan." In the *Memoirs* he explains that he chose "Formosa . . . that I might take occasion publickly to acknowledge, as it were by a third hand, the falsehood and imposture of my former account of that island."[47] Anonymity, the "third hand," is of course the best cure for infamy, the one that allows a continued production, just as forgetting is the analogous cure for memory.

Psalmanazar's deep return to Hebrew as the source of authentic language was a counter to his invention of Formosan characters. A decade earlier, he had played an important part in the writing of the *Universal History*, where he anonymously contributed chapters on the Jews, the Celts, the Scythians, the Greeks, the empires of Nice and Taubizon, the ancient Spaniards, Gauls, Germans, Thebans, and Corinthians. Psalmanazar's work for the *Universal History* replaced the self-aggrandizing particulars of his *Description* with self-effacing generalities. The goal of the *Universal History* was the integration of all historical cultures within a specifically Christian chronology. The preface to the first volume, dedicated to the duke of Marlborough, includes comparative tables of weights and moneys and goes on to explain: "works of this nature carry our knowledge, as Tully observes, beyond the vast and devouring Space of numberless years, triumph over Time and make us, though living at an immense Distance, in a Manner Eye-witness to all the Events and Revolutions which have occasioned astonishing changes in the World."[48] This was a world, a history, already known and already redeemed; it was in turn, of course, an ideal counter to the wild details of Psalmanazar's *Description*.

Thus what might also draw our attention here is the interplay between Psalmanazar's ethnography and his final works as an interplay between two rhetorical modes: the description/testimony and the confession/conversion. These two gestures—one reaching out to the world within a stance of distance and objectivity, the other reaching inward in a claim of transformation that in itself asserts or posits the very subjectivity that is its "motivating" cause—run in an obvious course from the halted narrative and ensuing lyricism of

Augustine's "confessions" to the paired volumes of ethnographic description and personal memoirs produced by anthropologists even today.[49] In fact, we might hypothesize that we find in these complementary rhetorics the ghost of eighteenth-century anthropology's missionary connections: the rhetoric of transformation projected here as a rhetoric of writing; the conversion of "experience" or "spectacle" into detail; the conversion of "the scene" into form; and the conversion, ultimately, of other into self, and self into other.

It is clear that these are interconnected sets of rhetorical modes, constantly bolstering one another in an attempt at persuasiveness and credibility. The confession is the narrative of the convert's fall and redemption, which of course achieves closure only at the moment of that redemption and so is, like tragedy, a narrative finished before it is begun. Furthermore, the confession acquires its integrity and value in proportion to its degree of detail and specificity. For every detail speaks to the authenticity generated by the "first hand," testifying as to the reliability of the speaker, lending authority to the speaker's self and capacity for truth. Thus it is obvious that the function of description in the confessional mode is not the replication of an "outside," an objective world unaffected by authorial consciousness, but the invention of the speaking subject as the location of veracity.

But these general features of confessional testimony, these qualities of "eye-witnessing" as "I-witnessing," are given a very specific form in Psalmanazar's texts. For Psalmanazar's conversions—from his native Catholicism to his imaginary "Formosan" religious practices; from "Formosan" to a feigned Anglicanism; and, finally, from a feigned Anglicanism to a true Anglicanism—must be read as conversions both from one set of cultural practices to another and from one set of subjectivities to another. Weaving in and out of doctrine, practice, appearance, and sincerity, these conversions effect a remarkable set of transformations even as surface changes. Yet it is only in Psalmanazar's final conversion—his conversion from a lie to "the truth" in the revelations of his memoirs and the habits of his later life—that he partakes of the religious, and often sexual, transformations of darkness and light, sin and salvation, familiar from the Augustine "break" with the world.[50] Here we must realize what tremendous power the feature of closure has on our acceptance of this rhetoric of "truth." There is no intrinsic reason to accept Psalmanazar's final account as being any more valid than his other accounts, but two features lend it a powerful credibility: the testimony of witnesses to his consistent practices of piety in his last years, and the power of death as the ultimate closure. Thus the corroboration of a "social" as the other to "self," the absolute otherness of death (its resistance to the manipulations of style and the frame), and the play on closure in the nonclosure of answerability and salvation that death assumes in Christian myth, all impress on us the authenticity of the "final account" as more than mere version.

We must remember that for an eighteenth-century writer, religion as a practice as well as a philosophy was a pressing, perhaps the most pressing, force of cultural differentiation; the relentless optimism of missionary work (of both the Jesuitical and Oxford varieties in Psalmanazar's moment) speaks to the relative unimportance of other signs of difference in the face of religious practices. In his *Memoirs*, just as in his rebuttals of objections to the *Description*, Psalmanazar still questioned the validity of religious doctrines, especially the issues raised by Catholic transubstantiation and Calvinist predestination. The singling out of these doctrines is not arbitrary, but a matter of the relationship such issues of appearance, reality, and free will had to his own transgressions and to his situation amid Jesuit, Anglican, and Calvinist influences. Indeed, the emphasis upon faith in miracles in his writings provides a repetitive clue to the problem of his own discourse—its failed referent and its insistent singularity. Swift's debts to Psalmanazar's geography and his accounts of human sacrifice are obvious, but we also see in Psalmanazar's vexed relation to doctrine the prototype of the niggling "bigendian" controversy in the Lilliput section of *Gulliver's Travels*. In Psalmanazar's *Memoirs*, religion's shifting grounds of argument are finally subdued by a general appeal for tolerance and, in a prescient "echo" of his own repentance, by a recognition of God as the "only true Author" of understanding: "the truth of a Christian doctrine is not founded on the opinion or authority of any men, but on the evidence of Holy Writ."[51] The specific form of Psalmanazar's final conversion—his turn toward the intensive study of Hebrew and his part in the writing of the *Universal History*—is designed to counteract the dispersed fiction of his *Description* with the substitute of an originary and encompassing scholarship of culture.[52] Even this work was haunted by questions regarding the relations between doctrine and practice and the integrity of sacred books.

Psalmanazar's five-hundred-page "History of the Jews," chapter 11 of the *Universal History*, takes us from the "return to Jerusalem" to the death of Christ and the "total destruction of Jerusalem and dispersion of the Jewish nation." Yet this history's strongly narrative impulse is mixed with techniques and concerns deriving from Psalmanazar's ethnography. We find Psalmanazar constantly questioning the grounds of an authentic culture and such a culture's relation to its sacred writings. At the beginning of his history, Psalmanazar traces the split between "authentic Jews" and the Samaritans, "who were a mongrel mixture, partly of the ten tribes, partly of revolted Jews." The former, he writes, remained adverse to idolatry, observing of the Sabbath, and "willing to suffer the most bloody persecutions, and horrid butcheries, with utmost courage and constancy, rather than violate their laws or fidelity."[53]

As Psalmanazar's history unfolds, we see this antithesis between the Samaritans and the Jews as one defined by differing relations to textuality. The Samaritans, he writes, unlike the Jews, "were guilty of the most flagrant forgery in corrupting their pentateuch in many places." Psalmanazar excuses those errors resulting from poor transcription and those resulting from explanatory interpolations, but concludes that "there are certainly several notorious ones, which could not but be designedly made to support their cause against their Jewish antagonists."[54] This was certainly a style of "doctored" argument familiar to Psalmanazar.

The hero of Psalmanazar's history is Ezra, who compiled the sacred books in order to restore the church's discipline and rites, "according to its ancient patterns, under its former prophets. In order of which, his first care was to collect and set forth a correct edition of the sacred books."[55] Ezra's followers, the "Caraim or Karraites," cited by Psalmanazar as the "scripturists or persons wholly addicted to the reading, and thoroughly versed in sacred writings," are singled out for discussion and shown to be completely faithful to the tenets of scripture. Psalmanazar writes that those scripturists "look upon the canonical books of the old testament as the only rule for their faith" and "expound scripture by scripture."[56] Here was a textual world that did cohere. But, of course, there is a tone of straining credibility and anticipation throughout the history: the anxiety of the *Description of Formosa* is still with Psalmanazar, if only in his frequent railings against textual corruption. At the start of his "History," we find an elaborate digression on the incorrectness of Bishop Hare's edition of the Psalms: "the greatest part of the alterations and corrections" offered by the bishop being "made for the sake of it."[57] And at its close, we find strong criticism of derivative histories of the Jews. Psalmanazar attacks "Bengorian," whose work is "stuffed with the most absurd falsehoods," and applauds Josephus, who "hath all the marks of a judicious and exact historian."[58] The qualification "hath all the marks" has a particular resonance here to the tragic situation of this reformed forger who must yet convince, by the expounding of text by texts, a writing whose marks would ostensibly, but only ostensibly, bear an authentic relation to their referents.

Psalmanazar turned away from ornament and detail at the end of his life in a systematic rejection of the accouterments of his fictional project. The more particular, the more finely "worked" the ethnography, the greater its claims to authenticity, but once the artificial grounds for those claims were exposed, Psalmanazar's project became a matter of stripping away—the stripping away of information and complexity, and of the identity he had fabricated as an author. No one, not even Johnson, presumably ever learned his "real name"; hence we are never given his "proper" name, the name that would locate him in time, space, and genealogy. His autobiography was posthumous, closed before it could be opened. Here he included his last will and testament, prescribing:

> I desire that my body . . . may be kept so long above ground as decency or conveniency will permit, and afterwards conveyed to the common burying-ground, and there interred in some obscure corner of it, without any further ceremony or formality than is used to the bodies of the deceased pensioners where I happen to die . . . and that the whole may be performed in the lowest and cheapest manner. And it is my earnest request that my body be not inclosed in any kind of coffin, but only decently laid in what is called a shell of lowest value, and without lid or other covering which may hinder the natural earth from covering it all round.[59]

In these requests to strip away all ceremony, ornament, rank, architecture, and identity—to ultimately dissolve the figure into the ground—we see the final resolution of Psalmanazar's ethnographic dilemma. For this dissolution marks the end of articulation as well as the end of utterance—the mute and invisible narrative of the unmarked grave and its terrible threat to difference as well as to identity.

Notes

The research for this essay was greatly aided by the resources of The Library Company of Philadelphia, by the staff of the British Library, and by my colleague Peter Tasch, who generously shared a set of references on Psalmanazar with me.

1. See, for example, Paul Rabinow, "Representations Are Social Facts," in *Writing Culture: The Poetics and Politics of Ethnography*, ed. James Clifford and George E. Marcus (Berkeley: University of California Press, 1986), pp. 234–61. According to Rabinow, "A return to earlier modes of unself-conscious representation is not a coherent position (although the news has not yet arrived in most anthropology departments). But we cannot solve it by ignoring the relations of representational forms and social practices either. If we attempt to eliminate social referentiality, other referents will occupy the voided position" (pp. 250–51).

2. Rodney Needham, *Exemplars* (Berkeley: University of California Press, 1985).

3. For a discussion of the relation of the narrative memoir to the ethnographic description, see Mary Louise Pratt, "Fieldwork in Common Places," in Clifford and Marcus, eds., *Writing Culture*, pp. 27–50.

4. For background on George Psalmanazar, I have used the following editions of his work: *Memoirs of ****, Commonly Known by the Name of George Psalmanazar; A Reputed Native of Formosa. Written by himself, In order to be published after his Death: Containing An Account of His Education, Travels, Adventure, Connections, Literary Productions, and pretended Conversion from Heathenism to Christianity; which last proved the Occasion of his being brought over into this Kingdom, and passing for a Proselyte, and a Member of the Church of England*, 2nd ed. (London: R. Davis, 1765); *An Historical and Geographical Description of Formosa, An Island Subject to the Emperor of Japan. Giving An Account of the Religion, Customs, Manners &c. of the Inhabitants. Together with a Relation of what happen'd to the Author in his Travels; particularly his Conferences with the Jesuits, and others, in several parts of Europe. Also the History and Reasons of his Conversion to Christianity, with his Objections against it (in defense of Paganism) and their Answers. To which is prefix'd, A Preface in vindication of himself from the Reflections of a Jesuit lately come from China, with an Account of what passed between them* (London: Printed for Dan. Brown, at the Black Swan without Temple Bar; G. Strahan, and W. Davis, in Cornhill; and Fran. Coggan, in the Inner-Temple Lane, 1704); and *The Second Edition corrected, with many large and useful Additions, particularly a new Preface clearly answering every thing that has been objected against the Author and the Book. Illustrated with several cuts To which are added, A Map, and the Figure of an Idol not in the former Edition* (London: Mat. Wotten, Abel Roper, and B. Lintott in Fleetstreet; Fr. Coggan in the Inner-

Temple Lane; G. Strahan and W. Davis in Cornhill, 1705). I have also relied upon Sidney Lee's entry on Psalmanazar in *The Dictionary of National Biography*, vol. 16 (London: Oxford University Press, 1917); A. R. Winnet, "George Psalmanazar," *The New Rambler* 110 (Spring 1971): 6–18; James L. Clifford, *Young Sam Johnson* (New York: McGraw-Hill, 1955), pp. 239–41; Thomas M. Curley, *Samuel Johnson and the Age of Travel* (Athens: University of Georgia Press, 1976); and James Boswell, *The Life of Samuel Johnson* (New York: John W. Lovell, 1884), vol. 4, p. 22.

5. Hester Lynch Piozzi, *Dr. Johnson by Mrs. Thrale: The "Anecdotes" of Mrs. Piozzi in Their Original Form*, ed. R. Ingrams (London: Chatto and Windus, the Hogarth Press, 1984), p. 117.

6. James Boswell, *Boswell's Life of Johnson*, ed. George Birbeck Hill and L. F. Powell (Oxford: Clarendon Press, 1934), vol. 3, p. 443.

7. Sir John Hawkins, *The Life of Samuel Johnson, LL.D.*, ed. Bertram Davis (New York: Macmillan, 1961), p. 245.

8. Johnson's complex and often contentious relations to patronage, subscription, and the booksellers are discussed in Alvin Kernan, *Printing Technology, Letters and Samuel Johnson* (Princeton, N.J.: Princeton University Press, 1987).

9. Needham, *Exemplars*, p. 112.

10. Ibid., pp. 114–15.

11. For a useful general introduction to eighteenth-century and later modes of literary production and reception, see Terry Eagleton, *The Function of Criticism: From "The Spectator" to Post-Structuralism* (London: Verso, 1984), pp. 29–43. See also Kernan, *Printing Technology;* and Elizabeth Eisenstein, *The Printing Press as an Agent of Change: Communications and Cultural Transformation in Early-Modern Europe* (Cambridge: Cambridge University Press, 1979), vol. 1, p. 132 passim.

12. Psalmanazar, *Memoirs*, pp. 182–83.

13. Ian Watt, *The Rise of the Novel: Studies in Defoe, Richardson and Fielding* (Berkeley: University of California Press, 1957), pp. 9–34.

14. James Sambrook, *The Eighteenth Century. The Intellectual and Cultural Context of English Literature, 1700–1789* (London: Longman, 1986), pp. 168–97.

15. These issues will be taken up in more detail in chapters 3 and 4, but for background see the discussion of the neoclassical epic in Samuel Wesley, "Essay on Heroic Poetry," in *Series Two: Essays on Poetry*, no. 2, ed. Edward N. Hooker (Los Angeles: Augustan Reprint Society, 1947), pp. 4–5. (The essay originally appeared in *The Life of Our Blessed Lord and Savior Jesus Christ: An Heroic Poem* [London: Charles Harper, 1697].) See also Peter Hagin, *The Epic Hero and the Decline of Heroic Poetry: A Study of the Neoclassical English Epic with Special Reference to Milton's "Paradise Lost"* (Bern: Francke Verlag, 1964; New York: Folcroft Press, 1970). On the ballad, see Sigurd Hustvedt, *Ballad Criticism in Scandinavia and Great Britain During the 18th Century* (New York: American-Scandinavian Foundation, 1916); James Macpherson, *The Poems of Ossian. With an Essay in which they are Authenticated, Illustrated and Explained by Hugh Campbell* (London: Sir Richard Phillips, 1822); E. H. W. Meyerstein's classic biography, *A Life of Thomas Chatterton* (New York: Scribner, 1930); Donald Taylor, *Thomas Chatterton's Art: Experiments in Imagined History* (Princeton, N.J.: Princeton University Press, 1978); Norval Clyne, *The Romantic Scottish Ballads and the Lady Wardlaw Heresy* (Aberdeen: A. Brown, 1859); and Sir Walter Scott, "Essay on Imitations of the Ancient Ballad," in *Minstrelsy of the Scottish Border*, rev. and ed. T. F. Henderson, vol. 4 (Edinburgh: Oliver and Boyd, 1932).

16. Quoted in William Appleton, *A Cycle of Cathay: The Chinese Vogue in England During the Seventeenth and Eighteenth Centuries* (New York: Columbia University Press, 1951), p. 129. I am indebted to Appleton's history for most of the account of Anglo-Chinese "literary relations" here.

17. Recounted in ibid., pp. 143–44.

18. Further discussion of "untutored geniuses" will be taken up in chapter 3.

19. Henri Lefebvre, *The Survival of Capitalism: Reproduction of the Relations of Production*, trans. Frank Bryant (New York: St. Martin's Press, 1976), p. 83. See also James H. Bunn, "The Aesthetics of British Mercantilism," *New Literary History* 11 (1980): 303–21.

20. Psalmanazar, *Memoirs*, p. 113.

21. Ibid., p. 115.

22. Donald Lach, *Asia in the Making of Europe*, vol. 2, book 2: *The Literary Arts* (Chicago: University of Chicago Press, 1977), p. 389.

23. Psalmanazar, *Memoirs*, pp. 144–45.

24. Ibid., p. 163.

25. Psalmanazar, *Description* (1704), p. 204.

26. Ibid., p. 208.

27. Malek Alloula, *The Colonial Harem*, trans. Myrna Godzich and Wlad Godzich (Minneapolis: University of Minnesota Press, 1986), p. xv.

28. Earl Pritchard, *Anglo-Chinese Relations During the Seventeenth and Eighteenth Centuries* (New York: Octagon Books, 1970), p. 98. For later accounts, see also Appleton, *Cycle of Cathay*, p. 166.

29. Donald Lach, *Asia in the Making of Europe*, vol. 2, book 1: *The Visual Arts* (Chicago: University of Chicago Press, 1970), p. 114. Ctesias's career as a forger is discussed in Anthony Grafton, *Forgers and Critics: Creativity and Duplicity in Western Scholarship* (Princeton, N.J.: Princeton, University Press, 1990), pp. 9, 37–38, 105.

30. Psalmanazar, *Description* (1704), pp. 231–32.

31. Jonathan Swift, *A Modest Proposal for preventing the children of poor people from being a burthen to their parents, or the country, and for making them beneficial to the public* (Dublin: S. Harding, 1729), p. 10.

32. John Locke, *An Essay Concerning Human Understanding* (New York: Dover, 1959), vol. 1, pp. 72–73.

33. Anthony Pagden, *The Fall of Natural Man: The American Indian and the Origins of Comparative Ethnology* (Cambridge: Cambridge University Press, 1982), pp. 81–89.

34. Joseph Addison and Richard Steele, *The Spectator*, ed. Donald F. Bond (Oxford: Clarendon Press, 1965), vol. 1, p. 65.

35. Needham, *Exemplars*, p. 89.

36. Psalmanazar, *Description* (1704), pp. 231–32.

37. Ibid., p. 223.

38. Psalmanazar, *Memoirs*, p. 151n. We must note, as Psalmanazar does, that this was the ironic exposure of a forger by a plagiarist—an exposure based upon the forger's inability to copy his own "knowledge": "I soon perceived him [Innes] to be a man of no small ambition, though he was so far from having any of the generous disposition which is mostly known to accompany it, that he was no less a slave to avarice; witness his arrogating to himself the credit as well as the advantage of that excellent treatise, intitled, *A Modest Enquiry After Moral Virtue*, for which he obtained

from the present bishop of London a very good living in Essex; but which the real and worthy author, a poor episcopal clergyman in Scotland, since obliged him publickly to disown and disclaim in print, as well as to comprise with him for the profit of the edition" (p. 151n.).

39. Ibid., pp. 114–15.
40. Ibid., p. 155.
41. Psalmanazar, *Description* (1704), pp. 70–71.
42. Ibid., p. 82.
43. Ibid., p. 104.
44. Ibid., p. 106.
45. Ibid., p. 119.
46. Psalmanazar, *Description* (1705), p. A2.
47. Psalmanazar, *Memoirs*, p. 287.
48. *An Universal History, from the Earliest Account of Time to the Present: Compiled from Original Authors; and Illustrated with Maps, Cuts, Notes, Chronological and Other Tables*, 2nd ed. (London: S. Richardson, T. Osborne, J. Osborn, A. Millar, and J. Hinton, 1738), The first volume, from which I have quoted, is missing a title page in the Library Company of Philadelphia copy.
49. See Pratt, "Fieldwork in Common Places." We should also note the vaunting ambition of the opening of *The Confessions of Jean-Jacques Rousseau* (New York: Modern Library, n.d.): "I am commencing an undertaking, hitherto without precedent, and which will never find an imitator. I desire to set before my fellows the likeness of a man in all the truth of nature, and that man myself" (p. 3). Rousseau's project, we should remind ourselves, is a self that is an effect of writing—an undertaking involving the complete confession that produces the unique self and not the reverse. For further examples and discussions of the confessional mode, see of course Augustine's stunning collapse from the temporality of third-person narrative to the atemporality of dialogic lyricism at the juncture of books 9 and 10 in *The Confessions* and, among secondary texts, Neil Hertz, "Flaubert's Conversion," in *The End of the Line: Essays on Psychoanalysis and the Sublime* (New York: Columbia University Press, 1985), pp. 61–74; and of course Michel Foucault's discussion in *The History of Sexuality*, vol. 1: *An Introduction*, trans. Robert Hurley (New York: Vintage Books, 1980), and in *Discipline and Punish: The Birth of the Prison*, trans. Alan Sheridan (New York: Vintage Books, 1979). See also Foucault's edition of the memoirs of Pierre Rivière: *I, Pierre Rivière, having slaughtered my mother, my sister, and my brother . . . A Case of Parricide in the 19th Century*, ed. Michel Foucault, trans. Frank Jellinek (New York: Pantheon Books, 1975).
50. I must also mention the important function of testimony in Sadian ethnology, which will be explored more fully in chapter 8. The closed world of the château at Silling, for example, with its costumes, customs, manners, ceremonies, and social ranks, presents us with a spectacle of narrative testimonies that refuse to realize themselves as "events." Psalmanazar in turn, in the preface to his *Memoirs*, blames his forgery and imposture on "various carnal considerations and the violent hurry of my passions" (p. 10). The impostor, of course, does not have the patience for either nature or history to produce its more proper, and seemingly desireless, forms of subjectivity. I have largely left aside the matter of Psalmanazar's "motivation," but like his counterpart, the fabricator of history Thomas Chatterton, this teen-age forger was stranded in the lower rungs of the middle classes (both could claim a lack of

inheritance from an "ancient, but decayed family") and suffered from an aberrant relation to the Oedipal situation: Chatterton's father died before his birth; Psalmanazar's parents were inexplicably separated, his father mysteriously incapacitated. In addition, both impostors suffered from an imbalance between the qualities of their education and their fortunes. In *The Family Romance of the Impostor-Poet Thomas Chatterton* (Berkeley: University of California Press, 1987), Louise Kaplan argues that Chatterton's activities, like those of other adolescent males drawn to imposture, are driven by the search for a father. As I will argue in chapter 5, this seems to be a key aspect of imposture, but is incomplete as an explanation of the relation these figures bear to writing and literary forms.

51. Psalmanazar, *Memoirs*, p. 44.

52. This redemption through Hebrew is suggestively echoed in the frontispiece of Father Lafitau's *Moeurs des sauvages amériquains* (1724) as described by James Clifford, "On Ethnographic Authority," *Representations* 1 (Spring 1983): "[The frontispiece] portrays the ethnographer as a young woman sitting at a writing table amidst artifacts from the New World and from classical Greece and Egypt. The author is accompanied by two cherubs who assist in the task of comparison and by the bearded figure of Time who points toward a tableau representing the ultimate source of the truths issuing from the writer's pen. The image toward which the young woman lifts her gaze is a bank of clouds where Adam, Eve and the serpent appear. Above them stand the redeemed man and woman of the Apocalypse on either side of a radiant triangle bearing the Hebrew script for Yahweh" (p. 118).

53. *Universal History* vol. 1, chapter 11, p. 2.

54. Ibid., p. 33.

55. Ibid., p. 13.

56. Ibid., p. 174.

57. Ibid., p. 16.

58. Ibid., pp. 291–92.

59. Psalmanazar, *Memoirs*, pp. 3–4.

3

Notes on Distressed Genres

Each generation is a natural and social product of the previous generation; but each generation separates itself from the previous one and, *as a material condition of its praxis*, transcends the objectification of the previous praxis, that is to say, the being of the previous generation, in so far as this being becomes, through this very transcendence, an inert object which needs to be rearranged.

Sartre, *Critique of Dialectical Reason* (1960)

Life may be in color, but it's much more real in black and white.   Wenders, *The State of Things* (1982)

On December 10, 1792, Benjamin West delivered "A Discourse to the Students of the Royal Academy on the Distribution of Prizes." The speech, written in a clear and evenhanded way, is nevertheless full of ambivalence regarding, first, the relations between commerce and immortality, and, second, the relations between genius and community. West applauds the prosperity brought about by the rise of empire and, at the same time, like many other English intellectuals from Dyer to Johnson to Gibbon, is painfully aware of the collapse written into the parabola of that rise. And, like Edward Young, he ponders the oxymoron of training geniuses, wondering, in fact, if originality can be nourished or if it is a kind of given.[1] Regardless of the ontology of art, the survival of artifacts is the only possibility for transcending time, he concludes:

> It is by those higher and more refined excellencies of painting, sculpture, and architecture that Greek and Roman greatness are transmitted down to times in which we are, as if they were still in existence: although many centuries have elapsed since both Greeks and Romans

have been overthrown and dissolved as a people; while those nations, by whom those refinements were not known, or not cultivated, are erased from the face of the earth.[2]

Here appear a number of issues—an anxiety regarding materiality, a hope in the transcendence of art as either material or concept, a fear of erasure, a belief in art's capacity to reflect its contextual origins—that will be taken up in the essays that follow. But first I want to focus upon the phenomenon of the "new antique," which arose during the late seventeenth and early eighteenth centuries, a phenomenon that can be construed as an attempt to bypass the contingencies of time: by creating new antiques, the author hopes to author a context as well as an artifact. I shall refer to such imitations of older forms as "distressed genres" in order to emphasize their artifactual nature—that is, their guise of self-referentiality. The period's deepening historical awareness of the classical world was supplemented by a rising archaeology that demonstrated both the reappearance and disappearance of the past. Thus the desire to produce speaking objects, objects both in and out of time, seems an inevitable outgrowth of this development. And, perhaps more important, the endurance of archaeological, or found, objects emphasizes representation's stake in the dichotomy between language and action. The mediation posed by the artifact here offers a kind of knowledge that must be supplemented by documentation, evocation, and narrative. The eighteenth century, and the enduring legacy of its sensibility, found in such objects an intrinsicality very much like that held by property and the money form itself. But this illusion of intrinsicality depended upon the erasure or deferment of historical agency. Imitations of the antique could not always generate the grounds for their intelligibility, and in this, perhaps ironically, lies their authentic parallel to those speaking, but authorless and context-free, objects that West and others so admired.[3]

To distress: in common usage (although, curiously, not in dictionaries), "to make old, to antique," particularly in reproducing material goods from previous times. Simultaneously, the dictionary definition: "to afflict, to place in a state of danger or trouble, bad straits." In law, *to distrain* is "to force by seizure of goods," coming from the Latin root *dis* (apart) + *stringere* (to draw tight or stretch): "to seize and hold property as security or indemnity for a debt." In such usage, "to distress" involves a process of appropriation by reproduction, or manipulation through affliction. All these meanings bear upon the distressing of genres—and in particular on the literary imitation of folklore forms. Like the distressing of objects, the distressing of forms involves a process of separation and manipulation serving certain ideological functions.

How does the present appropriate the past? How does our gaze upon the past, even when articulated as a desire to escape mediation, always separate us from the past? How do aspects of culture become periodized in time just as under tourism they become localized in space? How do certain forms become emblematic of ways of life? The reproduction of folklore forms by the literary tradition, particularly as practiced from the late seventeenth century on, provides a deeply historicized set of answers to such questions.[4] Such a reproduction appears as a process of appropriation, manipulation, and ultimately transformation for oral and literary forms alike. For literary imitations of folklore involve not only a set of characteristically superannuated themes, but also an attempt to recoup the voice of orality in all its presumed authenticity of context. Such literary imitations as the epic, the proverb, the fable, the fairy tale, and the ballad mime the oral's mode of production and project the authority of the oral world. But these imitations just as surely suffer from an inauthenticity of presentation, a loss ensuing from the very periodization that is the foundation of their aesthetic.

Of all the ways in which one could evaluate the significance of the literary appropriation of oral forms, the most mistaken would be to assume that literature thereby records the lost world of preindustrial culture. Instead, we find that to "rescue" a form in this sense would necessarily be a means of killing it off. Nor is this "murder" arbitrary in either content or style: when oral forms are transformed into "evidence" and "artifacts," they acquire all the characteristics of fragmentation, symbolic meaning, and literariness that are most valued by the literary culture. Furthermore, we must consider the complex historical juncture of such phenomena of reproduction. The imitation of oral forms includes, for example, the late-seventeenth-century French court's fascination with fairy tales and fables, the nationalist impulses of early-eighteenth-century British writers attempting to re-create an epic history for their countries, the bourgeois writer's endeavors to escape the limits of individual expression by creating proverbs, and the contemporary antics of folk festivals, revivals, and societies for "creative anachronism."

Such a list, already implicated in an ideology of functionalism perhaps as suspect as the ideology of distressing, is complicated further by the changing contexts of literary production. As I noted in the introduction to this study, the decline of patronage throughout the period is tied to a nostalgia for a waning feudalism and its aesthetics of the local. The emergence of commercial publishing, of a writing destined for strangers, effects a compensation in the form of the encapsulated sense of "community" implied in the reproduction of folkloric forms. And more abstractly, the modes of suspending being that literary writing came to pose throughout the eighteenth century—the rise of fiction, the restriction of literary convention to certain codes of production and reception, the creation of authorial rights and obligations, the consequent development of the concept of genius, and the development of criticism as a science of attribution—depended upon separating literary form from the contingencies of its temporal moment and spatial position. In this sense, folklore as "oral tradition" posed immortal forms for literature to borrow. Yet inversely, the imitation of folklore marked off a space for representation in which literature was able to make broad claims over the more "limited" temporal and spatial contexts of the oral. Of course the novel, with its fantastic capacity to represent, its necessarily incomplete ambition toward totality, becomes here both the antithesis of the "distressed" genre and the logical consequence of the distressed genre's claims. For the distressed genre's hope to *enter* time, to re-create, is the first step in a move to *transcend* time that will be the paradigm for literary idealism from Romanticism through modernism.

Furthermore, the distressed genre addresses an anxiety regarding place, desertion, and the irrevocable silence of the dead that we find in poems such as Gray's "Elegy Written in a Country Churchyard," Goldsmith's "Deserted Village," and even Thomson's strained allegorical readings of landscape in *The Seasons*. The attempts to raise the dead, to hear what has vanished, to reanimate the scene, become coupled with a desire to fix one's own history in perpetuity—that is, to control the future of language as well, as perhaps most brilliantly managed by Gray's reflexive epitaph at the

close of his "Elegy." Here the poet attempts to serve as undertaker
to his own subjectivity. Nevertheless, the history of the subject will
suffer from the same mute artifactuality characteristic of the abandoned landscape and its ruins. As we shall see, Piranesi makes an
important contribution to this discourse regarding the problem of
animation when he abandons referentiality for the posing of contradictions between presence and absence, voices and silence.

In appropriating folklore genres, the literary tradition is able to
create an idealization of itself through a separation of speech and
writing. Such a separation, anchored in a mimetic theory of representation, always posits speech as a form of nature. Thus throughout
the eighteenth century, the work of "untutored geniuses" becomes
the paradigm for the last gasps of an oral culture, a culture now seen
to be miming literary form—that is, producing a "natural" variant
of it rather than simply imitating it. The taste for the fragment
included this preference for individuals like Psalmanazar, severed
from context and collected from the lower classes by an aristocracy
eager to promote them. Yet this severance also depended upon the
real contingencies of enclosure, industrialization, and the end of the
old order of village culture.

The prototype of the untutored genius was of course John Taylor,
the seventeenth-century "water poet" of London, who published
his own works and gave them in exchange for favors and money. In
the eighteenth century we find such untutored geniuses as Stephen
Duck, the poetical thresherman, discovered by George Parker, Lord
Macclesfield; Henry Jones, the poetical bricklayer, discovered by
Philip Dormer Stanhope, Lord Chesterfield; James Woodhouse and
John Bennet, the poetical shoemakers, the first patronized by Wil-
liam Shenstone and the second by Thomas Warton; Ann Yearsley,
the poetical washerwoman and milkmaid, patronized by Hannah
More; and James Hogg, Sir Walter Scott's shepherd/bard of Ettrick
Forest.

Yet what could it mean for these figures—who, depending on
one's preferred theory of history, could be called peasants, folk, or
native talents—to be "untutored"? What daydream of writing and
culture is implied by such a term? It is a daydream we find elsewhere
in eighteenth-century aesthetics, particularly in the writings of
Thomas Warton, Hugh Blair, Richard Hurd, Thomas Percy, and
James Beattie: the daydream of the minstrel/bard, authoritatively

speaking for and to the culture, motivated by feudal values or, perhaps more accurately, by a newly invented Gothic aesthetics. If this minstrel/bard finds his antithesis in the period's commercial writer, it is equally unlikely that the actual productions of untutored geniuses were spoken without the "burden" of writing. John Taylor himself gave an account of his studies in rhymed form:

> I care to get good books, and I take heed
> And care what I do either write or read;
> Though some through ignorance, and some through spite,
> Have said that I can neither read nor write.
> But though my lines no scholarship proclaim
> Yet I at learning have a kind of aim;
> And I have gathered much good observations,
> From many human and Divine translations.[5]

Taylor goes on to list Ovid, Homer, Virgil, Godfrey of "Bulloyne," Du Bartas, Chaucer, Sidney, Spenser, Daniel, Nash, *The Golden Legend*, Plutarch, Josephus, Marcus Aurelius, Suetonius, Seneca, Fox, Holinshed, and others, before finishing with a discussion of the Bible, as influences on his work.

Stephen Duck worked overtime as a thresher so that he and a fellow worker could purchase a small library consisting of Milton, *The Spectator*, Addison's *Defence of Christianity*, an English dictionary with a grammar, Ovid, Bysshe's *Art of Poetry*, a Josephus in folio, Waller, Dryden's Virgil, Prior, Tom Brown, *Hudibras*, and the *London Spy*. He often carried *The Spectator* to work, reading between tasks. His reading and verse writing came to the attention of aristocrats in Wiltshire, and, at the same time, a bookseller pirated a collection of his verses. The bookseller printed a frontispiece of Duck holding Milton in one hand and a flail in the other, coming from the barn toward a table on which pen, ink, and paper are lying; pigs, poultry, and reapers appear in the background. The collection, called *The Thresher's Labour*, was shown to Queen Caroline, who became his patron, giving him thirty pounds a year and making him keeper of her library, "Merlin's Cave," at Richmond.[6] Duck's next volume was a set of imitations of Horace, significant not only because he has moved from representing the work of threshers to imitating the work of lyric poets, but also because he has moved from a lyric of direct address to the Horatian (that form most linked to writing), as opposed to the singing or chanting of the Pindaric (a form inversely popular with aristocratic poets of the period). Woodhouse wrote that Duck had become "grey in servitude and poorer under patronage"; he ended his days a proprietor of a book and stationery shop.

Southey wrote of Ann Yearsley, the poetical washerwoman and milkmaid of Bristol, that "her vocabulary was that of the books which she had read, her syntax that of the ignorant and vulgar with whom she conversed."[7] Southey's analysis of Yearsley's form, as well as Duck's title, *The Thresher's Labour*, emphasize the concept of literary production as *work*, and the nature of that work as one of allusion and combination. Hence we are confronted once again with West's oxymoron of the taught genius, Young's paradox of the imitative genius, and the recurring problem of a writing that generates forms of subjectivity.

When Hannah More met Ann Yearsley, More wrote that

> her [Yearsley's] remarks on the books she read are so accurate, and so consonant to the opinions of the best critics, that from this very circumstance they would appear trite and commonplace to anyone who had been in habits of society; for without having ever conversed with any body above her own level, she seems to possess the general principles of sound taste and just thinking.

Yearsley had read *Paradise Lost* and Young's *Night Thoughts*, a few of Shakespeare's plays, and a translation of the *Georgics*. She took the classical allusions in her poems from prints in a shop window. Hannah More corrected errors in her grammar and spelling, and her poems were published by subscription. The money made from the first edition was placed in funds under the names of Elizabeth Montagu and Hannah More, as trustees for Yearsley and her children. But this caused a rift in the relation between poet and patron, for Yearsley wanted to be a joint trustee. Yearsley broke with More and Montagu, published a fourth edition of her first volume in 1786, and in 1787 published a second collection of poems by subscription, opened a circulating library at Bristol Hot Wells, and wrote several tragedies.[8]

My point is not certainly the suppression of untutored genius, but the necessity of inventing it. Hannah More's delight in finding a common but uninformed taste expressed by Ann Yearsley is the fantasy of David Hume's "Of the Standard of Taste," with its constant deferral of the utopian moment of a universal standard of judgment, or of the hopeful concept of common sense promulgated throughout eighteenth-century aesthetic writings. The eighteenth century looked for a natural writing in nature itself, in the productions of imagination, and in the creations of such peasant/poets as these. But untutored geniuses both began and ended in the library, their speech already written.

Of course, at the time when literary patrons were "collecting" such figures, literary figures like Southey himself were "polishing" the tradition, producing imitations and reproductions of those speech genres that supposedly reign and disappear as natural forms. The literary tradition was able to conceive of its own context as being encapsulated within the form of representation, and at the same time to inversely imagine the literary as being taken up, and taken back, by a nature that literary culture had itself invented.

Thus we must search for a model of the evaluative relations between time and genre by focusing on a process that is both historical and historicizing. We find here gestures of suppression, absorption, and "unnatural" superannuation, gestures that emphasize the contradictions of a literary ideal constantly seeking to invent its own temporal grounds, mourning the loss of a nature that it is in the process of writing. Hence the simultaneity, abstraction, and stasis characterizing a transcendent writing from the Enlightenment through modernism can be reevaluated in the light of literature's historical transformation of its own evaluative terms. A model might be found in Mikhail Bakhtin's notion of the "valorized temporal category," as it appears in his essay "The Epic and the Novel":

> The absolute past is a specifically evaluating (hierarchical) category. In the epic world view, "beginning," "first," "founder," "ancestor," "that which occurred earlier," and so forth are not merely temporal categories but *valorized* temporal categories, and valorized to an extreme degree. This is as true for relationships among people as for relations among all the other items and phenomena of the epic world. In the past, everything is good: all the really good things (i.e. the "first" things) occur *only* in this past. The epic absolute past is the single source and beginning of everything good for all later times as well.[9]

Thus the cultural reproduction of value works by attaching itself to particular forms. The valorized temporal category is not a category or kind that is abandoned; rather, it is a kind that is summoned from the world of the dead for particular purposes and that assumes a particular status by the very fact of its anachronism. Thus distressed forms show us the gap between past and present as a structure of desire, a structure in which authority seeks legitimation by recontextualizing its object and thereby recontextualizing itself. If distressed forms involve a negation of the contingencies of their immediate history, they also involve an invention of a version of the past that could only arise from such contingencies. We see this structure of desire as the structure of nostalgia—that is, the desire for desire in which objects are the means of generation and not the ends. Hence the polymorphic possibilities of forms compelled to *mean* historically. Turning to specific examples of such historicized forms, we find that they have been pried from a context of function and placed within a context of self-referentiality. The irony here is that the literary "voicing" of folklore forms emphasizes their new textuality all the more.

Epic

It is a commonplace of epic criticism to begin with the distinction between the authentic epic (oral epics such as the *Iliad,* the *Odyssey, Beowulf,* the *Song of Roland*) and the literary epic (the *Aeneid, Os Lusiadas, Gerusalemme Liberata,* and *Paradise Lost*). This preliminary distinction, of course, partakes of the equation of the oral/Homer with the natural as well as of the equation of the literary with both a revival of and a falling away from that place of privileged origin, the place of authentic voice. Although we have several examples from ancient epics of the immediacy of the form in context, by the time of *Beowulf* an elegiac mood appears in the epic. This mood depends upon a distance from the past and a sense of "the greatness of [the Danish] kings in old days."[10] Here we can reinterpret Horace's dictum that the epic must begin *in medias res* as a sense that in the epic everything has already *happened.* As C. M. Bowra has noted, the epic poet displays a kind of necessary detachment, for he writes in the last days or aftermath of nations or causes and hence is "melancholy and laden with responsibilities."[11]

Built into the thematics and form of the epic is an effort to overcome and incorporate distance, an effort to recapture the speech and thereby the very *epos* of a particular historical moment now lost. Thus the hero of the literary epic is always to some extent the author. Already in the Heroic Age of Greece, the epic bards are credited with being able, by special inspiration, to transcend the limitations of sense and to rescue the past from oblivion. Thus the bard's blindness serves both to obliterate the limitations of immediate context and, anachronistically perhaps, to imply the distancing of audience that will be implicit in mechanical modes of literary production. The gesture toward authentication in epic narrative is always an inside out and an outside in: we find a progressive synecdoche of the father whereby the face of Virgil is filled in by the accumulation of his bardic descendents, at the same time that Aeneas stands for Rome, Goffredo for Christian chivalry, and Adam for the state of all mankind.

This inclusive capacity of the epic depends upon a capacity for objectification as well as for distancing. The epic gathers and incorporates, in a reverent way, what has gone before it. Thus the epic marks the objectification or artifactualization of literature: literature as document, not so much absorbed into its context of production as a survival or remnant of that context. (Here we might think of the *Parsifal* of Syberberg, with its reverence for the disembodied heads of the fathers.) The literary epic, like the chronicle and the etiological legend, exists as an authenticating document and as such rests upon the literary self-consciousness of antiquarianism. Hence Tasso's *Gerusalemme Liberata* is "made," not born.[12] The author is here an assembler of history and parallel to that other history maker, the hero, inspiring and commanding others in the work of disembodiment preceding the establishment of a new order. The Virgilian model for the epic is both thematic and rhetorical: Virgil's production of a poem on the Roman character, made by linking Aeneas to the living patron Augustus, sets the precedent for establishing the authority of national culture by correspondingly linking that culture to the eternal and spiritual.[13]

Just as the epic collapses author and hero, so it also collapses history and value, particularly legitimating the moral and ideological forms of its age by means of its historical narrative.[14] Epic theory from the Renaissance on is quite explicit about the epic's moral basis. For example, Tasso prescribes (1:3:5–8):

So we, if children young diseased we find,
Anoint with sweets the vessel's foremost parts
To make them taste the potions sharp we give:
They drink deceived, and so deceived, they live.[15]

The literary epic, be it chivalrous or Puritan, is characterized by a refusal of the sensual, an inheritance that it received from Virgil and Augustan views on sexual morality and that is recapitulated in the high and transcendent aspect of its form.[16] As Bakhtin concludes, the refusal of laughter is a refusal of the body and its capacity for regeneration, novelty, and the juxtaposition of double-voicedness. The univocality of the epic is a moral refusal of the sensual and its fluctuating firsthand experience of temporality.

To focus on the epic, which is a distressed and antiquated genre from its very inception as a literary form, we might nevertheless take a closer look at its final stages, its period of decline. The most distressed form of this distressed genre is the epic of the eighteenth century, an epic specifically designed to combat laughter. Whereas classical epic embodies cause in the hero, the eighteenth-century epic is so oriented toward a moral and didactic function that the hero becomes ancillary to the cause. The subject of Blackmore's *Prince Arthur* is not the hero himself, but his mission to defeat the Saxons, those heathen oppressors of Britain, and to establish a great Christian kingdom. Analogously, Blackmore writes in the preface to another epic, *King Arthur*, that "'tis the Diversity of the Action, and not of the hero that diversifies the poem," and Glover was able to write a sequel to *Leonidas* even though he had killed his hero in the first work. The preface to the first *Leonidas* claims "to illustrate the following poem, to vindicate the subject from the censure of improbability, and to show by the concurring evidence of the best historians that such disinterested public virtue did once exist."[17]

The principal epics of the late seventeenth and eighteenth centuries—Blackmore's *Prince Arthur* (1695), *King Arthur* (1697), *Eliza* (1705), and *Alfred* (1723); Glover's *Leonidas* (1737); Wilkie's *The Epigoniad* (1757); Ogden's *The Revolution* (1790); and Ogilvie's *Britannia* (1801)—typically focus upon either historical or classical subjects, the former in Blackmore and Ogden, the latter in Glover and Wilkie, and a rather fantastic mixture in the work of Ogilvie. Yet these works simultaneously historicize the classical and classicize the historical, justifying the classical heroism of Xerxes (*Leonidas*) and Diomedes (*The Epigoniad*) by imposing a Protestant morality, and legitimating the classical status of Britain through stories about the founding of the nation, about the legendary kings of its prehistory, and about the inheritance of "freedom" duly protected by Elizabeth and the prince of Orange.

Although on the surface these epics, with their anti-Catholicism and antiquarianism, may seem to resemble their sometime contemporary, the Gothic romance, they in fact appear as the romance's opposite. Like the other epics mentioned here, they are an exaggeration of the already happened; they are designed to set the record straight and thus have a rhetorical purpose directly opposed to the deliberate mystification, half-shadowing, dubious paternity, and dubious motives brought to the fore by the Gothic romance. Hence the clarifying role of prophecy in these epics: Leonidas has been chosen from birth to fight against tyranny, so it is only fitting that his "heart exulting answers the call" of heaven to fight against Xerxes. And for the task of founding a new empire, of initiating the long and glorious history of British rule, heaven selects the Trojan Brutus to reclaim the land from the unruly control of the giants. Peter Hagin suggests that "if we recognize the hero's being anointed by Heaven as his most characteristic trait, we understand that this new type of heroism need not necessarily be associated with heroic deeds on the battlefield."[18] William of Orange appears on the battlefield only in the last book of Ogden's *The Revolution,* but we understand that he is chosen by God to execute heaven's cause— the promotion of English Protestantism. Similarly, Blackmore was able to make Elizabeth his heroine. The career of Blackmore well illustrates the relation between anachronistic hero and anachronistic author at work on this project. We see Blackmore's much appreciated contribution to the swelling bourgeois morality of his century in John Hughes's dedication to his poem "A Triumph of Peace" (1698). Hughes wrote that Blackmore "had given the world a novel Instance that good morals and good Poetry are very consistent."[19] Yet Blackmore equally cut what was considered to be a ridiculous figure, particularly in his debate with the Wits as he attempted to defend public virtue against the barbs of satire. We find him in his later career turning with the air of a martyr completely to biblical subjects in *Job* (1700) and *Creation: A Philosophical Poem Proving the Existence of God* (1712).

The epic hero is the antithesis of the hero of development whom we find in the early novel. The epic hero is the same at the beginning as at closure. He is against the proper name, against change and the contingencies of immediate context. He is a character of the sacred text, of the beginning Word, and not a character of speech or the street. As Blackmore makes clear in his essays railing against wit ("The Satyr Against Wit," "Nature of Man," and "Essay upon Wit"), the epic hero and the epic author are against laughter: Blackmore proposes the establishment of a "Bank and Mint of Wit" to ensure that it will be refined and purified. Retrospectively, we can see that the anti-Shaftesburian impulse here is meant to strengthen a religious worldview, given and whole. But such high seriousness eventually turns to the valorization of tears and sentimentality—and ultimately, of course, to parody and inauthenticity.

Macpherson's *Ossian* poems of the 1760s, the most famous of all literary forgeries of the antique, are poems "full of tears," "written" by the last of the Fienne and designed to record the *epos* of that dying race.[20] It is not surprising that after these declining epic forms of the eighteenth century, we see the epic revived within milieus of nostalgia or neoclassicism: the epics of William Morris (*The Life and Death of Jason*) and Matthew Arnold (*Sohrab and Rustum, Balder Dead*) are *against novelty*. These works refuse the imperative of the present, just as the classical and biblical subjects of cinematic epic (Charlton Heston is, of course, the index here) attempt to overwhelm the potential self-consciousness of the audience by the sheer mass of a cast of thousands contained within an absolute and distanced frame. That anonymous crowd is history itself casting up a transcendent hero/father. And the television epic, from "Roots" to "The Winds of War," may be seen as a similar gesture, extended quite authentically over succeeding nights and told beside or, even more accurately, *replacing* the very domestic hearth it legitimates.

Fable

If the epic has always already happened, the fable has always already been dead.[21] B. E. Perry, perhaps the foremost historian of the fable, wrote: "If fables are to be likened to withered leaves when their function is rhetorical . . . then we shall have to conclude that the fable was already dead in the earliest period to which we can trace it." The fable, according to Perry, presents an inversion of the common procedure of oral into written: the rhetorical collections of fables were used as both oral and written rhetorical devices before the use of fables in concrete situations such as we find in Aesop and others.[22] Thus the fable, as appropriated from the late seventeenth century on, is a form already bearing the marks of textuality. Most significant, the fable always tends to the pictorial and the limits of spatial enclosure.[23] It is a tableau form, oriented toward stasis and an eternally transcendent meaning, a meaning by which every element of the plot is encompassed and accounted for.[24] It combines thereby the systematicity of allegory with the totalizing power of symbol; our experience is one of a closure that only becomes stronger as we read the moral back into the narrative. In this, the temporal experience of the fable mimes the work of the historian: the function of time is revealed to be the classification, the ordering, of objects. Furthermore, all narratives appear to be the *consequences* of their morals. Thus the historian's task is legitimated by a history whose teleology is inscribed by a "reading back" of lessons now revealed, yet seeking historical legitimation.

The history of the literary fable rather closely parallels that of the literary epic. Like this form of epic, the fable emphasizes the didactic over the novel, an emphasis that at times even surpasses the epic's hypermorality. John Dennis wrote in 1700 that "the very first thing he who makes a fable does is to fix upon his Moral." He carried on a correspondence with Blackmore wherein he argued that the moral should therefore precede the narrative. Blackmore had suggested that one should invent a narrative and then draw from it a moral, assuming, of course, that a moral could be drawn from any narrative.[25] In the French neoclassical revival of the fable, the form also stands against novelty. To write fables meant to translate and adapt from the existing fables inherited from Aesop by way of Phaedrus and others. For La Fontaine, at least, an original fable could not be an Aesopian fable.[26] Thus the fable was used as ammunition by the Ancients in their war on the Moderns.[27]

Yet despite the position of La Fontaine within the Academy and despite the fable's place in that great debate, the seventeenth- and eighteenth-century fable holds the status of another neoclassical invention: literature for children. The fable, with its versification of morals, also must be closely allied to the ancestor of this literature: Renaissance courtesy books, with their elaborate moral instructions.[28] As didactic forms, the fable and the courtesy book differ from their relatives, the emblem book and the proverb. The latter forms involve an esoteric element, an element of "puzzling" or "figuring," whereas the literary fable and the courtesy-book lesson bear their morals in quite obvious ways. In this sense, the fable already has experienced a certain failure in membership: that is, the distance of bourgeois and aristocratic culture from the worlds of childhood and the working classes is so pronounced as to make explication necessary.[29]

Into the nineteenth century, the fable was considered a worthwhile vehicle for the conveyance of morality to children and the working classes, particularly in England and Germany. But Herderian nationalism and the Romanticism of the Grimm brothers presented a contrasting claim for the fable by linking it to what Herder considered to be "the raw prophetic powers of Nature." Herder, in the footsteps of Lessing, contended that La Fontaine and the neoclassical fabulists had turned "the great teacher of nature and educator of mankind, the fable, into a gallant chatterer or childish fairy tale," and the Grimms suggested that while the fable, like the epic, was "inherently instructive," it should perform such instruction in conformity with nature.[30] Ironically, Romantic theories of the fable could find no realization in practice, precisely because the Romantics argued that the fable was linked to an authentic and ancient nature, a nature now remote from contemporary experience and, unlike the folktale, already dead in the contemporary folk culture.

Regardless of these efforts to reawaken interest in it, the fable continued its cycle of decline from children's literature in the seventeenth century to children's literature in the nineteenth century. As a genre revered precisely for stasis, eternity, and closure, the fable is revived with the emergence of the neoclassical or whenever a desire for ideological completeness appears. For contemporary examples, we can turn to the anticommunist *Fables and Parables for Mid-Century*, published by Nym Wales in 1952,[31] or to recent Mobil Oil advertisements called "Fables" that prefer this naive voice form but seek to legitimate the appropriation of the natural by technology. Although we might distinguish between *fable*, which, centering on the animal, has traditionally been seen as more imaginary, and *parable*, which, centering on the human, has traditionally been considered more practical, we see that the fabular form redesigns nature according to human notions of intention and causality, and that the parable form in text and context naturalizes human actions, particularly in that its audience is typically the child and the underclasses.

Hegel contended that the fable appears at the moment of the decline of "the Divine will, which is self-revealed in its essential nature to mankind through natural events, and their religious import. We have nothing more than a quite ordinary course of everyday occurrences from the isolated reproduction of which we are able to abstract in a way commonly intelligible an ethical *dictum*."[32] This humanization of the natural, this naturalization and eternalization of the commonsensical, has become therefore quite suited as a background for the adages of monopoly capitalism. The fable's moral theology provides a structure of rationalization, a legitimation of an end that only the present can bring to consciousness, and hence, a celebration of novelty under the guise of a timeless wisdom.

Proverb

In his discussion of the fable, Hegel further notes that

> the original form of the fable leaves upon it . . . the impress of most naiveté, because in it the didactic aim and the deduction of general significances of utilitarian colour do not appear to be that which was the original intention of the narrator, but rather something which turned up afterwards.[33]

The fable is only one of a number of genres employing what might be called a "naive voice." Naiveté of voice always implies separation from immediate context, a deliberate "unawareness" of history as it mediates the relation between then and now, an authority based upon the absence of a contamination that is the effect of actual practice, and the making over of nature into culture.[34] The voice of the proverb, like the voice of the fable, is also the voice of both everyone and no one. As everyone, it bears upon the situation with the weight of tradition and traditional authority; as no one, it escapes the limitations and contingencies of biography and historical context. Thus like the fable, the proverb is already accomplished, already dead; change and novelty could only diminish the proverb by qualifying its capacity for transcendence. Hegel concludes of proverbs: "These are not modes of comparison of the type that the general significance and the concrete phenomenon are opposed to one another in separation, but the former is immediately expressed in the latter."[35] The proverb thus presents a paradigm for all ideological forms, in that it subordinates the concreteness of lived relations to an idea that thereby substitutes and cancels the unruly detail and flux of experience. The proverb marks the resolution of confusion, the end of history, and speaks with a voice that is both time-honored and superannuated. Hence the irony of a genre worn thin and the proverb's always dubious status within contemporary culture.

In its oral form the proverb is "worn," in both the positive and negative senses, because of its status as a transcendent and time-proven form of discourse. A new proverb would be as unimaginable to tradition as an original Aesopian fable or a private fad. Thus the literary tradition of the proverb takes one of two paths—that of new collections of previously known proverbs, or that of invented proverbs that never survive to be applied to concrete situations. We must remember that the status of the proverb as another's words makes the collection of proverbs serve a function of memorializing remnants of the literary culture, and that thereby the "newly minted proverb" always has the status of a forgery. In making "original proverbs," autograph literature seeks to pass itself off as collective wisdom. We see evidence of the proverb's function in maintaining and articulating the literary tradition particularly in the introduction of Hellenistic literature into Rome, where such literature served a legitimating function for the aristocratic culture and, more practically, operated as a training school for the Forum. This Hellenistic influence was opposed by the lower classes and the rural aristocracy,[36] which reveals the relation of the proverb as literary allusion not only to a generalized ideology, but to the particular ideology of class. Hence from Erasmus's *Adagia* to Martin Tupper's nineteenth-century handbook *Proverbial Philosophy*, proverbs were *condimenta* used by literate young men to spice their conversations with the authority of the antique.[37]

Archer Taylor, the great scholar of proverbs, has traced for us the rather pathetic history of literary proverbs: "a curious accompaniment of long familiarity with proverbs often appears in the belief that new proverbs can be invented. . . . In almost every case the results have given lie to the belief." Among such failures is James Howell's 1659 collection of "divers centuries of new sayings, which may serve for proverbs to posterity," none of which found a place in either oral or literary tradition. Franklin's *Poor Richard's Almanac* (1732–58) may carry the reputation of having invented a few proverbs (for example, "A penny saved is a penny earned"), but Taylor is able to trace each of them to either earlier oral forms or older collections. We might also note the tragedy of K. F. W. Wander, who compiled an enormous lexicon of German proverbs. When he subsequently issued equally enormous volumes of new proverbs, doubt was cast on his original lexicon. In this century, Alexander F. Chamberlain, editor of the *Journal of American Folklore,* collected and invented maxims suggested by modern life and science, none of which survived his own articles.[38] If proverbs form a singular example of a truly collective genre, a genre of anonymous authorship, the coining of proverbs seems ironically to be destined to remain a singular example of idiolectal genre.

Like the epic and the fable, the proverb is reproduced as an antique at moments in need of ideological closure: its rhetorical form lends itself to didacticism and defined meaning, the sublimation of occasion to rule. Characteristically, these are monologic rather than dialogic forms. Once the proverb is uttered, there is nothing more to say. When these oral forms appear as monologue, they tend toward abstract subjects expressed with singular concentration.[39] Therefore, it is not surprising that contemporary proverb collections are as obsolete as the interjection of traditional proverbs into conversation. Yet as recently as 1946 the Textile Machine Works Company of Reading, Pennsylvania, published a work called *The Wisdom of the Ages: A Collection of Proverbs illustrated photographically which, during the period 1936–1946, formed the basis for the advertising of Textile Machine Works.* The company president wrote in the preface that "we could think of no stronger way to start men thinking about progress, profit and obsolescence than to repeat the counsel of the wise men of the ages." This text, which clearly follows the courtesy-book tradition, includes the sections "Proverbs Pointing to the Value of

Keeping Machines in Condition" and "Proverbs Pointing to the Lesson of Patience while Waiting for New Machines."[40]

Fairy Tale

Thus far we have examined forms in which the motivation for distressing—that is, both reproducing and antiquating—genres for ideological purposes is quite apparent. The epic, fable, and proverb all bear a rhetorical closure that is absolute and fixed in its antiquity. These forms declare their distance from immediate context and immediate historical perspective, and at the same time are used to legitimate a particular account of origins and the natural. The remaining two genres to be considered, the literary fairy tale and the literary ballad, are much newer historically, the former dating from the late seventeenth century, and the latter from the early eighteenth. Both correspond to rising conceptions of the vox populi that linked the peasant with the child, concepts contributing to the invention of "the folk" in the West and to the collection and appropriation of the oral tradition by the leisure classes as part of a larger nostalgic reaction against industrialism.[41] Their distance from the present is used to legitimate the origins of the personal and familial— the domestic hearth of childhood and a domesticated agrarian past.

The Wife of Bath mentions King Arthur and the fairies in the same breath, and Straparola's *Le Piacevoli Notti* (1550–53) had been translated into French by the late sixteenth century. Yet despite these appearances, and considering that there was certainly a tradition of fairy lore within the European oral tradition, the term *fairy tale* is a rather recent literary invention, dating to the publication of Madame d'Aulnoy's *Contes des fées* in 1698, a year after the appearance of Charles Perrault's *Contes du temps passé*. In 1699 Madame d'Aulnoy's book was translated into English as *Tales of the Fairys*. What should draw our attention in this French context is its transformation of the ambivalent and vigorous popular tradition into a literary form inseparable from the world of the antique, the child, the pastoral, the moral, and the fantastic. Although Perrault is often heralded as an early folklorist in that he preserved both dialectal words and superfluous vestigial passages in his texts, we must remember that he published the tales under the name of his third son, Pierre Darmancour; that he ends each tale with a rhymed *moralité;* and that he felt that the "modern" French fairy tales of Mother Goose were "cleaner" than similar stories from antiquity (such as *The Golden Ass* of Apuleius).[42] Philippe Ariès has pointed out the complex ideological functions served by this late-seventeenth-century fashion in fairy-tale telling. Fairy tales appear at the same time as the invention of childhood, but like all children's literature then and since, such tales reflect the adult conception of childhood. Yet we may extend Ariès's point beyond what he has called the "falsely naive" voice of these tales for children.[43] The false naiveté of the tales is an escape from time in another sense. These distressed tales—"Little Red Riding Hood" without cannibalism, "Sleeping Beauty" without eroticism—must also be placed within the context of the court of Louis XIV and the mythological dream, the tableau of a Jupiter in "Paris, France, la Rome moderne," in which both Perrault, the civil servant and academician, and his tales, especially popular at Versailles, played a role.[44]

Between the late-seventeenth-century tales of Perrault and Madame d'Aulnoy, written for the amusement of aristocrats under the pretext of educational reform, and the mid-eighteenth-century *Magasin des enfans* of Madame Jeanne le Prince de Beaumont, the agreeable was largely supplanted by the useful, while the dialogue between fantasy and didacticism that characterizes the development of the literary fairy tale even today had begun. Although by the end of the eighteenth century fairy tales had come to be looked upon, in the style of Boileau, as an affront to the rational mind, the advent of Romanticism and Romantic nationalism again brought a new interest and focus to the fairy tale, both popular and literary. The fate of the fairy tale in England, where Protestantism channeled its traditional ambivalence to more didactic purposes, only exaggerates the role of Romanticism in "restoring" the fairy tale's overdetermined qualities of narrative and, at the same time, revising its language.

In German Romanticism particularly, we see both a burgeoning scientific interest in transcribing the tales and a new didactic interest in such tales as pedagogical and ideological tools. The Grimms, who, we must remember, called their collection *Kinder und Hausmärchen*, were eager to use the tales as evidence of a scientific theory of language. Their desire to transcribe the tales accurately from oral tradition reflected a nationalistic aesthetic that linked the artifact to a particular moment in historical evolution. In contrast, Hans Christian Andersen, the first author of fairy tales to come from the peasant classes, published *Household Stories* and *Tales for Children*, collections that were both newly minted and strongly didactic.[45] Here the nineteenth century's nostalgic concept of an agrarian past connected with the face-to-face communication of the hearth and the household world of childhood. Whereas the neoclassical fairy tale was characterized by neat morality and a focused closure, the Romantics supplemented the seventeenth-century tale with translations of Oriental and Celtic literature and a taste for the Gothic occult. Romantic writers—Coleridge, Nodier, Gautier, and George Sand, for example—preferred melancholy themes, a search for an ideal such as passionate love or absolute beauty, and a uniformly literary language.[46] Thus in their return to an idealized nature, they turned away from didactic closure, but were removed as well from the language of oral tradition.

Following the nineteenth-century fairy-tale literature of the Romantics, the diminutive tradition remains the exclusive provenance of the child. In *A Study of Fairy Tales* (1916), Laura F. Kready advanced six reasons why fairy tales were valuable to education, from (1) "Fairy tales bring joy into child life," to (6) "In the home fairy tales employ leisure hours in a way that builds character."[47] In the recent "debate" over fairy tales promulgated by Bruno Bettelheim and others, there is no question that such narratives belong to childhood. Furthermore, we might note that the most popular contemporary writer for children, Maurice Sendak, relies upon plots borrowed largely from the folk- and fairy-tale corpus, and that his celebrated drawings are always distinctly uncontemporary in both themes and execution. For example, his children rarely appear in dress more recent than that of the early twentieth century and most often appear in that of the eighteenth.

Ballad

Just as the fairy tale characterizes the invention of the child, so does the ballad characterize the invention of the folk. Theories of the ballad—from individual-genius positions to communal positions contending authorship by singing and dancing throngs—have always provided analogies to the prevailing conceptions of the folk held by the middle and upper classes. Like the fairy tale, the literary ballad appears in both transcribed and imitated form. Among the early-eighteenth-century imitations, Thomas Tickell's "Lucy and Colin" was declared by Gray and Goldsmith, themselves imitators, to be one of the best ballads in the English language. Such early imitations patterned themselves on broadsides and dealt mainly with village tragedies.[48] Oliver Goldsmith, Thomas Chatterton, and the collector Thomas Percy all attempted poetic imitations before the more famous imitations of the Romantics. In this early- and mid-eighteenth-century period of emulation of folk genres, we must also place Chatterton's "Rowley poems," a set of fabricated works that Chatterton contended were written by a fifteenth-century Bristol poet named Thomas Rowley.[49] Chatterton offered three of these poems to the publisher Dodsley and sent a history of painting in England, also "by Rowley," to Horace Walpole, who was temporarily deceived. A suicide at seventeen, Chatterton had been a student of Bristol antiquities since childhood. It would seem more appropriate to consider him an expander of the Renaissance repertoire than a simple forger. I shall take up his case in some detail in chapter 6.

Aside from the textual fidelities of Joseph Ritson, the attitudes of eighteenth-century ballad editors were either to "clean up" a "genuine" folk ballad by improving it or to invent an imitation that would bear applied marks of authenticity. Percy's *Reliques of Ancient English Poetry*, appearing in 1765, contended that ballads are rude survivals of the past, deserving of a certain amount of attention as illustrations of belief and custom, although of little intrinsic value as poetry. Thus Percy felt free to alter or improve his collected texts in order to make them "fit for the perusal of cultivated readers."[50] Percy's manipulated texts set the scene for his own counterfeit ballads as well as for the great ballad scandals of the late eighteenth and early nineteenth centuries, which we will consider in chapter 4. For just as the Renaissance specialized in classical forgeries, so did Romanticism find new inspiration for forgery in "primitive" and "lost" literature.[51]

Perhaps the best introduction to these scandals comes from one who participated in them: Sir Walter Scott's "Essay on Imitations of the Ancient Ballad." Scott's literary career began with his translation of a German ballad by Bürger, "Lenoré" (1795), which was soon followed by his imitations, "Glenfinlas" and "The Eve of St. John." What these imitations are imitations of, however, is not the popular ballad that Scott sometimes collected from the oral tradition of the Border, but "the vein of Ossian," whereby he considered himself "liberated from imitating the antiquated language and ruder rhythms of the Minstrel ballad." Scott cites Percy and Robert Burns as repairers and restorers of ballads, and criticizes Lady Wardlaw's "Hardyknute" and Chatterton's "Sir Charles Baudwin [*sic*]" as examples of forgeries.[52] He concludes:

> The art used to disguise and misspell the words only overdid what was intended and afforded some evidence that the poems published as antiques had been, in fact, tampered with by a modern artist, as the newly forged medals of modern days stand convicted of imposture from the very touches of the file by which there is an attempt to imitate the cracks and fissures produced by the hammer upon the original.

Scott says that he himself has tried such imitations, but concludes that

> a modern poet engaged in such a task, is much in the situation of an architect of the present day who, if acquainted with his profession, finds no difficulty in copying the external forms of a Gothic castle or abbey; but when it is completed, can hardly by any artificial tints or cement, supply the spots, weather-stains and hues of different kinds, with which time alone had invested the venerable fabric which he desires to imitate.[53]

Chapter 4 will investigate more deeply Scott's relation to the ballad scandals and the role these scandals played in the development of an authenticating criticism.

Parody

Scott's half-hearted "confession" brings us to the point we have been suppressing: the point of parody. As soon as we hear the distressed genre, its high seriousness, its inflexible form, its reverent tone, and its venerable language, we also hear the works that undermine it. For the epic, there is the mock epic—the epic form stripped of its content, a content replaced by a battle of frogs and mice, the rape of a lock, or the rural games of Gloucester. Similarly, the bastard child of the ballad is the antisentimental ballad opera, which, with its emphasis upon mixing generic categories, defying patronage, and depicting the failure of the father, might be seen as one of our most vivid models of an antiauthoritarian genre. Furthermore, we must consider the impossible task of distressing the novel, a genre that is heir to Elizabethan mixed modes rather than seventeenth- and eighteenth-century French neoclassicism. Attempts to distress the novel range from Erica Jong's recent "eighteenth-century novel" *Fanny* (which erupts into satire by the second page as a spaniel vomits its way through an eighteenth-century interior), to "serious" imitations such as John Barth's *Sotweed Factor,* also an "eighteenth-century" work, and "Leonie Hargrave's" *Clara Reeve,* an imitation of the kind of Gothic novel Clara Reeve herself would have written. It is the reduction of the novel to a skeletal form, either at its point of origin in the eighteenth century or in the highly formulaic period of the Gothic novel, combined with the reader's knowledge of the work's contemporary status (here the frame tale struggles against the paperback cover for our credibility), that makes such works parodies, no matter how seamless they might appear.

Furthermore, whereas parodies of high forms, such as the mock epic, depend upon the transposition of content within an inflexible form, the very novelty of the novel means that a parody or antinovel must attempt to make the form itself inflexible. Thus it is only the periodization of the novel that makes it susceptible to distressing. And that periodization, which the novel aesthetic constantly struggles against in its rejection of classicism, always falls into parody once the marks of distressing are applied, for the novel by its very "nature" is against the valorization of temporality.[54] For an analogy, we might look to the popular music tradition, which, with its emphasis upon improvisation, always presents the pure revival act like the new Big Band or Sha Na Na with a certain sensation of bad faith, tempered by a certain sensation of loss.

Because of the shadow of parody, the gesture made in distressing genres is an ambivalent one: it implies defamation as well as veneration. Whereas parody works by historicizing or contextualizing transcendence and authority, the distressed genre entertains the possibility of transcending the limits of historical circumstance. Here we see the irony of the distressed genre's relation to speech and writing, for any genre that in literature attempts to "pass itself as" the oral is destined to appear in ill-fitting clothing. The literary's nostalgia for oral forms is a nostalgia for the presence of the body and the face-to-face, a dream of unmediated communication that, of course, could never be approximated even in the oral—a dream of an eternalized present, a future-past. Thus distressed genres often exaggerate a movement of time into space on several simultaneous levels. First, such a movement characterizes the transformation of the temporality of speech into the spatiality of writing. Second, the movement of time into space is often a device for the legitimation of territory and property, both private and national, by means of narrative or textual evidence. Hence the legitimating function of Macpherson's *Ossian* for Scottish nationalism.[55] And hence Robert Chambers's collection *The Popular Rhymes of Scotland, Chiefly Collected from Oral Sources* is designed to create a documentation of place; although they are "humble ratt rimes," these pieces are "divided into rhymes on localities, characteristics of localities, popular reproaches (toward localities and families), rhymes upon families of distinction, family characteristics, slogans of families and towns, rhymes appropriate for superstitions and miscellaneous rhymes."[56] Third, the lived duration of history is replaced, through a transcendent voice, with the eternalized present of objects in space. In William Collins's "An Ode on the Popular Superstitions of the Highlands of Scotland, considered as a Subject for Poetry" (1749), for example, Collins advises his friend the Reverend John Home, an aspiring Scottish dramatist, to turn to "that soil . . . whose every value / shall prompt the poet":

> There must thou wake perforce thy Doric quill;
> 'Tis Fancy's land to which thou sett'st thy feet,
> Where still, 'tis said, the fairy people meet
> Beneath each birken shade on mead or hill.
> There each trim lass that skims the milky store
> To the swart tribes their creamy bowl allots;
> By night they sip it round the cottage door,
> While airy minstrels warble jocund notes.
> There ev'ry herd, by sad experience, knows
> How, winged with fate, their elf-shot arrows fly;

> When the sick ewe her summer food foregoes,
> Or, stretched one arth, the heart-smit heifers lie.
> Such airy beings awe th'untutored swain:
> Nor thou, thou learned, his homelier thoughts neglect;
> Let thy sweet Muse the rural faith sustain:
> These are the themes of simple, sure effect,
> That add new conquests to her boundless reign,
> And fill, with double force, her heart-commanding strain.

Here history, landscape, and poetic topic expand into a trove of awakened possibilities. The rhetoric of Collins's "Ode" contends that if Home will only see his connection to the substratum of folk belief, untutored poets, and the enduring tradition of minstrelsy, he will alike awake an affinity to Spenser, Shakespeare, and Tasso. Furthermore, Collins assures his friend that he will never run out of subjects for his writing:

> Proceed! in forceful sounds and colors bold,
> The native legends of thy land rehearse;
> To such adapt thy lyre and suit thy pow'rful verse.[58]

Yet the nostalgia of the distressed genre is not a nostalgia for artifacts for their own sake; rather, it is a nostalgia for context, for the heroic past, for moral order, for childhood and the collective experiences of preindustrial life. Thus we can understand why it makes little difference whether the artifact itself is real or a forgery: distressed genres are characterized by a counterfeit materiality and an authentic nostalgia. In fact, such genres point to the immateriality of all nostalgic objects. These artifacts of memory, these mnemonics, are artifacts of appearance, both partial and allusive. Their evocation lies in their surface (therefore many souvenirs are tied to the sensuality of touch), while their depth arises not from intrinsicality, but from the narrative of the subject they engender. Souvenirs must typically be economically worthless in order to serve the narrative of the personal; otherwise, they are a contradiction of the personal. However, distressed genres as temporal artifacts are not such relics or archaeological remains, the kind of enduring and typical forms West had hoped for. Instead, their analogy in space is to the prefabricated souvenir of tourism, an object that incorporates into its manufacture a particular reference to place that is largely the invention of the very system of objects to which it belongs. Our analogy is clearer if we note that such souvenirs, regardless of their referents, are most often made in Japan. As newly minted souvenirs of periodization, "everybody's souvenirs," distressed genres are close to kitsch objects, artifacts of exaggerated surface and collective experience. It is important to note this antipersonal dimension of the distressed genre, a dimension that coincides with its naive voice and forged status as gestures against the limitations of the self and the self's limited access to history. Furthermore, this erasure of the self, in both deferring to and creating a sense of anterior authority, is a movement against self-consciousness. Thus it is a movement against irony and irony's multiple accounts of the origins of history.

In distressed genres we see a mode of production in conflict with itself, an autograph literature that, by means of anonymity or even forgery, seeks for a collective authorship and the moral authority of community. Thus its politics always tend toward revisionism in its rejection of the present. The popularity of distressing cinema by producing in black and white, for example, might be seen both as a gesture against the opulent "color" of commercial films (as it is in Wim Wenders's *The State of Things*) and as an attempt to reconcile theme and form (as it is in Fassbinder's grainy *Effie Briest* and glossy *Veronica Voss* or the nostalgia films of Woody Allen).[59] To become familiar with the past here is simultaneously to become alienated from the present.

The desire to wake and honor the dead must always be reconciled to inappropriate modes, inappropriate contexts. The rejection of the present in the distressed genre operates on the level of form, theme, and intention, yet it can never surmount the present's control over the influence of context. Whereas the avant-garde is characterized by a struggle against generic constraints (indeed, its very anticlassicism depends upon classicism's refusal of the mixed category), the distressed genre is characterized by a struggle against history as it impinges upon the thematics of meaning. Distressed genres characterize periods of nostalgia juxtaposed by upheaval, revolution, and cultural distress. We should here consider the rise in popularity of antiques and antique reproductions as well as the rise of that carnival of distress, the American folk festival, in the period following World War I.[60] Similarly, the rural fair's nineteenth-century function as an exposition of technological change has been largely replaced by a nostalgic hypostatization of tradition in the face of a centralized agribusiness. And amusement-park motifs have similarly turned toward an exaggerated natural ("Great Adventure") and a naive account of origins (Busch Gardens' "Old Country" with three choices: France, Germany, and England). Furthermore, the peculiar mixture of medievalism, laissez-faire economics, Nietzschean heroics, and sexual discipline in contemporary science fiction and fantasy games and literature often rests upon a conceit of a future-past following a nuclear disaster.[61]

The closely guarded thematics of distressed genres—heroism, paternity, the domestic past, the rural/agrarian, the tribal/communal, the "primitive," and the child—are radically separated from their mechanical reproduction. In contrast to the art forms of the avant-garde, which are antihierarchical, international, and multilingual by definition, and in contrast to the classic and the "higher" forms of modernism, which seek to ignore the contingencies of history altogether, these forms search for a univocal voice within a centripedal culture. Historically, they have promoted a world purged of laughter and irony. Bakhtin concludes his study of the epic by writing that "the dead are loved in a different way. . . . In the high genres all authority and privilege, all lofty significance and grandeur, abandon the zone of familiar contact for the distanced plane. . . . It is in this orientation toward completeness that the classicism of all non-novel genres is expressed."[62] It is only with a sense of distress that we realize the incompleteness of this sensation of completeness: the gap between desire and object that in fact has generated, necessitated the invention of, this object. And if it has become the task of postmodernism to avoid a totalizing heroics, it has also become postmodernism's task to pose a critique of temporality that is deeply aware of the constraints of periodization.

Notes

1. Benjamin West, *A Discourse delivered to the Students of the Royal Academy on the Distribution of Prizes, December 10, 1792, by the President* (London: Thomas Podell, 1793), p. 11.

2. Ibid., p. iv.

3. For further discussion of the archaeological in relation to knowledge and action,

see Manfredo Tafuri, *The Sphere and the Labyrinth: Avant-Gardes and Architecture from Piranesi to the 1970s*, trans. Pelligrino d'Acierno and Robert Connolly (Cambridge, Mass.: MIT Press, 1987), p. 39.

4. This study differs from much contemporary genre criticism in its emphasis on the historical transformation of genres and their valuation. For a survey of current, and for the most part synchronic, approaches to genre in the study of verbal art, see Dan Ben-Amos, ed., *Folklore Genres* (Austin: University of Texas Press, 1976). Particularly helpful is Ben-Amos's own essay, "Analytical Categories and Ethnic Genres," pp. 215–42. A discussion of the relation of folklore to authenticity appears in Richard M. Dorson, *Folklore and Fakelore* (Cambridge, Mass.: Harvard University Press, 1976); my interest, however, is precisely in "fakelore" and its history—a subject Dorson seems to feel is best avoided. In a recent essay, "The Fabrication of Fakelore," Alan Dundes argues that fakelore is motivated by a "national, psychic need" (*Folklore Matters* [Knoxville: University of Tennessee Press, 1989], p. 50). Although nationalism is often tied to the artificial oral form, I find this explanation inadequate. First, it disregards the problematic historical relation between literature and folklore; second, "national psychic needs" seem to be as mystical in their conception as any bit of fakelore. William S. Fox's earlier essay, "Folklore and Fakelore: Some Sociological Considerations" (*Journal of the Folklore Institute* 17 [1980]: 244–61), provides a suggestive analysis of the relations between "fakelore" and ideology and critiques folklorists' concerns with authenticity as a matter of the reification of their discipline. I would draw the reader's attention to Marjorie Levinson, *Keats's Life of Allegory: The Origins of a Style* (Oxford: Basil Blackwell, 1988), and its argument that art that becomes aware of its own inauthenticity and seeks to represent such a contradiction might be characterized as "dis-eased" or "disarticulated." Levinson writes, in response to an earlier version of this essay, "perhaps the dis-eased work *is* the distressed work set within a dynamic social field where its contradictions start disclosing their purposes" (p. 93, p. 27).

5. Robert Southey, *The Lives and Works of the Uneducated Poets*, ed. J. S. Childers (London: Humphrey Milford, 1925), p. 25.

6. Ibid., p. 107

7. Ibid., p. 127.

8. For the full history of Ann Yearsley from which these remarks are taken, see ibid., pp. 125–34.

9. Mikhail Bakhtin, *The Dialogic Imagination*, ed. Michael Holquist, trans. Michael Holquist and Caryl Emerson (Austin: University of Texas Press, 1981), p. 15.

10. For example, in the eighth book of the *Odyssey* the Phaeacian bard Demodocus sings, at the request of the disguised Odysseus, the story of the Trojan horse. Similarly, the first book of the *Aeneid* finds Aeneas and his men confronted in Carthage with the walls of a newly built temple inscribed with scenes from the siege of Troy. For an account of Beowulf's divergence from these examples, see Paul Merchant, *The Epic* (London: Methuen, 1971), pp. 2–3.

11. C. M. Bowra, *From Virgil to Milton* (London: Macmillan, 1948), p. 28.

12. A. Bartlett Giamatti (*The Play of Double Senses: Spenser's Faerie Queene* [Englewood Cliffs, N.J.: Prentice-Hall, 1975], pp. 22–24) discusses "the traditional claim to be making an innovation here. . . . Epic poems, were since Antiquity the noblest

form of poetry, for which the high style was reserved, must contain and include all that went before" (p. 23). See also Bowra, *From Virgil to Milton*, pp. 13–15.

13. As Juliusz Kleiner has noted, "An undefined time and undefined place of occurrences are characteristic of tales, whereas epics are characterized by a clear definition of both. . . . However gradually as the emotional approach toward the past is intensified and expands, even the memory of past occurrences is penetrated by dreams. Slowly memory cedes to imagination and a fiction about the past grows up. This fiction contrasts with and complements the truth about the past, giving rise to an epos" ("The Role of Time in Literary Genres," *Zagadienia rodzajow literackich* [*Les Problémes des genres littéraires*] 2 [1959]: 6–7).

14. Theoretical discussion of the epic was stimulated by the translation of Aristotle's *Poetics* from Greek to Latin (1498, 1536); by 1549 this text had appeared in Italian as well.

15. Quoted in Bowra, *From Virgil to Milton*, p. 17.

16. Ibid., pp. 24–26. Bowra records that "the later writers of epic (i.e. those of the Reformation and Counter-Reformation) could not and would not laugh at the ideals which they proclaimed. There is no laughter in Tasso, who seems to regard it as particularly pernicious; for when the knights prepare to rescue Rinaldo from Armida, they are warned against a fountain which makes men laugh" (p. 26).

17. Richard Glover, *Leonidas* (1814; reprint, Baltimore: Neal, Wills and Coles, n.d.), preface. This movement toward the abstraction of moral cause parallels a substitution of allegorical/biblical subjects for classical heroes. Samuel Wesley writes in his 1697 "Essay on Heroic Poetry": "But this [Homer's manner] being now antiquated, I cannot think we are oblig'd superstitiously to follow his Example, any more than to make Horses speak, as he does that of Achilles. If a poet lights on any single Hero, whose true Actions and History are as important as any Fable that ever did or can produce, I see no reason why he may not as well make use of him and his Example to form the Manners and enforce any Moral Truth, as seek for one in Fable for that purpose" (*Series Two: Essays on Poetry*, no. 2, ed. Edward N. Hooker [Los Angeles: Augustan Reprint Society, 1947], pp. 4–5). (The essay originally appeared in *The Life of Our Blessed Lord and Saviour Jesus Christ: An Heroic Poem* [London: Charles Harper, 1697].)

18. Peter Hagin, *The Epic Hero and the Decline of Heroic Poetry: A Study of the Neoclassical English Epic with Special Reference to Milton's "Paradise Lost"* (Bern: Francke Verlag, 1964; New York: Folcroft Press, 1970), pp. 111–12.

19. John Hughes, "The Triumph of Peace, a Poem" (1698), quoted in Richard C. Boys, *Sir Richard Blackmore and the Wits* (New York: Octagon Books, 1969), p. 26.

20. See especially James Macpherson, *The Poems of Ossian. With an Essay in which they are Authenticated, Illustrated and Explained by Hugh Campbell* (London: Sir Richard Phillips, 1822). See also Edward Davies, *The Claims of Ossian, Examined and Appreciated* (London: Longman, 1825). The most comprehensive biography of Macpherson is still Bailey Saunders, *The Life and Letters of James Macpherson* (London: Swan Sonnenschein, 1894). Two more recent studies, however, show the complex background of authentic Gaelic sources, changing aesthetic and scientific values, and historical-political forces to Macpherson's "forgeries": Derick S. Thomson, *The Gaelic*

Sources of Macpherson's "Ossian" (Edinburgh: Oliver and Boyd, 1952); and Fiona J. Stafford, *The Sublime Savage: A Study of James Macpherson and the Poems of Ossian* (Edinburgh: Edinburgh University Press, 1988).

21. Note that the fable is often cited as the "little brother" of the epic. For example, Herder wrote in his essay "Aesop and Lessing" (1767–68), "I regard the fable as a source, a miniature of the great poetic genres" (quoted in Thomas Noel, *Theories of the Fable in the Eighteenth Century* [New York: Columbia University Press, 1975], p. 127).

22. B. E. Perry, "Fable," *Studium Generale* 12 (1959): 24.

23. For a fuller discussion of this point, see David Richter's study of ideological fictions, *Fable's End: Completeness and Closure in Rhetorical Fiction* (Chicago: University of Chicago Press, 1974).

24. Here we might be reminded of Perrault's 1675 work, *Labyrinthe de Versailles,* a short description of the Versailles gardens, decorated with an ensemble of fountains and sculptures designed to illustrate thirty-eight of Aesop's fables. Thus the perfect visual order of the gardens, followed by the ideological closure of the short poem, provides a projection of the emblem book into the landscape and vice versa.

25. Noel, *Theories of the Fable,* p. 21.

26. Ibid., p. 16.

27. We find La Fontaine writing

> Mon imitation n'est point un esclavage
> Je ne prends que l'idée, et les tours, et les lois,
> Que nos maîtres suivaient eux-même autrefois.

in "Epitre à Monseigneur L'Evéque de Soissons, En Lui Donnant Un Quintilien de La Traduction D'Oratio Toscanella" (quoted in Agnes E. Mackay, *La Fontaine and His Friends: A Biography* [New York: Braziller, 1973], pp. 145–46). We see this quarrel taken up in Johann Christoph Gottsched, *Attempt at a Critical Poetics for Germans* (1730). Gottsched suggested a compromise whereby the Aesopian fable was recommended for children and the common man, while the upper and educated classes could be given original morals without such a superimposed fiction. Noel writes that in later years Gottsched suffered from accusations of anachronism and obsequious imitation, in that he proposed the introduction of seventeenth-century French classicism into eighteenth-century German literature. His followers, Daniel Wilhelm Triller and Daniel Stoppe, wrote "new" Aesopian fables in which "diverse edifying moral lessons and useful rules of conduct were expounded in metrical speech." Triller lamented that the dearth of noteworthy fables in Germany paralleled a lack of accomplishment in the epic (Noel, *Theories of the Fable,* pp. 48–50).

28. Note the proximity of Caxton's *Book of Courtsye* (1497) and *Aesop's Fables* (1484).

29. For example, although Edward Moore declared that his *Fables for the Female Sex* were meant only for amusement, it was clear to a contemporary scholar such as Johann Jakob Bodmer that "his secret aim, in the midst of amusement, is to teach useful rules, how a female, in a manner becoming her sex, can arrange her life for her greater well-being and enjoyment" (quoted in Noel, *Theories of the Fable,* p. 65). Moore's text is arranged with each story followed by an illustrating or analogous poem. "The Poet and the Patron," for example, tells the story of a married woman who no longer cares how she is dressed, and is followed by a poem depicting a poet

who neglects his craft once he has a patron. Moore begins his collection with a fable celebrating transcendent knowledge, "The Eagle and the Assembly of Birds":

> Truth under fiction I impart
> To weed out folly from the heart
> And shew the paths, that lead astray
> The wandering nymph from wisdom's way.

(Fables for the Female Sex, 3rd ed. [London: J. Listee, 1766]). For another aviary fable, see Samuel Johnson, "Fable of the Vultures," *The Idler,* no. 22 (September 1758), wherein a mother vulture talks to her young about the evils of war in particular and humans in general.

30. Quoted in Noel, *Theories of the Fable,* pp. 145–46.

31. Nym Wales, *Fables and Parables for Mid-Century* (New York: Philosophical Library, 1952).

32. G. W. F. Hegel, *The Philosophy of Fine Art,* trans. F. P. B. Osmaston (London: Bell, 1920), vol. 2, pp. 114–15.

33. Ibid., p. 115.

34. This is the "child as swain" motif so brilliantly analyzed in William Empson, *Some Versions of Pastoral* (New York: New Directions, 1974), pp. 253–94.

35. Hegel, *Philosophy of Fine Art,* p. 124.

36. Max Lerner and Edwin Mims, Jr., "Literature," in *Encyclopedia of the Social Sciences* (New York: Macmillan, 1933), vol. 9, p. 533. Lerner and Mims's article is also of interest for the study of distressed genres in general, in that it suggests that literary evolution follows a path of "rebarbarization." Here they borrow from Viktor Šklovskij's concept that all literary genres derive from "subliterary" genres. For a more recent study of "subliterary systems," see Itamar Even-Zohar, *Papers in Historical Poetics* (Tel Aviv: Porter Institute for Poetics and Semiotics, 1978). To become a classic, the "high" genre must often be popularized; hence the position of *Robinson Crusoe,* a text that is presently found far more often in abridged than in full form.

37. Rosalie Colie (*The Resources of Kind: Genre Theory in the Renaissance,* ed. Barbara Lewalski [Berkeley: University of California Press, 1973]) links the adage and proverb tradition to the emblem-book tradition and traces through these caption forms the influence of the hieroglyph: in all there is the notion that something is concealed and accessible only by means of particularized and esoteric knowledge. Colie finds that the decline in esoteric elements was marked by a rise in didactic function (pp. 33–34). A work such as John Bunyan's *Divine Emblems for Children* (1686) as well might be seen as fabular in its impulse to fill out the meaning completely. Thus as the fable moved from written to popular to revived (written) and again to popular tradition, so did the emblem-book tradition circle from proverb and the popular/oral to esoteric to popular tradition once again. For Erasmus, the proverb may be a *condimentum* to be used in effective writing and speaking, but for Bunyan its understanding implicates the fate of the soul. Blake's proverbs, by contrast of course, remind us of the fragmentary quality of any totality; their contradictory and ambivalent content makes them serious and profound parodies of the proverb form.

38. Archer Taylor, *The Proverb* (Cambridge, Mass.: Harvard University Press, 1931), pp. 174–76.

39. Such univocality and abstraction is even typical of the most ambivalent oral form, the riddle, once it is put into literary form (Archer Taylor, *The Literary Riddle Before 1600* [Berkeley: University of California Press, 1948], p. 4). Yet when these forms appear in juxtaposition or dialogue with one another, they historically tend to move toward parody and the obscene. For example, the Old English Salomon and Saturnus, growing out of the Old Testament legends of the wisdom of Solomon, is a serious religious disputation. But over time, Solomon's opponent in dialogue becomes his fool; by the time of the medieval dialogue of Solomon and Marcolf, a shrewd fool tops each of Solomon's sayings with an obscene proverb or parody (Taylor, *Proverb*, pp. 177–78).

40. Textile Machine Works, Reading, Pa., 1946.

41. George Boas, *Vox Populi: Essays in the History of an Idea* (Baltimore: Johns Hopkins University Press, 1969).

42. Jacques Barchilon and Peter Flinders, *Charles Perrault* (Boston: Twayne, 1981), p. 81. See also Philippe Ariès, "At the Point of Origin," in *The Child's Part*, ed. Peter Brooks (Boston: Beacon Press, 1969), pp. 15–23; and Marc Soriano's great psychoanalytic project, *Les Contes de Perrault: culture savante et traditions populaires* (Paris: Gallimard, 1968), and *Le Dossier Perrault* (Paris: Hachette, 1972).

43. Ariès, "At the Point of Origin," p. 23. See also Zohar Shavit, *Poetics of Children's Literature* (Athens: University of Georgia Press, 1986), pp. 3–32.

44. The first literary fairy tale in French literature is generally recognized to be the "Isle de la Félicité," in Madame d'Aulnoy's novel *Histoire d'Hippolyte* (Paris: Sevestre, 1690), pp. 143–81. That transcendent and atemporal island in the midst of historical and novelistic flux is transposed without great difficulty to the position of Versailles itself.

45. In *Breaking the Magic Spell: Radical Theories of Folk and Fairy Tales* (London: Heinemann, 1979), Jack Zipes explains that in eighteenth- and nineteenth-century Germany we also find, in contrast to the oral tradition, the literary concept of "limited enlightenment . . . instead of folktales, the newspapers, weeklies, yearbooks and anthologies were filled with, and flooded the market with, didactic stories, fables, anecdotes, homilies and sermons which were intended to sanctify the interests of the emerging middle class" (pp. 24–25). For discussions of imitations of fairy tales, see also pp. 14–15 and Jack Zipes, *Victorian Fairy Tales: The Revolt of the Fairies and Elves* (New York: Methuen, 1987), pp. xiii–xxix. A recent study by Heinz Rölleke exposes the nationalist and sentimental assumptions that kept scholars from recognizing the French influences upon, and bourgeois provenance of, some of the Grimms' tales ("The 'Utterly Hessian' Fairy Tales by 'Old Marie': The End of a Myth," trans. Ruth Bottigheimer, in *Fairy Tales and Society: Illusion, Allusion and Paradigm*, ed. Ruth Bottigheimer [Philadelphia: University of Pennsylvania Press, 1986], pp. 287–300).

46. Edith Cummings, "The Literary Development of the Romantic Fairy Tale in France" (Ph.D. diss., Bryn Mawr College, 1934), pp. 90–91.

47. Laura F. Kready, *A Study of Fairy Tales* (Boston: Houghton Mifflin, 1916), pp. 3–9.

48. Sigurd B. Hustvedt, *Ballad Books and Ballad Men* (Cambridge, Mass.: Harvard University Press, 1930), pp. 22–23.

49. Edmund K. Chambers, *The History and Motives of Literary Forgeries* (1891; reprint, New York: Burt Franklin, 1970), pp. 32–33. Chambers adds that "the dawn

of the romantic movement in France presents an instance of a literary forgery parallel to those of Chatterton and Macpherson. . . . In 1803 a man named Vanderbourg published a volume of poems by Clotilde de Surville. It was stated that the authoress was a Provençal lady of the fifteenth century. . . . The language, the metre, and the orthography are not of the fifteenth century, and the ideas expressed are markedly later. Thus there are allusions to Sappho, Lucretius and Catullus, none of whom were discovered until the end of that century, and others which imply a knowledge of the writings of Voltaire and of an astronomical fact first ascertained in 1789" (p. 34).

50. Hustvedt, *Ballad Books and Ballad Men*, p. 23.

51. Chambers, *History and Motives of Literary Forgeries*, pp. 35–36. Chambers also lists "M. de Villemarqué's Breton ballads, the Macedonian songs of M. Verkovitch, and the collection of Illyrian translations published by Prosper Mérimée under the title *La Guzla*. Mérimée is responsible too for the *Théâtre de Clara Gazul*, an imaginary Spanish actress. His motive for these *supercheries* was a purely artistic one; he prided himself on his skill in catching 'local colour,' and enjoyed seeing it deceive the critics" (p. 35).

52. Walter Scott, "Essay on Imitations of the Ancient Ballad," in *Minstrelsy of the Scottish Border*, rev. and ed. T. F. Henderson (Edinburgh: Oliver and Boyd, 1932), vol. 4, pp. 10–11.

53. Ibid., p. 13.

54. Furthermore, "costume novels" such as those of Sir Walter Scott always suffer from the implicit comic threat of characters continually lapsing into modernity. We might add that in Scott's work the number of characters who burst into ballads, as one bursts into song in musical comedy, illustrates a notion of the subliminal folk culture ready to burst at any given moment (but particularly at moments of closure) through the surface of the contemporary. In contrast, opera assumes a sung world into which speech/text is occasionally intersected. The contradictions of the ballad imitations are suggestively echoed in the current controversy regarding authenticity and the performance of "early music." In "The Spin Doctors of Early Music" (*New York Times*, 29 July 1990, sec. 2, p. 1), Richard Taruskin of the University of California at Berkeley argues that the "revival" of early music derives from a modernist aesthetic of shock, novelty, and estrangement. Thus, he contends, the "authentic" presentation of early music does not so much link us to the past as confirm a radical otherness between past, present, and future. For a discussion and critique of this argument, see Charles Rosen, "The Shock of the Old," review of *Authenticity and Early Music*, edited by Nicholas Kenyon, *New York Review of Books*, 19 July 1990, pp. 46–52.

55. Stafford shows Macpherson's work within a matrix of Highland clan loyalties, Jacobite ambition, Scottish nationalism, and, at the same time, a rather decadent and sentimental aesthetic derived from anticlassical impulses in the academic and literary culture of the Lowlands and England (*Sublime Savage*, pp. 6–39, 151–62). In Hugh Campbell's official authentication of Macpherson's poem, the work's validating function, relying upon genealogy, geography, and history, is quite clear. Campbell not only dedicates his authentication to the marquis of Hastings, whose own genealogy has a stake in the authenticity of Ossian, but also mentions that the references to the traditional ancestor of the clan Campbell in the poem are "but natural and not to be doubted." The model that Ossian presents of authenticity and authority by virtue of territory and genealogy, the model of property and paternity, might even

be seen in the Gaelicized mythology of the antebellum South presented in such twentieth-century family epics as Margaret Mitchell's *Gone with the Wind*. Campbell writes: "It is encumbent upon me to add one more observation before I conclude— namely, that the natural, though rather singular *mound* called Tara, in the county of Meath, is generally considered by Irish antiquaries—who have implicitly followed O'Flaherty and one another—as the site of the regal palace of the O'Neill's" (Macpherson, *Poems of Ossian*, vol. 1, p. lxxxii). Genealogy was also a key element—and eventually the downfall—of William Henry Ireland's Shakespeare forgeries of 1794 to 1795. In addition to the forged Shakespeare plays, *Vortigern and Rowena* and *Henry II*, Ireland created a set of fake Shakespearean documents on genuine Elizabethan parchment. These documents included a number of pieces claiming that one of Ireland's own ancestors had rescued Shakespeare from drowning and that Shakespeare had consequently sent the ancestor gifts, dedicated some lines to him, and drawn a sketch of his house (Ian Haywood, *The Making of History* [Rutherford, N.J.: Fairleigh Dickinson University Press, 1986], pp. 185–89; J. A. Farrer, *Literary Forgeries* [1907; reprint, Detroit: Gale Research, 1969], pp. 161–74).

56. Robert Chambers, *The Popular Rhymes of Scotland, Chiefly Collected from Oral Sources* (Edinburgh: William Hunter, 1826).

57. William Collins, "An Ode on the Popular Superstitions of the Highlands of Scotland," in *Eighteenth-Century Poetry*, ed. Patricia Meyer Spacks (Englewood Cliffs, N.J.: Prentice-Hall, 1964), p. 221.

58. Ibid, p. 226.

59. In fact, in *Effie Briest* film seeks to distress itself into an earlier mode of production, in that it presents an imitation of the book's material features.

60. David E. Whisnant, *Folk Festival Issue: Report from a Seminar*, JEMF Special Series, no. 12 (Los Angeles: John Edwards Memorial Foundation, University of California at Los Angeles, 1977). See also Ellen Stekert, "Cents and Nonsense in the Urban Folksong Movement: 1930–1966," in *Folklore and Society: Essays in Honor of Benjamin Botkin*, ed. Bruce Jackson (Hatboro, Pa.: Folklore Associates, 1966), pp. 15–18. For a more "sincere" and perhaps more amusing example, see Jean Thomas, *Ballad Makin' in the Mountains of Kentucky* (New York: Holt, 1939).

61. Dungeons and Dragons, for example, offers a series of "mythos" to choose from, including Babylonian, Celtic, Central American, Chinese, Egyptian, Japanese, Indian, Greek, Norse, and Sumerian (James Ward and Robert Kuntz, *Advanced Dungeons and Dragons: Special Reference Work, Deities and Demigods Cyclopedia* [Lake Geneva, Wis.: TSR Games, 1980]). Piers Anthony's *Kirlian Quest* (New York: Avon Books, 1978) presents a world of nobles, dukes, heralds, horse-drawn carriages, exorcists, dueling swords, and characters wearing tartans and is marked by climactic hunt scenes, siege scenes, and chivalric customs in general. Analogously, Anne McCaffrey's *Dragonsinger* (New York: Bantam Books, 1977) presents the Land of Pern, with its hierarchy of Masterharpers, Journeymen, and Apprentices. In his reference work to the Martian stories of Edgar Rice Burroughs, *A Guide to Barsoom* (New York: Ballantine Books, 1976), John Flint Roy writes that "the Barsoomians place a high value on convention, including gallantry and dignity. Customs have been handed down by ages of repetition and the punishment for ignoring a custom is a matter for individual treatment by a jury of the culprit's peers" (p. 131). I am grateful to my student John August for these and many other references to contemporary science-fiction works.

62. Bakhtin, *Dialogic Imagination*, p. 20. In what might be considered a parody of the gesture of distressing, Witter Bynner and Arthur Davison Ficke, under the names Manuel Morgan and Anne Knish, published from 1916 to 1918 a series of poems meant to exaggerate the features of the avant-garde. Imagism particularly was the victim of this series of modernist "forgeries," called by its perpetrators "The Spectra Hoax." It is interesting to note that these forgeries succeeded to some degree in actually *being* avant-garde poems. That is, while the intention may have been parodic, the poems were seriously evaluated and considered by such modernist luminaries as Harriet Monroe. Furthermore, the end of the hoax and the revelation of the parody came about only with the production of parodies of the parodies. After a group of University of Wisconsin undergraduates calling themselves "the Ultra-Violet Movement" published poems by "Manual Organ" and "Nanne Dish," Bynner and Ficke admitted to the hoax and the "Spectrists" disappeared (William Jay Smith, *The Spectra Hoax* [Middletown, Conn.: Wesleyan University Press, 1961]).

Scandals of the Ballad

The entry for "The Ballad" in *The Concise Cambridge History of English Literature* somewhat vehemently states that "the genuine ballad" has

> these special marks of character: (1) it is a narrative poem without any discernible indication of personal authorship; (2) it is strong, bare, objective and free from general sentiments or reflections; (3) it was meant originally for singing, and, as its name implies, was connected at some time with dancing; (4) it has been submitted to a process of oral tradition among unsophisticated people fairly homogenous in life, habit, and outlook, and below the level at which conscious literary art appears.

The Cambridge *History* goes on to explain that "no verse of this sort can be produced under the conditions of modern life" and that "the three hundred and five ballads represented by some thirteen hundred versions in F. J. Child's collection (1882–98) set the patterns which later revivals and recoveries tended to follow."[1]

If we look closely at this account, we find, in fact, not so much the definition of a genre, but another, far more ambivalent, history of the kind outlined in the survey of distressed genres in chapter 3. We find that a genre can arise in a particular historical context and can just as particularly disappear. We find that the literary tradition, in rescuing a "folk" tradition, can just as surely kill it off. We find that in order to imagine folklore, the literary community of the eighteenth century had to invent a folk, singing and dancing "below the level" of "conscious literary art." And perhaps the same thing: we find that the advent of modern literary scholarship, with its task of genealogy—the establishment of paternity and lines of influence—and its role in the legislation of originality and authenticity, depended upon the articulation of a "folk" literature that "literature" was not.

Thus the eighteenth-century development of an "author" and the eighteenth-century crisis in authenticity must be situated within a history of the establishment and legislation of spheres of originality and accountability for writing. Focusing broadly on the period between the Scottish vernacular revival of the early part of the century and the criticism of Robert Chambers more than a hundred years later, this chapter will examine the development of a ballad genre that often supplanted the oral tradition, and that of a ballad scholarship that arose as the cure for the anxiety produced by this supplanting—an anxiety centered around the period's various "ballad scandals." In the early part of the eighteenth century, we find writers such as Allan Ramsay eagerly considering almost any "song" or "poem" as an example of the traditional ballad, but by the 1840s we find writers such as Chambers doubting the authenticity of nearly everything. It is not so much that the ballad scandals of the eighteenth century were the *products* of rules regarding forgery, authenticity, plagiarism, and originality as that the ballad scandals helped *produce* such rules.[2] In order to understand how the contradictions of literary ballad production erupted at this time, we might begin by looking at why one would want to "collect" folkloric forms such as the ballad in the first place.

Verbal art had been collected artifactually since the sixteenth century for a variety of reasons: to establish a corpus of texts that would reflect nationalist impulses and hence lend validity to a vernacular heritage in contradistinction to a classical one; to "rescue" forms that seem to be disappearing—that is, to effect a kind of archaeology of speech forms parallel to the rescue of what is properly known as "material" culture; to place such "specimens" as curiosities, characterized by fragmentation and exoticism, against the contemporary and so use them to establish the parameters of the present, much as any form of collecting does. However, the collector's attempt to transform speech into writing resulted, and continues to result, in a set of quite vivid contradictions regarding the collecting impulse.

The conversion of speech into writing, while a change in form, is not a matter of producing a fixed form; instead, we might say that the transformation of oral forms into collected, written forms is always a matter of releasing the oral from such fixity. Such a separation of speech from its particular moment may result in a singular text, but this text goes on to become symptomatic. It is a fragment of a larger whole that is a matter not only of other versions, but of the entire aura of the oral world—such a world's imagined presence, immediacy, organicism, and authenticity. Thus it is important to note the materiality of the signifier regardless of its oral or written form: the notion that writing endows the oral with materiality is another facet of the collector's interest in establishing the ephemerality of the oral, an interest that puts the oral in urgent need of rescue. In other words, the *writing* of oral genres always results in a residue of lost context and lost presence that literary culture, as we have seen, imbues with a sense of nostalgia and even regret. We might consider the writing of folklore in this sense to be, then, a method for making oral genres extinct, just as the zeal for trophies might ironically (with an irony having its own sweet pleasures of acquisition) both celebrate and eradicate a species. Consequently, these appropriations invest the oral with a new, and necessarily literary, mythology.

Because language is not a matter of wresting form out of nature, our sense of the differences between orality and writing cannot rest upon such a simple juxtaposition of ephemerality and materiality. This "ephemerality" of speech has nothing to do with the intrinsic qualities of folkloric forms. In fact, we might just as easily suppose that the features of folkloric forms (and such a list is always a matter of reduction)—the "presence" of the speaker, the foregrounded materiality of the signifier in nonsense verses, phonemic "choruses" and burdens, mixed performance modes such as the cante-fable, the realization of the affective relations of speaker and hearer in call and response, and the generalized collaboration of all such oral performances—make them enduring, "written" into the world, so much as "erased from memory," as the literary tradition might sometimes have it. For here materiality, the collected form, invents an ephemerality that legitimates its own sense of temporality and subjectivity. In the eighteenth century, this contradiction in the process of writing the world—which we may see as a certain crisis in the notion of representation—generated its own set of solutions to the problems of the material reproduction of writing.

Why and how does authenticity become an issue? First, it is clear that authenticity is possible as a concept only in a situation that, in fact, *has* an external history. The problem of authenticity arises in situations where there is a self-conscious perception of mediation; a sense of distance between one era and another, one worldview and another; a sense of historical periodization, transformation, and even rupture. The term *authentic* explores this problem from its inception in Greek, Latin, and Old French, in all cases implying the notion of firsthandedness; the Greek meaning, "one who does a thing himself, a principle, master, autocrat," was the meaning carried over and assimilated in the sixteenth century. From the fourteenth- and fifteenth-century emphasis upon the authenticity of the Bible, the sixteenth-century sense of "firsthand" becomes opposed to *copying*, to a sense of authentic documents, and to the seventeenth-century sense of "authentic laws." Swift's *Drapier's Letters* (1724–25), for example, contain a reference to "some short plain authentick Tract [that] might be published, for the Information both of petty and grandjuries."[3]

The artifactualization of the ballad is coterminous with the commodification of literature: the broadside dates to Wynken de Worde and the onset of printing in England. Although the notion of authenticity does not extend to these early broadside productions in their context, a problematic of authenticity does emerge once the historical sensibility of antiquarianism is combined with the materiality of printed ballads. Yet authenticity becomes most foregrounded in its encounter with contradiction—from the sixteenth-century crisis regarding the copies of mechanical reproduction to the eighteenth-century search for a merger of speech and context, for a utopian ballad world characterized by "survivals" and thus by transcendence over past and present.

The external history of the ballad is thus inextricably bound up with the emerging notion of the ballad as artifact and the crisis in authenticity that results from the severing of this artifact from its performance context. In collections ranging from the sixteenth-century Bannatyne manuscript[4] to the Sherburn Castle collection and Samuel Pepys's two thousand ballads, based on an early collection by the antiquarian John Selden, we see early examples of this impulse toward artifactuality.[5] These are largely broadside collections, for the materiality of the broadside places it among other potential antiquities, even though the ballads of the oral tradition were of course for the most part of older vintage. It is not until the eighteenth century that the method of collecting from oral tradition becomes predominant as a response to the crisis of authenticity brought about by imitation and artifactuality. Moreover, the notion of authenticity here is significantly influenced by the history of eighteenth-century ballad collecting itself. Thus we can characterize the features of the "traditional" ballad, but to do so is to recapitulate, as Vladimir Propp did with the folktale, those features that were formulated by means of the collecting process. In other words, there is no "natural" form here, but a set of documents shaped by the expectations that led to their artifactualization in the first place.

When the literary culture reproduces folklore, the result is a seepage of inauthenticity from the stranded folkloric form to the stranded subjectivity of the author. For autograph literature, the authenticity of *volkspoesie* must always be derivative: the possibilities are a matter of the collected artifact or, in a desperate attempt at appropriation, the collected collective, as displayed by the ushering in of those "untutored geniuses" discussed in chapter 3. Yet just as these quite tutored untutored geniuses left a record of their reading and writing, so in the case of Sir Walter Scott's Ettrick shepherd/bard, James Hogg, do we have a record of how the literary community sought an idea of folklore more than the actuality of folkloric materials themselves:

> I must confess that, before people of high rank, he [Scott] did not much encourage my speeches and stories. He did not then hang down his brows, as when he was ill pleased with me, but he raised them up and glowered, and put his upper lip far over the under one, seeming to be always terrified at what was to come out next, and then he generally cut me short, by some droll anecdote, to the same purport of what I was saying. In this he did not give me fair justice, for, in my own broad homely way, I am a very good speaker, and teller of a story too.[6]

James Beattie's "shepherd swain" as minstrel may approach realization in these examples, but as we saw in chapter 3, this approach is blocked by the constant presence of writing itself and writing's idealization of speech. As is the case with the "discoveries" of talent scouts, the "natural" is always denatured by discovery, and history becomes a kind of novelty act. Allan Ramsay accounted for this relation between history and novelty in his preface to *The Ever Green: A Collection of Scots Poems* (1724):

> I hope also the Reader, when he dips into these poems will not be displeased with this Reflection, that he is stepping back into the Times that are past, and that exist no more. Thus the Manners and Customs then in Vogue, as he will find them here described, will have all the air and charm of Novelty: and that seldom fails of exciting Attention and pleasing the Mind.[7]

By the mid-eighteenth century, the tautology of discovery lay in its recovery of a national identity, a tracing back to a point of origin that would be the very landscape of the present. On April 13, 1763, Thomas Percy wrote to his friend David Dalrymple, Lord Hailes, with reference to his (Percy's) "Miscellaneous Poems Relating to the Chinese": "I am much mistaken if we are not on the eve of some great discoveries that will surprise the world."[8] For Percy and others, this great tautological "discovery" would center more and more on the ballad and its contingent subjectivity—a ballad most often providing an etiological narrative of a subject "bound" by history, and a ballad performed by a "minstrel" author completely immersed in a context of (imaginary) feudalism. The ballad's historical exoticism promised, through the theory of minstrel origins, an authentic authorship and a legitimating point of origin for all consequent national literature. But all this depended upon the invention of a historical rupture, a separation that would enable the "discovery" of the ballad and the authentication of that discovery as in fact a recovery.

To trace these developments of the ballad scandals is not necessarily to rely on some true or more authentic account of the history of the ballad as a genre. For it is impossible to separate the genre from this external history, impossible to locate some purer form outside this tradition. Indeed, it is a methodological imperative to avoid such a search, for constantly to seek an intrinsic form is to recapitulate the very tragedies of the scandals themselves. And it is equally difficult to preserve a domain of scholarship outside these valorizations of historical modes; as the ballad scandals make clear, scholarship itself often arises in response to a crisis in authenticity, here representing its own interests in teleology, replicability, and documentation. The scandal of the ballad is in its very revival: the production of a ghost, freed of a history that scholarship will take on as its duty to supply.

It is difficult to talk about the ballad as having a particular set of immutable characteristics. One can speak of ballad meter and then begin to list the many "traditional" exceptions, and one can speak of ballad thematics, but to do so is simply to fix the antithesis of an infinitely possible parody. Yet it is possible to speak of a genre without reducing the concept to a kind of abstracted history of rules, and to do so is to recognize that the concept of the genre is always emergent historically. One can thus outline a historical process whereby what is valued and thereby made permanent within the genre becomes foregrounded, and conclude that the genre emerges as a form, and thereby develops its permutations, through time. In other words, what is "variation" gets determined by the mutual specification of what is "stored." Furthermore, the discourse regarding a genre—including its valuations, its imitations, parodies, revivals, and disparagements—should be considered as the appearance of certain aesthetic problems that, once brought to completion, will also be likely to disappear.[9]

MacEdward Leach's summary of ballad history offers a gloss on these problems: "Ballads as a form, as a distinct genre . . . emerged in England and in most of West Europe in the late Middle Ages and in this form the ballad continued to be composed and to exist in diminishing numbers through the 19th and into the 20th centuries."[10] More specifically, the period of generation for the traditional ballad is generally agreed to extend from the middle of the sixteenth century to the end of the seventeenth; those appearing on broadsides and in broadside style reached their peak in the period 1750 to 1850. Throughout the eighteenth and nineteenth centuries, we see the emergence of imitations, forgeries, and scholarship in a complex interrelation. Imitation arises as a scandal, forgery as a style of genius, and scholarship as a cure.

Putting aside a persistent and appropriately Gothic rationale for the minstrel origins of the ballad, Leach concludes that "the evidence from numerous records as far back as the Middle Ages points rather to the middle class [as the ballad folk]: small farmers, shoemakers, village schoolteachers, nursemaids, tinkers, wives of small tradesmen, innkeepers, drovers."[11] Leach contends that the broadside, too, is a middle-class form and one even more directly tied to middle-class modes of production. The broadsides themselves took their final shape in the offices of printers who employed hack writers to churn them out; often thousands of copies were printed. As a genre that emerges at the point of transition between a feudal and a capitalist/industrial order, the ballad moves from its so-called traditional narrative form to the mixed modes of the broadside—which include such narrative ballads as well as songs, lyrics, dirges, and elegies—and thence to a form characterized by either revival or imitation.

The internal process of ballad making, like the process of forming any genre through time, is a matter of syncretism and mixed modes, of novelization in the sense that conflicting social values and social forms come into play. This mixing is evident formally as varieties of song genres are incorporated into broadside productions, and as narrative distance is replaced by lyricism in the sense that temporality is deemphasized in favor of argument. And this mixing is evident thematically in the changing structural and social relations portrayed by the ballad through time. A. L. Lloyd gives examples of a thematics of cross-class sexual relations and a profusion of lower-class heroines, comparing the feudal lady and the foot page in "Glasgerion" and the bourgeois lady and the sailor in "Jack the Jolly Tar."[12] Although this is not the place for a full thematic analysis of the ballad, it is important to note that the thematic of the genre is breaking into a discursive heterogeneity homologous to the transformations of the form itself within its historical milieu. Lloyd's examples stand in contrast to the traditional ballad's concerns with incest and adultery. If incest, adultery, and domestic murder appear as the taboos of an insulated and even "pure" ballad form, alterity and multiplicity of voice appear as the transgressions of the ballad's later developments.[13]

We see as well in the ballad's external history an eroticization of boundary. The climactic moment of "discovery" when one finds, as one might find a true love or secret self, a "genuine" ballad singer and his or her repertoire; the transference from performer to author and back again; the revival of ghosts through genealogy; and the very concrete metaphor of "the border" in the Anglo-Scots tradition—all serve as examples supplementing such thematic crossings. In his "Essay on the Ancient Minstrels," Percy points out this recurrence of "the border" as place of origin:

> I cannot conclude this account of the ancient English Minstrels, without remarking that they are most of them represented to have been of the North of England. There is scarce an old historical song or Ballad wherein a Minstrel or Harper appears, but he is characterized by way of eminence to have been "of the North Countreye": and indeed the prevalence of the Northern dialect in such compositions, shews that this representation is real. On the other hand the scene of the finest Scottish Ballads is laid in the South of Scotland; which should seem to have been peculiarly the nursery of Scottish Minstrels. In the old song of Maggy Lawder, a Piper is asked, by way of distinction, Come ye frae the Border?—The Martial spirit constantly kept up and exercised near the frontier of the two kingdoms, as it furnished continual subjects for their Songs, so it inspired the inhabitants of the adjacent counties on both sides with the powers of poetry. Besides, as our Southern Metropolis must have been ever the scene of novelty and refinement, the northern countries, as being most distant, would preserve their ancient manners longest, and of course the old poetry, in which those manners are peculiarly described.[14]

For Percy, this task of antiquing the region is tantamount to an erasure of the border as separation and hence the melding of a "national" (i.e., "British") tradition.

Percy deserves attention here not simply because he was the "compiler/author" of the *Reliques of Ancient English Poetry*, but also because his ambivalence about compilation and authorship is a key to the role of the ballad revival in the invention of literary scholarship. Before Percy, ballads had been printed by Ambrose Philips (*A Collection of Old Ballads*, 3 vols., 1723–25)[15] and Allan Ramsay (*The Ever Green*, 1724; *Tea-Table Miscellany*, 1724) and occasionally imitated: Lady Wardlaw's infamous "Hardyknute," David Mallet's "William and Margaret," William Shenstone's "Jemmy Dawson," John Gay's "Molly Mog," Matthew Prior's "The Thief and Cordelier."[16] If the ballads themselves do not always employ the thematics of nationalism,[17] such a thematic often accompanies the gesture of collecting. When the Scottish chancellor, James Ogilvy, Earl of Seafield, signed the Act of Union in 1707, he made his

famous declaration, "Now there's ane end of ane old song."
Throughout the period, the ballad continued to negotiate the border
between two mutually exclusive nationalistic claims (one "Scottish,"
the other "British") even as it posed its erotics of transgression.
Allan Ramsay wrote in his preface to *The Ever Green:*

> When these good old Bards wrote, we had not yet made use of
> imported trimmings upon our Cloath, nor of foreign Embroidery in
> our Writings. Their Poetry is the Product of their own Country, not
> pilfered or spoiled in their Transportation from abroad: their Images
> and nature, and their Lanskips domestick; copied from those Fields
> and Meadows we every Day behold.[18]

Despite the doubts of the meticulous Joseph Ritson, Thomas
Percy did hold in his possession a collection of ballads dating probably to the mid-seventeenth century, and the story of his acquisition
of this collection is legendary. As John W. Hales and Frederick
Furnivall wrote in the foreword to their edition of the folio manuscript, Percy found the manuscript

> lying dirty on the floor under a Bureau in the Parlour of his friend
> Humphrey Pitt of Shiffnal in Shropshire, being used by the maids
> to light the fire. He begged it of Mr. Pitt and kept it unbound and
> torn till he was going to lend it to Dr. Johnson. Then he had it bound
> in half-calf by the binder, who pared off some of the top and bottom
> lines in different parts of the volume.[19]

The mixed attitudes of this "rescue" reflect the eighteenth century's varying sensibility toward ballad texts. Following the somewhat hedged admiration of Sir Philip Sidney ("Apologie for Poetry")
and Joseph Addison (*The Spectator,* no. 70, 1711),[20] the ballad's valuation is a matter of mixed judgments. In Allan Ramsay's introduction to his *Tea-Table Miscellany,* he blithely explains: "My being
well assured how acceptable new words to known tunes would prove,
engaged me to the making verses for above sixty of them . . . about
thirty more were done by some ingenious young gentlemen."[21] In
a note to the folio manuscript, Hales and Furnivall record that before
Percy learned "to reverence the manuscript," as he says,

> he scribbled notes over its margins and put brackets for suggested
> omissions in its texts. After he reverenced it, he tore out of it the
> two leaves containing its best ballad, "King Estmere," which he had

evidently touched up largely by himself. As to the text, he looked on it as a young woman from the country with unkempt locks, whom he had to fit for fashionable society.

They add: "He puffed out the 39 lines of the 'Child of Elle' to 200; he pomatumed the 'Heir of Lin' till it shone again; he stuffed bits of wool into 'Sir Cawline' and 'Sir Aldingar'; he powdered everything."[22] At the end of his career, long after he had made many claims for the authenticity of his versions, Percy still held that "without [such emendations] the collection would not have deserved a moment's attention."[23]

It is clear that throughout Percy's literary endeavors, authenticity was not a value in itself and was certainly not a consideration equal to that of aesthetic value or taste. Percy's first letter to Thomas Warton describes the folio manuscript and his plans for it and asks Warton to send him ballads, "but such as have some higher merit than that of meer antiquity."[24] Even more suggestive is a postscript to Warton in a subsequent letter:

> I cannot prevail on myself to close up the packet without mentioning a wish, that has been long uppermost in my heart, it is (pardon the liberty I take) that you would complete the Squire's Tale of Chaucer.—It is a task worthy of your genius, and to which I know none of our present poets equal, but yourself:—that pleasing cast of antiquity which distinguishes your compositions would be finely adapted to such a subject. Let me add, the undertaking would do no injury to your reputation. Besides; the novelty of such a performance would be a means of recovering to poesy that attention which it seems in great measure to have lost.[25]

Much like Collins in his "Ode on the Popular Superstitions of the Highlands of Scotland," Percy saw the reproduction of past forms as a way of animating a continual and illustrative history of the national literature.

The notion of "touching up," and a consciousness of the ways in which documents transcend their immediate historical circumstances, is evident as well in Percy's practices regarding his own letter writing. Percy would ask his correspondents to return his letters, whereupon he would frequently "correct" them.[26] The point here is that, for Percy, integrity is bestowed by closure and not by a proximity to a state of nature still incomplete as a cultural invention. Percy's rather Menardian suggestion to Warton should be juxtaposed with his requests to Warton (June 18, 1763)[27] and to Lord Hailes (April 17, 1763)[28] that they finish "The Child of Elle." He wrote to Hailes:

> You will also observe that the conclusion even of this copy is wanting. I am tempted to add a few stanzas of my own by way of conclusion and would beg your opinion whether I shall make it end happily in the Old Baron's being reconciled to the match or otherwise.

After Percy himself wrote an ending for the ballad (November 3, 1765), he asked Hailes "to perfect and improve it."[29]

For Percy, what is unfinished here is not simply the individual ballad, but the history of a national literature that men of letters are obliged to complete or fill out in a variety of ways, including invention and imitation. Percy is writing from a sensibility within which the notion of individual genius is not so important as the notion of the integrity and antiquity of a national tradition. His first letter to Warton makes it clear that his interest in the ballad has to do with a desire to show the English origins of the Arthurian cycles. And on the eve of the publication of *Reliques* (June 2, 1764), he writes that his collection is nearly complete: "I wish, sir, you would furnish me with a subject for a general frontispiece: this is a favor I am soliciting from all my friends. It shall be in the Gothic style, no classical Apollo, but an old English Minstrel with his harp."[30] Here is the antiquarian motivation that we find from William Camden's *Britannia* on: the sense of a national culture and the impulse to legitimate that culture through documents and artifacts. And here we see the recurring motif of a role for the author, a role that at this point gets "authored" as the location of the performing subject within an imaginary feudalism—in other words, an inversion of the conditions of authorship in the literary culture of the late eighteenth century. The feudal world is imagined as one where the author's position is a natural one; the organic validity of the minstrel and his discourse arise from his position within a social matrix. However, the eighteenth-century author, caught between the decline of patronage and the rise of commercial publishing, produces a discourse gradually legitimated by a system of property and separation. The emergence of copyright rules will sever the author's body from his or her discourse and legitimate that discourse by the intricate structures of *more* discourse—the law.[31]

Percy's project here echoes Macpherson's, for *Reliques* satisfied, albeit in skewed manner, the eighteenth-century search for an English epic. Macpherson's ambitious plan to create an analogous epic for Scotland was accompanied by a more limited agenda to establish the genealogies of certain clans, such as the Campbells. (Hence we might suppose the passionate defenses of Macpherson's own authenticity by Hugh Campbell.)[32] Percy, the bishop son of a grocer, held a similar interest in giving an account of the Percy family genealogy, and his ballad imitation "The Hermit of Warkworth" (1771) is "a tribute to the ancient line of the Percies."[33]

In looking at the ballad imitations, it is thus obvious that ballad and epic become confused as genres precisely because of the relation between the "minstrel theory" and this imperative of genealogy. Percy's frontispiece of the "old minstrel" is explicated in his prefatory remarks to *Reliques:* "The reader is here presented with select remains of our ancient English Bards and Minstrels, an order of men, who were once greatly respected by our ancestors, and contributed to soften the roughness of a martial and unlettered people by their songs and music."[34] The minstrel origins theory legitimates thereby the professional status of the bard/author. It legitimates the notion of a national literature and its corollary genesis in the naturalized categories of feudalism, poses the security and fixed identity of patronage against the flux and anonymity of the literary marketplace, and allows such a decorous mixture of form and theme that the ballad becomes imitable in a variety of genres—epic, lay, elegy, and tragedy.[35] This emphasis on the martial quality of the ballad is a constant feature of the imitation and no doubt speaks to the ballad revival's hope to uncover a continuous and unified national tradition. (One is reminded here of the complex alliances of the Tories and Country Whigs.) Percy wrote to Thomas Warton on May 28, 1761, that "ballads about King Arthur . . . seem to have been as current among our plain but martial Ancestors, as the Rhapsodies of Homer were among his countrymen."[36] But this picture contrasts sharply with the thematics of the ballad as collected from oral tradition, for, risking generalization, such traditional ballads constantly explore the psychological tensions of the family, the humor of social stratification, and the tragic dilemma of individual desire pitted against the social good.

The character of the minstrel thus becomes as marvelous and opportune an invention as that of the ballads themselves. In his "Essay on the Ancient Minstrels," Percy includes a sixteenth-century description of a "personation" of an "ancient minstrel" who entertained Queen Elizabeth at Kenilworth Castle with "his cap off; his head seemly Tonster-wise," and adds that, along with other "venerable customs of the ancient Lord Percys," the presence of minstrels attached to the House of Northumberland was continued by the "late Duke and Duchess."[37] This dual etiology of the feudal ballad in the cultures of the monastery and the court must have appealed to a bishop with bardic aspirations, just as the schoolboy tonsure and robe of Thomas Chatterton were to abet the invention of his fifteenth-century alter ego, the poet/monk Thomas Rowley.[38]

But the ballad imitator is confronted by the irony of all costuming: the contamination of the natural, the dissolution of the integrity of the underlying category. The labor of simplicity is always belabored. In 1759, in his "Enquiry into . . . Polite Learning," Oliver Goldsmith recommends, "Let us, instead of writing finely, try to write naturally."[39] And John Aikin's "Essays on Ballads and Pastoral Songs" of 1774 gives directions for making modern imitations: "simplicity in thought and style, to the avoidance of both vulgarity and over-refinement."[40] Such suggestions put the author into a certain jeopardy. Thus we find John Pinkerton (alias Robert Heron) in his pseudonymous "Letters of Literature" (1785) noting that "perhaps in fact nothing can be more heroic and generous in literary affairs than a writer's ascribing to antiquity his own production; and thus sacrificing his own fame to give higher satisfaction to the public."[41] Considering the historical milieu of these remarks, we find that Pinkerton's renunciation is equally a piece of self-promotion and a recapitulation of the crux of the ballad imitation—that is, the fact that the nostalgic collapse of the author into history is always ironically underlain by the discursive invention of that history and its corollary, an "inauthentic" subjectivity bolstered only by the referentiality of a proper name that it continually hopes to escape. Neither costume nor pseudonym nor false mustache can enable one to flee the inevitable separations of temporality.

Pinkerton's remarks are more plea than theory for a more pressing reason. In August 1778, an anonymous commentator on Chatterton's *Miscellaneous Prose and Verse* had announced, "He deserves to be branded as the worst of imposters, who obtrudes anything upon the world, under the venerable name of antiquity, which has not an honest title to that character."[42] By 1784 Joseph Ritson was drawing similar claims against Pinkerton, denouncing him in the *Gentleman's Magazine* as a forger "to be ranked with other Scottish imposters like Lauder and Macpherson." Just as *Ossian* had inspired many "folkloric" imitations, so did the exposure of Macpherson contribute to the development of an apparatus of exposure—a scholarship equipped to examine the materiality of documents and their internal structure and thematics in an effort to situate them in their "proper" historical context. We see this consciousness in Johnson's letter to Boswell of February 25, 1775, where he explains that there is no written "Erse" and reprimands Boswell for his ingenuous appreciation of "ancient" Scottish poetry:

> You then are going wild about Ossian. Why do you think any part can be proved? . . . Macpherson is, so far as I know, very quiet. Is that not proof enough? Everything is against him. No visible manuscript; no inscription in the language; no correspondence among friends; no transaction of business, of which a single scrap remains in the ancient families.[43]

What is missing here is evidence, the accumulation of materials authenticated by learning that will place the author's claims within the legal matrix. But Johnson also felt that such works should be dismissed on their lack of aesthetic qualities alone. In a famous quip, he said of *Ossian* that such verse might be written by "many men, many women, and many children."[44] Reciprocally, Percy is said to have been particularly annoyed by Johnson's parody of "The Hermit of Warkworth":

> I put my hat upon my head
> And walked into the Strand
> And there I met another man,
> With his hat in his hand.[45]

Pinkerton had of course completed in his *Scottish Tragic Ballads* a second part to "Hardyknute," the ballad composed by Lady Wardlaw and Ramsay that was to become the most scandalous of all the ballad scandals. Pinkerton claimed that this ballad, which was first published in a folio sheet at Edinburgh in 1719, dated to "the end of the 15th century," a date he was sure was appropriate for "the antique parts of this noble production."[46] Following further publication in Ramsay's *Ever Green* and *Tea-Table Miscellany*, "Hardyknute" was accepted by Percy for the second edition of *Reliques*.[47] In a letter of August 1, 1763, to Lord Hailes, Percy wrote:

> The Ballad of Hardyknute being about to be sent to the press, among the pieces for the second Volume of Mr. Dodsley's Collection of ancient Ballads, I have thrown together a few lines by way of introduction: which, as they are chiefly extracted from a Letter you formerly honored me with, I think it incumbent on me to submit for your corrections.[48]

Percy explained in a headnote: "She [Lady Wardlaw] professed to have discovered it written on shreds of paper; but a suspicion arose that it was her own. Some able judges pronounced it modern, and the lady in a manner acknowledged it to be so by producing the last two stanzas beginning 'There's nae light.' "[49]

Thus for Lord Hailes and Percy, the aesthetic merits of the ballad were not necessarily linked to its antiquity; in fact, Percy's note to the ballad makes clear that Lady Wardlaw is the author and has been proved to be by her addition of "matching stanzas." But by the early nineteenth century, her authorship of this ballad had contaminated the confidence placed in all "traditional" ballads. Robert Chambers declared in *Chambers' Edinburgh Journal* for 1843 that at least twenty-five traditional ballads were composed by her, adding:

> I have arrived at the conclusion that the high-class romantic ballads of Scotland are not ancient compositions—are not older than the early part of the eighteenth century—and are mainly, if not wholly the production of one mind. Whose was this mind is a different question, on which no such confident decision may for the present be arrived at; but I have no hesitation in saying that, from the internal resemblances traced on from Hardyknute through Sir Patrick Spence and Gil Morrice to the others, there seems to me a great likelihood that the whole were the composition of the authoress of that poem— namely Elizabeth (Halkett) Lady Wardlaw of Pitreavie.[50]

This was a border crossing that Chambers found intolerable. Yet it is obvious that the motivation of Lady Wardlaw (1677–1727) and her later compatriot Carolina Oliphant, Baroness Nairne (1766–

1845), was quite different from that fueling other ballad imitators. In Scotland, the production of ballad literature by aristocratic women, often done pseudonymously or anonymously, was part of the political and aesthetic production of the home and not part of a literary circle's attempts to validate a national literary tradition. We find here the Jacobite desire to turn back the clock of history within a domestic scene miming the artisanal culture of feudalism. Norval Clyne writes that Lady Wardlaw

> pretended she had found this poem written on shreds of paper employed for what is called the bottoms of clues. The authoress was described by her relations as "a woman of elegant accomplishments, who wrote other poems, and practiced drawing, and cutting paper with her scissors, and who had much wit and humour, with great sweetness of temper."[51]

Indeed, it might be wise to reconsider all ballad imitators as a variety of fancy paper cutters and embroiderers writing from their vernacular allegiances, rather than as "an order of men" in a "martial" context. We are reminded of Percy's find under the bureau, as well as Thomas Chatterton's mother's interest in the bundles of parchment manuscripts from St. Mary Redcliff: "for use for new thread papers."[52] In a letter from Robert Purdie, regarding her song "The Mitherless Lamme," Baroness Nairne is advised:

> If it meets the author's approbation I should like the word *children* left out as it gives the Idea of something so trifling. The song is really pretty and will be sung by grown up people with much pleasure. Besides this, Mr. Dun says (for I have seen him this Evening) that the first part is too low set for children, as he offers his name as having put the accompaniment this will be in favor of the sale, but this is only if quite agreeable to the Ladies.[53]

For at least two generations, Scottish gentlewomen produced songs in the vernacular: the works of the first wave of songwriters, Lady Wardlaw and Lady Grizel Baillie (1665–1746), were recorded in collections such as Ramsay's *Tea-Table Miscellany*. The works of the second group, Jean Elliot of Minto, Baroness Nairne, Alicia Cockburn, Susanna Blamire (who was in fact from Cumberland, but acquired her taste for Scottish songs on visits to Perthshire), and Lady Anne Barnard, often did enter into the oral tradition. The ballad is thus constantly being rescued not so much from "history," as from a generalized oblivion of the feminine—the maids lighting the fire, Lady Wardlaw playing "clues," the baroness composing "trifling" children's songs, and Mrs. Chatterton's sewing.

Once we look beyond the invention of the minstrel tradition, we find a genre predominantly continued by women in both its "authentic" and imitated forms. A turn-of-the-century guidebook to Edinburgh reads:

> To the Jacobite gentlewomen of Edinburgh we owe many of our best known Scottish songs. Baroness Nairne was of the old Jacobite and Episcopalian family of the Oliphants of Gask, and lived at Dudingston. . . . Mrs. Cockburn, the author of "The Flowers of the Forest," lived at one time in a close on the Castle Hill . . . and Baroness Nairne was the sister of Scott's friend Mrs. Keith of Ravelston.[54]

In his book *The Balladists*, John Geddie similarly cites Lady Anne Barnard's compositions.[55] Furthermore, the majority of the singers of traditional ballads who donated versions to contemporary collectors and anthologists were women. Just as Lady Wardlaw and Baroness Nairne were often the focus of discussions of scandals of the ballad, so were such "natural" balladeers as Mrs. Farquharson and Mrs. Brown of Falkland the focus of ballad restoration in works such as Scott's *Minstrelsy of the Scottish Border*.[56]

Although ultimately no one but Chambers came to take seriously the idea that Lady Wardlaw had written all the traditional ballads of Scotland, his theory illustrates a change that had occurred by the end of the eighteenth century regarding authenticity and orality— a change resulting in a new emphasis upon collecting from oral tradition. Yet such a "science" of collecting from life rather than from documents had its own ambiguities and slippages. Alan Bruford, in his study of Alexander Carmichael's treatment of oral sources, argues that late into the nineteenth century the imperative of writing down the actual words of an "informant" was not yet keenly felt:

> True, Campbell of Islay and his collectors tried to take down and then publish the story-teller's words as accurately as they could, given the difficulties of writing from dictation. But his predecessors, from the Brothers Grimm on, had had no more scruples about "correcting" or "improving" a story to fit it for the printed page than Burns had about writing new verses for a bawdy folk-song or Scott about in-

venting a line or two (at least) to patch up an incompletely remembered ballad.

A writing seeking to erase itself as writing, a writing dreaming of
animation—this becomes the "ethic" of a science of folklore. Yet
the shadow of the mark continues to haunt this writing. Bruford
notes of Carmichael: "The only way in which Carmichael seems an
exception . . . is the thoroughness with which, having taken down a
complete text, he revised every sentence, almost as if he were trying
to evade copyright restrictions."[57]

Perhaps the most serious blow to documentation in the eighteenth
century was struck by the Rowley controversy. The exposure of
Thomas Chatterton's elaborate and imaginary invention of a Bristol
past necessitated the invention of a machinery for exposure, a machinery of scholarship. Just as Percy played a part in the attribution
of "Hardyknute" to Lady Wardlaw, so did he play a part in uncovering Chatterton's hoax; in both cases he expressed admiration for
the literary skills of the "impostors." On September 6, 1773, he
wrote a postscript to a letter to Thomas Barrett-Lennard, Lord Dacre, explaining that the forged Rowley documents (two parchments
that William Barrett had given to Dacre to show to Percy) were
coming to London with Sir Robert Chambers, who was on his way
to India:

> After all tho' I think from the style of the Composition arises as Strong
> Evidence that the Poetry cannot be ancient, as does even from the
> forged spurious Writing, itself—yet still it may be highly deserving
> of Publication, not only on account of the Poetical Merit of the Poems,
> but also to show what human Invention is capable of performing:
> And I am persuaded that if all the undoubted Pieces of Chatterton
> were collected into a Volume, they would prove him not only capable
> of writing these Poems attributed to Rowlie, but considering his early
> youth and the disadvantage of his Education, to have been one of
> the greatest geniuses that ever existed in the World—For my own
> part, I would subscribe to such a publication with as much pleasure
> as if the Pieces could be proved to be Rowlie's own: and would lend
> all the assistance in my power to promote the sale and formation
> ["execution" crossed out, at first writing, in one of Percy's corrections]
> of such a work.[58]

In the slip of "execution" and the remedy of "formation," we see
all the moral ambiguities faced by the teen-age Chatterton as he

experimented with yellow ocher and an antiqued handwriting: the ambivalence of the frame tale in Horace Walpole's works; the mixtures of invention, collection, and supplementarity in the publications of Ramsay and Pinkerton as well as Percy; the promulgation of a genius untutored within the literary tradition itself. In a letter to William Mason on May 25, 1772, Walpole wrote,

> Somebody, I fancy Dr. Percy, has produced a dismal dull ballad, called "The Execution of Sir Charles Bawdin," and given it for one of the Bristol Poems, called Rowley's—but it is a still worse counterfeit, than those that were first sent to me; it grows a hard case on our ancestors, who have every day bastards laid to them, five hundred or a thousand years after they are dead. Indeed Mr. Macpherson, etc., are so fair as to beget the fathers as well as the children.[59]

The aristocracy of the ballad was envisioned as a pure and uncorrupted one—the ballad was to be steeped in history, yet locked within an impenetrable feudalism, hence an arrested history. Thus despite the ballad's actual place in history—its absorption of the ongoingness of temporality through details, innovations, borrowings, fragmentation, and changes in form—and despite the evident appearance of the ballad within contemporary traditional culture, the collectors and anthologists of the ballad continued to look for an uncorrupted and seemingly transcendent form. In expressing his doubts about the Scottish ballads, Chambers had criticized "Sir Patrick Spens" (which he refers to as "Spence") as especially dubious and most likely to be another of Lady Wardlaw's compositions. He lists "cork-heeled shoes, hats, fans, and feather beds, in addition to the inapplicability of the ballad to any known event in Scottish history" as anachronistic details showing the inauthenticity of the ballad.[60] Such a statement betrays a lack of understanding of oral tradition and reveals as well the consequences of a purely textual scholarship of the ballad. As James Hogg wrote to Sir Walter Scott regarding "Lord William":

> I am fully convinced of the antiquity of this song; for, although much of the language seems somewhat modernized, this must be attributed to its currency, being much liked, and very much sung in this neighborhood. I can trace it back several generations, but cannot hear of its ever having been in print.[61]

The ballad arrested, integral, and impervious is the ballad as artifact; thus, ironically, those ballads that most fulfill the eighteenth-century ballad ideal are precisely those ballads so carefully "pomatumed" and "stuffed." These "ballads-in-drag," as we might call them, find their most exaggerated and exemplary forms in such fabrications as Chatterton's "Bristowe Tragedie" and Sir Walter Scott's *Lay of the Last Minstrel,* for these works take on a scenic relation to history in which all roles are carefully articulated. In contrast to the terse narrativity of the traditional ballad, history is arranged here as a location of pageantry and spectacle in which performer, audience, and narrative are mutually enfolded in a decorative "pastness." Here the ballad is a machine for re-creating context, and the only true ballad tragedy is the constant failure or breakdown of that machinery, its impossible relation to authenticity.[62] These two works in fact put the problems of "staging" folklore into high relief for us.

Turning first to "The Bristowe Tragedie," we must consider it in light of Chatterton's biography, particularly as it establishes the relations between the poet Rowley and the patron William Canynge, an imaginary relation between imaginary figures that Chatterton comes fruitlessly to seek in a number of real patron/father figures. And we must consider the work as well in light of Chatterton's entire oeuvre, as just one in a series of "documents" designed to validate an imaginary Bristol history. Yet there are several features of its structure and thematic that are relevant to its status as a ballad scandal. For among the many qualities that distinguish it from the traditional ballad, the most dominant is its relentless spatiality—a spatiality continually tied to the transcendent view of "Kynge Edwarde." Here symmetry replaces repetition: the symmetry of the pageant; the symmetry of the crowd's reciprocal tears in response to the hero's blood; and, most dramatically, the closing alignment of the four symmetrical parts of the body upon the four points of the town. One might contend that the ballad internalizes the problematic of the imitation by continually artifactualizing history. Bawdin's speech of apotheosis claims:

> 'Whatte tho', uphoisted onne a pole,
> 'Mye lymbes shall rotte ynne ayre,
> 'And ne ryche monument of brasse
> 'Charles Bawdin's name shall bear;

'Yett ynne the holie booke above,
'Whyche tyme can't eate awaie,
'There wythe the sarvants of the Lorde,
'Mye name shall lyve for aie.'[63]

The book offers a transcendent, if forever arrested, form of life once
the body is itself a relic, the voice dispersed, and the organic made
textual.

We find an analogous scenario in the structure of Scott's *Lay of
the Last Minstrel*, which, although not properly a ballad imitation,
must be considered as a kind of manifesto, or perhaps a parting
statement, of the ballad revival spurred by Percy and of that revival's
concomitant invention of the minstrel figure. As in "The Bristowe
Tragedie," the aristocracy becomes the proper audience of the narrative: "The Maid's pale shade, who wails her lot"; "The phantom
Knight, his glory fled"; "The Chief, whose antique crownlet long /
Still sparkled in the feudal song"; "All mourn the Minstrel's harp
unstrung, / Their name unknown, their praise unsung."[64] Even more
strikingly, the "lay" is formed by the juxtaposition of the frame
sections situating the minstrel's context within the rather conventional love story of divided houses and within what might be seen
as the dominant narrative—the theft and reclamation of the mystical
book of the wizard Michael Scott. This book, if taken from Scott's
grave,

would not yield to unchristen'd hand
Till he smear'd the cover o'er
With the Borderer's curdled gore;
A moment then the volume spread.[65]

Brought to life by death and its symbolic, ancestral blood, this mystical book must be seen as an analogue to the persistently Gothic
architecture of the lay itself: Melrose Abbey's arrested life

Nor herb, nor floweret, glisten'd there,
But was carved in the cloister-arches as fair
· · ·
Thou would'st have thought some fairy's hand
'Twixt poplars straight the ozier wand,
In many a freakish knot, had twined;

> Then framed a spell, when the work was done,
> And changed the willow-wreaths to stone[66]

becomes the antithetical complement to the minstrel's skill at awakening the dead: "In sooth, 'twas strange, this old man's verse / Could call them from their marble hearse."[67] Nature petrified and inscribed; stone awakened by a song—it is obvious that this must be "the last minstrel"; otherwise, there might be no reason for Sir Walter Scott to exist to invent him, for these reciprocal "awakenings" project an imagined history that Scott, as a national "figure," must relentlessly supply.[68]

These texts, the culmination of the ballad scandals, in turn provoke the question of why the ballad had such an appeal as a genre to be revived, for the ballad as it existed in popular tradition did not fit this scenario of feudalism and arrested, sentimentalized nature. Nevertheless, there were intrinsic features of the ballad tradition that made it an appropriate solution to the problems of authorial subjectivity at the onset of the widespread mechanical production of literature.

First, the location of voice within character in the ballad—a voice inseparable from the ongoingness of dialogue—situates the ballad in antithesis to the spatiality and stasis of the document and the document's devices of framing. Consider, for example, the dialogue/testament form of a ballad such as "Edward," which was recorded in Percy's *Reliques*:

> "Why dois your brand sae drap wi bluid, Edward, Edward,
> Why dois your brand sae drap wi bluid,
> And why sae sad gang yee O?"
> "O I hae killed my hauke sae guid, Mither, mither,
> O I hae killed my hauke sae guid,
> And I had nae mair bot hee O."[69]

In Percy's version, the ballad tells the story of a patricide, and Edward's testament states that his mother will receive "the curse of hell" for her "sic counseils." A ballad such as "Edward" immerses one immediately in a voiced context: the ballad singer in turn takes the form of each of the "characters" in a ventriloquistic fashion. Even when a traditional ballad works by means of third-person narration, the speaker "voices" quotes and makes statements with the authority of an observer in context or witness. The ballad is thereby a form continually marked by immediacy—immediacy of voice, immediacy of action, immediacy of allusion.

Second, the dissolution of the performing self in the performance style (the Anglo-Scots tradition of holding the body rigidly still and letting the ballad speak *through* oneself)[70] promises a total immersion of personality in context that is the antithesis of the literary author's separation from both the local and the living presence of audience. It is not merely that the ballad occurs "out loud," as would be the case with any folkloric form, but as well that we have the appearance of tradition speaking through someone. Now other forms, particularly proverbs, also work this way, and we might also note that the novel's dialogism analogously, in the eighteenth century, if not in later practice, presents a world that seems to come to life beyond the signature of any particular authorial style or voice. But the ballad singer is praised for fidelity, not for originality. The panoply of ventriloquized voices presented in the novel is still attributed to the authority of a central consciousness: the novelist is a kind of puppeteer. For writers such as Scott, the ballad came to represent an idyllic context of representation in which the Scottish tradition would "voice" Scott himself—the inverse of the animation of ghosts that was his true stock-in-trade.

Third, the ballad's erotic of transgression, its exploration of the subject's tragic relation to the social, and its recurrent closure of death transformed by testament, all contributed to its value for eighteenth-century literary culture. What endures, according to the progress of ballad narrative, is the form of the recanting—the testament of the genre itself. "What will you leave?" "What shall I tell?" These common ending refrains of the ballad emphasize that the true hero of the narration is the one who distributes the inheritance and the message. Here, ultimately, was a role for the eighteenth-century author quite different from that offered by patronage, professionalism, and the parodies of ventriloquism. But this role was destined to collapse into self-parody because of its impossible claims of authenticity. We might invert the *Cambridge History*'s contention and assert that "no life of this sort can be produced under the conditions of modern verse." For history itself is always a mixed mode, traversing the "integrity" of the authorial subject in a drama that nonetheless has all the features of a relentless, perhaps even authentic, tragedy.

Notes

The completion of this essay was aided by the kind assistance of the curators of the British Library, and the National Library of Scotland, the Edinburgh University Library, and the Folklore Archives of the School of Scottish Studies at Edinburgh—particularly Alan Bruford, director of the archives, and Joan MacKenzie, the archives secretary.

   1. George Sampson, ed., *The Concise Cambridge History of English Literature*, 3rd ed. (Cambridge: Cambridge University Press, 1970), p. 90.
   2. See also Eric Hobsbawm, in *The Invention of Tradition*, ed. Eric Hobsbawm and Terence Ranger (Cambridge: Cambridge University Press, 1983).
   3. *Oxford English Dictionary*, s.v. "authentic"; Jonathan Swift, *The Drapier's Letters and Other Works, 1724–1725*, ed. Herbert Davis (Oxford: Basil Blackwell, 1941), p. 173.
   4. *Ancient Scottish Poems: Published from the Manuscript of George Bannatyne. MDLXVIII* (Edinburgh: A. Murray and J. Cochran, 1770).
   5. For a discussion of some of these collections, see "The Preface" to Thomas Percy, *Reliques of Ancient English Poetry*, ed. Edward Walford (1794; London: Frederick Warne, 1880), pp. xxvii–xxviii.
   6. James Hogg, *Domestic Manners of Sir Walter Scott*, with a "Memoir of the Ettrick Shepherd" by the Reverend J. E. H. Thomson, D.D. (Stirling: Eneas Mackay, 1909), p. 86.
   7. Allan Ramsay, ed., *The Ever Green: A Collection of Scots Poems. Wrote by the Ingenious before 1600* (1724; reprint, Glasgow: Robert Forrester, 1876), vol. 1, p. ix.
   8. Thomas Percy to David Dalrymple, Lord Hailes, 13 April 1763, Percy–Hailes Correspondence, British Library #32,331 (1762–83), f. 24.
   9. See Mikhail Bakhtin's discussion of the "valorized temporal category" in *The Dialogic Imagination*, ed. Michael Holquist, trans. Michael Holquist and Caryl Emerson (Austin: University of Texas Press, 1981), p. 15, and Theodor Adorno's discussion of Croce's classicism in *Aesthetic Theory*, trans. C. Lenhardt, ed. Gretel Adorno and Rolf Tiedemann (London: Routledge & Kegan Paul, 1970): "Since time immemorial art has sought to redeem and promote the particular. Accomplished works everywhere were those in which specificity was pushed to the limit. Granted, general concepts of aesthetic genres kept cropping up in the form of norms, but they were probably always inspired by didactic considerations reflecting a desire to abstract universal characteristics from important works so as to be able to obtain a general standard for judging others. Of course, these characteristics did not have to be what was most essential in those works. Still, a genre can be said to store up part of the authenticity of individual works" (p. 287).

10. MacEdward Leach, *The Ballad Book* (New York: Barnes, 1955), p. 29. See also Alan Bold, *The Ballad* (London: Methuen, 1979); A. L. Lloyd, *Folk Song in England* (New York: International Publishers, 1967), pp. 11–90, 134–68; and MacEdward Leach and Tristram P. Coffin, eds., *The Critic and the Ballad* (Carbondale: Southern Illinois University Press, 1961).

11. Leach, *Ballad Book*, pp. 8–9.

12. Lloyd, *Folk Song in England*, p. 165.

13. One is reminded of Jane Gallop's discussion of Freud's *Dora: An Analysis of a Case of Hysteria:* "Sexual relations are with someone whose alterity is limited within the confines of a larger circle. Exogamy, marrying outside the larger circle, is equally a violation of the incest taboo. Marriage outside of class or race might represent a contact with a non-assimilable alterity, thus like actual incest bringing unmitigated heterogeneity within the family circle. Freud's nurses and governesses might represent just such otherness, the very otherness that can also be represented by the violence of class conflict" (*The Daughter's Seduction: Feminism and Psychoanalysis* [Ithaca, N.Y.: Cornell University Press, 1982], p. 145). Some further implications of these issues of alterity will be taken up in chapter 6.

14. Thomas Percy, "An Essay on the Ancient Minstrels in England," in *Reliques of Ancient English Poetry*, with memoir and critical dissertation by G. Gilfillan, ed. Charles Cowden Clarke (1794; Edinburgh: William P. Nimmo, 1869), vol. 1, pp. lv–lvi. Percy's preparation of *Reliques* and the social background to his career are fully explicated in a new biography: Bertram Davis, *Thomas Percy: A Scholar-Cleric in the Age of Johnson* (Philadelphia: University of Pennsylvania Press, 1989).

15. The 1727 copy of these volumes in the British Library has Percy's marginal notes.

16. R. S. Forsythe, "Modern Imitations of the Popular Ballad," *Journal of English and Germanic Philology* 13 (1914): 89–90. Forsythe presents a taxonomy of ballad imitations by theme, but he also makes a useful distinction between imitations of ballad form and imitations of specific ballads. This raises interesting questions regarding the poet's apprenticeship by "copying" and, at the same time, prohibitions against plagiarism.

17. Indeed, it can be argued that the popular ballad always espouses a local politics over a politics of the state. Leach points out that ballads are usually concerned with "local battles," rarely with "great battles," and that "fully half the ballads can be classified under the subject category: local happenings of a dramatic character" (*Ballad Book*, p. 15).

18. Ramsay, *Ever Green*, vol. 1, p. vii.

19. Thomas Percy, *Bishop Percy's Folio Ms. Ballads and Romances*, ed. John W. Hales and Frederick Furnivall (London: N. Trubner, 1868), vol. 1, p. xii.

20. Joseph Addison and Richard Steele, *The Spectator*, ed. Donald F. Bond (Oxford: Clarendon Press, 1965), vol. 1, May 21 and 25, 1711. Percy was also the first to attempt a complete textual edition of *The Spectator*.

21. Allan Ramsay, ed., *Tea-Table Miscellany: A Collection of Choice Song Scots and English* (Glasgow: Robert Forrester, 1876), p. viii. The index to the volume is marked as to "new words by different hands; the author's unknown; old songs; old songs with additions."

22. *Bishop Percy's Folio Ms.*, pp. xvi–xvii.

23. Thomas Percy to Robert Jamieson, 4 April 1801, quoted in Sigurd Hustvedt, *Ballad Criticism in Scandinavia and Great Britain During the 18th Century* (New York: American-Scandinavian Foundation, 1916), pp. 198–99.

24. Thomas Percy to Thomas Warton, 28 May 1761, Percy–Warton Correspondence, British Library #42560 (1761–70), f. 69.

25. Percy to Warton, 26 August 1762, f. 97.

26. See Percy correspondence as well as comments by A. Watkin-Jones, "Bishop Percy, Thomas Warton, and Chatterton's Rowley Poems, 1773–1790," *PMLA* 50 (1935): 772. Ironically, this constant "covering" has had the effect of obscuring Percy's personality, as Bertrand Bronson complains in *Facets of the Enlightenment: Studies in English Literature and Its Contexts* (Berkeley: University of California Press, 1968), p. 186.

27. Percy to Warton, 24 November 1763 (referring to letter of 18 June 1763), f. 121.

28. Percy to Lord Hailes, 17 April 1763, f. 25.

29. Percy to Hailes, 3 November 1765, f. 41.

30. Percy to Warton, 2 June 1764, f. 129.

31. See Michel Foucault, "What Is an Author?" in *Textual Strategies*, ed. Josué Harari (Ithaca, N.Y.: Cornell University Press, 1979): "But it was at the moment when a system of ownership and strict copyright rules were established (toward the end of the eighteenth and beginning of the nineteenth century) that the transgressive properties always intrinsic to the act of writing become the forceful imperative of literature" (pp. 124–25). For Foucault, this marks the author's entry into transgression; analogously we note the move from this midcentury imitation of oral forms to Romanticism's freer renditions of them. Mark Rose ("The Author as Proprietor: *Donaldson v. Becket* [*sic*] and the Genealogy of Modern Authorship," *Representations* 23 [Summer 1988]: 51–85) argues that at the same time the law was undergoing "a period of increasing idealization and rationalization in legal thinking" (p. 59). It is not surprising that this idealization of legal discourse accompanied the invention of genius, no more so that the Critical Legal Studies movement's current attack on such formalist theories of law accompanies the poststructuralist critique of the author. For an attack on formalist approaches to the law, see Roberto Mangabeira Unger, *The Critical Legal Studies Movement* (Cambridge, Mass.: Harvard University Press, 1983), p. 2.

32. James Macpherson, *The Poems of Ossian, with an Essay in which they are Authenticated, Illustrated and Explained by Hugh Campbell* (London: Sir Richard Phillips, 1822).

33. Quoted in Hustvedt, *Ballad Criticism in Scandinavia and Great Britain*, p. 188. See the Percy–Wharton Correspondence, which includes a notebook of Percy's on poets and painters (a book linking him further to the interests of Walpole and Chatterton) accompanied by a family tree of the Percies.

34. Percy, *Reliques* (1869), p. 11.

35. In his 1880 edition of *Reliques*, Edward Walford adds the further comment: "Doubtless what was true in one country was true more or less in every other; as the manners of each people become more refined, their ballads come to embrace a wider range of subjects. The songs were no longer confined to the rehearsal of deeds of valour, but began to include all sorts of tales of adventure, wild and marvellous, and occasionally became the vehicle of sentiment and passion" (p. 19).

36. Percy to Warton, 28 May 1761, f. 67.

37. Percy, "An Essay on the Ancient Minstrels in England," p. liii. He notes, however, the already fallen status of the minstrel in this "personation": "Toward the end of the 16th century this class of men had lost all credit and in Elizabeth's 39th year a statute was passed by which 'minstrels, wandering abroad' were included among 'rogues, vagabonds, and sturdy beggars' " (p. liii–lix).

38. E. H. W. Meyerstein, *A Life of Thomas Chatterton* (New York: Scribner, 1930): "The uniform of the Hospital was a blue robe, with an orange-colour lining, a band, and a blue bonnet, with orange-colour stockings; each boy had a number, wore a brass badge bearing the founder's crest, a dolphin; and he 'had the tonsure.' In that last bare fact, I believe, lies the genesis of Thomas Rowley, the monk" (p. 36). Meyerstein also notes that the tonsure is shown in Nicholas Pocock's 1784 sketch of the child Chatterton being conducted by Genius to her altar, with St. Mary Redcliff in the background.

39. Quoted in Hustvedt, *Ballad Criticism in Scandinavia and Great Britain*, p. 206.

40. Ibid., p. 241.

41. Ibid., p. 253.

42. Ibid., p. 230.

43. James Boswell, *The Life of Samuel Johnson* (New York: John W. Lovell, 1884), vol. 3, pp. 86–87.

44. Quoted in Hustvedt, *Ballad Criticism in Scandinavia and Great Britain*, p. 214.

45. Quoted in Sir Walter Scott, "Essay on Imitations of the Ancient Ballad," in *Minstrelsy of the Scottish Border*, rev. and ed. T. F. Henderson (Edinburgh: Oliver and Boyd, 1932), vol. 4, p. 20.

46. Hustvedt, *Ballad Criticism in Scandinavia and Great Britain*, p. 247.

47. One should state at the outset, however, that the unacknowledged authorship by Lady Wardlaw should be attributed as well to another convention—that of the pseudonymous "female author." Baroness Nairne's songs were similarly motivated by Jacobite and nationalist sympathies and were also "unavowed" (Lady Nairne Collection, National Library of Scotland #980–986). "Hardyknute" became a motif in a subsequent antic of inauthenticity. In *Curiosities of Literature* (Paris: Baudry's European Library, 1835), D'Israeli records: "George Steevens must again make his appearance for a memorable trick played on the antiquary Gough. This was the famous tombstone on which was engraved the drinking-horn of Hardyknute to indicate his last fatal carouse, for this royal Dane died drunk! To prevent any doubt, the name in Saxon characters, was sufficiently legible. Steeped in pickle to hasten a precocious antiquity, it was then consigned to the corner of a broker's shop, where the antiquarian eye of Gough often pored on the venerable odds and ends; it perfectly succeeded on the 'Director of the Antiquarian Society.' He purchased the relic for a trifle, and dissertations of due size were preparing for the 'Archaeologia!' " (vol. 3, p. 282). D'Israeli adds in a note that he has "since been informed that this famous invention was originally a flim-flam of a Mr. Thomas White, a noted collector and dealer in antiquities. But it was Steevens who placed it in the broker's shop, where he was certain of catching the antiquary." Steevens plays a role in many scenes of inauthenticity, taking part in the exposure of Ireland's Shakespeare forgeries and Chatterton's Rowley poems, as well as forging a letter of George Peele describing a meeting with Shakespeare. Steevens also invented the fabulous "Upas" tree, allegedly described by a Dutch surgeon at Samarang in 1773. This tree was said to have existed

in Java, with properties so poisonous as to destroy all animal and vegetable life to a distance of fifteen or sixteen miles around it—an appropriate symbol, perhaps, of the forger's "blasted" relation to historical context.

48. Percy to Hailes, 1 August 1763, f. 29.

49. Percy, *Reliques* (1880), p. 188.

50. Quoted in Norval Clyne, *The Romantic Scottish Ballads and the Lady Wardlaw Heresy* (Aberdeen: A. Brown, 1859), p. 36.

51. Ibid., p. 7.

52. Esther Park Ellinger, *Thomas Chatterton, the Marvelous Boy to which is added The Exhibition, a Personal Satire* (Philadelphia: University of Pennsylvania Press, 1930), p. 14.

53. Robert Purdy to Carolina Oliphant, Baroness Nairne, "Monday, April 5," Lady Nairne Collection, #980 (1763–1873). See also David Masson, "Lady Wardlaw and the Baroness Nairne," in *Edinburgh Sketches and Memoirs* (London: A. and C. Black, 1892), pp. 110ff. The National Library of Scotland also has the manuscript copy (not apparently a shred of paper used for "clues") of Lady Wardlaw's "Hardyknute" (Pitfirrane Collection, #6503).

54. *Edinburgh. Painted by John Fulleylove. Described by Rosalind Masson* (London: Adam and Charles Black, 1907), pp. 100, 148.

55. John Geddie, *The Balladists* (Edinburgh: Oliphant, Anderson and Ferrier, 1896).

56. See "Introduction" to Scott, *Minstrelsy of the Scottish Border*, vol. 1, pp. 55–176, especially pp. 170–71.

57. Alan Bruford, " 'Deirdire' and Alexander Carmichael's Treatment of Oral Sources," *Scottish Gaelic Studies* 14, part 1 (1983): 3–4.

58. Thomas Percy to Thomas Barrett-Lennard, Lord Dacre, 6 September 1773, Percy Literary Correspondence, British Library #32,329 (1762–80), f. 75. Percy was given to interesting slips, as when he often wrote "Islandic" rather than "Icelandic" when mentioning Northern epics.

59. Horace Walpole to William Mason, 25 May 1772, *Horace Walpole's Correspondence with William Mason, 1756–1779*, ed. W. S. Lewis, Grover Cronin, and Charles Bennett (New Haven, Conn.: Yale University Press, 1955), p. 36.

60. Robert Chambers, *The Romantic Scottish Ballads: Their Epoch and Authorship* (1849; reprint, Folcroft, Pa.: Folcroft Press, 1969), pp. 6–7.

61. Quoted in Clyne, *Romantic Scottish Ballads and the Lady Wardlaw Heresy*, pp. 28–29. See also Thomson, "Memoir of the Ettrick Shepherd," in Hogg, *Domestic Manners of Sir Walter Scott*, pp. 9–50.

62. Obviously the "pageantlike structure" of these works speaks to the hybrid Gothicism of Ossian and, even earlier, to the neoclassical epics of Blackmore, Glover, Wilkie, Ogden, and Ogilvie discussed in chapter 2. In contrast, Chatterton's sense of humor in his work as a whole, if not in "The Bristowe Tragedie" particularly, should not be underrated. When we consider the wildly parodying possibilities of Chatterton's "Ossianics" as "copies" of "genuine" Macphersons, we realize that Chatterton was shrewdly aware of the Ossianic as *style*. In *Thomas Chatterton's Art: Experiments in Imagined History* (Princeton, N.J.: Princeton University Press, 1978), Donald Taylor quotes from a parody Chatterton sent to John Baker on March 6, 1769, written two days after the composition of "Ethelgar," his first published Ossianic piece: "my friendship is as firm as the white Rocks when the black Waves

roar around it [*sic*], and the waters burst on its hoary top, when the driving wind ploughs the sable Sea, and the rising waves aspire to the clouds teeming with the rattling Hail; so much for Heroics: to speak in plain English, I am and ever will be your unalterable Friend" (p.273). For further discussion of the relation between ballad and epic, see Ralph Cohen, "On the Interrelations of Eighteenth-Century Literary Forms," in *New Approaches to Eighteenth-Century Literature*, ed. Phillip Harth (New York: Columbia University Press, 1974), pp. 33–78; and Walter Morris Hart, *Ballad and Epic: A Study in the Development of the Narrative Art* (1907; reprint, New York: Russell and Russell, 1967).

63. *The Complete Works of Thomas Chatterton*, ed. Donald S. Taylor with Benjamin B. Hoover (Oxford: Clarendon Press, 1971), vol. 1, p. 13.

64. Sir Walter Scott, *The Lay of the Last Minstrel*, new ed., with the author's latest corrections (New York: C. S. Francis, 1854), p. 136.

65. Ibid., p. 87.

66. Ibid., pp. 65–67.

67. Ibid., p. 132.

68. From the costume novel to the feudal accoutrements of Abbotsford, Scott's role in the culture becomes more and more that of an archivist charged with the invention of the archive. It is not surprising to see Scott rushing to the still-warm scene of Waterloo for the express purpose of gathering souvenirs. In a suggestive reading of Scott's relation to legality, Daniel Cottom suggests that Scott saw in the world of face-to-face, spoken communication an older, more intimate, and hence for Scott more honorable bond among men: "Etiquette makes enemies and violence creates intimacy. . . . This understanding does much to explain the general pattern of romance in Scott's novels by which women are won only after the hero has endured situations of physical conflict, whether or not they are directly connected to his love; but the psychology represented in this pattern . . . is by no means peculiar to Scott or to Gothic writers, it is rather the product of the most tenacious of historical traditions, which holds the spoken word and the unmediated appearance of one individual to another to be the authentic forms of human relationship. As it leads to a demand for personal bonds in place of legal codes, this belief is especially aristocratic and is based on an ideal of hierarchical and reciprocal duties transmitted more by blood than by writing" (*The Civilized Imagination: A Study of Ann Radcliffe, Jane Austen, and Sir Walter Scott* [Cambridge: Cambridge University Press, 1985], p. 180). Here, then, the blood that awakens the ancestral book of the wizard can be tied to aristocratic/primal violence, and, more abstractly, we see the connection between revivalist aesthetics and a hereditary, nonparliamentary theory of power.

69. Percy, *Reliques* (1869), vol. 1, p. 59.

70. Roger Abrahams, "Patterns of Structure and Role Relationships in the Child Ballad in the United States," *Journal of American Folklore* 79 (July–September 1966): 448–62. In *Anglo-American Folk Song Style* (Englewood Cliffs, N.J.: Prentice-Hall, 1968), Roger Abrahams and George Foss observe: "The singer [in Anglo-American song traditions] views himself as a voice for whatever piece he is performing: he places himself in the background, letting the piece speak for itself" (p. 12).

The Birth of Authenticity in the Progress of Anxiety: Fragments of an Eighteenth-Century Daydream

Distortion may lend itself . . . to all the paranoiac ambiguities, and every possible use has been made of it, from Arcimboldi to Salvador Dali. I will go so far as to say that this fascination complements what geometral researches into perspective allow to escape from vision.

How is it that nobody has ever thought of connecting this with . . . the effect of an erection? Imagine a tattoo traced on the sexual organ *ad hoc* in the state of repose and assuming its, if I may say so, developed form in another state.

How can we not see here, immanent in the geometral dimension—a partial dimension in the field of the gaze, a dimension that has nothing to do with vision as such—something symbolic of the function of the lack, of the appearance of the phallic ghost?

Lacan, *The Four Fundamental Concepts of Psycho-Analysis*[1]

At the beginning of the eighteenth century, Sébastien le Prestre, the marquis de Vauban, reintroduced a three-dimensional military architecture to the West; his heavily armed tower bastions and enclosed casements were designed as protection against explosive mortar bombs and, especially, "ricochet fire." Ricocheting was a technique that Vauban had also invented, whereby round shot was lobbed at low velocity into open bastions and bounced about, thus dismantling and mangling both guns and defenders.[2] The marquis laid out his designs in his two-volume work of 1718, *Manière de fortifier*. Notably, he follows this text with a systematic and extensive "Traité préliminaire de principes de géométrie," pages of geometry exercises revealing the origins of all fortifications in the material spatiality of the line and, equally important, in the psychological imagery of individuality and its vulnerability to contagion and dispersal:

> L'art de fortifier a été inventé pour conserver le droit des gens. La communauté des biens ne pouvoit subsister qu'avec l'innocence des hommes: les vices s'emparant de leurs coeurs, il fallut faire des partages: l'intérêt fit naître les démelez; le fort devint ambitieux: les foibles se firent des retraites. Voilà l'origine des Villes, & des Fortifications, dont on va traiter.[3]

This is not a retelling of the Edenic expulsion; rather it is a description of the construction and maintenance of an ego (and the ego/city here is obviously already Rome) that always threatens to collapse from internal decay or external suffocation. For, as Vauban notes, there is a relation here between the projection of a set of surfaces—the ego, the fortification, the city—that will form the principle "props" of a scene the eighteenth century seems compelled to repeat. I am thinking here of the Rome of Gibbon[4] and Piranesi, the aesthetic of the ruin, the century's array of impostors and forgers, and the dazzling rise of an "ephemeral" prose fiction as a cultural phenomenon. What has been constructed is also what has been taken down; what is built is what disappears; and the tragic reciprocity of the strong and the weak as a social relation gets played out as a subjective relation between self-consciousness and the repression of identity. In other words, we find that the identity of any material with itself is always undermined by temporality—a problem clearly outlined in the notion of the ruin, as well as in the metaphor of time's "ravaged face," the house that is a tomb, the line inscribing stone and also wearing it away. The aesthetic, obviously, becomes the sphere most aptly signifying this relation between materiality, temporality, and identity, for, to echo the epigraph from Lacan, what is "realized," what is "revived" or made "vivid," comes to represent, tragically and in due course, what is not: the foreground of the material survival immediately dissolved into the irretrievable background of the necessarily immaterial past; the ghost so "true to life" and yet in that very "truth" always in a relation of slippage to life.

I am not so interested here in the specificity of Vauban's forms as I am interested in the formal possibilities of their specificity. Vauban's account of the origins of the fortification has a particularly telling "ricochet fire" with regard to two other speculations on origins—Husserl's remarks on the origins of geometry, and Freud's theses regarding the daydream's relation to "creative writing." Here I want to construct a speculation, using several eighteenth-century "figures," about these concurrences: a daydream capable of surprising itself by means of the revelation of its purely social character, just as one experiences both excitement and diminishment in the realization that one's dream belongs as well to another.

"A tower has no strength," quoth my Uncle Toby, "unless 'tis flanked."   Sterne, *Tristram Shandy*[5]

To flank—"to cut out from the joint; to surround." Flanking is an action common to all theoretical and fictional practices. There exists, as always, a prior text for such a formulation and here it is *Tristram Shandy*, the book whose title is a displacement in the form of a birth, yet whose true subject is an unmentionable wound, healed by a narrativity that only the text itself can supply. We should remember that while Trim's *enabling* wound—the wound that occasions his meeting with the fair Beguine—has come from "a ball," Toby's wound has come from a fortification, the fortress of Namur: "[H]e got it, Madam, by a blow . . . from a stone, broke off by a ball from the parapet of a horn-work at the siege of Namur, which struck full upon my uncle Toby's groin."[6]

If this stone has ricocheted directly from Vauban's designs to Toby's digression, it is because the wound is always received as an inheritance: the walls are up; the city is already polluted. The relation of Toby's wound to the past is the relation of the child to the phallus and to the phallic weight of a language that is pregiven and yet incomplete. Toby, we should remember, is wounded when he is an eyewitness to an exposure, and his frustrated relation to realization—his relation to memory, reverie, digression, and narratability—comes from the impossibility of "filling in" that scene: the impossibility of conquering history and materiality as actual constraints, and the necessity of constructing a compensation in the form of ghosts, fables, idealizations. Ghosts, fables, and idealizations can be recognized thereby as the accouterments of legend, that narrative form most strongly allied to place. The etiology here is the false reasoning of etymology: the narration of a fall from grace into mere language, from mythic time into mere history, from intrinsic relations into merely asserted ones. Hence we see the ways in which the Oedipus narrative is truly a legendary one, attached to a prior scene that could not be "filled in." It is the task of the Oedipal legend to stock this scene with characters and the relations among them, to designate such characters by proper names, and to situate a gaze *within*, rather than without, the scene.

Let us look more closely at a well-known passage explaining the background to Toby's wounds:

> I must remind the reader, in case he has read the history of King William's wars—but if he has not—I then inform him, that one of the most memorable attacks in that siege, was that which was made by the English and Dutch upon the point of the advanced counterscarp, between the gate of St. Nicholas, which inclosed the great sluice or water-stop, where the English were terribly exposed to the shot of the counter-guard and demi-bastion of St. Roch: The issue of which hot dispute, in three words, was this; That the Dutch lodged themselves upon the counter-guard—and that the English made themselves masters of the covered-way before St. Nicholas-gate, not withstanding the gallantry of the French officers, who exposed themselves upon the glacis sword in hand.[7]

Who is speaking this passage? It is the narrator, ostensibly Tristram; it is the author, quoting from Tindal's *History of England,* itself a compilation of other sources, in this instance.[8] This legendary scene—in which Toby as eyewitness cannot appear, since he is in fact the focus of it—dissolves from the shocking actuality of exposure to the regressive and protective materiality of the accompanying objects. The gaze, unable to follow a narrative trajectory here, follows an architectural one instead. Constantly deferred, "glanced" from its location or narrative end, the gaze fixes on the accouterments of the scene, the accompanying forms, cavities, and categories, which function as compensation for that stricken look:

My uncle Toby was generally more eloquent and particular in his account of it; and the many perplexities he was in, arose out of the almost insurmountable difficulties he found in telling his story intelligibly, and giving such clear ideas of the differences and distinctions between the scarp and the counterscarp—the glacis and the covered-way—the half-moon and ravelin—as to make his company fully comprehend where and what he was about. . . . To speak the truth, . . . 'twas a difficult thing, do what he could, to keep the discourse free from obscurity.[9]

It is Toby's task, therefore, to keep his daydream from becoming a nightmare. For the daydream, as it leaps into the future, as it builds itself forward from the articulated materials of the past, is a building of clean lines: deliberate, purposeful, the intentional scene designed to eclipse its antithesis—that obscure and disarranged sight/site of the mother that one inevitably has "fallen into."

I then made some short observations upon *the psychological differences between the conscious and the unconscious*, and upon the fact that everything conscious was subject to a process of wearing away, while what was unconscious was relatively unchangeable; and I illustrated my remarks by pointing to the antiques standing about in my room. They were, in fact, I said, only objects found in a tomb, and their burial had been their preservation: the destruction of Pompeii was only beginning now that it had been dug up.—Was there any guarantee, he next enquired, of what one's attitude would be towards what was discovered? One man, he thought, would no doubt behave in such a way as to get the better of his self-reproach, but another would not.—No, I said, it followed from the nature of the circumstances that in every case the affect would be overcome—for the most part during the progress of the work itself. Every effort was made to preserve Pompeii, whereas people were anxious to be rid of tormenting ideas like his.

Freud, "Notes upon a Case of Obsessional Neurosis"[10]

"The best-known productions of phantasy," writes Freud, "are the so-called 'day dreams' . . . imagined satisfactions of ambitious, megalomaniac, erotic wishes which flourish all the more exuberantly the more reality counsels modesty and restraint."[11] The daydream, with its refusal of the "break," has a constantly realizable content, as opposed to the extinguishable content of the nightmare.[12] It is therefore not surprising that Toby's "works" are built at the expense of the house: the leaden gutters, the melted-down pewter shaving basin, the weights from the sash windows. And in this sense the digression—whose intention is always "the full articulation," the clarification—is built at the expense of the position. The digression, as compensation for the obscurities of narrative form, inevitably leads to an obfuscation that is "mere" form. Here we see that the primary formal quality of the daydream is its indomitable syntax—its insistence upon the production of the sentence without concession, without a nod to either consideration or constraint, as it takes up its elements in its insistent march toward an impossible closure, *foreclosed* in that it would have to end in judgment or abstraction.

Freud's comments on the daydream have a certain surface logic—that the daydream takes its stance oblivious to reality; that the daydream satisfies unconscious wishes or fantasies regarding eroticism (as Freud claims, in women) or ambition (as Freud claims, in men); that the creation of fiction in general repeats this process:

> They are the raw material of poetic production, for the creative writer uses his day-dreams, with certain remodellings, disguises, and omissions, to construct the situation which he introduces into his short stories, his novels, or his plays. The hero of the day-dream is always the subject himself, either directly or by an obvious identification with someone else.[13]

In Freud's notes, quoted earlier, we witness a dramatic scene in which logic is undermined by an underlying desire. Hence the whole passage works as a parable of its opening statement: "the fact that everything conscious was subject to a process of wearing away, while what was unconscious was relatively unchangeable." Freud's interlocutor reminds him that the clarity of objects, of "illustration by pointing," is subject to an already implicated and already ambivalent interpretation, and Freud himself takes up this reminder and brings it back to the interlocutor as an aphorism of his own. Yet in doing so, in making his second "illustration by pointing," Freud's aphorism is itself split into its unhappy reverse: that Pompeii cannot be wholly preserved, that anxiety cannot wholly rid us of torment.

Thus on closer look, Freud's speculations on the daydream themselves begin to vanish in the style of the *Luftschlösser*, his conclusions fading into one another with irrepressible fluidity. The identifying "content" of the daydream is elided by the surplus of its syntax. The willed, imagined quality of the daydream gets lost as Freud imagines such dreams as the source of neurosis: "such unconscious day-dreams are thus the source not only of night-dreams, but also of neurotic symptoms." Hence some daydreams are conscious, others unconscious.[14] Yet Freud also concluded: "we do not experience or hallucinate anything in them but imagine something, we know we are having a phantasy, we do not see but think."[15] Thus the status of the daydream is something Freud is constantly unwilling to articulate, as if the establishment of its epistemology were its banishment.

In an equally obvious contradiction, we find Freud attempting, with a blatant ambivalence, to both establish a reality principle and typify the location of the daydream within some developmental frame: "These day-dreams appear in the prepubertal period, often in the latter part of childhood even. They persist until maturity is reached and are then either given up or maintained to the end of life." What can it mean to say that they are "either" maintained or given up? We sense a ritual of renunciation or else a taking of vows. What kind of commitment does the subject make to his or her own delusions? Implicit to the argument here, yet never articulated and hence emphasized, is the collapse of context. Freud draws up each point into its own negation in a megalomaniacal gesture miming its theme.

If agency and stance are thus refused in Freud's reverie, if the unconscious and the conscious are indistinguishable here, the slippage of his argument is even more strongly marked in his gestures toward a differentiation of the sexes through the daydream. In the two major essays on the daydream, "The Paths to Symptom Formation" (1917) and "The Relation of the Poet to Day-dreaming" (1908), the most absolute judgments are turned into the most astonishing as Freud performs a kind of magic act of collapsed categories, all the while preserving, insisting upon, the shell of "the category" as a notion. In "The Paths to Symptom Formation" he writes:

> In young men the ambitious phantasies are the most prominent, in women, whose ambition is directed to success in love, the erotic ones. But in men, too, erotic needs are often enough present in the background: all their heroic deeds and successes seem only to aim

at courting the admiration and favour of women. They are either, each of them, dropped after a short time and replaced by a fresh one, or they are returned, spun out into long stories and adapted to the changes in the circumstances of the subject's life.[16]

Here again the either/or becomes the either/and, the daydream's power absorbing all content and refusing the finite. What seemed to be ambition, other, was "simply" desire, gratification; and, most dramatically, what seemed to be male was female. Nevertheless, in "The Relation of the Poet to Day-dreaming" Freud writes:

> in young women erotic wishes dominate the phantasies almost exclusively, for their ambition is generally compressed in their erotic longings; in young men egoistic and ambitious wishes assert themselves precisely enough alongside their erotic desires. But we will not lay stress on the distinction between these two trends; we prefer to emphasize the fact that they are often united.[17]

Hence a problem: the relation that association bears, or cannot bear, to identity. Here, as in Locke, association appears as a *train* of thought, a train that necessarily is moving temporally and yet never arrives at a scene, rather being continuous under the sign of its own intelligible movement. The temporal movement of the *Luftschlösser* constantly undermines its own affirmation—"one thing leads to another," as in all forms of desire. But what remains is the issue (concept) and the issue (consequence) of mastery. The behind/ before of the daydream, as it takes up the materials of the past in a singular projection, poses as the answer to the riddle of what one might possess as one's own (i.e., as only one's own). And this riddle, rooted in the ambiguities that precede the formation of subjectivity, suggests that mastery is a metaconceptual and transcendent drive whose formation, or defense against the social, once fallen, is a matter of usurping the social. When Freud writes that the daydreams are "usually concealed with some shame, as though they belonged to the person's most intimate possessions,"[18] we realize that the etiology of shame is not in the directives received from a pregiven Other, but in shame's function for the generation of a defense—an ego to be shamed. Thus the introvert turns away from the social and asserts a self-sufficient subjectivity under the sign of the social's abandonment. This is the mastery that leads not to recognition but to delusion, the mastery that others, in their refusal, as surely affirm, as the daydreamer incorporates all positions, including that of the Other. Therefore, the realization that will dismantle, "burst," this castle in the air is a crucial step between repression and the clarity of censorship. Yet it is this very gesture of a totalized incorporation that reveals the incorporeality of the daydream, its completely created quality; the daydreamer's mastery, like the narcissist's, undermines itself with each move toward the limits of its claims.

We have seen Freud's discourse as a daydream itself, a daydream hoping to collapse the categories of development, the categories of gender—indeed, all categories of "content." In the argument of "Hysterical Phantasies and their Relation to Bisexuality" (1908), Freud collapses the boundaries between illness and health, the aberrant and the normal. As implied earlier, he posits the daydream at the origin of a teleology of neurosis: "The common origin and normal prototype of all these phantastic creations [i.e., "the delusional fantasies of paranoics," the scenarios of "perverts," "the hysterical fantasies of psychoneurosis"] are the so-called daydreams of adolescence."[19] However, in this essay Freud sees the daydream not merely at the origin of neurosis but at the origin of all sexuality: "Now an unconscious phantasy has a very important connection with the sexual life of the person: it is actually identical with the phantasy which served the person in his sexual gratification during the period of masturbation."[20] And later:

> to resolve the symptom one has, on the contrary, to deal with two sexual phantasies, of which one has a masculine and the other a feminine character, so that one of these phantasies has its source in a homosexual trend—it may represent two libidinal phantasies of an opposite sexual character. . . . A quite analogous condition occurs when anyone in his conscious masturbatory phantasies pictures himself both as the man and the woman in an imagined situation.[21]

Once again, Freud's thoughts on the daydream turn to an elision of the possibility of content—and a reification of position and category. But what goes unrecognized in the construction of the latter formulation regarding masturbation is that the dreamer/masturbator imagines himself or herself not as a gendered subject so much as the spectator of the doubling, self-canceling view. Hence the structure being collapsed here is not so much that of gender (although this would in itself be noteworthy and quite useful to Freud's contemporary reputation), as that of the actor/acted-upon speculation of the sadomasochistic relation whereby the sadist, in inhabiting the position of his or her victim, assumes a position that is precisely the masturbatory position: that of taking up all the roles, including the role of the taker, the viewer.

Now we find here, as Freud did, the obvious analogy to the writer, the one who produces a discourse that legitimates his or her position as the source of that discourse. We need no more obvious example than that of Freud himself producing a theory of the daydream that aspires to the absorption of all themes and conflicts in a gesture proclaiming its own theoretical mastery. But, as Freud has warned us, the daydream bursts because it has no relation to reality—that is, no relation to topography/context or temporality/history. So the collapse of the daydream precisely serves the interests of realizing these alterior conditions as something external, something beyond volition. It hypostatizes them as the ghost of a history that we know only through textuality. The lie of writing is not simply the arbitrary generation of an author, but the displacement of another writing, the repetition of a necessarily unimagined "before" to which it thereby gives testament.

Thus we find the final daydream of Freud's work on the day-dream—the maintenance of the boundary between "fiction" and "reality"—as a preservation of the reality of theoretical speculation. This reality, for Freud, was not rooted in biology, but in the un-folding of temporality and the overdetermined relations of historical understanding. The interjection of the social in the mirror phase becomes the obvious prototype of the truth of what Samuel Weber, in *The Legend of Freud,* has called "reality as repetitive alteration."[22] Thus although there is a tangled ambiguity in Freud's remarks on the relation of the daydream to literature, there is yet the privileging of the latter as a repetition, a kind of typical fantasy that serves to mediate the boundary between the subject and the social. "Why do we feel repulsion when hearing phantasies, but attraction when experiencing them in literature: the essential *ars poetica* lies in the technique by which our feeling of repulsion is overcome, and this has certainly to do with these barriers erected between every individual being and all others."[23]

In writing's alteration of the daydream (and hence quite literally in its intrinsic alteration of form), the daydream acquires the badge of sociality. A formal change is a social change. But it is also a denial of the shifting temporality underlying the materiality of writing itself. We therefore see the process at work on this secondary level, a process whereby one daydream (the dream of textual coherence and social intelligibility) replaces another (the dream of individual gratification and pure mastery). When we "surrender" our daydreams to reality, we are in fact trading them in for the grounds of their intelligibility.

> The silence of prehistoric arcana and buried civilizations, the entombment of lost intentions and guarded secrets, and the illegibility of the lapidary inscription disclose the transcendental sense of death as what unites these things to the absolute privilege of intentionality in the very instance of its essential juridical failure.
>
> Derrida, *Edmund Husserl's Origin of Geometry*[24]

I will claim, therefore, that it is appropriate to find an analogy here to another account of the relation of pure objects to understanding—that of Husserl's "Origin of Geometry." It is, of course, impossible to read this text by now without reading the altering repetition that Derrida has attached to it. Husserl is interested in the ontology of certain ideal objects—geometrical space, mathematical time—not in their historical specificity, as in the sense of a descriptive, philological, or historical account of their origin, but as an account of the accomplishment of an "ideal" objectivity through the practice of tradition. For Husserl, this is a matter of the historical development of pure abstraction and hence the freeing of the concept from its spatiotemporal matrix into a realm of truth:

> The Pythagorean theorem, [indeed] all geometry, exists only once, no matter how often or even in what language it may be expressed. It is identically the same in the "original language" of Euclid and in all "translations"; and within each language it is again the same, no matter how many times it has been sensibly uttered, from the original expression and writing-down to the immemorial oral utterance or written and other documentation.[25]

In the utterance of such pure forms, argues Husserl, we see the transformation of the intrapersonal (these forms in their transcendent objectivity being free, from the beginning, from an existence as "something personal") to the interpersonal, in that they are "objectively there" "for everyone" and hence are taken up by tradition. Husserl's initial account of this process is the familiar, and cheery, phenomenological scenario of the community of language taking up the interpersonal both passively and actively (i.e., in the sense of "reawakening"): "In the contact of reciprocal linguistic understanding, the original production and the product of one subject can be actively understood by the others."[26] But once Husserl turns to writing as the vehicle of communication, a certain problem emerges that, within a few pages, turns into a "danger," the danger we have already encountered in *Tristram Shandy* and in Freud's writings on the daydream—that of association:

> The important function of written, documenting linguistic expression is that it makes communications possible without immediate or mediate personal address, it is, so to speak, communication made virtual. . . . Accordingly, then the writing-down effects a transformation of the original mode of being of the meaning-structure [e.g.], within the geometrical sphere of self-evidence, of the geometrical structure which is put into words. It becomes sedimented so to speak.[27]

In other words (and other words have by now become the problem), the writing form itself comes to awaken its own familiar significations and thus take the place of an active experience with the ideality. For Husserl, this becomes a matter of the human, "personal" trajectory: "the originally intuitive life which creates its originally self-evident structures through activities on the basis of sense-experience very quickly and in increasing measure falls victim to the *seduction of language*. Greater and greater segments of this life lapse into a kind of talking and reading."[28]

The remedy that Husserl recommends is not a return to the primacy and privacy of sense impressions, but a commitment to the rigors of univocity:

> In view of the unavoidable sedimentation of mental productions in the form of persisting linguistic acquisitions, which can be taken up again at first merely passively and be taken over by anyone else, such constructions remain a constant danger. The danger is avoided if one not merely convinces oneself *ex post facto* that the particular construction can be reactivated, but assures oneself from the start, after the

self-evident primal establishment, of its capacity to be reactivated
and enduringly maintained. This occurs when one has a view to the
univocity of linguistic expression and to securing . . . the results which
are to be univocally expressed.[29]

In other words, this remedy is the result of a social agreement
regarding univocity, a matter of an effect of predication. As Derrida
reminds us, the impossible balancing act of univocity is always a
matter of an assumed historicity, an assumed subjectivity, an assumed translatability:

> Thus a subjectless transcendental field is one of the "conditions" of
> transcendental subjectivity. . . . But all this can be said only on the
> basis of an intentional analysis which retains from writing nothing but
> writing's pure relation to a consciousness which grounds it as such,
> and not its factuality which, left to itself, is totally without signification
> . . . if there is no purely juridical possibility of it being intelligible for
> a transcendental subject in general, then there is no more in the
> vacuity of its soul than a chaotic literalness or the sensible opacity of
> a defunct designation, a designation deprived of its transcendental
> function.[30]

There is thus always a gap in consciousness that myths of tran-
scendentality can address, but not overcome. We are reminded of
Socrates' argument in the *Charmides* that a relation to self can never
be totalized, since it is impossible for a property of something to
relate to itself. And we are reminded that the Derrida passage just
quoted appears immediately before the epigraph regarding the silence of "prehistoric arcana and buried civilizations." We thus arrive
at an anxiety regarding language's ideal objectivity that is analogous
to Freud's anxiety regarding his daydream of the daydream. This
anxiety attaches itself to the problematic relation between subjectivity and socialization, on the border between the megalomania of
an inarticulate yet replete universe of sensation and a fully articulated, fully categorizable, and consequently empty universe of the
purely symbolic. Yet as Derrida supposes, this is not a matter to be
negotiated dialectically, for to do so would simply bind us in the
impossible relation between those two terms we wish to escape.
Rather, following Husserl's and Derrida's logic, we must examine
the grounds for this split as the impossibility enabling the very
possibility of writing: "a subjectless transcendental field" as "one

of the 'conditions' of transcendental subjectivity." It is association that enables the recognition of originality; it is an anxiety regarding ontology that establishes the grounds for an assumption of grounds. But, as was the case with Freud's transcendent categories, such grounds can never be given a historical location or they will lose their capacity for the absolute.

Hence we return to the notion of the daydream as it is on the brink of effecting its own disaster. To imagine seeing ourselves seeing; to imagine taking all roles including that of the taker; to enter into a dream of one's own death; most radically, to attempt to live the daydream—these are the anxious margins of the daydream's work, its end in both senses of the term.

I have argued some of the historical conditions surrounding the eighteenth-century anxiety regarding authenticity, but obviously such conditions are neither sufficient nor uniform in their effect upon an eighteenth-century writing practice. The novel, for example, emerges as a positive embracing of the problem of a subjectless transcendental field; as Mikhail Bakhtin contends, it ventriloquizes all available social voices both in a mélange and dialogue of language and, at the same time, in the notion of the hero— an animated subjectivity obviously artificial and obviously "real," taking place in time, the new novelistic temporality of everyday life.[31] But such novelistic confidence is belied by other genres of the period, such as the essay/fragment, the artificial document, the imitation epic and ballad. We thus are compelled to rediscover the tenuous margin between authority and imposture—a margin difficult to maintain in persons or documents.

In the study of past events our curiosity is stimulated by the immediate or indirect reference to ourselves; within its own precincts a local history is always popular; and the connection of a family is more dear and intimate than that of a kingdom, a province, or a city.   Gibbon, *Memoirs of My Life*[32]

Let us consider more closely the ways in which imposture appears as a solution to a set of interrelated problems. The impostor is, of course, self-made. In overthrowing the relation to the rule of the proper name, the impostor becomes his or her own mother and father, and it is the task of the imposture to supply the details of

that new, invented genealogy. We find here the reason for the
impostor's frequent attention to minor details of his or her "character," and at the same time a complete disregard for the more
obvious "external" facets of that character's history. As Phyllis
Greenacre noted in her psychological portrait of the impostor,

> although they [impostors] are quick to pick up details and nuances
> in the lives and activities of those whom they simulate and can some-
> times utilize these with great adroitness, they are frequently so utterly
> obtuse to many ordinary considerations of fact that they give the
> impression of mere brazenness or stupidity.[33]

Like his or her counterpart "character" the literary figure, contends Greenacre, the impostor has a "seamed" identity, an un-
evenness in knowledge, detail, and skill. But we must not be too
readily willing to accept this formulation, for in fact any identity is
seamed, and it is the task of the ego to integrate it and to appear
to integrate it. Furthermore, we immediately become aware here of
the social formation of the ego, for an imposture, like any "identity,"
is necessarily a matter of collaboration. The impostor makes his or
her person with the help of an audience willing to participate in it.
Thus the impostor's failed attention regarding the more obvious
details of his or her history can be seen as the summoning of a
superego that is otherwise deficient.

Quite specifically, this failure of the "censor" results from an
aberrant relation to the phallic order. The impostor typically effects
an inappropriate superseding of the father, writes Greenacre.
Thomas Chatterton, we must remember, was a posthumous child.
George Psalmanazar's father left the scene when Psalmanazar was
six. The symptoms of this relation are manifold. We might consider
the "scrambling," or anagrammatic, nature of the impostor's identity: the infamous Titus Oates's anagrammatic Testis O, for instance, and Psalmanazar's reworking of his pseudonym into I.
Palmer; E. H. W. Meyerstein wrote of Chatterton: "Though afire
to have his name blown about, not a single printed contribution by
him stands signed with it . . . [he] seldom seems to have advanced
nearer his surname than the initial C (T. C. were also the initials
of his friend Cory) and when not anagrams, rejoiced in a plurality
of pseudonyms."[34] More abstractly, the anagrammatic quality of the
impostor's attempt to rework the conditions of his or her existence

into a new mixture capable of inventing a new context frequently results in a codified identity whose referent is split between a kind of proper arbitrariness and a genuine, yet unreadable, referentiality.

Furthermore, the impostor feels an impulse toward totality and giganticism. Greenacre writes that when a child has "an uncontested supersedence over its father . . . an illusory enlargement of the phallus becomes indeed a kind of local imposture involving the organ."[35] Here Greenacre confuses the penis and the phallus, but by insisting upon their separation we in fact arrive at the aberrant relation to language and cultural rule involved in all impostures. We also can readily see the relation of imposture to hysteria and to the omnipotence of daydreaming. The skewed relation of the impostor to the phallic order results in an identification with the illusory and scenic "dimensions" of the mother's phallus and hence an inmixing of identities. Typically, the impostor's task, like the daydreamer's, is to take up all positions, male and female, historical and contemporary, child and adult, self and social, moment and context.

But this totalitarian daydream, this gigantic lie unanchored in any material reference, must consequently result in an anxiety whose only relief is accomplished by exposure. Thus what is manufactured and presented by the impostor, that elaborate and oversized identity, is in fact successful only as long as it is not visible, as long as it remains unrepresentable. Yet it can reach closure only at the moment when it is seen and hence dissolved. One of the most affecting details of Greenacre's study is her finding that often, once the imposture collapses, it is followed by the onset of amnesia.[36] Now the remedy of the imposture, as we can see, is not the uncovering of some true identity, but the erasure of its location of production. In Chatterton's case, suicide was the inevitable, and of course authenticating, apparatus of this closure. In Psalmanazar's case, conversion satisfied the social objections to his imposture. But at the same time, the invisibility of any "true identity" for this historical character leaves him remembered as a kind of open wound. Psalmanazar's pious scholarship, his return to the patrimony of Hebrew, his simple coffin—all these details of closure present us with a site of submission and not with the articulation of some "personality."

In the narrative structure of the imposture, we "see" once again what cannot be seen and so must be forgotten—the site of the invisible phallus. For the mother's absent phallus presents the phantasmagoric ontology of difference, while the father's "present" phallus presents the phantasmagoric ontology of symbolization. Therefore, we also find here the imposture's reliance upon façade, display, the scenic, the frontal view—a showmanship wholly designed for the purposes of concealment. The divestiture of the phallus engaged in by the impostor thus becomes the divestiture of all aberrant relations to the linguistic order. The rule of language, the rule of law, no longer is one's proper inheritance. Thus a legend regarding genealogy, the failure and loss of that inheritance, comes to take the place of the proper name. We return therefore to the legendary as the form of language most involved in authenticating position and at the same time most suspect in its relation to history and materiality.

> Let the island of castles lament, for the dead bodies of her
> keeps are carried away in the blackwaters of Severn.
>   Chatterton, "The Hirlas I"[37]

Let us turn more closely to the legend of Chatterton as an example of this narrative of imposture. What was the nature of Chatterton's daydream? Chatterton's fabrications focused upon three exotic sites: the Rowleyan world of medieval Bristol; the historically and geographically sublime world of the Ossianic; and, in his last works, a world of African place names and slaving ports. But to begin with such points of reference is rather absurd, for of course all these "sites" are sites of writing. They are representations of the economy of Chatterton's consciousness and not of some "external" history or nature.

Thomas Chatterton, the poet's father, was a "writing master" at the ancient church of St. Mary Redcliffe at Bristol. We might note from the beginning not only the portentousness of this title, but also the other interests of this absent father: music and magic.[38] Meyerstein's *Life of Thomas Chatterton* records that Lambert, the attorney to whom the younger Chatterton was apprenticed at fourteen, once found Chatterton "sitting up very late at night attempting to raise spirits from the instructions of a book of magic."[39] Chatterton's attempts to raise the dead, to animate the past; his writing full of splashing sprays, storms, and golden showers; his ventriloquistic services as a writer of love poems for other boys—all appear as evidence of a proper name as an inauthentic repetition, an identity both aggrandized and rootless.[40]

Chatterton took as his first task the invention of a Bristol history. Thus his earliest efforts were designed to bring glory to his neighborhood, St. Mary Redcliffe, his father, and his successive patrons, the local antiquaries William Barrett and George Catcott.[41] Chatterton's "literary works," the poems and fragments themselves, are perhaps not so important here as those texts he designed in order to provide them with contexts: the first Rowleyan document, "Extracts from Craishes Herauldry," connects Chatterton, his friends, and Bristol to noble families, coats of arms, and historical events of great importance. But as Donald Taylor notes in his study of Chatterton's "art," Chatterton stops as soon as he starts, giving the fullest account only for the Chatterton family and the family of his girlfriend Polly Rumsey, the only name listed after the "C's"![42] Chatterton's collection of forged documents, manufactured between 1768 and 1769, satisfied the needs of other peoples' imaginations as well as his own. His temporary duping of Horace Walpole with "The Ryse of Peyncteynge, yn Englande, Wroten bir 'T'. Rowleie, 1469, for Mastre Canynge" is a good example of the collaborative nature of imposture, as is the fact that Barrett wanted to accept his "Battle of Hastynges, written by Turgot the Monk, a Saxon, in the tenth century, and translated by Thomes Rowlie, parish preiste of St. John in the city of Bristol in the year 1465," despite the obvious error in the date.[43]

It is quite clear that Chatterton's authenticating Rowley documents—his "Yellow Rolle," with its "Englandes Glorye revyred in Maystre Canynge beinge some Accounte of his Cabynet of Auntiaunt Monumentes"; his "Purple Rolle," containing "Explanyneals of the Annexed Yellowe Rolle"; his "The Rolle of Seyncte Bartlemeweis Priorie"; and his marginalia and footnotes—are all designed to serve as a genealogy for Chatterton's own situation. But it is also important to note the strange temporal inversion by which the daydream is etiology and the invention is a projection of memory. In other words, we find here the drawing of a scene that cannot be made present, the animation of ghosts who never lived. For Chatterton is in the anxious position of inventing his own inheritance. Such a scheme of projection is in fact mimed by the collaborations noted above, as Chatterton constantly anticipates responses, readily assuming the role of his audience as well as the role of his authorial subjects.

Thus Chatterton is not taking part in an Oedipal scene where he would supplant the Father, nor is he simply legitimating him, so much as he is attempting to fill the absence of his authority. But because there is no referent here, we have a great deal of authority with very little authenticity. And rather than establishing a reputation, Chatterton's "career" becomes a series of humiliations and expulsions culminating in his suicide in London at the age of seventeen. That career serves as a paradigm for the predicament of a talented charity-school boy looking for the conditions of a literary fortune at a moment of radical upheaval in literary production. Chatterton was caught between two models of authorship: the medieval and Renaissance model of the patron, and the newly emerging contemporary schema of commercial publishing centered in London. His production is split along the same lines: his reverentially historical works designed for the former audience, his satires and commentaries characterizing his brief stint in London before his death.

If the realities of the marketplace ultimately supplanted the idealized fantasy of patronage and authentic place that Chatterton borrowed (as he borrowed their equally suspect techniques) from Macpherson, Percy, and Walpole, so did the daydreams of Chatterton condense within a fantasy of idealized materiality. In his Rowley works, and as well in his Ossianics and the African eclogues, a thematic of heroism, sacrifice, and vengeance reworks his particular drama with great violence.[44] Consider, for example, the progress of "Elegy, Written at Stanton Drew," which tells of a poet viewing a "druidic" stone circle and imagining a pagan ceremony as his thoughts turn to an erotic memory of his dead "Maria."[45] Suddenly the poem shifts to an actual sacrifice in which a Druid priest's knife is metonymic to Death's "doubly armd dart," which has killed Maria and will now kill the poet.[46] Chatterton's ballad on the sacrifice of Sir Charles Bawdin, his frequent threat to go to Africa as a kind of renunciation,[47] land the opening of his "Narva and Mored," with its account of "Chalma's ground" where "the warriors circle the mysterious tree; / Till spent with exercise they spread around / Upon the op'ning blossoms of the ground"—all link eroticism and sacrifice, the dominant terms of the Oedipal drama.[48] In his 1770 "Exhibition," a satire of Bristol society written a week after his move to London, Chatterton presents a sexual history, including accusations of impotency, of Alexander Catcott, couched in the terms of Catcott's geologic treatise *The Deluge*; a medical attack on exhibitionism as a threat to the prosperity of doctors; and a mockery of Barrett's Bristol history mentioning in line 168 "The Vengeance of the Lifted Quill."[49] Chatterton's final personal satire, "The Revenge," also written in 1770, again takes up this theme.[50] Yet the revenge here is not a matter of the Father's threat of castration exercised upon the erotic desires of the child; rather, it is an attack on the rule of law voiced in the exhibitionary scene of the Father's absence—that is, the absence of the phallus centered in the figure of the Mother—an assertion of divestiture, dissemblance, a robbing of the "family jewels" that Chatterton sees as a just inheritance of recognition.

Thus the revenge sacrifice is not functioning to restore the Father's name. To the contrary, the revenge is always a matter of usurpation, for the restoration of the Father's name is a matter of making a claim for the revenger's thus derived identity; the revenge marks the restoration of the abstract relation and in this way suppresses the importance of the Father's body itself. Hence the anxiety in Chatterton's daydream: in restoring his genealogy, Chatterton is still simply reclaiming the self that has no audience other than that grounded in the conditions of the daydream itself. Just as pain articulates the surface of the ego, Chatterton's insistent and rambling discursions on sacrifice continually inscribe a deprivation he is unable to surmount. The "lifted quill" is in this case an unanchored phallus, and while Chatterton can take on all available voices, he cannot surmount the loss of time and place that is his birthright.

Idealized views of materiality thus come to play an important part in all his work. The mysterious tombs and sculptures of St. Mary Redcliffe that loomed in his childhood imagination are supplemented by a discourse illuminating them. But inevitably such a discourse, the scraps of parchment left to the Chatterton family by the dead father, is nevertheless fabricated by a process of deliberate erasure and reinscription. This is quite literally Chatterton's process. Meyerstein recounts the fate of the manuscripts that were originally found in the muniment room or treasury over the north porch of St. Mary Redcliffe, opened in 1727 and "exposed as of no value, some taken by a woman to clean her furniture," others used by Chatterton, Sr., to cover presentation copies of Bibles, and by Mrs. Chatterton, as noted earlier, for "thread papers, dolls, and patterns." Chatterton, as he grew older, learned to streak these parchments with yellow ocher, then rub them on the ground and crumple them with his hand, suggesting that "that was the way to antiquate it." Chatterton then took a variety of terms from Bailey's *Dictionary*, Speght's *Chaucer*, Percy's *Reliques*, Hughes's *Spenser*, Hearne's *Robert of Gloucester*, and other sources in order to construct his "medieval" works. We must remember that Chatterton's "forgeries" were textual forms of imposture; although they pose as ancient documents, they are in fact new originals and not copies of some preexisting texts. The parchment deeds, erased and reinscribed as authenticating documents (rolls, descriptions, accounts), and the poetic works are betrayed only by the inauthenticity of their materiality and of their conditions of production and reception. They share with Chatterton himself an imaginary and altered relation to time.

Thus it is not surprising to find, in addition to the heroic and genealogical thematic of Chatterton's work, an ongoing critique of materiality—particularly an attack on money. In this sense, Walpole was exactly wrong when he feared that, with encouragement of his artistic forgeries, Chatterton might eventually turn to writing bad checks. For Chatterton hoped that the documents would provide a way to circumvent the need for money, garnering for him a world of prestige and patronage at odds with that commercial life to which he had been apprenticed and by which he had been, since birth, humiliated. From the earliest Rowley documents on, Chatterton critiques the world of commercial gain. Donald Taylor has noted that one of the predominant characteristics of the character Chatterton draws for Canynge is his "imaginative use of riches"[51]: Canynge is drawn as piously munificent and as a benefactor adhering to the maxim "From each according to his ability." Another Rowley poem, "The Worlde," criticizes the miser on his deathbed. "The Gouler's Requiem" discusses the wrong use of riches. And "An Excelente Balade of Charitie" contrasts a limiter's charity with the greed of an abbot. The motif of secret hoarded wealth in Chatterton's work echoes to the parchments of the muniment room. Chatterton drew up a description of the Chatterton arms, decorated with nine pairs of Chatterton escutcheons. Here was his inheritance, family jewels of an invisible nature, waiting to be inscribed by the posthumous son of a writing master. A small detail from Meyerstein's biography comes to mind here: "At Colston's Hospital, where the seven year old Chatterton studied until his apprenticeship, the principal fields of study were writing and business arithmetic."[52] Thus Chatterton once again appears caught between the haughty but dissembling scene of an inheritance and the brute facts of commercial gain. He brilliantly moves between two literary genres, legend and satire, as he constructs these disparate worlds. And just as his life ended in a scene of contemporaneity, so does satire become the dominant genre of his last works. As the opening to "Memoirs of a Sad Dog," his long satire written in the last months of his life, states with a suggestive ambivalence in the possessive pronoun: "The man who sits down to write his own history, has no very agreeable task to execute."[53]

Things, in their fundamental truth, have now escaped from the space of the table; instead of being no more than the constancy that distributes their representations always in accordance with the same forms, they turn in upon themselves, posit their own volumes, and define for themselves an internal space which, to our representation, is on the exterior. It is from the starting-point of the architecture they conceal, of the cohesion that maintains its sovereign and secret sway over each one of their parts, it is from the depths of the force that brought them into being and that remains in them, as though motionless, yet still quivering, that things—in fragments, outlines, pieces, shards—offer themselves, though very partially, to representation. And from their inaccessible store, representation can draw out, piece by piece, only tenuous elements whose unity, whose point of connection, always remains hidden in that beyond.   Foucault, *The Order of Things*[54]

If the literary impostor represents a marginal yet exemplary case of the eighteenth century's problematic relation to authenticity, it is not so much that the impostor is typical as that imposture, in its relief, enables us to reexamine an assumption of a natural authority, a natural authenticity, of context. In order to maintain imposture as a notion, we must also maintain a fiction of seamless subjectivity. But authoring in general, with its requirements of genealogy, citation, and system, reminds us of the complex relation between the body and its objects, between the ego and the social, between artistic and other forms of consciousness. This is not to deny the existence of imposture; it is rather to claim the manufactured and collaborative, as well as contradictory, nature of all identity, and, just as we can see obscenity as an utterance out of place, to see imposture as an identity out of place. That imposture should appear as a minor epidemic in the eighteenth century quite obviously refers to the tremendous uprising in contexts, transformations of the relations between literature and its audience, cultures, and histories, typical of the period.

Vauban had written that geometry was characterized by three dimensions: "longeur, largeur et profondeur." If such impostors as Psalmanazar and Chatterton represent for us the dimensions of the articulation of time and space with regard to the geometry of history, Piranesi's work appears as a profound meditation on these problems, an exploration of the limits and depths of subjectivity and representation whose unity nevertheless remains caught within the contradictions of a "personality" to which we can never have further access.

There are several "truisms" with which we should begin any discussion of Piranesi's work: that he depicted the decaying monuments of Rome; that he contributed greatly to eighteenth-century archaeology and was the first etcher of ruins to use measurements and numbers to clarify his drawings, and yet at the same time willfully distorted the perspective conventions of his day; that he worked in two lights, the full sunlight and bright moonlight of the Roman *campagna;* that he passionately argued a mistaken theory contending the Etruscan origins of Greek art; that he was a commercial success and came to control the entire process of his artistic production; that the *Prisons* are aberrant but entirely original works of genius.

I would like to begin instead, however, with a deceptively simple feature of Piranesi's work—the scenes of Piranesi as a relation between outside and inside. For rather than seeing the *vedute* (views), the *capricci* (caprices), and the *carceri* (prisons) as three periods of Piranesi's oeuvre, I would contend that we must see these works as a kind of anxious turning between axes of time, space, façade, and depth, a turning by which an authorial gaze is finally positioned as the trajectory of that necessary distortion. We might see an analogy here between Freud's daydreaming discourse on the daydreams compared with his more complex account of fantasy in his later essays (particularly "The Economic Problem of Masochism" and "A Child Is Being Beaten"), and the early views of Piranesi compared with the final plates of the *Prisons*. This is not, however, a narrative of an intellectual and artistic evolution toward some totalized consciousness. For just as Freud's daydream crumbles immediately under the terms of its own argument, so were the *carceri* shadowing the views as early as 1743. Rather, we can see that out of the material transformations of work, the shape of the work as well as the shape of its representation become clearer. And as such a clarity is itself denied, it is just as surely affirmed.

Chatterton's villain, Walpole, speaks in his *Anecdotes of Painting in England* (1765) of "the sublime dreams of Piranesi."[55] We know too that in many ways, from Thomas De Quincey's *Confessions* to William Beckford's *Dreams, Waking Thoughts and Incidents* (and, of course, the vast halls of *Vathek*), and perhaps even to Aldous Huxley's *Themes and Variations*, Piranesi can be linked to the ongoing sublime of English Romanticism.[56] Yet it is not the historical cult of the sublime that might interest us here so much as the link Piranesi bears to a Kantian—that is, a psychological—sublime, that point where concept and nature bifurcate, where pleasure and pain, mastery and submission flower in a contradictory relation, a conflict of the faculties in which what we can imagine and what we can accomplish must split. Now this account of the sublime maps quite well (and here we must recognize in "map" not so much a daydream of identity as the inevitable split between a territory and its representation) into that split subject we know from "The Economic Problem of Masochism" and "A Child Is Being Beaten," a subject whose identity cannot simply be an effect of an act of aggrandizement, that hyperbolic subject who is the fantasy of Freud's studies regarding creative writing and daydreams. Instead, it is this subject made aware of the other side of that hyperbole, the subject of erotogenic masochism, phallic divestiture, and abasement. If in Chatterton the satiric foundations of the heroic ultimately overwhelm it, in Piranesi the full contradictions of a subject who moves between conscious and unconscious desires, the subject articulated on the boundary of a limit within the economy of consciousness—inside and outside, pain and sociability—are worked through in their scenic dimensions.

But what can "scenic" mean here other than the unrepresentable, the impossibility of a totalized view? It is Piranesi's task to work out this impossibility through processes that form an exact counterpart to the Kantian sublime: in the *vedute,* this is the view that overflows the margins of the plate and so signifies the infinity that is temporal consciousness. In the *carceri,* this becomes a matter of the blocked view, the view arrested. Furthermore, in a dialectic that finds a rather exact counterpart in what Derrida has called Hegel's "pit" and "pyramid"—the relation between divine and human law, and that between the unconscious and rationality[57]—Piranesi turns as well from subterranean and imaginative regions loosely based upon Roman cisterns, crypto-porticos, foundation works, and cellars to the stairs and monuments of broad daylight that nevertheless, in their exposure, are constantly subject to vanishing. Manfredo Tafuri has asked in his important study of Piranesi's architectural practice:

> Is Piranesi the "archaeologist" interested in caves, underground passages and substructures purely by chance then? Rather, cannot this interest in "what is hidden" in ancient architecture be interpreted as a metaphor for the search for a place in which the exploration of the "roots" of movements meets with the exploration of the depths of the subject?[58]

These speaking ruins have filled my spirit with images that accurate drawings, even such as those of the immortal Palladio, could never have succeeded in conveying, though I always kept them before my eyes.   Piranesi[59]

The views of Piranesi take as their subjects the monuments of ancient Rome, monuments that were already in Piranesi's time fifteen centuries old. Neglected, they often served as quarries for contemporary buildings; today approximately a third of those ruins Piranesi depicted no longer exist.[60] But the movement toward venerating them, in which Piranesi was to play such an important role, was stimulated by the archaeological discoveries of Herculaneum in 1738 and Pompeii in 1740. Piranesi (1720–78), the Venetian who gave Anglo-American tradition its most enduring picture of Rome, derived his sense of the Eternal City from three paternal sources: the legends of Rome from his brother Angelo, a Carthusian monk; expertise in the engineering of ancient aqueducts and other structures from his uncle Matteo; and a sense of stone itself as a permanent material, subject to slow decay, from his stonecutter father. Consider, for example, the first of many views overflowing the boundaries of the plate, the "Arch of Janus" from the "Archi Trionfali." Here and in the consequent arch plates of the series—"Arch of Constantine," "Arch of Titus," "Arch of Septimius Severus"—façade is constantly crumbling away to reveal an interior that then becomes more façade. Inscriptions are shadowed and highlighted until they are indecipherable; weeds and small branches sprout from the tops and sometimes the sides of the arches; ornate carvings and, in the case of the "Arch of Septimius Severus" (figure 5), what seem to be armies of figures approximate the size of those "real figures" and goats positioned in the shadows at the base of the arches.

We become aware of the ways in which a ruin refuses habitation, refuses enclosure; it has been wrested from itself by nature, specifically by weather through the wearing away of materials, the process of transformation in time. These tiny eighteenth-century figures—courtiers, goatherds, bandits, cripples, hunchbacks, and beggars, or perhaps *not*, because of the partial illumination that gives them shape without definition—have as their task the continuation of their particular movement. They course through and light upon the ruins as a matter of fact, adding to our sense that the view within the frame continues in all directions—out the back in the infinite vistas opened through or beside the arches, to the sides in many directions of sky, and across planes guiding our gaze from monumental surface to adjacent structures, trees, horizons. We are aware of the permeability of the entire surface, but we are also aware that the only gaze that the figures do not take part in is our own: their task, unlike ours, is to inhabit the present.

We could contend, as does Marguerite Yourcenar in her classic essay "The Dark Brain of Piranesi," that what we are viewing here is a manifestation of the baroque—its "shifting volumes, its breakdown in equilibrium, its manifestation of the superhuman."[61] Yet we would also need to consider the debt here to the theatrical architecture of Bibiena and Pannini—an architecture whose primary quality is not the establishment of definite volumes, but impermanence and ornament. Here Piranesi's is not an art of essences, but an art of resemblances; his arches open unto a differentiated space; in this they are theatrical but have no conclusive theatrical

Figure 5

Giovanni Battista Piranesi. "Arch of Septimius Severus." From *Views of Rome* (*Vedute*). (Courtesy of The Library Company of Philadelphia)

content. His "speaking ruins" are the representations, as he implies, of the limits of representation—the Kantian split between concept and presentation, and the ephemerality of materials in time. Tafuri concludes that in Piranesi's insistence on contradiction and invention lies a critique of referentiality, a profound insistence on negation particularly with reference to rationality:

> The dissolution of form and the void of the signifieds are thus the presentation of the negative as such. The construction of a *utopia of dissolved form*—what has been naively called Piranesian eclecticism—constitutes the recuperation of this negation, the attempt to utilize it. . . . Architecture is nothing more than a sign and an arbitrary construction, then; but this is intrinsic to Piranesi's discovery of the absolute "solitude" that engulfs the subject who recognizes the relativity of his own actions.[62]

However, in light of the dialectic between inside and outside, the relativity of all projected surfaces, and the fabulous sociality of all languages, architecture appears here as the prime metaphor of an inscription torn between action and appearance—that problem of artifactuality and temporality we have encountered in each of the cases of this study.

Thus the views confront us with a mysterious semiotic of inarticulate but gesticulating figures, indecipherable inscriptions, signs, symbols, arms. We become aware of the irony of these inscriptions of the disappearance of inscription, particularly when we remember Piranesi's frontispieces, always framed as inscriptions within the frame of the ruin, or when we remember his careful delineation of what we are seeing/not seeing in his notes and captions. Illumination is thus tied into an inevitable historical process of obfuscation. For midcentury and later writers, this proximity of death and life, this inevitable decay, was a rather gloomy prospect, but we must remember that for Piranesi it was closely tied to the concept of *rinnova,* the idea of cultural rejuvenation he had taken from Vasari and Vico. If time was the enemy of history, making transparent that historical narrative that once had integrity and entelechy, Piranesi's goal was to lay, by means of perspective and delineation, the groundwork for history's renovation. Thus we can see that Piranesi is always working here toward the accumulation of fragments that give evidence, attempting to piece together a context within which the integrity of Roman law, Roman building, Roman culture can "speak," can take place within a semiotic replete with nuance and comprehensibility.

Piranesi's daydream of *rinnova* is not the same as the wish for a totalized and singular view, nor is it thereby subject to parody as are concepts of restoration. His views, layer upon layer, inscription upon inscription, stone wearing away to stone, volume opening upon volume, are the perfect form for the representation of this non-totalizable representation. As they mime the layering and dispersal of materiality that characterize temporal processes, they are subject to decay and loss of meaning in time, yet they evoke thereby a mode of self-consciousness that escapes idealization and nostalgia. In other words, Piranesi's task is, quite literally, to enact the labor of a birth: the movement between inside and outside as *worked* through time; the falling away of an old order, the simultaneous articulation of that order in such a "falling away"; and the pressure by which content emerges from the decay of forms.

Hence I would argue the importance of a related set of figures in Piranesi's work—the frame, the arch, and the shell, for example. For Piranesi's aim is to show the form of history in its incompleteness, its hollowness. The frame recurs to the temporal aporia of the theater, the arch to that architectural space most obviously subject to traversal and an impermanent habitation, and finally the shell as an allusion to Etruscan ornaments and as symptomatic of the speaking ruin—the abandoned place of habitation.[63]

If the *Views* are flooded by time, the *Prisons* are flooded by space, but precisely not the infinite space suggested by the vistas of the *vedute*, imagined or "real." Instead, the space of the *carceri* suggest the overwhelming volume of the agoraphobic's nightmare, following by means of detail to an equally horrible nightmare of claustrophobia—an infinite and relentless closure. We are thus immediately aware of a first and second "look" in these etchings; the totalized view is, before our eyes, dissolved into a view of impossible, but finite, detail. We therefore return to the idea of blockage, with its obvious connection to the primal scene and the invisible phallus of the mother. The mutilations within the views are quite decipherable, even if those mutilated forms are not. And in the *Prisons* we see the price of their representation. For we are caught within volume, within a space of representation whose concreteness is undermined by the abstraction of its limits. Staircases, catwalks, ladders, bridges, ropes, planes, balconies seem to go somewhere, but dissolve, returning us to ourselves, the point of origin (figure 6). We are reminded of De Quincey's secondhand description of what must have been the spiraling, in fact shell-like, enclosures of plate 7.

> Many years ago, when I was looking over Piranesi's "Antiquities of Rome," Mr. Coleridge, who was standing by, described to me a set of plates by that artist, called his "dreams," and which record the scenery of his own visions during the delirium of a fever. Some of them (I describe only from memory of Mr. Coleridge's account) represented vast Gothic halls; on the floor of which stood all sorts of engines and machinery, wheels, cables, pulleys, levers, catapults, etc. etc. expressive of enormous power put forth, and resistance overcome. Creeping along the sides of the walls, you perceived a staircase; and upon it, groping his way upwards, was Piranesi himself: follow the stairs a little further, and you perceive it come to a sudden and abrupt termination, without any balustrade, and allowing no step onwards to him who had reached the extremity except in the depths below. Whatever is to become of poor Piranesi, you suppose, at least, that his labours must in some way terminate here. But raise your eyes, and behold a second flight of stairs still higher, on which again Piranesi is perceived, but this time standing on the very brink of the abyss. Again elevate your eyes, and a still more aerial flight of stairs is beheld; and again is poor Piranesi busy on his aspiring labours; and so on, until the unfinished stairs and Piranesi both are lost in the upper gloom of the hall. With the same power of endless growth and self-reproduction did my architecture proceed in dreams.[64]

If we do not find in De Quincey's account a credible record of any of the *Prisons* plates, we do find an exact account of that anxiety dream in which flight and chase become merged in purposeless and unceasing motion. This is a dream in which we experience a spatial blockage that is in fact a blockage of time, for we are both before and behind in this merging of flight and chase—we are running away from the past and running toward a future that is pursuing us. Hence the abyss confronting us here, which is the one brought about by the transparency of time and materiality, and the inevitability of that abstraction awaiting us in the form of a death that can have no particular form outside its temporal presentness. The power of "endless growth and reproduction" characterizing the architecture of such

Figure 6
Giovanni Battista Piranesi. "An Immense Interior with Numerous Wooden
Galleries and a Drawbridge in the Center." From *Prisons* (*Carceri*). (Courtesy
of The Library Company of Philadelphia)

dreams is that of the daydream's relentless syntax, its absorption of reference into the terms of its own delusion.

We thereby arrive at the link between the daydream, the necessary inauthenticity of representation, the correspondingly split subjectivity of the dreamer, and, most striking, the temporal quality of anxiety. Although Freud at times literalizes the notion of anxiety by linking it to the castration threat per se, he anticipates the Lacanian position on anxiety—anxiety as fear of the unrepresentable—in his account of the etiology of anxiety in the structure of absence. In *Inhibitions, Symptoms and Anxiety* (1926), he critiques his original assumptions regarding the birth trauma (those assumptions taken up consequently by Rank) and develops an explanation of the origins of anxiety as being located in an increase of tension that arises from experiences of the nongratification of needs. Freud contends that the content of anxiety shifts from the loss of the maternal object that gratifies such needs to fear of castration to dread of the power of the superego; thus fear of castration develops into dread of conscience—that is, into social anxiety. He concludes, in his ever present effort to distinguish the sexes, that hysteria has a greater affinity with femininity, just as compulsion neurosis has with masculinity. Therefore, the loss of love plays a role in hysteria similar to the threat of castration in the phobias and of dread of the superego in compulsion neuroses.[65]

Here we have the "economic" Freud of the later essays and not the simplistic notions of reference as wish-fulfillment in the daydream essay. But we also see a number of issues tied to the temporality of anxiety. Anxiety's most functional qualities—its role in adaptation and in protecting the organism from danger—result from its flexibility of reference, from the fact that the mechanism operates under a translatable and necessarily changing content. Hence, just as sexuality offers the paradigm for all laws of association, anxiety would seem capable of attaching itself to anything. But unlike sexuality, anxiety's content comes to be precisely those absences that are unrepresentable. To be able to represent the threat, we would be able to define it and to thereby rationalize it by means of a consciousness no longer anxious. Thus, as Freud contends, anxiety must be a function of the ego and cannot be a function of the superego, whose very task is the refining and defining of objects and the appropriate—the superego as that aspect of the law with the capability of censorship, restriction, and limitation. Perhaps more important, we thereby realize it is anxiety that serves the interest of truth—that is, authenticity—in the functioning of the ego, taking it in bearable degrees toward a relation with the Real.

We cannot speak of flight as a defensive mechanism in this case (flight from instinctual demand, on the one hand, or the censorship of the law, on the other) once we consider these two positions as already caught within the economy of the ego. Freud contends that "any kind of behavior on the part of the ego will result in an alteration in the instinctual process as well."[66] Thus flight is a tautological process, returning us to the same structure under modified terms. Obviously, in Piranesi's account of blockage we find a graphic depiction of this relation. Yet another analogue exists between the temporal translations of anxiety's referent and the relentless spatialization of the prisons in contrast to the transparent and overflowing emptiness of the views. Thus in the anxiety of the *Prisons*, we witness a mechanism of replacement, amply evidenced by De Quincey's "mistaken" and replacing account. In the amnesia of the *Views*, we witness a mechanism of loss, the flooding overdetermination of temporality.

Certain details of the *carceri* thereby begin to preoccupy our argument—the inscriptions from Livy on the founding of the Mammertine prison, and the ambivalent justice of Tullus on the columnar reliefs of plate 16 (figure 7), or the names of those punished unjustly by Nero in the portrait reliefs above the scene of torture in plate 2.[67] As John Wilton-Ely has noted, such details support Piranesi's argument against the Greeks by reflecting upon the decline in Roman law under a philhellene emperor.[68] But we can also conclude that we are witnessing the unrepresentability of the law—the operation of a structure of law with no content representable outside of time. Thus it is the fluidity, the unrepresentability of this structure—as opposed to the attempts at numeration, notation, measurement, and fixity symptomatic of the views' paraphernalia—that gives rise to anxiety. Piranesi imagines a scene in which an ego is bound by what must be rationalized.

Thus, following Yourcenar, we can note the perfectly ordinary quality of the machines depicted in the *Prisons* series, and at the same time note their inevitable association with torture.

Figure 7
Giovanni Battista Piranesi. "A Wide Hall with Low Timbered Roof in the Foreground from Which Hangs a Lantern." From *Prisons* (*Carceri*). (Courtesy of The Library Company of Philadelphia)

These subterranean chambers resemble the ancient reservoirs of the Emissarium of Lake Albano or the Cistern of Castel Gandolfo; these trophies at the foot of the splendid staircases of Plate VIII suggest those of Marius on the ramp of the Capitol; these posts linked by chains derive from the façades and the courtyards of Roman palaces where they quite banally serve to keep out carriages; these staircases whose balusters flight after flight encage the abyss are, but on a nightmare scale, those which princes and prelates of Baroque Rome mounted and descended every day . . . these bronze rings between the teeth of granite masks are there not so much to tether weak captives as to moor Caesar's galleys.[69]

In this context such machines become the possibilities of tethering, incision, wracking—all the ways of binding a subjectivity implicit in the blocked trajectories of the *carceri*'s lines of perspective. Furthermore, we note how brilliantly Piranesi has employed the two primary senses displayed in anxiety reactions—the distanced and distancing senses of sight and hearing—and collapsed their possibilities of flight into a terrifying proximity to all limits. Thus what seems to be an unlimited volume closes resoundingly into finite space, and the minuscule quality of the figures only emphasizes the echo of their movements exaggerated through that cavernous volume. One is reminded, of course, of the cries of the Athenians imprisoned in the Orecchio di Dionyso at Siracusa—perhaps for Piranesi, as it was for Caravaggio, an image of the binding, and empty, shell of the law. Thus, as Tafuri implies in his study of the *carceri*, we are confronted by the silence of all architecture.[70] But we are also made acutely aware of the moment when the intelligible becomes voiced and when mere noise becomes articulated as a cry. Our attempt to see figuration in the *carceri* must be linked to our attempt to distinguish in general and to hear in particular.

We might also recall Derrida's gloss on Hegel for its insight into the relations between the sensory and intelligible as an architectonic, or inside–outside, relation:

> This phonic relationship between the sensory and intelligible, the real and the ideal, etc., is determined here as an expressive relationship between an inside and an outside. The language of sound, speech, which carries the inside to the outside, does not simply abandon it there, as does writing. Conserving the inside in itself as it is in the act of emitting it to the outside, speech is par excellence that which confers existence, presence (*Dasein*) upon the interior representation, making the concept (signified) exist. But, by the same token, insofar as it interiorizes and temporalizes *Dasein*, the given of sensory–spatial intuition, language lifts existence itself. . . . It makes sensory existence pass into representative or intellectual existence; the existence of the concept. Such a transition is precisely the moment of articulation which transforms sound into voice and noise into language.[71]

Piranesi thus returns us to the etiology of the daydream not in the facts of conscious life that seem to be its transformed content, but in the unrepresentable fears, the prelinguistic noise, of an alterity. It is his genius to have left us with these scenes of the relations between consciousness and the unconscious as a heritage of a necessary distortion. For the view that we come to examine is not the trajectory of overdetermination or blockage emergent in the dialogue between the *Views* and the *Prisons*, but a sense of the heterogeneity, the split quality, of our looking. In the half-worn inscription, in the windswept vegetation breaking through the masonry of the ruin, in the simultaneously ordinary and sinister set of referents for the details of the prison series, and, finally and most importantly, in the layered cumulative quality of these prints destined to decay in the very process of reproduction, we become radically aware of the tragedies and inevitabilities of temporal consciousness. In the style of Piranesi's frontispiece, we might inscribe a moral from these fragments—the moral of the persistence of allegory, psychoanalytic or otherwise, at the expense of temporal particularity, and that of the triumph of temporal particularity over the abstract laws of allegory. But such a moral would necessarily appear upon a stone already subject to the vicissitudes of weather.

Notes

This essay was aided by the kind assistance of the staffs of The Library Company of Philadelphia and the British Library.

1. Jacques Lacan, *The Four Fundamental Concepts of Psycho Analysis*, trans. Alan Sheridan, ed. Jacques-Alain Miller (New York: Norton, 1981), pp. 87–88.

2. Simon Pepper and Nicholas Adams, *Firearms and Fortifications: Military Architecture and Siege Warfare in Sixteenth-Century Siena* (Chicago: University of Chicago Press, 1986), p. 26.

3. Marquis de Vauban, "Traité préliminaire des principes de géométrie," in *Véritable manière de fortifier. Où l'on voit de quelle méthode on se sert aujourd'hui en France, pour la fortification des places* (Amsterdam: Jannsons à Waesberge, 1718), vol. 2, p. 35. For a complementary discussion of Vauban's importance for eighteenth-century French writing, see Joan DeJean's richly informative study of Rousseau, Laclos, and Sade: *Literary Fortifications* (Princeton, N.J.: Princeton University Press, 1984). DeJean focuses on the relations between pedagogy, liberation, and defensiveness in these discourses as they convey "the shadow of the fortress" from classicism to, she argues, Flaubert's modernism. Another work of relevance for this essay is Laurence Goldstein, *Ruins and Empire: The Evolution of a Theme in Augustan and Romantic Literature* (Pittsburgh: University of Pittsburgh Press, 1977). Goldstein traces the theme of the ruin in English literature from Thomas Browne through British and American Romanticism. Goldstein's discussion of the influence of Gibbon on this writing is especially detailed and helpful.

4. Although Edward Gibbon will not be treated as a separate figure here, there

are obvious motifs in his work that are central to my argument. Consider the following details from *Memoirs of My Life*, ed. Georges A. Bonnard (London: Thomas Nelson, 1966): first, his concern regarding Fielding's ancestor Basil Fielding, second earl of Denbigh, who got an unscrupulous antiquary to link the Fieldings to the Hapsburgs, and so was able to (falsely) claim for himself the title of the fifth count of Hapsburg (pp. 232–33n.); and second, Gibbon's explanation of the consequences of his grandfather's involvement in the South Sea Bubble: "on these ruins, with the skill and credit of which Parliament had not been able to despoil him, my grandfather, at a mature age erected the edifice of a new fortune; the labours of sixteen years were amply rewarded, and I have reason to believe that the second Temple was not much inferior to the first" (p. 16).

5. Laurence Sterne, *Tristram Shandy*, ed. Howard Anderson (New York: Norton, 1980), p. 95.

6. Ibid., p. 48. For a description and map of the siege, see J. W. Fortescue, *A History of the British Army* (London: Macmillan, 1879), vol. 1, pp. 341, 378.

7. Sterne, *Tristram Shandy*, p. 58.

8. Theodore Baird, "The Time-Scheme of *Tristram Shandy* and a Source," *PMLA* 51 (1936): 804–6.

9. Sterne, *Tristram Shandy*, p. 58.

10. Sigmund Freud, "Notes upon a Case of Obsessional Neurosis" (1909), in *Standard Edition of the Complete Psychological Works of Sigmund Freud*, trans. and ed. James Strachey (1955; reprint, London: Hogarth Press, 1975), vol. 10, pp. 176–77.

11. Sigmund Freud, "The Paths to Symptom Formation," in *Introductory Lectures in Psychoanalysis*, trans. and ed. James Strachey (New York: Norton, 1977), p. 372.

12. Sigmund Freud, "The Relation of the Poet to Day-dreaming" (1908), in *Character and Culture*, trans. I. F. Grant Duff, ed. Philip Rieff (New York: Collier Books, 1963), pp. 34–43.

13. Freud, "Paths to Symptom Formation," p. 99.

14. Ibid., p. 372.

15. Ibid., p. 98.

16. Ibid.

17. Freud, "Relation of the Poet to Day-dreaming," p. 37.

18. Sigmund Freud, "Hysterical Phantasies and their Relation to Bisexuality," in *Dora: An Analysis of a Case of Hysteria*, trans. Douglas Bryan, ed. Philip Rieff (New York: Collier Books, 1963), p. 146.

19. Ibid., p. 145.

20. Ibid., p. 147.

21. Ibid., p. 151.

22. Samuel Weber, *The Legend of Freud* (Minneapolis: University of Minnesota Press, 1982), p. 142.

23. Freud, "Relation of the Poet to Day-dreaming," pp. 42–43.

24. Jacques Derrida, *Edmund Husserl's Origin of Geometry: An Introduction*, trans. John P. Leavey, ed. David B. Allison (Stony Brook, N.Y.: Nicolas Hays, 1978), p. 88.

25. Edmund Husserl, "The Origin of Geometry," in ibid., p. 160.

26. Ibid., p. 163.

27. Ibid., p. 164.

28. Ibid., p. 165.

29. Ibid.

30. Derrida, *Edmund Husserl's Origin of Geometry*, p. 88.

31. Mikhail Bakhtin, *The Dialogic Imagination*, ed. Michael Holquist, trans. Michael Holquist and Caryl Emerson (Austin: University of Texas Press, 1981), and *Speech Genres and Other Late Essays*, trans. Vern McGee, ed. Caryl Emerson and Michael Holquist (Austin: University of Texas Press, 1986).

32. Gibbon, *Memoirs of My Life*, p. 6.

33. Phyllis Greenacre, "The Impostor," *Psychoanalytic Quarterly* 27 (1958): 363. In *The Family Romance of the Impostor-Poet Thomas Chatterton* (Berkeley: University of California Press, 1987), Louise Kaplan builds on Greenacre's theories of imposture and applies her own insights into psychoanalytic work with adolescents to the materials of Chatterton's biography. Peter Ackroyd's witty novel *Chatterton* (New York: Grove Press, 1987) explores Chatterton's case by weaving the facts of his life through various fictional screens—creating a kind of academic and highly allusive mystery story out of what is known and not known about Chatterton's life and death.

34. Greenacre, "Impostor," p. 370; E. H. W. Meyerstein, *A Life of Thomas Chatterton* (New York: Scribner, 1930), p. 324. It is an interesting irony that the last line of John Bunyan's "advertizement" to *The Holy War* (Philadelphia: Presbyterian Board of Publication, 1803), attesting to the originality and authenticity of *The Pilgrim's Progress*, abruptly "scrambles" his name: "witness my name, if anagrammed to thee, / The letters make, Nu honey in a B" (p. xv). We might note the obvious point here—that the anagram, in its coded nature, shows all texts to be generating from a single point of authority. Unscrambled, they lead us inevitably to the proper name and hence reify it. In contrast, the pseudonym (and here we might think of Kierkegaard) shows the fragility of singular consciousness and a mind subject to choice and change.

35. Greenacre, "Impostor," p. 369.

36. Ibid., p. 364, n. 4.

37. Thomas Chatterton, "The Hirlas I," in *The Complete Works of Thomas Chatterton*, ed. Donald S. Taylor with Benjamin B. Hoover (Oxford: Clarendon Press, 1971), vol. 1, p. 403.

38. Meyerstein, *Life of Thomas Chatterton*, pp. 7, 63.

39. Ibid., p. 68.

40. See as well Chatterton's impersonation of an unknown girl in his "obscene" text "The Letter Paraphrased," in *Complete Works*, vol. 1, pp. 686–87, and vol. 2, pp. 1134–35.

41. The situated nature of his history is obvious as well in a work only marginally connected to Rowley—"Account of the Family of the DeBerghams from the Norman Conquest to this Time"—providing an authenticating genealogy of another patron, Henry Burgum (Donald Taylor, *Thomas Chatterton's Art: Experiments in Imagined History* [Princeton, N.J.: Princeton University Press, 1978], p. 71). One branch of the pedigree showed that in the fifteenth century the Burgum and Chatterton families had intermarried (Esther Parker Ellinger, *Thomas Chatterton, the Marvelous Boy to which is added The Exhibition, a Personal Satire* [Philadelphia: University of Pennsylvania Press, 1930], p. 18)!

42. Taylor, *Thomas Chatterton's Art*, p. 53.

43. J. A. Farrer, *Literary Forgeries* (1907; reprint, Detroit: Gale Research, 1969), p. 156.

44. Wylie Sypher, "Chatterton's African Eclogues and the Deluge," *PMLA* 54 (1939): 246–60. Sypher, following Meyerstein, draws a suggestive parallel to Coleridge's "Kubla Khan." We should be reminded of that poem's dissolving context, its untotalizable landscape, throughout the discussion of the daydream here. For additional discussion of the relations of Chatterton and Macpherson to Romanticism, see Marjorie Levinson, *The Romantic Fragment Poem: A Critique of a Form* (Chapel Hill: University of North Carolina Press, 1986), pp. 34–51.

45. Chatterton, "Elegy, Written at Stanton Drew," in *Complete Works*, vol. 1, pp. 379–80.

46. Taylor suggests that the poem deals thereby with the suppression of erotic feeling (*Thomas Chatterton's Art*, p. 269).

47. Sypher, "Chatterton's African Eclogues," p. 260. Bristol was a slavery port, and Africa was, for Chatterton, linked to slavery. See this theme in his "Heccar and Gaira: An African Eclogue," in *Complete Works*, vol. 1, pp. 432–35.

48. Chatterton, "Narva and Mored: An African Eclogue," in *Complete Works*, vol. 1, p. 544.

49. Chatterton, "Exhibition," in *Complete Works*, vol. 1, pp. 546–59. See also Ellinger, *Thomas Chatterton*.

50. Chatterton, "The Revenge," in *Complete Works*, vol. 1, pp. 606–31.

51. Taylor, *Thomas Chatterton's Art*, pp. 149–50.

52. Meyerstein, *Life of Thomas Chatterton*, p. 27. Thomas Eakins was the son of a writing master, too, and of course took quite an opposite approach to authenticity.

53. Chatterton, "Memoirs of a Sad Dog," in *Complete Works*, vol. 1, p. 651.

54. Michel Foucault, *The Order of Things: An Archaeology of the Human Sciences* (New York: Pantheon Books, 1970), p. 239.

55. Horace Walpole, *Anecdotes of Painting in England* (1765; reprint, New York: Arno Press, 1969), vol. 1, p. xvi. For Walpole's further remarks on Piranesi's engravings, see also vol. 4, pp. 217–18.

56. William Beckford, *Dreams, Waking Thoughts and Incidents*, ed. Robert J. Gemmett (Rutherford, N.J.: Fairleigh Dickinson University Press, 1971): "various are the prospects I surveyed from this imaginary exaltation, and innumerable the chimeras which trotted in my brain. . . . I shot swiftly from rock to rock, and built castles, in the style of Piranesi, upon most of their pinnacles" (p. 83); and: "snatching my pencil, I drew chasms and subterraneous hollows, the domain of fear and torture, with chains, rocks, wheels, and dreadful engines, in the style of Piranesi" (p. 124). Here the tourist cannot "see" nature without the titles of Piranesi's etchings. Aldous Huxley ("Variations on *The Prisons*," in *Themes and Variations* [London: Chatto and Windus, 1954], pp. 192–208), reflects upon the ways in which the prisons are "purely abstract art" (p. 205), "combining pure geometry with enough subject-matter, enough literature, to express more forcibly than a mere pattern can do, the obscure and terrible states of spiritual confusion and *acedia*" (p. 206).

57. G. W. F. Hegel, *Phenomenology of Spirit*, trans. A. V. Miller (Oxford: Clarendon Press, 1977), p. 286; Jacques Derrida, "The Pit and the Pyramid: Introduction to Hegel's Semiology," in *Margins of Philosophy*, trans. Alan Bass (Chicago: University of Chicago Press, 1982), p. 77, n. 7. This argument receives full exposition in Derrida's *Glas* (Paris: Editions Galilée, 1974).

58. Manfredo Tafuri, *The Sphere and the Labyrinth: Avant-Gardes and Architecture from Piranesi to the 1970s*, trans. Pelligrino d'Acierno and Robert Connolly (Cambridge, Mass.: MIT Press, 1987), p. 38.

59. Quoted in John Wilton-Ely, *The Mind and Art of Giovanni Battista Piranesi* (London: Thames and Hudson, 1978), p. 12. The translation is from *Piranesi: Drawings and Etchings at the Avery Architectural Library, Columbia University* (catalogue of a circulating exhibition, October 1975–December 1978) (New York: Arthur M. Sackler Foundation, 1975).

60. Marguerite Yourcenar, *The Dark Brain of Piranesi and Other Essays*, trans. Richard Howard (New York: Farrar, Straus & Giroux, 1984), p. 99. My discussion of Piranesi is much indebted to this work and Tafuri's, as well as to Wilton-Ely, *Mind and Art of Piranesi; Piranesi: Etchings and Drawings*, introduction by Roseline Bacon (Boston: New York Graphic Society, 1975); *The Prisons (Le Carceri) by Giovanni Battista Piranesi: The Complete First and Second States*, introduction by Philip Hofer (New York: Dover, 1973); *Piranesi: The Imaginary Views*, ed. Miranda Harvey (New York: Crown, 1979); Arthur M. Hind, *Giovanni Battista Piranesi: A Critical Study* (1922; reprint, London: Holland Press, 1978); *Le carceri: Giovan Battista Piranesi*, ed. Mario Praz (Milan: Biblioteca Universale Rizzoli, 1975); and William L. MacDonald, *Piranesi's "Carceri": Sources of Invention*, Katherine Asher Engel Lectures of 1978 (Northampton, Mass.: Smith College, 1979). MacDonald illustrates in some detail Piranesi's use of the "stage designer's arrangement of major forms in a *scena per angolo*. In this, the Renaissance principle of a single, centered perspective frame is abandoned in favor of a system of powerful diagonals receding, like tightly stretched tent ropes, right and left in overlapping sequences—a method of construction expounded in detail in Ferdinando Bibiena's architectural treatise of 1711 . . . as the whole is to be seen obliquely, and in perspective, the artist's grid is made up of a series of lozenges. . . . This particular method of presenting forms in perspective on flat surfaces is part of a system of projection called Baroque mechanics, and Piranesi mastered it very early on. By adding a low spectator's viewpoint to this technique of drawing, the subject is made to loom above the view, and Piranesi regularly did this in order to emphasize the scale and grandeur of his buildings. The effect can be rather like that of seeing the bow of an ocean liner from a rowboat. We rarely are allowed to look down" (pp. 14–15).

61. Yourcenar, *Dark Brain of Piranesi*, p. 97.

62. Tafuri, *Sphere and the Labyrinth*, p. 54.

63. In *Mind and Art of Piranesi*, Wilton-Ely suggests that "the modern designer should learn from antiquities to borrow from nature" (p. 80). Wilton-Ely shows Etruscan vase forms drawing inspiration from several natural patterns, particularly shells.

64. Thomas De Quincey, "Confessions of an English Opium Eater, etc.," in *A Selection of the Best Works*, ed. W. H. Bennett (London: David Stott, 1890), vol. 1, pp. 167–69. This is perhaps the most opportune moment to mention that Freud's description of hysterical narrative from *Dora: An Analysis of a Case of Hysteria*, "an unnavigable river whose stream is at one moment choked by masses of rock and at another divided and lost among shallows and sandbanks" (p. 30), may apply quite closely to the geologic thematic of much of Chatterton's writing and, perhaps more

important, quite exactly to the structural strategy of De Quincey's remarkable digressions. For a more general discussion of the topography of streams and blockage in Freud's work, see Henry Sussman, *The Hegelian Aftermath: Readings in Hegel, Kierkegaard, Freud, Proust, and James* (Baltimore: Johns Hopkins University Press, 1982), pp. 168–75; and Neil Hertz, "The Notion of Blockage in the Literature of the Sublime," in *Psychoanalysis and the Question of the Text: Selected Papers from the English Institute, 1976–1977*, ed. Geoffrey Hartman (Baltimore: Johns Hopkins University Press, 1978), pp. 62–85.

65. Sigmund Freud, *Inhibitions, Symptoms and Anxiety* (1926), trans. Alix Strachey, ed. James Strachey (New York: Norton, 1959), pp. 58–69.

66. Ibid., p. 72. The issue of temporality in relation to the formation of the ego in Freud is suggestively presaged in Kierkegaard's discussion of anxiety and subjectivity in "Journals and Papers": "To use a new expression for what has been said, anxiety is really the *discrimen* (ambiguity) of subjectivity. It is therefore very clear that 'future' and 'possibility' correspond to this; but if one speaks of being anxious about the past, this seems to invalidate my use of language, for the ambiguity of subjectivity has nothing that is past. If I were now to suggest that subjectivity is not completed all at once, and that insofar as one might speak of a reappearance of this ambiguity, then this would not be favorable to my position, assuming that it actually is justifiable to speak of anxiety about the past. But if we ask more particularly in what sense it is possible to speak of anxiety about the past, everything becomes clear" (Søren Kierkegaard, *The Concept of Anxiety: A Simple Psychologically Orienting Deliberation on the Dogmatic Issue of Hereditary Sin*, ed. and trans. by Reidar Thomte, with Albert Anderson [Princeton, N.J.: Princeton University Press, 1980], p. 197).

67. Yourcenar notes that the Mammertine was a completely different kind of prison, though, resembling a grave more than the terrifyingly infinite spaces of Piranesi's *carceri*, which are often presented as both underground and freshly exposed, hence the psychological allusion to a birth in one sense and an awakened corpse in another (*Dark Brain of Piranesi*, p. 109).

68. Wilton-Ely, *Mind and Art of Piranesi*, p. 89.

69. Yourcenar, *Dark Brain of Piranesi*, p. 114.

70. Tafuri, *Sphere and the Labyrinth*, p. 49.

71. Derrida, "Pit and the Pyramid," p. 90.

6

Exogamous Relations: Travel Writing, the Incest Prohibition, and Hawthorne's *Transformation*

Incest

One must travel to find a mate. That is, one must not look too closely, and one must not look too far afield. This aphorism links two projects—travel writing and the prohibition of incest—that have to do with the articulation and maintenance of cultural boundaries in time and space. If we look to the notion of such a "link," we find a rule of metaphor: that a point of comparison must be artic- ulated within an acceptable field, yet must be novel enough to be "striking," to make a sign of difference. Such a rule of metaphor is thereby also a rule of writing, or marking, that must be recognizable to others and meaningful to one's kind.

Let us begin by considering some of the ways in which the pro- hibition of incest operates, not so much in culture as in cultural thought, on the bounds—not quite out of bounds—of this rule of metaphor. First, as Claude Lévi-Strauss has explained, the incest prohibition is the cultural rule appearing at the limit of cultural rule— that is, the one most resembling the oxymoronic possibility of a rule of nature:

> Suppose that everything universal in man relates to the natural order, and is characterized by spontaneity, and that everything subject to a

norm is cultural and is both relative and particular. We are then confronted with a fact, or rather, a group of facts, which, in the light of previous definitions, are not far removed from a scandal: we refer to that complex group of beliefs, customs, conditions and institutions described succinctly as the prohibition of incest, which presents, without the slightest ambiguity, and inseparably combines, the two characteristics in which we recognize the conflicting features of two mutually exclusive orders. It constitutes a rule, but a rule which, alone among all the social rules, possesses at the same time a universal character.[1]

Thus the incest prohibition appears as the vehicle of an impossible translatability between nature and culture, a vehicle motivated by a kind of deferred tenor—a position that must always appear as an unarticulatable given of a cultural order irremediably with us. Dramatically, of course, we immediately realize that such a cultural order must then constantly be reinscribed by its own gesture of self-consciousness as something natural and universal.

Furthermore, the incest prohibition extends in all directions of time and space. As Lévi-Strauss contends, all exceptions (Egypt, Peru, Hawaii, Azande, Madagascar, Burma, etc.) are "relative": for "from another's perspective; [the incest prohibition] might be temporary or ritual marriage allowed."[2] The prohibition has its "real" and "metaphorical" forms in that one can be prohibited from marrying a parent, for example, and prohibited from marrying someone old enough to be one's parent, or, inversely, one is prohibited from violating minors.[3] The prohibition is simultaneously endogamous (defining those within the marriageable pool) and exogamous (defining those without it). The prohibition extends spatially to the boundaries of social groups and temporally through the organization of generations. It can be articulated positively as the scope of claims of entitlement and eligibility, and articulated negatively as the renunciation of a privilege, as E. B. Tylor expressed in a well-known conclusion: "marry out or be killed out."[4]

There are many ways in which this natural rule of the cultural, appearing as it does as the cultural rule of the natural, is made suspect, but none of them serves to eliminate it. For example, the current explosion of debate surrounding the increased reportage of the violation of minors and parent–child incest in the industrialized West takes as its point of attack the formulation of Freud, who contended that violation of the rule was imaginary rather than real in most cases.[5] The debate does not attack the formulation of the incest prohibition itself. The rule is not subject to attack precisely because there are no grounds of intelligibility for reproduction outside its reign. In other words, the prohibition of incest and consequently the articulation of kinship are both descriptive and classificatory; hence what contradicts them still falls within their rule, while what falls outside their rule is promiscuity, anarchy, wildness, and nonmeaning.

Exogamous relations therefore pose a contradictory set of cultural solutions. On the one hand, they define one's membership, and by completing one's needs for otherness pose an imaginary wholeness, a completed gaze or circuit. But on the other hand, as in Tylor's "be killed out," they define one's subjection, the renunciation of "spontaneous" desires, the "castration" one experiences under the rule of all cultural law, and the reinscription of all novelty into the domain of tradition. Obviously, I am borrowing here a formulation from Lacan: the necessarily separating function of the visual, and the alignment and articulation of subjectivity under the rule of language. Specifically, I want to borrow this theory of the visual and the spoken in order to examine the rhetoric of a particular form of literature—the writing of travel—so as to study the negotiation of cultural meaning and the "staking" of intelligibility in such writing. And even more specifically, I want to use this problem of the stake of intelligibility as a pretext for a reading of Hawthorne's enigmatic *Transformation*, the novel we know as *The Marble Faun*, in order to "go the long way around" so as to arrive at a reading of a novel that meditates on the relation between exogamy, gazes, resemblances, and formlessness in a systematic attempt to elide the cultural rule of the incest prohibition.

Writing Travel

It is by now something of a commonplace within the theory of travel writing to acknowledge the ways in which travel is a form of writing and writing a form of travel. Travel, as the traversal of a space, calls forth notions of memory propelled by desire and of the movement of a body through a landscape that is called upon to mean. Michel

Butor reminds us of flags planted, the markings of arrival, and the "thick tissue of traces and marks" by which the movements of travelers leave their inscription on nature.[6] As for the second notion—that writing is a form of travel—we acknowledge the exodus of all writing into the undifferentiated whiteness of the page, writing as sign of habitation and movement—a kind of territorial marker like the bent twigs left by others on the paths before us.

Yet to see travel and writing as metaphors for each other is also to note the relentless metaphorizing nature of thought. The churning of one thing into another within an acknowledgment of difference is perhaps the central task of travel writing as the inscription of views both familiar and strange. And although such views may risk unintelligibility, the writing of them may not. Just as the movement of writing takes place within a history of forms and possibilities for excursus, so does the movement of travel have its pregiven genres: the one-way and the round trip, the stopping by wayside, the return home, the journey into outer space and the journey around one's room, the business trip and the holiday, the pilgrimage and the march to the sea. Similarly, the resting places of significance in travel are either those centers of mixing and dialogue and consequently danger—the inn and the crossroads—or those places of seclusion and silence where one confronts an interior consciousness made of external censors—the forest, the holy site, the shrine, and the temple.

Now in this tension between public and private we see a fundamental problem in the writing of travel: its necessary and founding disjunction—a disjunction that on the one hand locates us all the more squarely within the necessarily liminal world of travel, and a disjunction that, on the other hand, makes the very idea of a theory of travel writing suspect. For travel writing reminds us of its own temporality: it always balances its metadiscursive properties, its aphorisms, against the contingencies of the next experience. It offers us the view of a person on the road—the mounted view, a view too low to be transcendent and too high to be in the scene. If one of the most vivid moments in Goethe's *Italian Journey* is the description of the girl in Catania who runs beside the mule of the *vetturino* "chattering and spinning her thread at the same time,"[7] it is because this talking picture is moving at the speed of, and alongside, the traveler, presenting us with a dream of the end of mediation, a dream nevertheless merging with the accomplishment of distance. Hence she represents a perfected form of temporal exogamy, perfectly poised between this side and that and moving with us, all at the same time.

The ways in which the inscription of a gaze results in a writing of the self are recapitulated in the very history of travel writing. Between the eighteenth and the nineteenth century, the paradigm for travel writing shifted from supposedly "disinterested" observation to biographical narrative.[8] Another way of accounting for this is to say that a literature of exploration involving the cataloguing of curiosities surrendered to a literature of travel involving the transformation of a subject through firsthand experience. The latter is the kind of travel writing we find described by Mikhail Bakhtin, when he writes that "the author's own real homeland serves as an organizing center for point of view, for scales of comparison," and that "the hero of such a work is the public and political man of ancient times, a man governed by his sociopolitical, philosophical, and utopian interests. . . . [Here] biography is the crucial organizing principle for time."[9]

But this public figure is without his or her public. Even while under assault, the home culture serves as a unit of measurement, and so we find the travel writer imagining, in isolation from home, an intimate and domestic audience. The epistolary form of the travel piece, ranging from the imagining of letters to family or friends to the frequent American convention of sending travel letters to one's hometown newspaper, thus satisfies a need here that the seeming disinterestedness of the journal or note form does not. The product of too much cultural noise is loneliness. Thus the traveler is caught between the desire for self-transformation, for the search for wider horizons of consciousness (consciousness being, of course, a landscape), and the desire to be a faithful witness, a steady point of comparison and accountability. Thus travel experience, in its endless search for meaning, must also be without irrevocable meaning: it must find a meaning in time, the very meaning of time implicit in such ideas of flight, escape, search, transgression, and reparation alternately at the center of the travel narrative.

In the American travel writing of the nineteenth century that serves, for our purposes, as a backdrop to Hawthorne's project, we find a rich discussion of these paradoxes of the traveler's biography:

the problems of coming too close or going too far, the problems of
staying too long or leaving too quickly, the problems of rigidity and
provinciality on the one hand and promiscuousness and contamination on the other. Margaret Fuller's tripartite typology of the
servile (or gluttonish), the conceited (or unchanging), and the thinking (or admirable) tourists obviously prefers the thinker whose
knowledge arguments and enriches those selective experiences to
which he or she is subject.[10] Similarly, Henry Theodore Tuckerman
makes the following suggestions in *Isabel; or Sicily, a Pilgrimage*
(1839):

> In truth, no ideas can be more false than many of those which it
> requires at least one sojourn of an American in Europe to correct.
> There is a vague notion prevalent among the untravelled, that abroad
> there are many and peculiar means of enjoyment. In one sense this
> is true: but is it enough borne in mind, that the only worthy pleasures
> peculiar to Europe, are those of taste, and that to enjoy these, a
> certain preparedness is requisite? The truth is the legitimate grati-
> fications of Southern Europe are eminently meditative. They are alike
> incompatible with a spirit of restless ambition or gainful passion. They
> address themselves to the imaginative and enthusiastic, to the con-
> templative and intellectual . . . to those who have faith in the refining
> influences of art and culture.[11]

One is reminded of Gibbon's lengthy instructions in his *Memoirs*
for preparing oneself for a visit to Rome. Gibbon suggests that one
begin with indefatigable vigor of mind and body and then progress
through knowledge of classics, history, and music to the possession
of a flexible temper and independent fortune and finally to a knowledge of all national and provincial idioms as well as all arts of conversation.[12] The complete tourist would be so completely cultured
that he or she would not need the corrective of culture contact—
indeed, would become the place itself. We should consider at this
point the fate of the idealized European tourist, the Count di V—,
described in James Fenimore Cooper's *Excursions in Italy* (1838).
Cooper explains that

> in this age of cosmopolitanism, real or pretended, so many people
> travel that one is apt to ask who can be left at home; and some aim
> at distinction in this era of migration by making it a point to see
> everything. Of this number is a certain Count di V—, whom I met
> in America just before leaving home. This gentleman went through

the United States, tablets in hand, seeming to be dissatisfied with himself if he quitted one of our common-place towns with an hospital unexamined, a mineral unregistered, or a church unentered. It struck me at the time that he was making a toil of a pleasure, especially in a country that has so little worth examining.

Cooper concludes this anecdote by noting that the count traveled all over the world and eventually "lost his life by falling into a boiling spring on the island of Batavia."[13]

The fetishistic activities of the Count di V— and his fall into nature make his story a parable of the problem of traveling too far. The count's venture into the wild contrasts sharply with the travel activities of nineteenth-century Americans journeying to Europe. The predominant number of such Americans—Protestant preachers, lawyers, doctors, businessmen, society women, educators, abolitionists, actors, health seekers, and young wanderers—were searching for culture and a matrix within which to articulate a new American identity.[14] Thus their travels are marked by activities of comparison and judgment and a frequent fear of conversion. This fear is particularly evident among Protestant travelers to Italy. By relentlessly aestheticizing Italian life, these travelers were able to protect themselves from the full implications of the contexts of Italian art. The ways in which many Protestant travelers still prefer to think of Italy's churches as museums testifies to the endurance of this aestheticizing gesture. By making all travel experiences metonymic to aesthetic experiences, travel writers could separate themselves from dialogue and the obligations of reciprocity, with the latter forms of the spoken thereby saved for an audience of cultural peers. Furthermore, the late-eighteenth-century and nineteenth-century American's view of Italy was already mediated by British aesthetics of the period. From Gothicism to Romanticism, Italy represented what might be called a contaminated site of representations ranging from classicism to Catholicism to revolution.

Speaking Pictures

Although there obviously are many suggestive aspects to the attempt of travel writing to appropriate and contain cultural forms and values, I would like to focus upon the ways in which a central problem of

eighteenth-century aesthetics—the relation between the plastic arts
and writing—comes to be renegotiated in the tension in this travel
writing between description and narration. And more significantly,
in the tension between aestheticism (and the separating function of
the gaze) and ethics (and the implicating function of the dialogic)
that is reflected in the stasis of depiction and the moving judgment
of language as uttered in time. Thus the formal tension of travel
writing as the temporal inscriptions of views and scenes suits it well
to the thematic of forging identity and the critique of cultural relations motivating such accounts in the first place.

The subtext here is obviously Lessing on the Laocoön, and consequently Schiller. Along with the Apollo Belvedere, the Capitoline
Venus, and the Dying Gladiator, the Laocoön was one of a handful
of classical works familiar to American artists, thanks to casts brought
to New York at the turn of the century and later copied in Philadelphia as part of Charles Wilson Peale's attempt to make Philadelphia "the Athens of the West."[15] The problems posed by the
Laocoön—the impenetrability of static art and the temporality of
verbal art; the temporality of one's viewpoint; the silence, even
indifference, of history—are central to the traveler's experience of
nineteenth-century Italy. The Laocoön is a work that casts its
shadow strongly upon those texts we will focus on: Rembrandt
Peale's *Notes on Italy, Written During a Tour in the Years 1829–1830*;
David Dorr's *A Coloured Man Around the World* (1858); Washington
Irving's *Tales of a Traveller* (1824); and, finally, Hawthorne's *The
Marble Faun* (1860), formed during his sojourn in Italy in 1858 and
1859 and heavily indebted, especially in what we might call its
departures, to the structure of his *Italian Notebooks*.

These texts are quite self-conscious about the problems of travel
writing as a narrative of the self. Perhaps not so coincidentally,
Hawthorne's famous description of a romance as the product of a
romancer who can "dream strange things and make them look like
truth" is presaged by Rembrandt Peale's insistence upon the dream-
like character of "his" Rome. The beginning of *The Marble Faun*
contains a well-known passage:

> Side by side with the massiveness of the Roman past, all matters that
> we handle or dream of nowadays look evanescent and visionary alike.

It might be that the four persons whom we are seeking to introduce
were conscious of this dreaming character of the present, as compared
with the square blocks of granite wherewith the Romans built their
lives.[16]

When the Napoleonic Wars kept Rembrandt Peale from going to
Italy in 1807 and again in 1810, he became obsessed with seeing
Italian paintings in England, Paris, and America. "Italy," he writes,
"which was my reverie by day, became the torment of my dreams
at night,"[17] adding: "the idea that my dreams of Italy were never
to be realized seemed to darken the cloud which hung over the
prospect of death itself."[18]

Once Peale had arrived, he contended that Rome "is indeed a
delicious dream, but a dream that must be repeated by the artist
until its impressions are confirmed into records of truth and usefulness."[19] The problem then becomes, as it is in managing any dream,
the subjection of the ego to the demands of the law, the testing of
the daydream against reality and of idealizations against practice,
and most significant, the posing of issues of reproduction and representation. If such a problem speaks to the situation of the relation
between the New World, which is, as the Count di V— discovered,
all nature and newly articulated law not yet subject to experience,
and the Old World, which is by now a land of pictures, an archaeological site with so many shifting and fusing layers of meaning that
all is art rather than rule, we have dreamed this dream before. And
perhaps as much as any other feature, this artistic dream is characterized by its vagueness, its refusal of cultural definition. For the
most part, the picture is Italy and not a celebration of particular
works or paintings. When the Pennsylvania Academy opened in
1807, many of the "Old Masters" came without labels, and Peale
and his father had some trouble attributing them.[20]

Contemporary tourism markets its views as compositions of ways
of life and thereby exaggerates the leisure of the tourist as he or she
observes others working. From this retrospective viewpoint, one of
the most startling aspects of nineteenth-century American travelers'
accounts of Italy is how squarely they are framed within the paradigm
of the aesthetic view. Yet we are also made aware of how relentlessly
these discourses explore the implications of the problems of representation arising out of the picturesque: What do these views stand

for? What do they mean? How will their history be completed? What stance should the viewer take with regard to them? These are the problems plaguing Peale and the problems arising from the aesthetic issues addressed in Hawthorne's *Italian Notebooks*, later played out in the condensations and displacements of *The Marble Faun* itself. For Peale, trained in the realistic genres of historical painting and portraiture, a Protestant moralism led to a taste for allegory, as in his most successful painting, *The Court of Death*. And since this viewpoint would preclude a Catholic reading of the Old Masters, turning to landscape as painting, even a painting that only referred further to painting, was a likely move.

Just as the landscape is conceived as an allegorical canvas within this literature, so does the notation of Italian types call for moral conclusions. In his 1858 volume *A Coloured Man Around the World*, David Dorr recorded the following observations regarding the connection between volcanoes and immorality:

> I don't think that one contented man can be found in the whole city of Naples, with its 450,000 souls. Every time this growling, burning mountain roars it jars the whole city; organ grinders give themselves as little trouble about Vesuvius as any other class, and the streets are full of them. . . . Naples is yet the most wicked city on the face of the globe. . . . To see a club-slain man in Naples is no object of pity . . . their mind is forever placed on wholesale calamities.[21]

In the prostitution district of Naples, Dorr's *lazzarone* gives twenty-five cents to a group of women in payment for exhibiting themselves: "as many as wished to claim stock in the 25 cents commenced showing their nakedness, to the horror of man's sensual curiosity. I saw fifty women show what I had never legally seen before. I must end the chapter and commence another."[22] Dorr's anxiety is the anxiety of volitional sight: to have license to see is also to claim a responsibility for seeing. To claim that one has seen is to posit one's originality, to admit that one is not merely recognizing.

Yet the innocence of the picturesque view is always suspect, already framed by another picture. This travel writing is thus relentlessly intertextual. Dorr's narrative, for example, borrows directly from Cooper's, particularly in its historical descriptions of the Palatine. And it is difficult to believe that Cooper had not read Rembrandt Peale when we compare their passages on quack doctors.

Peale records "an eloquent quack doctor, who proclaims his skill from the seat of his carriage, or . . . the dexterity of a dentist who, on horseback, draws teeth."[23] Cooper writes of a quack doctor who "extracts a tooth from a peasant without dismounting,"[24] thus condensing Peale's image. And whereas Cooper has derived his impressions of "picturesque-looking bandits" (who later turn out to be friendly peasant-farmers) from Washington Irving, Washington Irving's picture of "The Italian Banditti" in his *Tales of a Traveller* (1835) has no doubt come from Mrs. Radcliffe:

> They wear jackets and breeches of bright colors, sometimes gaily embroidered; their breasts are covered with medals and relics; their hats are broad-brimmed, with conical crowns, decorated with feathers, or variously-coloured ribands; their hair is sometimes gathered in silknets; they wear a kind of sandal of cloth or leather, bound round the legs with thongs . . . a broad belt of cloth or a sash of silk net, is stuck full of pistols and stilettoes; a carbine is slung at the back; while about them is generally thrown, in a negligent manner, a great dingy mantle, which serves as protection in storms, or a bed.[25]

The prostitute, the quack doctor, and the bandit represent in this empire of signs the profusion of a semiotic outside the boundaries of law and expectation, and at the same time are already written, always inscribed by a previous view. They thus promise exogamy within the constraints of an already written order.

There is no virgin sight or site: the slippery types at the edge of the law are symptomatic of a writing whose referent will not remain fixed or pure. Goethe sees his friend Kniep substitute for the middle and foreground of an "awful" view an "elegant and delightful set borrowed from Poussin," and writes, "I wonder how many 'Travels of a Painter' contain such half-truths."[26] And we are similarly struck when we read, without attribution, Laurence Sterne's account of the Spanish pilgrim weeping over his donkey in Peale's *Notes on Italy*. There (as in my Penguin edition of *A Sentimental Journey*, p. 62), we find: "A poor ass fell down under a heavy load, cut its side, and dislocated its hind leg. As soon as the poor man, who led him saw this, he looked sadly, then sobbed aloud, and burst into the most piteous grief and lamentations." Although the origin of this incident seems to lie in the Indian folktale of the washerman and the queen, we might see the intertextual allusion to travel

characters as the more likely one here, as well as some poetic justice
regarding Sterne's own infamous tendency to plagiarize.

Thus ironically, the traveler finds that, although firsthand, his or
her experience is all the more inscribed in an already written order.
Hawthorne notes in *The Marble Faun* "a party of English or Americans paying the inevitable visit by moonlight [to the Colosseum],
and exalting themselves with raptures that were Byron's, not their
own."[27] Peale suggests, "I have preferred the simple task of describing only those things which I saw, as they may be seen by other
persons in my situation, and have pretended no opinions or judgments but such as forced themselves upon me."[28] But he is unable
to sustain this benevolent and passive relation to his sense of realism
and nature. It is as if the tiny figures in the shadows of Piranesi's
monuments had become gigantic and thereby too vivid: the prostitute's nakedness; the shifting rhetoric and obliviousness to pain of
the quack doctor; the almost feminine deadliness of the gaudy bandit—these present the traveler with a surplus of information, a type
exceeding the bounds of its own cultural propriety, its own cultural
landscape. Such vivification is thus a reminder of the customs house
and of the worldliness of exchange. And it is also a reminder of the
darker side of exchange—the side of contagion and contamination.
The traveler, like the characters in Tuckerman's *Isabel* and like Peale
entering Naples, was frequently subject to quarantine, so the themes
of decay and disease signified a quite literal threat as well as a
metaphorical reading of the breakdown of an old order.

Furthermore, death results from the sacrifice the picturesque
makes in diminishing its subjects. In an inversion of the Galatea
story, the Italians surrounding art and occupying the landscape are
either aestheticized within it or purged from it. When Peale observes
contemporary life in a scene near Michelangelo's *David,* he has an
interest in creating a disjunction between life within the view and
life outside it: "These objects of fine art are daily seen without
emotion by the greater part of the people who pass or frequent the
place, occupied with bales of goods near the customhouse, bargain-
ing for straw hats or horses, surrounding a foolish buffoon, or a set
of dancing gods."[29] Tuckerman's hero Vittorio says, "how unutter-
ably sad . . . that so fair a heritage, should be so unhappily peopled—
that superstition and ignorance should overshadow so rich a domain."[30] Obviously, the aestheticization of context enables the trav-

eler's interpretation of the work of art to gain a kind of formal integrity. Hence what is made original is not the work, but the view of the traveler. And it is not accidental that the native view must be thereby suppressed. Hawthorne has Kenyon give a little speech in the Colosseum:

> The Coliseum is far more delightful, as we enjoy it now, than when eighty thousand persons sat squeezed together, row above row, to see their fellow creatures torn by lions and tigers limb from limb. What a strange thought that the Coliseum was really built for us, and has not come to its best uses till almost two thousand years after it was finished![31]

Yet following our discussion of the respective anxieties attending propinquity and distance, we can see that such writers were attempting to contain and articulate a kind of American originality. What would it mean for Americans to produce an art that was not a mere reproduction, or cast, of a previously completed European corpus? How could such an art acquire qualities of novelty, animation, and authenticity? For Hawthorne, the remedy for such a problem lay in a tension between fidelity to nature (although a nature to be found in art so much as anywhere else) and a kind of spiritual animation, an animation arising from a particularly Protestant notion of the individual view.

In this sense, the art of the past is always liable to improvement, including the improvements effected by reproductions and copies. American imitations of European masterpieces are hence seen to reawaken their spirituality, now drowned in the malaria of a corrupted European context. The narrator explains that Hilda's copies are valued because she does not attempt to reproduce the whole of a masterpiece, but only "some high, noble, and delicate portion of it, in which the spirit and essence of the picture culminated." He adds:

> If a picture had darkened into an indistinct shadow through time and neglect, or had been injured by cleaning, or retouched by some profane hand, she seemed to possess the faculty of seeing it in its pristine glory. The copy would come from her hands with what the beholder felt must be the light which the old master had left upon the original in bestowing his final and most ethereal touch. In some

instances even . . . she had been enabled to execute what the great
master had conceived in his imagination, but had not so perfectly
succeeded in putting upon canvas.[32]

Hawthorne's *French and Italian Notebooks*, as well as *The Marble Faun* itself, are preoccupied with negative judgments of European art. The Trevi Fountain is "absurd" and full of "artificial fantasies, which the calm moonlight soothed into better taste than was native to them";[33] Hilda "began to suspect that some, at least, of her venerated painters had left an inevitable hollowness in their works, because, in the most renowned of them, they essayed to express to the world what they had not in their own souls. . . . A deficiency of earnestness and absolute truth is generally discoverable in Italian pictures, after the art had become consummate"; the narrator suggests, "who can trust the religious sentiment of Raphael, or receive any of his Virgins as heaven-descended likenesses, after seeing, for example the Fornarina of the Barberini Palace, and feeling how sensual the artist must have been to paint such a brazen trollop of his own accord, and lovingly?"[34] Elsewhere in *The Marble Faun* criticisms of Guido's archangel and Titian's Magdalen are offered. Thus Hilda's metonymic relation to the Old Masters becomes a technique that Hawthorne valorizes for any "copy," including the selective relation between American and Italian culture. His proposal is that the Old World not be reproduced but selectively copied, so that the spiritual can be excised and remade under the conditions of a Protestant novelty. And Hilda, whose whiteness is itself metonymic to an abstracted spirituality, twice removed from nature as an aestheticization of the aesthetic, herself becomes the figure most copied in the book: she is copied by other copyists as she spends her days in the picture galleries, and her white hand is copied by Kenyon.[35]

Now the latter case brings to mind the relation between copying and metonymy in the "novel" as a whole. For the novel is often copied out of Hawthorne's travel notebooks, as noted earlier. The impressions of the traveler in those notebooks are themselves largely formed by previous travelers' accounts. Furthermore, Hawthorne copied his characters from life: Kenyon is based on the American sculptor William Wetmore Story, and Hilda herself on Hawthorne's wife, Sofia, whose work as a painter was supposedly limited by her proclivity to copying the works of Salvator Rosa and others. The characters in the novel are copies of art as well: Miriam's self-portrait

resembles Guido's Beatrice (which, the novel claims, could not resemble the real Cenci so much as Hilda's spiritualization of the
portrait does); and of course Donatello wavers between a copy of
Praxiteles' faun (which the Murray guidebook that Hawthorne used
would have identified as a copy of a Greek bronze original) and a
copy of a real (i.e., mythologically natural) faun. And just as, in the
chapter "A Walk on the Campagna," the assembly of the buried
archaic Venus ("either a prototype or a better replica of the Venus
of the Tribune") falls apart, becoming "a heap of worthless fragments," once Kenyon's thoughts turn away from art and toward the
consequences of a "human affection," so do the pieces of *The Marble
Faun* ultimately refuse closure. This chapter is, in fact, importantly
mimicked by the final elements of the novel's "structure," for Kenyon integrates the statue by putting a head on it, characterizing it
thereby. And yet on second look, its artificiality compels his gaze
to disassemble. Analogously, the narrator of the novel becomes a
character in the novel itself, meeting and wandering with the characters in the novel's closing sections. By this gesture, the narrator
completes the outside/in movement, the recapitulating functions of
copying, that the novel takes as its subject, hence underscoring the
romance and dream aspects of the form and at the same time emphasizing the novel's celebration of abstraction and its attack on
sensuality and nature.

In this attack on secularism and naturalism, *The Marble Faun* is
quite typical of American travel writing's refusal to acknowledge the
contexts of Italian art and its distaste for any art that imitates a
grotesque nature. Especially revealing are Peale's remarks on the
waxworks in Florence's Museum of Natural History:

> I expected to find the waxworks representing the plague which de-
> populated Florence large and anatomically correct—On the contrary,
> they are in three small boxes, each with a sheet of glass in front, and
> containing figures only a few inches long, arranged in groups to pro-
> duce the effect of pictures, and expressly calculated to excite horror
> in the imagination rather than to represent truth. It is a disgusting
> exaggeration, the toy of a demon and a gossip's tale.[36]

In order to understand that Peale's quarrel is with the representation
and not with death itself, we might remember his father's innovative
experiments with taxidermy, and his (Rembrandt's) only mention

of a souvenir or relic, from his trip to the Catacombs of Santa Maria della Vita near Naples:

> the flesh of fifteen hundred years was still of such tenacious though pliant fibre that it required a sharp knife to cut off a piece. The guide showed us the heads of some of these early Christians with the tongues still remaining in them, but would not permit us to take them away.[37]

In contrast, when Cooper observes waxworks in Bologna, he says they have a "horrible truth [yet] are odious as spectacles in their disgusting accuracy."[38]

Finally, we should recall that both the figure of Donatello and the plot of *The Marble Faun* turn real at the moment when the model is killed. The model's murder is effected by Miriam's glance and by Donatello's acting upon a scene he can no longer stand to view. Later the dead model reappears as a kind of awakened waxwork, a corpse made so real to life that it horrifies as an overly real representation as much as evidence of the crime. This is another point at which Hawthorne both uses and reflects upon the concept of metonymy to great effect. For the feet of the corpse become for Kenyon quite literally feet of clay:

> "Those naked feet!" said he. "I know not why, but they affect me strangely. They have walked to and fro over the hard pavements of Rome, and through a hundred other rough ways of this life, where the monk went begging for his brotherhood. . . . It is a suggestive idea, to track those worn feet backward through all the paths they have trodden, ever since they were the tender and rosy little feet of a baby, and (cold as they now are) were kept warm in his mother's hand."[39]

These worn feet, soiled by time and the corrupted dust of Rome, lead the sculptor, retrospectively, to a hand that will become the white hand of Hilda—a hand he has "photographed" by heart (just as Hilda "photographed" the portrait of Beatrice) and then kept from contamination in an ivory coffer. These traversing metonymical images—of course, the coffer then moves forward and backward to the "grave" of the Venus with the "dirt between her lips" in the *campagna* chapter)[40]—thus become symptomatic of Hawthorne's design for an art that copies, and thus isolates itself from chaos, and that also abstracts a spirituality from a prelapsarian version of art—an art before materiality, hence an art destined to vanish by its closure.

For Hawthorne especially, everyday life might be picturesque from a distance, but it appears too vivid, even stained, upon firsthand examination. Representations can therefore suffer from a surplus of reality. Emblems of nature in *The Marble Faun*, such as the buffalo calf accompanying Kenyon on his walk across the countryside, the distilled sunshine wine, the traditional peasants of carnival, are emphatically denatured. As the title of *Transformation* makes clear, history will not allow nature to remain unemblematic; allegory resounds.[41] And it is impossible for an American artist, literally compelled by the morality of allegory, to see nature in any other way. When Hawthorne continually claims that nature imitates art, and again when he valorizes the notion of copying, he has taken from travel writing two strategies that are in perfect accord with his aims as an artist. And in the metonymic traversals already outlined, he as well claims his victory over time: the victory of the "consummate artist" that Kenyon is not—an artist who distills a spirituality out of fragments beyond the claims of nature and beyond the claims of any art merely reproducing nature.

Obviously, the nature that imitates art is already another form of art. It is a nature of cliffs, valleys, crags, and other uneven spaces, just as William Gilpin had specified in his essay "On Picturesque Travel" (1792): "The imagination can plant hills, can form rivers and lakes and valleys, can build castles and abbeys, and if it find no other amusement, can dilate itself in vast ideas of space." The landscape appears as a canvas; even the built environment seems to be a form of sculpture.[42] In fact, we might attribute the taste for Rome and the Roman *campagna* by moonlight, stretching in touristic discourse from Piranesi to Edith Wharton, to the desire to solidify such masses and to excise the distractions of their contemporary context—as well as, of course, to the desire for a meditative epiphany in the style of Gibbon's own moonlit inspiration for his masterpiece.[43] According to both Peale and Cooper, English-speaking tourists spent a great deal of their recreational time playing at charades, *tableaux vivants*, and other speechless theatrical entertainments, all of which can be seen as another level of "playing" at the nonreciprocity, silence, and visual closure of the touristic experience.[44]

Let us look at some scenes of nature imitating art. From Peale:

During our ride to Borelli, I remarked effects of atmosphere, such as I had never seen in nature before, But recognized as true in the picture of Claude and Vernet—a hazy horizon—masses of mountains resembling clouds in colour pale and grey—the front objects more and more distinct.

Peale complains that there are not enough peasant cottages for sketchers to rest in.[45] Tuckerman's characters similarly see art everywhere they look. In Messina,

> the broadly undulating shapes of the Sicilian mountains come clothed with the vivid verdure of the lemon and orange trees, and the darker evergreen of the olive. On their tops, at intervals, volumes of pearly mist reposed, and elsewhere the edge of their summits was marked with the distinctness of a chiselled line upon the clear background of the horizon.

When Tuckerman's character Clifford Frazier sees an old woman's face near Etna, "it reminds him of some of the Dutch portraits he had seen in the collections of Italy."[46] And when a peasant fetches chestnuts for Isabel, the heroine, "she wished there had been time to sketch the curious picture."[47] Cooper often shows the pervasive influence of Salvator Rosa and Poussin in his descriptions, and sees the background to Bologna as "the view . . . which the old Italian masters sometimes put to their religious subjects."[48]

In our post-snapshot age, it is perhaps difficult for us to see how relentlessly writing and drawing were connected for these authors—particularly in the temporal/spatial conflation brought about by joining these two activities. Peale had written in his 1835 textbook *Graphics* (figure 8): "writing is little else than drawing the forms of letters [just as] drawing is little more than writing the forms of objects."[49] We might remember Goethe noting in his *Italian Journey* that one evening he found himself using his sepia drawing ink for writing.[50] This mixture of the sketcher's and writer's art is particularly served by the notion of nature as itself a kind of painting, now copied within the temporal movement of the line. Hilda's most successful copy, her drawing of Guido's Beatrice Cenci, is accomplished by writing with her eyes. Since the "Prince Barberini" forbids copies of the painting,

> I had no resource but to sit down before the picture, day after day, and let it sink into my heart. I do believe it is now photographed

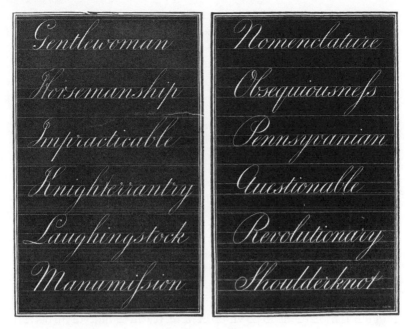

Figure 8
Samples of handwriting that illustrate the letters *G* to *S*. Note the absence
of *J* and the misspelling of *Pennsylvanian*. From Rembrandt Peale, *Graphics:
A Manual of Drawing and Writing for the Use of Schools and Families*. (Courtesy
of The Library Company of Philadelphia)

> there. . . . Well, after studying it in this way, I know not how many
> times I came home, and have done my best to transfer the image to
> canvas.[51]

Beatrice's "red-rimmed gaze" reminds us of the historicity of sight.
It is impossible to look afresh; all seeing is contaminated by knowledge, all seeing is a form of action. Hence the intertwining of a
series of "scenes": the scene of original sin, the scene of the crime,
the scene of the painting. Throughout *The Marble Faun*, seeing/
reading becomes a matter of the consequences, or effects, of impressions—their contaminating possibilities, their capacity for implica-
tion, their linking of gazes and actions, their relation to originality
and authenticity.

We arrive once again at the crucial issue of copying for the Amer-

ican tourist/aesthete. The aestheticization of Italy—its language a
music, its people a portrait, its landscapes a painting—was part of
a very generalized tracing of an aesthetic genealogy from the classical
world: more specifically, the classical world now traversed by a Christian and democratic myth seeming to run backward from Rome to
Athens to Jerusalem. Peale concluded his travel account:

> In leaving Milan, I may bid farewell to the arts of Italy! An Italian,
> not exempted from bigotry, discovered a new world for the eman-
> cipation of man. May America in patronising the arts, receive them
> as the offspring of enlightened Greece, transmitted through Italy,
> where their miraculous powers were nourished in the bondage of
> mind. Let them in turn be emancipated and their persuasive and
> fascinating language be exalted to the noblest purpose and be made
> instrumental to social happiness and national glory![52]

Any marriage between America and Europe depended upon a separation of generations and a translation of classicism into indigenous
terms. Peale, born on Washington's birthday, the son of the painter
whom he calls "the first painter of the Western world," traveled
through Italy carrying his own portrait of Washington. He displayed
the portrait throughout his trip to dignitaries and artists, and had
given instructions that if he died during the journey, he was to be
buried with the portrait placed on his coffin. Peale himself appears,
therefore, in his search for culture as a case of nature imitating art.

But we should look more closely at this portrait, which shows
Washington through a perforated screen of ornamented stonework,
beneath a Phidian head of Jupiter. This perforated screen through
which we view the "father of our country" is strangely reminiscent
of several other screens, such as the golden, even erotic, one through
which Goethe observes the statue of the Virgin in the side altar of
the church at Monte Pellegrino, outside Palermo. (Goethe refers to
her as a "beautiful lady who seemed to be reclining in a kind of
ecstasy"—an almost willful refusal to "read" her native meaning,
especially considering the presence of a "cherub, fanning her with
a lily.")[53] And here are two examples from Hawthorne: the "iron
lattice of a prison window" through which Kenyon seems to observe
the carnival at the close of *The Marble Faun*, and the iron grating of
the Vatican sculpture gallery through which Hawthorne observes the
Laocoön for the first time.[54] The *Notebooks* record three views of the

Laocoön: this first, hurried view; a second, where Hawthorne compares the sculpture to the "tumult of Niagara, which does not seem to be a tumult because it keeps pouring on, forever and ever";[55] and a third, derivative view at the Uffizi, where a copy of the sculpture does not impress Hawthorne "with the sense of might and terrible repose... growing out of the infinitude of trouble"[56] that he had felt in the original.

If American culture was to copy Italian culture, the challenge would be to avoid being a mere valorization of the original, as the Uffizi statue seemed to be. There is a moving scene in Irving's travel narrative when he tells of his feelings upon seeing the statues in the Pitti Palace, for his father had had etchings of them in the house when he was growing up: "the views, the wrestlers, the dancing faun and the knife-grinder, four of my oldest acquaintances on paper, now stood before my eyes, looking like living beings."[57] But the risk taken in bringing the statue to life is its irreversibility; the very feature that makes it no longer a representation, but something subject to mortality, is what will come back to haunt us.

Transformation, or The Marble Faun

The Marble Faun, as a novel of glances and resemblances, plays out this paradoxical desire for an artistic animation of history as a tension between the morality of allegory (the possibility that the signs of art can be made to cohere within judgments regarding the ethical) and the neutrality of aestheticism (the play of resemblances as an unending and empty comparison). In "Scenes by the Way," a chapter essential to this theme (though importantly, quite minor to that minor player in Hawthorne's romance—the plot), we find a passage exemplifying this tension between the allegorical and the aesthetic, the American and the Italian. First the narrator writes:

> A pre-Raphaelite artist might find an admirable subject in one of these Tuscan girls, stepping with a free, erect, and graceful carriage. The miscellaneous herbage and tangled twigs and blossoms of her bundle, crowning her head (while her ruddy, comely face looks out between the hanging side festoons like a large flower), would give the painter boundless scope for the minute delineation which he loves.

He then explains a few sentences later:

Nothing can be more picturesque than an old grape vine, with almost
a trunk of its own, clinging first around its supporting tree. Nor does
the picture lack its moral. You might twist it to more than one grave
purpose, as you saw how the knotted serpentine growth imprisoned
within its strong embrace the friend that supported its tender infancy
and how (as seemingly flexible natures are prone to do) it converted
the sturdier tree entirely to its own selfish ends, extending its innumerable arms on every bough, and permitting hardly a leaf to sprout
except its own.[58]

Of course, to "twist" the picture to this grave purpose would be to
be condemned to repeat it.

At this point the American sculptor Kenyon, who will ultimately
find what Hawthorne poses as an American form of happiness by
marrying Hilda the copyist, thinks of how "the enemies of the vine,
in his native land, would here see an emblem of the remorseless
gripe which the habit of vinous enjoyment lays upon its victim."[59]
Hawthorne seems to abandon this passage by changing the subject
in his next paragraph. Yet on closer look, Hawthorne has in fact
reinscribed the problem he has borrowed from Lessing: the relation
between imitation, indication, and action, implicit in the contradiction between the stasis of the view and the temporality of narration.
This relation between seeing and acting is further emphasized by
the contrasts between Miriam and Kenyon. Miriam becomes emblematic of the fluid and temporal medium of paint; Kenyon becomes
emblematic of the static and permanent integrity of marble. Miriam's
gaze ties her to the literal "execution" of her model. In contrast,
with a verbal command Kenyon is able to have his assistants bring
stone to life.

It is part of the studied brilliance of *The Marble Faun* that this
gripping image of the vine is only glancingly a repetition of the
Laocoön, as are the whole series of central problems in the novel:
Donatello's achievement of life through his break with resemblance
and the wrongful action of the murder; Miriam, whose crime is, as
the conclusion puts it, "after all merely a glance," weighted by the
novel's closure with the full ethical implications of a meaningful
look; the facility and superficiality of the copyist's matching and
distanced perception; and the active relation between hands and
eyes that produces, for Hawthorne, a genuine art. Finally, the little
passage on the vine mimes Lessing's point regarding tragedy: that

we enter into a view of the struggle with the serpent in the moment before the cry, and that we also already know the narrative and are powerless before it.

The complexity of this problem and the ways in which it in effect entwines the rule of the incest prohibition with the inevitably over-determined consequences of culture are particularly brought forward by Hawthorne's chapter on what are appropriately called "Fragmentary Sentences." Here a symbolic relation is established between the scene of original sin, the crime of Beatrice Cenci, and the predestined yet unarticulated plot of *The Marble Faun* itself. Significantly, this is the only location in the text (and we should note that most chapters are, as they are in guidebooks, locations) where the model speaks.

Hawthorne establishes immediately the incommensurability of the relation between the characters of Miriam and the model:

> owing, it may be, to this moral estrangement—this chill remoteness of their position—there have come to us but a few vague whisperings of what passed in Miriam's interview that afternoon with the sinister personage who had dogged her footsteps ever since the visit to the catacomb. In weaving these mystic utterances into a continuous scene, we undertake a task resembling in its perplexity that of gathering up and piecing together the fragments of a letter which has been torn and scattered to the winds. . . . Yet unless we attempt something in this way, there must remain an unsightly gap, and a lack of continuousness and dependence in our narrative; so that it would arrive at certain inevitable catastrophes without due warning of their immanence.[60]

In fact, this conversation, although "depicted" by Hawthorne, is depicted with so much fidelity that it is necessarily fragmented by time and hence can be known only through its effects. It represents the culminating moral crisis of the novel, for it alludes to every crime: the fascination of the model for Miriam, being "such as beasts and reptiles of subtle and evil nature sometimes exercise upon their victims"; the "iron chain" linking them, which "must have been forged in some such unhallowed furnace as is only kindled by evil passions and fed by evil deeds"; or their relation, which, the narrator contends, is among "the most insoluble riddles propounded to moral comprehension."[61]

By the time we arrive at Miriam's first words in this scene—"You follow me too closely. . . . You allow me too scanty room to draw my breath. Do you know what will be the end of this?"—we are well aware of the allusions to original sin as separation, a separation resulting of course in the fall from nature that, as the ontology of mediation, permits all representation to "take place." And we are aware of the redundant propinquity of incest and its riddles—the "too close" journey of the Other that results in the "chill remoteness" of an unnatural relation. Miriam bursts forth in "vehement passion": "Oh, that we could have wandered in those dismal passages till we both perished, taking opposite paths in the darkness, so that when we lay down to die, our last breaths might not mingle!" The model replies: "In all that labyrinth of midnight paths, we should have found one another out to live or die together. Our fates cross and are entangled. The threads are twisted into a strong cord, which is dragging us to an evil doom." As the conversation ends, the model grasps her hand and notes that although it "looks very white," he has "known hands as white, which all the water in the ocean would not have washed clean." "It had no stain," retorts Miriam bitterly, "until you grasped it in your own." The narrator claims that the rest of their conversation blew away on the wind, but adds that "in their words, or in the breath that uttered them, there seemed to be an odor of guilt, and a scent of blood."[62]

Miriam has reminded the model that death will sever their relation; this is of course the answer to the riddle of the sins of the fathers—the consequence of crossroads and of too much familiarity, too much knowledge. Hawthorne, however, will not allow us access to that plot, because he would necessarily have to present a grotesque copy, too close to nature and hence too far from the abstracted spirituality that he has convinced himself is the only redeeming value of art. The "fragmentary sentence" is thus here a kind of death sentence that is indirectly received: the kind of death sentence imposed on all men and women as a result of original sin.

The multiple allusions to the model's madness and the hints of Miriam's notorious genealogy all lead us to believe that the model might be a child of incest rather than a practitioner of it. And significantly, the Beatrice Cenci plot overdetermines, and itself incestuously mixes, the positions of victim and criminal, inheritor and perpetrator. Hilda is ready to quickly accuse Beatrice, just as she is ready to quickly accuse Miriam; Miriam, who acts out of an originality struggling against the burden of its inheritance, realizes the complexity of Beatrice's crime and the full implications of the redundancy of being both sinned against and sinning. The Cenci plot continues as Hilda is commissioned to give another packet of "fragmentary sentences" to an unknown recipient at the Palazzo Cenci. This packet contains what remains of Hawthorne's plot; its message, revealed to no one other than an unknown referent, explains Miriam's history and actions. But Hilda is not privileged to this information; she remains in "the land of pictures," as is emphasized by the ways in which this episode of the packet and Hilda's consequent disappearance are repeatedly inscribed as an invisibility. The narrator teases the reader with claims that "Hilda had been permitted, for a season to converse with the great, departed masters of the pencil, and behold the diviner works which they have painted in heavenly colors. Guido had shown her another portrait of Beatrice Cenci, done from the celestial life"; Perugino shows her "a woman's face . . . so divine . . . that a gush of happy tears blinded the maiden's eyes before she had time to look"; and Raphael "had taken Hilda by the hand . . . and drawn aside the curtain of gold-fringed cloud that hung before his latest masterpiece. On earth, Raphael painted the Transfiguration. What higher scene may he have since depicted, not from imagination, but as revealed to his actual sight!"[63] But as this passage illustrates, such a celestial art would be completely empty: it would be so abstract that it would have no intelligibility, no referent other than its own self-evidence.

Critics have attended to the Cenci theme in *The Marble Faun* as an allusion to Shelley's *Cenci*, an allusion to Byronic legends of incest, and an allusion to Hawthorne's own supposedly incestuous relation with his sister Elizabeth ("Ebe"), and retrospectively as itself an allusion in Melville's *Pierre*.[64] But as *The Marble Faun* itself demonstrates, mere allusion does not suffice outside a sphere of intelligibility and structure within which allusion is able to "resonate." Furthermore, allusion severed from its grounds becomes gratuitous detail. Thus I would conclude by remarking upon the ways in which the Cenci portrait is, for the novel, a kind of indeterminate center of overdetermination.

We should begin by noting that the Cenci portrait is now considered to be neither Beatrice Cenci nor a work by Guido.[65] But for Hawthorne, and for Sophia, the portrait was a central point on a

tour of Roman art. Hawthorne records in his *Notebooks* that in his
visit to the Barberini Palace, he passed quickly by Dürer's picture
Christ Disputing with the Doctors

> and almost all the other pictures, being eager to see the two which
> chiefly make the collection famous.—These are Raphael's Fornarini,
> and Guido's portrait of Beatrice Cenci. These we found in the last
> of the three rooms; and as regards Beatrice Cenci, I might as well
> not try to say anything, for its spell is indefinable, and the painter
> has wrought it in a way more like magic than anything else I have
> known.[66]

The picture, in Hawthorne's view, clearly achieves the goal of abstracted spirituality that he states as an aim throughout *The Marble
Faun*. He describes the figure in the portrait as being

> like a fallen angel, fallen, without sin. It is infinitely pitiful to meet
> her eyes. . . . It is the most profoundly wrought picture in the world;
> no artist did it, or could do it again. Guido may have held the brush,
> but he painted better than he knew. I wish, however, it were possible
> for some spectator, of deep sensibility, to see the picture without
> knowing anything of its subject or history; for no doubt we bring all
> our knowledge of the Cenci tragedy to the interpretation of the
> picture.[67]

Now here we find the traveler's wish for a completely aestheticized
context—a land of pictures unburdened by the stories of history—
that links Hawthorne's project to the central problematic of incest
as a relation between the overly propinquitous and the overly
alterior.

Beatrice is the perfect emblem for this problem, since she has
taken up the positions of both acted upon and actor, since she
has suffered from the temporal reflexivity of being too close to her
mate and from the spatial reflexivity of being too far from her kin.
The contamination of incest and the estrangement of fratricide and
parricide are the axes thereby of a circle of Western culture that
finds its narrative origins in the story of original sin, with its account
of too much knowledge and too much estrangement, and the story
of the founding of Rome, with its incestuous mixing of nature and
culture and its analogous coda of fratricide.

Each of the characters in *The Marble Faun* experiences this problem
of redundancy, overlap, and indeterminacy. The model, displaying

the ambiguity of other strangers encountered on the road, might be Miriam's brother or lover. He resembles nothing other than the portrait she had made of him and the demon in Guido's picture at the church of the Capuchins—a demon killed by St. Michael. A figure of replete liminality, the model hovers between life and death (here we are reminded of the Capuchin practice of mummification as another allusion to the novel's Galatea theme), between nature and art. The model is a kind of profoundly nameless relative who thereby introduces all the problems of relation without category. Furthermore, just as the Guido painting depicts the demon killed by the angel, so is this "demon" killed by a view. It is as if the model has been condemned to death by a painting: when Donatello acts upon Miriam's gaze, Miriam's gaze retrospectively alludes to the scene of Guido's painting and to other scenes we are not given access to, since we are not given their "stories." It is thus we readers who stand in the relation to this crime that Hawthorne asserted to be the ideal relation for the viewer of the Beatrice portrait—a relation uncontaminated by story.

Yet even those among us of "deep sensibility" must surely experience the anxiety of unintelligibility when confronted with such a view. It becomes our task to keep reading the symbols of the text against its overarching sets of allegory. Hilda and Miriam, for example, resemble the allegorical "light" and "dark" lady figures that recur in late-eighteenth- and nineteenth-century fiction from the Gothic novel to travelogues à la *Corinne* and the novels of Scott. But if we attend more closely and read back the allusion of the Cenci portrait, we find that these two figures break into the fragments of an overly condensed female image: Beatrice is a blond figure wearing a black hood. Furthermore, Hilda comes to symbolize the limitations of stasis; fixed in her tower, her art is immobile, completely dependent upon what is within range. And Miriam wanders so far afield that her actions become indecipherable, her work a revenge upon an unintelligible action.

The respective "mates" of these characters present us with a similar jumbling of what had seemed to be a symmetrical relation. Donatello mixes, like Romulus and Remus, the animal and human in his relation to the faun. The opening and closing "figure" of the hidden ears of the faun thus takes us to that border where the incest prohibition is first articulated. Yet even this figure is necessarily mediated by Donatello's resemblance to Praxiteles' faun, as noted earlier, and by his name, which makes him an allusion to an artist as well as to an artwork. In this sense, Donatello is mated to Hilda, who likewise is a copy as well as a copier. And consequently Kenyon is mated to Miriam, for their views, being those of original, if not "consummate," artists, are transformed to acts: Miriam's gaze, if not her paintings, effects her revenge; Kenyon's appropriation of Hilda's hand in marriage, if not in sculpture, completes his Roman project.

   The Marble Faun imitates, then, an anxiety regarding consummation. Incest, travel, and art are linked as actions threatening a closure that would mark the end of reproduction. It is rather easy to see the biographical import of this theme for Hawthorne. Once one attends to them, the most particular details in the text have the most general resonance. Consider, for example, the feet of the murdered model, which we earlier mentioned as a symbol of both experience and the worn trajectory of all paths in Rome. The symbol of the feet is readily linked to Hawthorne's earlier story of guilt and expiation, "The Ancestral Footstep"; to Hawthorne's visit to the legendary "bloody footstep" at Smithell's Hall in London; to Hawthorne's own lame foot in his youth; to Byron's affliction and metonymically, then, to Byron's experience of incest; and thereby to Oedipus's swollen foot as a mark of incest and patricide. We are reminded of other places in Hawthorne's fiction where to "dream strange things and make them look like truth" becomes a device for the conflation of act and symbol. For example, in "The Birthmark," in the story of an infant hand that reminds the bridegroom of a connection with animals. Or the moment in "Alice Doane's Appeal" when Leonard Doane, looking down at the face of the man he has murdered, Walter Brome, sees his dead father's face. Leonard has killed Walter because Walter has brought about the "shame" of Leonard's sister Alice. But Walter, it turns out, is also Alice's brother; Leonard has thus committed, in more or less literal and metaphorical degrees, incest, fratricide, and patricide.[68]

   All of Hawthorne's work—including his life, of course—is concerned with an inheritance of sin, with the reading of stains, with the consequences of views. Yet to reduce *The Marble Faun* to biography or anything else is to refuse the very problems of determination that the novel works to present. A consummate art would have no story to tell; in this sense, Hawthorne is struggling at the margins of such a possibility. Yet he is also presenting us with the particular ways in which such a possibility must necessarily fail. To travel in a land of pictures is to trade a being in time for a spatial illusion. The Laocoön itself is only intelligible because of the narrative Virgil has provided for reading it. Its perfected spatial form is thereby constantly put into motion by its representation of a punishment delivered in retribution for an unlicensed prophecy. We are not surprised to learn at the end of the novel that Hilda and Kenyon have abandoned art. Without the risk of contamination by narrative particularity, on the one hand, and the unintelligibility of abstraction, on the other, the transformations effected by the aesthetic have no meaning.

As with the experience of the Laocoön, the site to which all roads, including this one, lead, we have a relentless critique of aestheticism within a proclamation of the triumph of aestheticism. Although it may seem that Hawthorne aligns America with moralism and Italy with aestheticism, we find that he has in fact presented a devastating critique of the limitations of both—the sterility, the impossibility of closure and production, whenever art and action refuse each other. Hawthorne rather gloomily reminds us that to stay too long in Italy and away from America would lead to a "kind of emptiness," for we would "defer the reality of life, in such cases, until a further moment. . . and by then there are no future moments—or if we do return we find that. . . life has shifted its reality to the spot where we have deemed ourselves only temporary residents."[69] But he also reflects upon the meaning of the metaphors of emptiness—that emptiness of all travel writing having as its point the redemption of actions now subject to view.

Notes

1. Claude Lévi-Strauss, *The Elementary Structures of Kinship*, trans. James Harle Bell, John Richard von Sturner, and Rodney Needham (Boston: Beacon Press, 1969), pp. 8–9. Jacques Derrida discusses the paradox of this passage in light of Lévi-Strauss's entire oeuvre in "Structure, Sign and Play in the Discourse of the Human Societies," in *Writings and Difference*, trans. Alan Bass (Chicago: University of Chicago Press, 1978), pp. 278–94.
    2. Lévi-Strauss, *Elementary Structures of Kinship*, p. 9.

3. Ibid., p. 10.

4. Quoted in Ibid., pp. 42–43. See also Jack Goody, "A Comparative Approach to Incest and Adultery," in *Marriage, Family and Residence*, ed. Paul Bohannan and John Middleton (Garden City, N.Y.: Natural History Press, 1968), pp. 21–46. Goody cites Malinowski's treatment of incest, as the prohibition on sexual intercourse, and exogamy, the prohibition on marriage, as "being but two sides of a coin" (p. 22). He finds this position unsatisfactory, for he claims that it does not account for the asymmetry between in-group marriage rules and intragroup marriage rules, nor does it account for the asymmetry between marriage, which "affects the alignment of relationships between groups," and sexual intercourse, which when conducted in "semi-secrecy" does not affect such alignments (pp. 43–44). Although Goody's argument makes a strong methodological point regarding the anthropological study of incest and exogamy, this essay must necessarily deal with codes that are not "semi-secret"; hence exogamy and incest are treated as cognitive offenses and not "merely" sexual offenses.

Other standard readings on incest can be found in Emile Durkheim, *Incest, the Nature and Origin of the Taboo*, trans. Edward Sagarin (New York: Lyle Stuart, 1963); and E. B. Tylor, *Researches into the Early History of Mankind and the Development of Civilization* (London: T. Murray, 1870), and "On a Method of Investigating the Development of Institutions, Applied to Laws of Marriage and Descent," *Journal of the Royal Anthropological Institute* 18 (1888): 245–72. John T. Irwin provides a valuable paradigm for thinking about the relation between time, space, repetition, and repression in *Doubling and Incest/Repetition and Revenge: A Speculative Reading of Faulkner* (Baltimore: Johns Hopkins University Press, 1975). Other studies of the thematic of incest in literature include Sandra Sandell, " 'A Very Poetic Circumstance': Incest and the English Literary Imagination, 1770–1830" (Ph.D. diss., University of Minnesota, 1981); William Goetz, "Genealogy and Incest in *Wuthering Heights*," *Studies in the Novel* 14 (Winter 1982): 359–76; and W. Daniel Wilson, "Science, Natural Law, and Unwitting Sibling Incest in Eighteenth-Century Literature," *Studies in Eighteenth-Century Culture* 13 (1984): 249–70.

5. Sigmund Freud, *Dora: An Analysis of a Case of Hysteria*, trans. Douglas Bryan, ed. Philip Rieff (New York: Collier Books, 1963); Jane Gallop, *The Daughter's Seduction: Feminism and Psychoanalysis* (Ithaca, N.Y.: Cornell University Press, 1982); Charles Bernheimer and Claire Kahane, eds., *In Dora's Case: Freud—Hysteria—Feminism* (New York: Columbia University Press, 1985).

6. Michel Butor, "Travel and Writing," *Mosaic* 8 (1974): 1–16.

7. Johann Wolfgang von Goethe, *Italian Journey*, trans. W. H. Auden and Elizabeth Mayer (1962; reprint, San Francisco: North Point Press, 1982), p. 273.

8. Charles Batten, *Pleasurable Instruction: Form and Convention in Eighteenth-Century Travel Literature* (Berkeley: University of California Press, 1978); Michel de Certeau, *Heterologies: Discourse on the Other*, trans. Brian Massumi (Minneapolis: University of Minnesota Press, 1986), pp. 69–71; Percy Adams, *Travel Literature and the Evolution of the Novel* (Lexington: University Press of Kentucky, 1983); George B. Parks, *The English Traveler to Italy*, vol. 1: *The Middle Ages to 1525* (Stanford, Calif.: Stanford University Press, 1954).

9. Mikhail Bakhtin, *The Dialogic Imagination*, ed. Michael Holquist, trans. Caryl Emerson and Michael Holquist (Austin: University of Texas Press, 1981), p. 103.

10. Quoted in Allison Lockwood, *Passionate Pilgrims: The American Traveler in Great*

Britain, 1800–1914 (Rutherford, N.J.: Fairleigh Dickinson University Press, 1981), p. 150.

11. Henry Theodore Tuckerman, *Isabel; or Sicily, a Pilgrimage* (Philadelphia: Lea and Blanchard, 1839), pp. 15–16.

12. Edward Gibbon, *Memoirs of My Life*, ed. Georges A. Bonnard (London: Thomas Nelson, 1966), p. 135.

13. James Fenimore Cooper, *Excursions in Italy* (London: Richard Bentley, 1838), vol. 1, pp. 47–49. The complicated history of this edition of Cooper's travels is recounted in James Fenimore Cooper, *Gleanings in Europe, Italy*, ed. John Conron and Constance Ayers Denne (Albany: State University of New York Press, 1981), pp. xxvii–xxviii.

14. For a survey of these texts, see Harold E. Smith, *American Travellers Abroad: A Bibliography of Accounts Published Before 1900* (Carbondale: Southern Illinois University Press, 1969).

15. James Thomas Flexner, *The Light of Distant Skies: History of American Painting, 1760–1835* (New York: Dover, 1954), p. 160.

16. Nathaniel Hawthorne, *The Marble Faun, or The Romance of Monte Beni* (New York: Penguin Books, 1961), p. 14.

17. Rembrandt Peale, *Notes on Italy, Written During a Tour in the Years 1829–1830* (Philadelphia: Carey and Lea, 1831), p. 4.

18. Ibid., p. 5.

19. Ibid., p. 137.

20. Flexner, *Light of Distant Skies*, p. 161.

21. David F. Dorr, *A Coloured Man Around the World: By A Quadroon* (Cleveland: the author, 1858), pp. 104–5.

22. Ibid., pp. 106–7. Here Dorr's complaints about morality echo those of Stendahl: "A sense of duty . . . has no hold on the heart of the *lazzarone*. If, in a blind fit of anger, he should chance to kill his best friend, yet still his God, *San Gennaro*, will grant him forgiveness" (*Rome, Naples and Florence*, trans. Richard N. Coe [New York: Braziller, 1959], p. 124).

23. Peale, *Notes on Italy*, p. 205.

24. Cooper, *Excursions in Italy*, pp. 4–5.

25. Washington Irving [Geoffrey Crayon, pseud.], *Tales of a Traveller* (Philadelphia: Carey and Lea, 1837), p. 48.

26. Goethe, *Italian Journey*, p. 272.

27. Hawthorne, *Marble Faun*, p. 117.

28. Peale, *Notes on Italy*, p. 3.

29. Ibid., p. 205.

30. Tuckerman, *Isabel*, p. 31.

31. Hawthorne, *Marble Faun*, p. 118.

32. Ibid., p. 50.

33. Ibid., p. 109.

34. Ibid., p. 244.

35. For discussions of *The Marble Faun* and Hawthorne's views of aesthetic response, see John Dolis, "Hawthorne's Metonymic Gaze: Image and Object," *American Literature* 56 (October 1984): 362–78; Thomas Brumbaugh, "Concerning Nathaniel Hawthorne and Art as Magic," *American Imago* 11 (1954): 399–405; Jonathan Auerbach, "Executing the Model: Painting, Sculpture, and Romance-writing in Haw-

thorne's *The Marble Faun*," *ELH* 47 (1980): 103–20; Rita K. Collin, "Hawthorne and the Anxiety of Aesthetic Response," *The Centennial Review* 4 (Fall 1984): 28–29, 94–104; Carol Hanberry Mackay, "Hawthorne, Sophia, and Hilda as Copyists: Duplication and Transformation in *The Marble Faun*," *Browning Institute Studies* 12 (1984): 93–120; and Paul Brodtkorb, "Art Allegory in *The Marble Faun*," *PMLA* 77 (June 1962): 254–67.

36. Peale, *Notes on Italy*, p. 211.

37. Ibid., p. 52.

38. Cooper, *Excursions in Italy*, p. 17.

39. Hawthorne, *Marble Faun*, p. 140.

40. In the chapter "*The Marble Faun* and the Space of American Letters" (*High Resolution* [New York: Oxford University Press, 1989], pp. 129–51) Henry Sussman discusses the significance of this "goddess" as part of Hawthorne's "fictive program, in which the image is the source of energy and illumination" (p. 148). Furthermore, the story of Kenyon's miraculous discovery echoes that of the miraculous discovery of the Laocoön. Here, "uncovering" the art of the past is a form of animation more powerful than copying. Felice de Fredi, who discovered the Laocoön among the ruins of the Baths of Titus on January 14, 1506, has his good fortune recorded on his tombstone at the Aracoeli church.

41. The standard formulation for this problem remains Paul de Man, "The Rhetoric of Temporality," in *Interpretation: Theory and Practice*, ed. Charles Singleton (Baltimore: Johns Hopkins University Press, 1969), pp. 173–209.

42. William Gilpin, "On Picturesque Travel," in *Eighteenth Century Critical Essays*, ed. Scott Elledge (Ithaca, N.Y.: Cornell University Press, 1961), vol. 2, p. 1063. For material regarding the background to these views, see also Elizabeth Wheeler Manwaring, *Italian Landscape in Eighteenth Century England: A Study Chiefly of the Influence of Claude Lorrain and Salvator Rosa on English Taste, 1700–1800* (New York: Russell and Russell, 1965).

43. In *Memoirs of My Life*, Gibbon writes: "In my journal the place and moment of conception are recorded: the fifteenth of October 1764, in the close of evening, as I sat musing on the Church of the Zoccolanti or Franciscan friars, while they were singing vespers in the Temple of Jupiter on the ruins of the Capitol" (p. 136). The "surprise ending" of Edith Wharton's "Roman Fever" is in fact a pun on Gibbon's legend of "conception" (*Roman Fever and Other Stories* [New York: Scribner, 1964], pp. 9–24).

44. See, for example, Peale's account of a "scenic exhibition" of the "Tragedy of Desdemona" (*Notes on Italy*, pp. 161–63) and "the contrivance and exhibition of living pictures" at "the residence of a Scottish gentleman of fortune" (pp. 164–65), and Cooper's account of "an entertainment" involving the caricature of various "national traits" at an English residence in Tuscany (*Excursions in Italy*, pp. 50–51).

45. Peale, *Notes on Italy*, p. 188.

46. Tuckerman, *Isabel*, p. 32.

47. Ibid., p. 36.

48. Cooper, *Excursions in Italy*, p. 23.

49. Rembrandt Peale, *Graphics: A Manual of Drawing and Writing for the Use of Schools and Families* (New York: J. P. Peaslee, 1835).

50. Goethe, *Italian Journey*, p. 125.

51. Hawthorne, *Marble Faun*, p. 54.

52. Peale, *Notes on Italy*, p. 304.

53. Goethe, *Italian Journey*, p. 227.

54. The prison window is described in *The Marble Faun*, p. 317; the grating at the Vatican, in Nathaniel Hawthorne, *The French and Italian Notebooks*, Centenary Edition of the Works of Nathaniel Hawthorne, ed. Thomas Woodson (Columbus: Ohio State University Press, 1980), vol. 14, p. 86.

55. Hawthorne, *French and Italian Notebooks*, p. 125.

56. Ibid., p. 296.

57. Irving, *Tales of a Traveller*, pp. 43–44.

58. Hawthorne, *Marble Faun*, pp. 212–13.

59. Ibid., p. 213.

60. Ibid., pp. 72–73.

61. Ibid., p. 73.

62. Ibid., p. 76.

63. Ibid., p. 324.

64. Diane Long Hoeveler, "La Cenci: The Incest Motif in Hawthorne and Melville," *American Transcendental Quarterly* 44 (1979): 247–59; Frederick Crews, *The Sins of the Fathers* (London: Oxford University Press, 1966); Philip Young, *Hawthorne's Secret: An Un-Told Tale* (Boston: Godine, 1984); Gloria C. Erlich, *Family Themes and Hawthorne's Fiction: The Tenacious Web* (New Brunswick, N.J.: Rutgers University Press, 1984).

65. This point is mentioned in Young, *Hawthorne's Secret*, p. 42. Mackay ("Hawthorne, Sophia, and Hilda as Copyists," p. 116, n. 5) cites the following texts as questioning both the identity of the figure and the attribution to Guido Reni: Francesco Guerazzi, *Beatrice Cenci*, trans. Luigi Monti (London: National Alumni, 1906); Corrado Ricci, *Beatrice Cenci*, trans. Morris Bishop and Henry Longan Stuart (New York: Boni and Liveright, 1925), vol. 2, pp. 280–88; and Isabel Stevenson Monro and Kate M. Monro, *Index to Reproductions of European Paintings* (New York: Wilson, 1956).

66. Hawthorne, *French and Italian Notebooks*, p. 92.

67. Ibid., p. 93.

68. "The Birthmark," in *Hawthorne's Short Stories*, ed. Newton Arvin (New York: Knopf, 1961), pp. 177–93; "Alice Doane's Appeal," ibid., pp. 411–22. We should note that as the passage ends, Leonard decides to carry Walter's body off: "the face still wore a likeness of my father; and because my soul shrank from the fixed glare of the eyes, I bore the body to the lake, and would have buried it there. But before his icy sepulchre was hewn, I heard the voices of two travellers and fled" (p. 417).

69. Hawthorne, *Marble Faun*, p. 330.

7

Ceci Tuera Cela: Graffiti as Crime and Art

> The law permits me to write; it asks only that I write in a style
> other than *my own!* I am allowed to show the face of my mind,
> but, first, I must give it a prescribed expression. . . . Prescribed
> expressions mean only *bonne mine á mauvais jeu.*
>
> Marx, "Remarks on the New Instructions to the
> Prussian Censors" (1842)

> There is therefore a good and a bad writing: the good and
> natural is the divine inscription in the heart and the soul; the
> perverse and artful is technique, exiled in the exteriority of the
> body. Derrida, *Of Grammatology* (1967)

I have taken my title from Victor Hugo's self-conscious diversion in
Notre-Dame de Paris: "le livre tuera l'édifice." In this little essay,
Hugo contends that the mechanical reproduction of print will destroy
the monumental architecture of the Middle Ages, that the innovations of the press will thereby kill the solidity of the Church, and
that a change in mode of expression is a change in human thought.
Here Hugo takes as his subject the inverted teleology of certain
loss: "L'homme qui a écrit ce mot sur ce mur s'est effacé, il y a
plusieurs siècles, du milieu des générations, le mot s'est à son tour
effacé du mur de l'église, l'église elle-même s'effacera bientôt peut-
être de la terre."[1]

   If for Hugo history is a progressive erasure, from another perspective—that of postmodernism—history is a progressive, and self-
contradicting, accumulation. This accumulation of subjectivities,

practices, goods, and rationalities appears within the framework of a commodity system that can take up even its own negation and reinscribe it within the discourse of novelty. The capacity for the reinscription of negation as novelty is evident in a variety of postmodern cultural forms—*le mode rétro*, kitsch, the "functional" ornamentation of postmodern architecture[2]—but it is particularly evident in the axiological premises shaping graffiti as writing, painting, dirt, and crime.

These premises, formulating the boundary between practices and artifactuality, continue a debate we have encountered before in these studies, a debate at least as old as the *Phaedrus*, regarding a conflict between a divine and transcendent writing and a "bad" writing—laborious, human, and literal.[3] But more dramatically, such premises center on a current crisis in the situation of the artwork—a crisis modulated between the ephemeral and the classic, between the vernacular and the law, between the brand name and the signature, and between commodity production and artistic practices. If modernist aesthetic theory suffered from the disjunction between spirituality and sensuality,[4] postmodern aesthetic theory suffers from a disjunction between intention and necessity erupting in the relations between artistic reproduction and reception. For it is the nature of the commodity system, of its compelling systematicity per se, to replace labor with magic, intrinsicality with marketing, authoring with ushering.

Explanations or descriptions of axiological premises should take as their point of departure the locations of contradiction within those premises. Because at the present time graffiti are both outlawed and venerated, they provide such a point of departure. Radically taken up as both crime and art, graffiti have, in recent years, been the site of a conflict regarding the status of the artist and the artwork in contemporary culture. The production and reception of graffiti show how the articulation of the art object proceeds according to certain axiological practices. It is not that the dismissal and veneration of graffiti are two oppositional gestures; rather, these gestures are part of a reciprocal and interdependent system of axiological practices tied into the larger values of the commodity culture. The "criminal art" of graffiti could arise in its present form only from a crisis in the situation of art objects as commodities: while graffiti emerge as a statement of this conflict on the level of the culture of the street, we see the same crisis outlined in "high" art's inversion of art's commodity status through recent developments in environmental, conceptual, and performance art. We can here specify a process whereby consumer culture, which is literally in the business of inventing arbitrary value and of circumscribing intrinsicality, takes up what is "not valuable" precisely to reinforce the structure of that gesture of articulation.[5]

In this sense, the divergent attitudes toward graffiti are not only a matter of the interests of one social group or class posited against another, but can be seen as parts of a complex relationship among authorities, powers, institutions, and modes of artistic production in the broadest sense. Here then is, I believe, an analogy to the dramatic upheavals in artistic production at work in the decline of patronage and the ensuing transformations of subscription and commercial publishing witnessed from the early eighteenth century on. In that case, as the conditions for the production of writing in particular were transformed, so were new boundaries provided for the very conception of authoring and works. Problems of originality, collaboration, authenticity, nostalgia, and sentimentality certainly bridge these eighteenth-century and late-twentieth-century changes in conditions of production, but just as certainly these changes arise in specific and different circumstances. Thus to the extent that the plastic arts still rely on a system of patronage, there is a continuity in concepts of authoring and authenticity regarding the production of singular works.

The multiple reproduction of materials, however, makes originality appear in more and more abstract and conceptual ways. Graffiti in particular combine the remoteness, abstraction, and simultaneity characteristic of mechanical modes of production with the ethic of presence, signature, and individuality characteristic of handicrafts. As we shall see, they propose the ultimate daydream of consumer culture—the transformation of quantity into quality, and the redemption of individuality by means of a collectively held semiotic. The intensity of the struggle for space and resources within an urban environment makes the conflicts centered on graffiti particularly illuminating for a discussion of such artistic production. Surrounded by violently oppositional valuations, graffiti push us to a limit where the postmodern emergence and disappearance of such notions as quality, integrity, and taste may be described historically and specifically, without necessarily valorizing the a priori status of such terms, the kind of valorization found in modernism proper.

To focus on a sense of art as commodity—rather than, say, on a sense of art as play, or as experiment, or even as expression, fiction, invention, or the beautiful—enables us to examine how such categories as play, experiment, expression, fiction, invention, and the beautiful are summoned in the very process of canonizing this "crime" as "art." Methodology here must begin at a point where any intrinsic notion of the artistic is put into question or bracketed by social practices, rather than at a point where the phenomenon is already framed as art; in the latter case, the method can only reinscribe the conditions of its own attention. Obviously, this method is in conflict with any method that takes on a liberal pluralism of aesthetic judgments. This is at least in part a matter of the questions raised by the topic. The responses to graffiti make clear that in practices of production and apprehension, aesthetic valuation is a process of repression and emergence, erasure and reinscription. Thus it is also necessary to put into question any account of axiological practices that is transcendent and equivocal, if only because such a model itself is tied into notions of the classic and assumptions of transcendent consciousness.[6]

The goal here is to account for the *presentness* of the phenomenon at hand. Hence it is necessary to take into consideration the specificity of contemporary consumer culture. It is also necessary to take into consideration a set of manipulations and resistances to that culture, by which the culture's very structure marks off a closed arena of consumption. The theme of access—access to discourse, access to goods, access to the reception of information—has import for the creation of such a methodology in a profound sense, calling into question the relations between a micro- and a macro-analysis: the insinuating and pervasive forms of the mass culture are here known only through localizations and adaptations. Graffiti as a phenomenon vividly take on the form and thematic of that tension as graffiti writers or artists address the relation that those cut off from consumption bear to consumerism, and as they address the ways the consumer culture absorbs and reinscribes all other forms of cultural production.

It is not necessarily the intention of graffiti writers or artists to point to the paradoxes of consumer culture; rather, the paradoxes inherent in the production and reception of graffiti are paradoxes shaped by the contingencies of this historical conjuncture. Thus there is a certain risk of "trendiness"—or, just the same, a risk of datedness—in taking graffiti as a subject, but it is the very ephemerality of graffiti that is of interest here. Between May 1988 and May 1989, New York City officials declared New York's subways nearly, and then completely, free of graffiti. But meanwhile, graffiti appeared in new locations in New York and called forth new legal restrictions in London and Los Angeles.[7] The repression of graffiti in one location seems inevitably to be accompanied by their emergence in another. This sense of ephemerality, the sense that one's subject may disappear or relocate by morning, is itself the condition of writing through any aspect of a continually novelized economy.

Writing on graffiti, moreover, summons the specters of parasitism and "bad taste," for graffiti push us to a point that breaks down the very usefulness of notions of taste and originality and thus call for the relocation of *taste* within its historical (liberal/democratic) milieu.[8] Even the materiality of artworks such as graffiti must be historicized, for as Jean Baudrillard and Xavier Rubert de Ventós have shown us, the facility for "good taste" in the post-Puritan upper classes is a facility for the suppression of the sensual and the emergence of fine discrimination and careful mutability.[9] Thus the interplay between materiality, mediation, and erasure in graffiti provides a commentary on the relation that theories of taste bear to the structure of consumerism. The axiological model that depends upon the exercise of taste amid a panoply of objects no longer is suited to an object of study that takes as its very point or focus consumerism's patterns of suppression and emergence with regard to art objects. We here find the necessity of rejecting an axiological model in which elements have equivocal standing, mutuality, and reciprocity as items for consumption.[10] Even if awakened to the activities of discrimination, we are reminded by graffiti of the fleetingness of such judgments and of the embeddedness of the model under which they take place.

Who Is John Scott?

Since the 1960s, teenagers, mostly boys, in cities such as Philadelphia, New York, and Los Angeles (the loci of this strongly local

Figure 9
A variety of graffiti forms—tags, throw-ups, pieces—appear on this wall. Note, in particular, the commentary "UGLY" written on the *R* in *ERX*. (Photograph by Debora Kodish, Director, Philadelphia Folklore Project)

essay) have engaged in a practice of graffiti writing that is public and exterior and has a particular focus (figure 9). Using markers, pens, and/or spray paint, they have written their names, in the form of nicknames or special graffiti names called "tags," on subway cars, public buildings, walls, and many other exterior surfaces. For example, several early Philadelphia writers earned their legendary status by writing their tags on a jet at the airport and on an elephant at the Philadelphia zoo. Graffiti writers have distinctive codes of style and behavior, both individual (one's particular style of writing) and local (New York style, for example), that are readily recognized by those who practice graffiti. This style has only occasionally to do with the referent or legibility of graffiti. In fact, the term "wild style" is used for letters that cannot be read as anything except the mark of an individual's (now past) presence at the scene.

I will outline more specifically these practices, but it should be clear from the outset that I am not concerned here with the more hidden forms of graffiti writing, such as bathroom graffiti, that have often been the focus of psychological studies. Nor am I concerned with the writing one finds prior to this development, like the mark of a high-school prank ("Class of '58") or graffiti of the "John loves Mary" type. My point is not that there is no relation among these forms, but that the public and institutionalized production of the kind of graffiti I address, and its consistent emphasis upon the *name*, make it of quite different interest to us here. Perhaps a counter-example will help clarify my neglect for now of the earlier forms; whereas such forms are anonymous messages to an abstract public, the forms I will discuss are the personal signatures of an individual style, designed to be read by a particular audience in particular ways.

A Philadelphia madman named John Scott has, over the past ten years or so, placed red "bumper stickers" printed with black letters reading "Who Is John Scott?" in hundreds of locations throughout the city. If we juxtapose the practice of John Scott with the practices of contemporary graffiti writers, we might conclude that the key to John Scott's madness lies in the mass-production, the distanced compulsion, of his question; for John Scott has no style, no hand-writing, coterminous with a private body. The question of John Scott's identity is a social question that Scott is compelled to reca-pitulate, virtually to map, as the ephemeral trace of his journeys across town; the radical alienation of Scott's gesture lies in its perfect merging, its perfect identification, with that exteriority. Scott's body is an extension of the machine that poses the question; the *himself* is the always deferred place or location of the question's posing. The fame of Scott has no referent other than the surface of its own repetition. It is as if someone had decided to mass-produce Haw-thorne's symbol of the footprint and to thereby erase its authentic context of "original" experience.

My point is to contrast Scott's gesture with the practice of the graffiti writer. (Graffiti "artists" call themselves "writers," so to avoid further confusion the more familiar term will be used.) The graffiti writer's goal is a stylization inseparable from the body, a stylization that, in its impenetrable "wildness," could surpass even linguistic reference and serve purely as the concrete evidence of an individual existence and the reclamation of the environment through the label of the personal. Here we see connections to the vaunting personal ambition of a figure such as Chatterton, caught between the conflicting worlds of feudal patronage and Grub Street. But we also are reminded that Chatterton's forgeries depended upon, and manipulated, local pride—that of either Bristol in particular or England in general. Furthermore, Chatterton's forgeries were tied to a patriarchal romance in which his personality could emerge only under the sponsorship of an idealized father. Graffiti artists who turn to the patronage system for the fine arts must either follow the inversions of the avant-garde promoted by the galleries or accept the dutiful civic realism promoted by the state. The only other alternative is to participate in the displacements offered by the criminal activity of graffiti, and so remain outside the sphere of artistic production as defined by the larger culture.

The "victims" of graffiti project a graffiti writer in the mode of John Scott, singular and disturbed. Yet ethnographies, perhaps in their own village, and village-making, tradition, characterize graffiti in contemporary urban environments as an indigenous or folk form carried out by a community of writers relatively homogeneous in age (nine to sixteen).[11] This community is structured by an explicit hierarchy: beginners (called "toys") work with master writers as apprentices. The toy generally progresses from writing simple "tags" on any surface to writing "throw-ups" (larger tags thrown onto inaccessible surfaces or the outsides of subway cars) to writing "pieces" (short for masterpieces: symbolic and/or figurative works such as landscapes, objects, letters, or characters drawn on a variety of surfaces).[12]

Given this social background to the practice of graffiti, the function of graffiti appears repeatedly, nevertheless, in the native scheme of things as a matter of individuation. One of the principle rules of the graffiti writer's code of ethics is that a writer cannot copy, or "bite," either the tag or the style of another writer without instigating a cross-out war or, more directly, a first-person fight. The reputation of the writer depends upon the recognizability of his or her style, but even more importantly upon his or her facility for "getting up," for making one's mark as frequently and extensively as possible. Although writers with "messy handwriting" are spoken of with contempt, the sloppiest writer whose name appears frequently throughout a city will have far more status than the most polished writer whose work is limited to just a few examples. Thus the honorific titles "King of the Line," "All City—Insides," and "King of the

City" are bestowed, regardless of style, on those writers respectively whose tags appear in every car of a certain subway line, on the insides of every subway car, and in as many locations as possible.

There is no question that graffiti's investment in frequency of production borrows from the methods of commodity advertising and publicity. The writer is his or her own "agent," and here agency as artistic expression is a tautological process of self-promotion miming the reflexive signifiers of fashion and "packaging." But as will become more and more apparent, this borrowing of advertising methods is a matter of adaptation, manipulation, and localization. As predicted in Andy Warhol's famous "everyone will be famous for fifteen minutes" maxim, "Fame" becomes "fame" as celebrity and appreciation are closely restricted to the esoteric codes of the folk community. Writers frequently mention the thrill of seeing their "tags" on the television news as backdrop to an event being filmed, and this is a particularly apt metaphor for graffiti's interstitial relation to the structures of the culture in general.

Because writing graffiti is illegal and quite specifically dangerous, the aesthetic criteria at work in the writers' schemes of evaluation are a matter of conception and execution more than a matter of judgments regarding the qualities of a final artifact. Writers will often make evaluative comments part of their "pieces," leaving a history of the constraints on their work: "Sorry about the drips," "It's cold," "Cheap paint," "Too late. Too tired."[13] Graffiti writers plan larger pieces, and practice smaller ones, in sketchbooks called "black books" or "piece books," and the execution of a large piece depends upon "racking up" or "inventing"—that is, stealing—sometimes hundreds of cans of spray paint and hundreds of markers before a piece can be begun.[14] The graffiti writer often must be an accomplished thief, athlete, and con artist; thus "personal" style itself is a matter applied not simply to the artifact, but to many aspects of the graffiti writer's everyday behavior. These obstacles to production are a major factor in the evaluation of graffiti by the folk community of writers, and a special weight is thereby given to frequency of production when such evaluations are made.

It is important to reemphasize that the art of graffiti is an art of the autograph; the tag is a signature adopted from the writers' given names, from nicknames, or from names chosen for their sound or appearance. For example, a Philadelphia writer chose the name PARIS, but after making a few tags decided that the *S* did not offer good visual closure, and so added an *H* because he felt the block letter of the *H* gave the name a more finished quality, hence his tag PARISH.[15] And black books serve as autograph books as well as sketchbooks: writers ask more accomplished writers to autograph their books; toys especially prize such collections and study the autographs to determine how individual effects are accomplished. In this sense, contemporary graffiti's antecedents would seem to be not only the privatized anonymity of indoor forms of graffiti, but also the slam books or autograph books that have been long a tradition of American adolescents—books used to define emerging identities within the adolescent social group, as teenagers collect the signatures, written in the most stylish handwriting, of their friends.

Finally we should note that the function of individuation, stylization, and uniqueness would also seem to be served by the appropriation of the metaphor of the robot in both graffiti and its sister art, break dancing. The distinctly geometric letters called "Robot Style," or styles with names such as "Computer" and "Mechanical" style,[16] find their complement in the mixture of freeze-frame stopping found in break dancing and its accompanying handmade "scratches" (moving a record back and forth on a turntable by hand).[17] This mixture of body movement and the imitation of mechanical action is mirrored as well in the homemade innovations that diversify the function of the graffiti writer's materials: improvised spray-can tops, improvised inks, and transformations of marker tips[18] all demonstrate the imposition of individualized style upon mass forms and tools. Writers do not conceive of their role as one within a larger narrative or historical structure other than this specific tradition of graffiti writing; rather, they place their arts within the interruptions of social life, marking off a physical space for a time and inscribing it within an individuality both unique and ephemeral. In this way, graffiti resembles the "cut" frame of cinema, refusing metonymy, refusing—here negating—an "outside" in favor of an "inside out," a focus on the separation. Here an argument Manfredo Tafuri has made regarding the technological objects to be found, rather than identified, in Piranesi's *Prisons* is illuminating:

The universe of pure *power*, of the absolute alienation of the subject, is not by chance a "mechanical" universe. A judgment on the part of Piranesi is implicit here. He sees the mechanical universe, kingdom par excellence of the artificial, as the place where there occurs the definitive loss of primordial organicity, of the union between the world of nature and the universe of human institutions.[19]

Here the graffiti writer is the logical end of organicity as well as the logical product of consumerism: the graffiti writer is produced by a repetition, an interstitial mark that defines the alterity of an alienation unrecouperable by older concepts of artistic production. The work's severance from the body and its "intimacy" with technology mime the systematization of labor and the projection of surface by means of repetition.

Graffiti as Dirt

It is easy to see how graffiti becomes dirt once we consider, in the mode of much recent cognitive anthropology, that dirt is something in the wrong place or the wrong time and consequently something ranked at the bottom of a hierarchical scale of values.[20] It is of course the fixity of the scale and the arbitrariness of its contents at any given point that provide the scale with its particular power. But more specifically, graffiti can be seen as a *permanent* soiling of the environment simply in their constant replicability, their emphasis upon repetition and replacement. Graffiti are widely considered to be a practice of *defacement:* an application that destroys the significance of their material base just as the defacement of coins invalidates their worth, their face value, and proves a threat to the monetary system as a whole.

The analogy to the defacement of money is particularly apt, for graffiti are considered a threat not only to the surface upon which they are applied, but also to the entire system of meanings by which such surfaces acquire value, integrity, and significance. Thus we find former New York mayor John Lindsay saying that he and his staff had never really wondered whether graffiti were "anything but defacement."[21] The Philadelphia City Ordinance banning the sale of spray paint to minors states that graffiti "contributes to the blight and degradation of neighborhoods, and even discourages the formation of business." And the head of the police gang-control unit in Los Angeles declares that "graffiti decreases property value, and signed buildings on block after block convey the impression that the city government has lost control, that the neighborhood is... sliding toward anarchy."[22]

This is graffiti as nonculture. Linked to the dirty, the animal, the uncivilized, and the profane, contemporary urban graffiti signify an interruption of the boundaries of public and private space, an eruption of creativity and movement outside and through the claims of street, façade, exterior, and interior by which the city is articulated. Graffiti make claims upon materiality, refusing to accept the air as the only free or ambiguously defined space. The practice of graffiti emphasizes the free commercial quality of urban spaces in general, a quality in contrast to the actual paucity of available private space. In this, graffiti hearken to what is a much older, and perhaps mostly Latin, sense of the street. For example, Helen Tanzer, in her study of the graffiti of Pompeii, notes this tradition:

> one reason why shops were tolerated in a residential district is that in the genial climate of Campania most of the time was spent out of doors, as is the case today, and the houses faced inward in the fashion familiar in the patio type of house throughout the Latin countries. The peristyle gave freedom and privacy to the household.[23]

We may extend Louis Kahn's contention that "the street is a room by agreement" to include the street as playground, ballfield, and billboard by agreement—or by conflict, subterfuge, and the exercise of power and privilege. A striking example of graffiti's dual obsessions with names and with publicity is an ongoing "masterpiece" along the main commuter-train tunnel of Philadelphia's Thirtieth Street Station. Here a series of ornamented tombstones have been drawn, each marking the death of a celebrity (John Belushi, Marilyn Monroe, among others). Furthermore, the "tombstones" are divided symmetrically so that those who died drug-related deaths appear to the right and those who died of other causes to the left (figure 10).

To think of the street in this way is to confront the interior world of domestic genres—the still life, the window display, the arrangement of consumable objects—with a radical exteriority. This exteriority is characterized by movement and direction, by a body set into motion like a machine—but, as noted earlier, a machine made

Figure 10
"Tombstone" graffiti ornament a wall to the east of the Thirtieth Street
Station, Philadelphia. (Photograph by Debora Kodish, Director, Philadel-
phia Folklore Project)

singular, stylized, and individual. The accouterments of lettering in
graffiti—the characters and arrows—serve as heralds to the name,
pointing to its fluidity and speed. This characteristic sense of motion
arises from the necessity of working quickly under terrific constraints
and thus is a matter of a thematic arising from the graffiti writer's
hounded scene of production. But it is also a sense of motion that
relates to the mobility of the name and the sense of an author who
traverses the city. The subway car is the perfect surface for graffiti:
a moving name is set into motion by this traveling billboard. A name
that "gets around," that "goes places," must be seen against a
background of the fixed society it traverses and that society's continually deferred promise of personal mobility.

     Graffiti writers often argue that it is ethical to write on spaces that
have been abandoned or poorly maintained; it is considered a sign
of amateurism, however, to write on churches, private homes and
automobiles, and other clearly "private" property. Writers sometimes extend this argument to a complaint about the "emptiness"

or lack of signification characteristic, in their opinion, of public and corporate architecture overall.[24] To these buildings characterized by height and anonymity, the graffiti writer attaches the personal name written by hand on a scale perceptible to the individual viewer. In this sense, the graffiti writer argues for the personalization of wall writing and for the appropriation of the street by those who primarily inhabit it. Here the presence of the writer is posited against absenteeism and neglect; graffiti writers espouse an antimonumental politics, contrasting to the monument's abstraction and stasis the signature's personality, mobility, and vernacular, localized audience.

Despite the implicit sexual metaphor of "getting up" one's name, contemporary exterior graffiti are rarely, if ever, obscene, since the entire practice and valuation of graffiti among writers centers upon the importance of the tag or name and its frequent appearance. Yet the public and the law often declaim the obscenity of graffiti, and we might conclude that in a general sense the obscenity here is, as earlier noted, an utterance out of place. All display is a form of exposure; just as the spaces of reproduction in society are maintained through the regulation, by means of taboo and legitimation, of places and times for sexuality, so in this case do writing and figuration in the wrong place and time fall into the category of obscenity. The more illegible, or "wild style," the writing, the stronger is the public's assumption that the message must be obscene.[25]

Unlike other forms of dirt, graffiti, as a kind of vandalism, are intentional; and, even worse in the eyes of the law, graffiti are not in any physical sense ephemeral. In fact, for durability of surface and materials, graffiti are a far more permanent art than, say, painting on canvas. Yet city governments must make the claim that graffiti, like other pranks, are reversible or erasable, in order to legitimate the vast resources the state has expended on "graffiti maintenance." The New York City Transit Authority alone has spent up to $10 million a year in what it calls "normal graffiti maintenance" and has been willing to experiment with toxic chemical paint removers that provide clear threats to the health of Transit Authority workers and residents of neighborhoods bordering on the train yards.[26] Of course, graffiti do not exist in the singular work, but in a process of rampant reproduction. Through such maintenance programs, city governments have simply cleared more space for writing and thereby provided a needed service to the writers.

The intentionality of graffiti is accommodated by attributing graffiti's production to gangs, criminals, and the insane (for the public, not always mutually exclusive categories). On August 19, 1972, in the *New York Times*, Mayor Lindsay claimed it was "the Lindsay theory that the rash of graffiti madness was 'related to mental health problems.' "[27] This claim amended an earlier statement by the mayor that graffiti writers were "insecure cowards."[28] The Los Angeles government, in anticipation of the Olympics, violated standard constitutional rights regarding evidence and trial by jury in forcing gang members to clean up graffiti or go to jail, regardless of whether they could be proved guilty of having written the graffiti.[29] And the Philadelphia police have adopted the phrase "hard-core graffiti writers" to describe those apprehended in recent "sweep" arrests.[30]

These responses to graffiti may seem extreme in light of prevailing social values, yet liberal approaches to graffiti writing are even more insidious, if we consider them in light of the values of writers themselves. For the predominant liberal solution to the "graffiti problem" is the demand that (1) the writers "erase" or paint over their own work or that of others, usually with white or beige paint, and thereby "whitewash" their work, or (2) the writers become art *students*—that is, work with brushes on static materials in a figurative style, thus subjecting themselves to a form of realism that would hardly be demanded of most contemporary art students proper.

This "encouragement" of the writer's creativity is in effect a matter of disciplinary punishment, a punishment that takes as its thematic a generalized representation and simultaneous suppression of the signature that had been at the center of the graffiti artist's work. The project of erasure offers a replication of the liberal position of presenting categories without the hierarchical determinations that are the work of history. Here erasure is a powerful metaphor for liberalism's dependence upon forgetting. For example, the director of the Philadelphia Anti-Graffiti Task Force has announced that graffiti writers will be asked to go to "vacant housing projects and paint venetian blinds, flowers, or figures of human beings on boarded-up windows."[31] In figure 11 we can see this "solution" in the barely illusionist "forest" covering a walkway wall in the vicinity of the other graffiti depicted here. Thus the trompe l'oeil of the middle classes, the façade of civic values, is to be maintained as a punishment by those whose initial project was the destruction of such an illusion.

Figure 11
Trompe l'oeil art by the Philadelphia Anti-Graffiti Task Force covers the wall of an underpass at Twenty-second and Market streets, Philadelphia. Note the tags on the wall perpendicular to the sidewalk. (Photograph by Debora Kodish, Director, Philadelphia Folklore Project)

The graffiti signature, which marked in unmistakable color the truth of desolation and abandonment, is here replaced by the mere illusion of presence and a remarkable sense of "public appearances."

Foucault has argued that the function of discipline after the pastoral innovations of the Reformation is to individualize the subject and thus to individualize a continual self-surveillance.[32] Yet in the contemporary practice of graffiti writing, a public and publicized subjectivity is the point or focus of the illegal act; reformist efforts hope that the redemptive and penitent activity of erasure or cleansing will produce such self-surveillance, or that the anonymity and subjection of apprenticeship to an alien tradition will check the writer's ego and prepare him or her for the long hierarchical process of becoming an artist through institutions. It is also an effort to distance writers from their own production—to force writers to see graffiti from the viewpoint of a mediating discourse hitherto unavailable to them: the history of the tradition (and not as presented in the black books).

In a profound sense, the current "crisis" regarding graffiti is symptomatic of a crisis in the status of the body. On the one hand, there is the inappropriate display of the body and its reproductive power implicit in graffiti's signifying practices. The affront to the façade in graffiti writing might be considered an extension of the tradition of the criminal's self-marking and self-mutilation. In that tradition, one rebels against the imposed environment by inventing a new surface—the body's exterior—for the inscription of one's identity, writing upon that surface a set of social relations denied by one's imprisonment: lovers, family, the names of exotic places, the mottos of one's value system.[33] The criminal's assertion of the tattoo offers some consolation thereby for the state's confiscation of his or her fingerprint and for the insult of the mug shot.[34]

On the other hand, there is the threat of graffiti, articulated by their "victims" as an attack or form of violence. Here, the façade that graffiti inscribe is clearly a projection or an externalization of the private body of the middle classes. It is private property that has maintained appearances, that has put its best face forward, and graffiti's confiscation of the urban environment, their relentless proclamation that what is surface is what is public, poses the threat to exchange, to business as usual, noted in ordinances and police statements earlier. Here graffiti's emphasis upon elegance, speed, grace, and the sensuality of the body must be contrasted to the abstractions of wage labor and mechanical production represented by the surfaces they inscribe. Graffiti writers have put their subjectivity in the wrong place; it must be properly reassigned by disciplinary measures. Marx noted in *The German Ideology:* "The exclusive concentration of artistic talent in particular individuals and its suppression in the broad mass which is bound up with this, is a consequence of the division of labor."[35] Such reforms are designed in a true sense to find for the graffiti writer "a place in life" where he or she can make, in most circumscribed fashion, his or her "mark."

Graffiti as Art

We do not find the current fashion of venerating graffiti as gallery art far from these reformist efforts. The avant-garde here appears as a quarrel in the house of the bourgeoisie. The appropriation of graffiti by the art establishment has meant the retention of the signature, but the mode of execution and reproduction, equally essential to the graffiti aesthetic, has been dropped. The point is to make graffiti a commodity; to do so, one must clearly define their status as unique objects. One must invent a self-conscious intentionality that places the artist intertextually within the tradition as it is defined by critics and the art establishment in general.

Let me clarify this point by emphasizing once more that graffiti writers themselves explain their tradition in terms of individual and regional styles, while the apprenticeship and black-book aspects of their work commit them to a certain linear and even patriarchal view of their place as writers. Furthermore, the writers readily recognize their debt to the iconography of billboards and other forms of advertising, and to comic strips, logos, and commercial calligraphy. But this iconography quite literally points to the writer's name in the configuration of the "piece," and the pointing is another gesture of localization within the graffiti aesthetic. Thus the graffiti writer's sense of the tradition here is not the same as the tradition of the Tradition, not the same as Sidney Janis's introductory remarks in the catalogue of his Post-Graffiti show: "urban-bred, the graffiti artist continues the tradition of Pop Art which he admires."[36] Thus this show announces the death of graffiti proper (hence "post-graffiti")

and the rejuvenation of the pop art tradition that the Janis Gallery
was instrumental in presenting in the first place.

A dominant number of the most successful graffiti artists are in
fact art students proper, often middle-class adolescents who have
had contact with and befriended street artists. Calvin Tompkins
suggests in the *New Yorker*:

> Crude as it may be in execution, the work of these artists (Keith
> Haring, Kenny Scharf, Jean-Michel Basquiat, Ronnie Cutrone) has
> a certain sophistication—an awareness of such antecedents as Dubuf-
> fet's *"art brut,"* Cy Twombly's elegant scribbling, and the comic-
> book imagery of pop artists. The graffiti artists lack this sort of ref-
> erence—when they spray paint on canvas, it does not look like other
> art. Nor does it much resemble the work they used to do on trains.[37]

Tompkins's remarks make clear that the two complementary axes
of the art establishment's appropriation of graffiti are tradition and
adaptation. But the claiming of tradition in this much documented
case has skipped the track of graffiti's own history. This history
might move from the graffiti of the Athenian agora, Pompeii, and
Arabic traditions of place marking and camel brands to medieval
cathedral inscriptions, through the whole history of public, anonymous, generally political forms of art.[38] But in an important sense,
the tradition should not be dated before the late 1950s and the early
1960s, when this kind of autograph graffiti and the writers sharing
its legibility specifically arose. In Tompkins's account, this tradition
is derailed onto the track of art history, specifically the history of
painting as institutionally canonized—that is, as a progression of
individual artifacts worked by individual masters.

Thus graffiti are continually linked with the spontaneous, the
primitive, the real of this tradition—a "real" located in nature and
the body. Here the invention of a tradition for graffiti, particularly
as a form of "folk art," is the product of both nostalgia and currency.
Graffiti are valued as a dying art form, the Romantic heir to abstract
expressionism and pop art; they are also valued as the newest and
most fashionable art form, hence their thematics are often ones of
youthful tragedy. Despite an ongoing practice, a technological so-
phistication, and a rather rigid apprentice system, graffiti are appropriated by a discourse applauding their "fresh and spontaneous"
nature (Dolores Neumann in the Janis catalogue) or, as Norman

Mailer describes it in *The Faith of Graffiti*, "the impulse of the jungle to cover the walled tanks of technology." Claes Oldenburg's famous description of subway-car graffiti as a "bouquet from Latin America" equally contributes to this process of naturalization and primitivization. The widely held assumption on the part of graffiti's opponents that graffiti are practiced by those of African-American and Latin descent is probably a matter of racism. Martha Cooper and Henry Chalfant have noted the complicated mixture of cultural backgrounds found among New York writers: for example, the "crew" or team of writers known as "The Vamp Squad" has members of Peruvian, Scottish, Italian, African, Jordanian, Puerto Rican, and Albanian descent.[39] The dean of the Moore College of Art in Philadelphia announced at the opening of a show by "Lady Pink" at that institution that "the art world has domesticated a formerly feral animal."[40] And the popularity of graffiti art in Europe may be attributed, certainly in part, to European notions of the American frontier, the American city, and the high-tech romance of a contemporary colonial culture.

The movement of graffiti to canvas and gallery space continues the process of substitution by which historical contingency is mythologized. Mediating figures such as art students become the new graffiti artists and thus enable the street artists to "die off." Social workers and photographers become spokespersons and publicists for graffiti writers.[41] Acceptable, readable, and apprehensible in scale, graffiti painting is enclosed within a proper space and time, and is delimited for consumption as a singular artifact, an artifact that now *stands for*, is metonymic to, an infinity of wild-style tags that would have been previously available only to a simultaneous consciousness that is the quintessential urban daydream. Thus what was formerly a matter of desecration and even violence is now modulated to a matter of domestic consumption: enter *taste*, for either one likes the individual work or one does not. In the latter case the work, like any other consumer good, can be left for someone else to take up. The virtues of the good are, of course, assumed by the consumer, for the commodity's magic always lies in the substitution of the "labor" of consumption for the labor of production.[42]

Graffiti on canvas, graffiti as artwork or art objects, clearly are the invention of the institutions of art—the university, the gallery, the critic, the collector. And they are an invention designed to satisfy the needs of those institutions to assert their own spontaneity, class-lessness, flexibility, and currency—all qualities that can emerge only through a self-consciousness that negates them. We might ask why the commodity system has taken up graffiti writing as painting, for this transformation provokes some interesting problems. Here graffiti are moved from a permanent surface, the granite of the bank or the metal of the subway car, to the less durable background of canvas. Here graffiti are transformed from something indelible calling for erasure to something eternal calling for curating. Here graffiti are halted in their self-perpetuating and rampant motion and framed quite literally as static objects.

Cooper and Chalfant note that

> a subway car is sixty feet long and twelve feet high. To do a top-to-bottom (to paint the whole train) in the yard, where there is no convenient platform to stand on, a writer must climb up the side of the car and hang on with one hand while painting with the other; or, if his legs are long enough, he can straddle the distance between two parked trains.[43]

Thus the writer never sees the entire "piece" until, and if, it pulls out of the train yard. The motion of writing, constrained by these conditions, forecloses the possibility of a far view. Here such absorption is translated into the contemplation and distance of gallery art. The valuation of graffiti is an effort to accommodate through adaptation a novel threat to the status of the art object in general. To the extent that graffiti writers move off the street and into the gallery, the threat will be met. But there is no room in the gallery for that many writers, so we arrive again at graffiti's most intimidating aspect: its sheer numbers.

Brand Names

It is important to remember that the crime of graffiti is a crime in mode of production. Unlike pornography, graffiti is not a crime of content. Paradoxically, in graffiti that sign of proper training, discipline, and Puritan control over the body—good handwriting—is elevated to a dizzying perfection, a triumph over the constraints of materials and surface. And certainly the high tradition of art has long recognized the ascendence of the signature, which has made graffiti possible; we have only to think of the secular's encroachment upon the triptych, and later of de Kooning and Rauschenberg's collaborative erasure.

Part of the threat of graffiti is their claim that anyone can be an artist. Graffiti's system of masters and apprentices is theoretically available to anyone. But unlike other forms of mass creativity from *proletkult* to *lifestyle*, graffiti promise and indeed depend upon a dream of the individualized masses. They have borrowed from the repetitions of advertising and commercial culture an antiepitaph: the name's frequent appearance marks the stubborn ghost of individuality and intention in the mass culture, the ironic restatement of the artist as "brand name." Graffiti celebrate the final victory of the signature over the figure, the sign over the referent, by making claims on the very subjectivity invented by consumerism. In this sense they have gone beyond pop art, which always took on the abstractions of the exchange economy solely as a matter of thematics.[44] For graffiti have reenacted, within a vernacular setting, that culture's style of simultaneous distribution, erasure of authenticity, and insistent superficiality. Thus graffiti have borrowed from consumer culture not simply an iconography, but an entire rhetoric. And in the localization of that rhetoric lies their resistance to their own absorption into the larger commodity system. The discourse of graffiti is a discourse, thereby, of euphemism: the ornament covering the surface appears not simply in the pieces themselves, but also in the graffiti writer's presentation of self and in his or her antilanguage, which substitutes the tag for the proper name, and words like *nasty*, *the death*, *vicious*, *bad*, and *dirty* for the standard terms of approval in evaluation.[45]

But the larger threat of graffiti is their violation of the careful system of delineation by which the culture articulates the proper spaces for artistic production and reproduction. As suggested earlier, those who call graffiti a form of violence are not only invoking the process by which all violence penetrates the materiality of the body, but also calling our attention to graffiti's disregard of the boundaries of all materiality. It is not so much that graffiti are, after all, a public art; rather, graffiti point to the paradox of a public space that belongs to no one and to the paradoxes of privacy and face, presentation and display, by which surface, space, and the frontal view are gestures of respectability and respect toward a generalized order for its own sake.

Graffiti's own emphasis upon insides and outsides, differentiating the kinds of tags and pieces that can appear on various kinds of interior and exterior surfaces, underlines the ways in which graffiti work toward turning commodity relations inside out. For graffiti attempt a utopian and limited dissolution of the boundaries of property. Within the manufactured environment of the city, they point to the false juxtaposition by which the artistic is made part of the private and domestic, while its figure or referent stands outside in nature.[46] Furthermore, they elaborate upon an earlier cultural moment when, in a gesture perhaps slightly less desperate than that of the criminal's tattoo, the "personal" space of the body became a site of creativity and innovation during the mid- to late 1960s. In this elaboration, it is the city itself that now appears as a body—not an artifactual body held in common and available for display, but a body known as our own bodies are known: piecemeal, fragmented, needing an image or a signature.

Graffiti may be a petty crime, but their threat to value is an inventive one, for they form a critique of the status of all artistic artifacts, indeed a critique of all privatized consumption, and carry out that threat in full view, in repetition, so that the public has nowhere to look, no place to locate an averted glance. That critique is paradoxically mounted from a relentless individualism, an individualism that, with its perfected monogram, arose out of the paradox of all commodity relations in their attempt to create a mass individual, an ideal consumer, a necessarily fading star. The independence of the graffiti writer has been shaped by a freedom both promised and denied by those relations—a freedom of choice that is a freedom among delimited and clearly unattainable goods. While that paradise of consumption promised the transference of uniqueness from the artifact to the subject, graffiti underline again and again an imaginary uniqueness of the subject and a dissolution of artifactual status per se.

It is the style of the writer, relentlessly and simultaneously appearing across and through the city, that is graffiti's triumph over property and history. It is precisely graffiti's mere surface, repetition, lack of use, meaninglessness, and negativity that give us the paradox of *insight* with regard to the billboard of commodity culture. And this is exactly the point: graffiti have no lasting value, no transcendent significance. If my project here has been the redemption of methodology from such larger and ahistorical assumptions, it has also been to emphasize the fleeting and vernacular nature of such a redemption.

Notes

1. Victor Hugo, *Notre-Dame de Paris* (Paris: Librairie de L. Hachette, 1869), vol. 1, p. 2. The essay "Ceci Tuera Cela" is in the same volume, pp. 255–74.

2. See Fredric Jameson's "standard" formulations regarding the postmodern affinities for pastiche, the image, and a commodified history in his interconnecting essays, "Postmodernism and Consumer Society," in *The Anti-Aesthetic: Essays on Postmodern Culture*, ed. Hal Foster (Port Townsend, Wash.: Bay Press, 1983), pp. 111–25, and "Postmodernism, or the Cultural Logic of Late Capitalism," *New Left Review* 146 (1984): 53–92.

3. Plato, *Phaedrus*, in *The Works of Plato*, trans. B. Jowett (New York: Tudor, n.d.), vol. 3, p. 447. See also Jacques Derrida's discussion of the *Phaedrus* in *Of Grammatology*, trans. Gayatri Chakravorty Spivak (Baltimore: Johns Hopkins University Press, 1976): "the writing of truth in the soul, opposed by *Phaedrus* to bad writing (writing in the 'literal' [*propre*] and ordinary sense, 'sensible' writing, 'in space'), the book of Nature and God's writing, especially in the Middle Ages; all that functions as *metaphor* in these discourses confirms the privilege of the logos and founds the 'literal' meaning then given to writing: a sign signifying a signifier itself signifying an eternal verity, eternally thought and spoken in the proximity of a present logos" (p. 15).

4. Theodor Adorno, *Aesthetic Theory*, trans. C. Lenhardt, ed. Gretel Adorno and Rolf Tiedemann (London: Routledge & Kegan Paul, 1970), pp. 14–22, 128–47.

5. Michael Thompson has made a valuable analysis of this process in *Rubbish Theory: The Creation and Destruction of Value* (Oxford: Oxford University Press, 1979). More recently, Barbara Herrnstein Smith has extended the discussion of reclassification as a matter of a facility for adaptation: "It may be noted here that human beings have evolved as distinctly opportunistic creatures and that our survival, both as individuals and as a species, continues to be enhanced by our ability and inclination to reclassify objects and to 'realize' and 'appreciate' novel and alternate functions for them" ("Contingencies of Value," *Critical Inquiry* 10 [September 1983]: 13).

6. For recent attacks on Kantian disinterestedness, see the fuller argument posed by Barbara Herrnstein Smith in *Contingencies of Value: Alternative Perspectives for Critical Theory* (Cambridge, Mass.: Harvard University Press, 1988), especially pp. 64–72; and Pierre Bourdieu, *Distinction: A Social Critique of the Judgement of Taste*, trans. Richard Nice (Cambridge, Mass.: Harvard University Press, 1984), pp. 485–500.

7. For announcements of the decline in graffiti, see *New York Times*, 6 May 1988, p. 1, and *New York Times*, 10 May 1989, sec. Al, p. L. On London, see *New York Times*, 13 October 1988, p. 9. For Los Angeles, see "Driver's License Suspension

Passed as Graffiti Penalty," *Los Angeles Times*, 26 May, 1989, p. 36. Declarations of the disappearance of graffiti are both a sign of increased vigilance on the part of the authorities and a rhetoric of public welfare promoted by the press.

8. See, for example, Paul Rabinow, "Representations Are Social Facts," in *Writing Culture: The Poetics and Politics of Ethnography*, ed. James Clifford and George E. Marcus (Berkeley: University of California Press, 1986): "I would add that if it arose in the 1960's in part as a reaction to the academic canonization of the great modernist artists, post-modernism, moving quickly, has itself succeeded in entering the academy in the 1980's. It has successfully domesticated and packaged itself through the proliferation of classificatory schemes, the construction of canons, the establishment of hierarchies, blunting of offensive behavior, acquiescence to university norms. Just as there are now galleries for graffiti in New York, so, too, there are theses being written on graffiti, break dancing, and so on, in the most avant-garde departments" (p. 248).

9. Jean Baudrillard, *Le Système des objets* (Paris: Gallimard, 1968), p. 43; Xavier Rubert de Ventós, *Heresies of Modern Art*, trans. J. S. Bernstein (New York: Columbia University Press, 1980), pp. 48–59.

10. See Raymond Williams, "Taste," in *Keywords* (New York: Oxford University Press, 1976), pp. 264–66.

11. Information in this section is abstracted from Craig Castleman's important and comprehensive study, *Getting Up: Subway Graffiti in New York* (Cambridge, Mass.: MIT Press, 1982); from Martha Cooper and Henry Chalfant, *Subway Art* (New York: Holt, Rinehart and Winston, 1984); and from a series of radio interviews conducted by Terry Gross at WUHY, Philadelphia, on the following dates: interview with "Cornbread" and "Parish" and interview with Henry Chalfant, February 10, 1984; interview with "Lady Pink," April 11, 1984; interview with Madeline Smith, Henry Chalfant, and call-in show, May 3, 1984. I am grateful to Danny Miller and Terry Gross of WUHY for providing me with recordings of these programs, and to Sally Banes for her comments on graffiti and break dancing when a preliminary version of this paper was delivered at the Tenth International Congress on Aesthetics in Montreal in August 1984.

12. Castleman, *Getting Up*, pp. 71–82.

13. Cooper and Chalfant, *Subway Art*, p. 38.

14. In *Getting Up*, Castleman records the term as "racking up." Norman Mailer's essay accompanying Mervyn Kurlansky and Jon Naar's photographs in *The Faith of Graffiti* (New York: Praeger, 1973), records the term as "inventing" (n.p.; see section 2).

15. "Parish," interview by Terry Gross, February 10, 1984.

16. For comments on style names, see Castleman, *Getting Up*, pp. 25–26, 55–65. In *Subway Art*, Cooper and Chalfant quote Kase 2, a "King of Style": "Wildstyle was the coordinate style and then computer. That's what I brought out. Nobody else can get down with it 'cause it's too fifth-dimensional. I call it the fifth dimensional step parallel staircase, 'cause it's like computer style in a step formulated way. It's just sectioned off the way I want. Like if I take a knife and cut it, and slice you know I'll slice it to my own section and I'll call it computer style" (p. 71).

17. See Robert Palmer, "Street Smart Rapping Is Innovative Art Form," *New York Times*, 4 February 1985, p. C-13.

18. In *Subway Art*, Cooper and Chalfant display a photograph showing the differ-

ence between "fat caps" and "skinny caps" and describe the way nozzles are fitted onto spray-paint cans to achieve different effects (p. 33).

19. Manfredo Tafuri, *The Sphere and the Labyrinth: Avant-Gardes and Architecture from Piranesi to the 1970s*, trans. Pelligrino d'Acierno and Robert Connolly (Cambridge, Mass.: MIT Press, 1987), p. 32.

20. See Mary Douglas, *Purity and Danger* (London: Routledge & Kegan Paul, 1966); Edmund Leach, "Anthropological Aspects of Language: Animal Categories and Verbal Abuse," in *Reader in Comparative Religion*, ed. William Lessa and Evon Vogt (New York: Harper & Row, 1972), pp. 206–20; and Thompson, *Rubbish Theory*, which explores the hierarchical aspects of systems of classification.

21. Quoted in Mailer, *Faith of Graffiti*, n.p., section 4.

22. "Clamping Down on the Gangs in the Graffiti Fight," *Philadelphia Inquirer*, 21 November, 1982, p. 2-A.

23. Helen H. Tanzer, *The Common People of Pompeii: A Study of the Graffiti* (Baltimore: Johns Hopkins University Press, 1939), p. 4.

24. Call-in show on graffiti, conducted by Terry Gross, May 3, 1984.

25. A passage from Donald Preziosi, *Architecture, Language, and Meaning* (The Hague: Mouton, 1979), provides an interesting gloss on the illegibility of graffiti: "Artifactual markings must satisfy requirements which seem, on the face of it, to be at cross-purposes. On the one hand, a mark must be sufficiently enhanced perceptually so as to be palpable to members of a group and to speak clearly to outsiders of passage and settlement claims. On the other hand, it should maintain sufficient opacity so as to be, to a certain extent, enigmatic; it may be necessary under certain conditions not to reveal too much about a group and its habits. In effect, architectonic objects may need to balance properties of synechdochic *caricature* and *camouflage*" (p. 39).

26. Castleman, *Getting Up*, pp. 150–57.

27. Edward Ranzal, "Ronan Backs Lindsay Anti-Graffiti Plan," *New York Times*, 29 August 1972, p. 66.

28. Quoted in Mailer, *Faith of Graffiti*, n.p., section 4.

29. See "Clamping Down on the Gangs," *Philadelphia Inquirer*.

30. See, for example, "Ten Arrested in City War on Graffiti," *Philadelphia Inquirer*, 26 July 1988, p. B-2, and "Eleven Arrests in Graffiti Probe," *Philadelphia Inquirer*, 25 June 1986, p. B-4.

31. Edward Colimore, "Vandals Fire Back in Graffiti War," *Philadelphia Inquirer*, 25 January 1984, p. B-2. In a complex, and ironic, development, graffiti writers hired by the Anti-Graffiti Task Force for such painting have finally received their pay after months of protest and even demonstrations on their part. Embezzling and financial irregularities characterized the administration of the program, now under investigation ("For Youths, City Jobs Turn Sour," *Philadelphia Inquirer*, 25 August 1986, p. B-1; "Graffiti Workers Go Unpaid," *Philadelphia Inquirer*, 4 September 1986, p. B-1; "Graffiti Workers to Be Paid Today, Officials Decide," *Philadelphia Inquirer*, 5 September 1986, p. B-7).

32. Michel Foucault, *Discipline and Punish: The Birth of the Prison*, trans. Alan Sheridan (New York: Vintage Books, 1979).

33. For a variety of accounts of these practices, see Floyd Salas, *Tattoo the Wicked Cross* (New York: Grove Press, 1967), a novel set in a reform school where young Mexican- and African-Americans are incarcerated; Sylvia Ann Grider, "Con Safos:

Mexican-Americans, Names, and Graffiti," in *Readings in American Folklore*, ed. Jan
Harold Brunvand (New York: Norton, 1979), pp. 138–51; and A. J. W. Taylor,
"Tattooing Among Male and Female Offenders of Different Ages in Different Types
of Institutions," *Genetic Psychology Monographs* 81 (1970): 81–119, a study of tattooing
among New Zealand criminals, Borstal boys and girls, and some Maori analogues.

34. I am grateful to my colleague Bill Van Wert for this point.

35. Karl Marx, *The German Ideology*, in *Marx, Engels, on Literature and Art*, ed. Lee
Baxandall and Stefan Morawski (New York: International General, 1977), p. 71.

36. *Post-Graffiti* (exhibition catalogue) (New York: Sidney Janis Gallery, 1983).

37. Calvin Tompkins, "The Art World: Up from the I.R.T.," *New Yorker*, 26
March 1984, p. 101. More recently, the Museum of Modern Art staged a show
(October 1990–January 1991) celebrating the influence of graffiti and other "low art"
forms, such as caricature, comics, and advertising, on the "high art" forms of modernism and postmodernism. Again, emphasis is placed on the continuity of "high
art" history and the thematization of "low art" in that history (Kirk Varnedoe and
Adam Gopnik, *High and Low: Modern Art and Popular Culture* [New York: Museum
of Modern Art, 1990], pp. 69–99, 375–82).

38. See, in addition to her *Common People of Pompeii*, Helen H. Tanzer, *Graffiti
in the Athenian Agora* (Princeton, N.J.: American School of Classical Studies in Athens,
1974); Henry Field, *Camel Brands and Graffiti from Iraq, Syria, Jordan, Iran, and
Arabia* (Baltimore: American Oriental Society, 1952); and Violet Pritchard, *English
Medieval Graffiti* (Cambridge: Cambridge University Press, 1967).

39. Cooper and Chalfant, *Subway Art*, p. 50.

40. Ann Kolson, "Subways Were Her Canvases, a Spray Can Her Brush," *Philadelphia Inquirer*, 13 April 1984, p. E-1.

41. Henry Chalfant, interviews by Terry Gross, February 10 and May 3, 1984.
For a discussion of the social worker Hugo Martinez's involvement with the United
Graffiti Artists in New York, see Castleman, *Getting Up*, pp. 117–26.

42. A patron of graffiti writers in Great Neck, New York, who had her children's
room covered with graffiti murals, told the press: "It's individual, it's very personal.
It's spontaneous" (Dinah Prince, "The New Chic in Decorating? Graffiti in the
Home," *Philadelphia Inquirer*, 23 December 1982, p. 3-D). The individual she has
in mind is, not surprisingly, herself—the consumer and the personality she exercises
through choice, taste, and eclecticism. Yet we might also note that, as is frequently
the case in the adaptation of primitive and working-class cultural forms, the children's
room is the repository of savagery here.

43. Cooper and Chalfant, *Subway Art*, p. 34.

44. For a discussion of the theme of money in pop art, see Nancy Marmer, "Pop
Art in California," in *Pop Art*, ed. Lucy Lippard (New York: Praeger, 1966), pp. 156–
57. In an argument of relevance here, Jean Baudrillard discusses the ascendence of
the signature and its relation to value in the twentieth century in "Gesture and
Signature: Semiurgy in Contemporary Art," in *For a Critique of the Political Economy
of the Sign*, trans. Charles Levin (St. Louis: Telos Press, 1981), pp. 102–11.

45. Castleman, *Getting Up*, p. 25. In *Subway Art*, Cooper and Chalfant provide a
glossary of terms, noting: "Writers have a specialized vocabulary, often metaphors
for war and violence, such as 'bomb,' 'hit,' and 'kill' " (p. 27). The euphemistic and
sublimating aspects of this vocabulary become foregrounded when one considers the
graffiti writer's generally antithetical relation to gangs (for a discussion that contrasts

the gang member's vested interest in territory with the graffiti writer's vested interest in mobility, see Castleman, *Getting Up*, pp. 91–115) and often pacifist politics (cf. the famous *Stop the Bomb* whole-car masterpiece of Lee Quinones, a member of the Fabulous Five graffiti team).

46. I take this point from de Ventós, *Heresies of Modern Art:* "When our entire environment is a manufactured one, we cannot pretend that the 'artificial' activity of the artist can and should remain restricted to the private domestic sphere, as in periods when privacy was synonymous with 'culture' and environment with 'nature' " (p. 134).

Figure 12
An anonymous witness testifies before the Attorney General's Commission on Pornography. (Meese Commission *Report*, Department of Justice)

8

The Marquis de Meese

Madamina, il catalogo è questo
Delle belle che amò il padron mio,
Un catalogo egli è che ho fatt'io,
Osservate, leggete con me.
　　　Ponte, *Don Giovanni* (1787)

There is always something statistical in our loves and something
belonging to the laws of large numbers.
　　　Deleuze and Guattari, *Anti-Oedipus* (1972)

Pleasures of Comparison: The Bureau of Statistics

The pornography debate occupies a prominent site of contradiction
in contemporary culture: a site where the interests of cultural feminism merge with those of the Far Right, where an underground
enterprise becomes a major growth industry, and where forms of
speculation turn alarmingly practical. Another more problematic con-
fluence occurs as a result of this debate. That is, by juxtaposing the
1986 *Final Report* of the Attorney General's Commission on Pornography (known informally as the Meese Commission *Report*) and
the Marquis de Sade's *120 Days of Sodom*, we will see how pornography and the public discourse on pornography have the same comparative logic. An examination of such a logic shows how the
pleasures of comparison—its gestures toward control, limit, and transcendence—are always balanced by its failures, even tragedies: the
realization of the situated nature of all measurement, juxtaposition,

235

subordination, and hierarchization. Thus this essay is designed to both discuss and illustrate a series of issues implicit in pornography's predicament: the impossibility of describing desire without generating desire; the impossibility of separating form and content within the process of sublimation; and, most important, the impossibility of constructing a metadiscourse of pornography once we recognize the interested nature of all discursive practices. We cannot transcend the pornography debate, for we are in it. But by writing through it, by examining its assumptions, we can learn a great deal about the problems of representing desire and the concomitant problems of a cultural desire for unmediated forms of representation.

The Meese Commission *Report* and *The 120 Days of Sodom* constitute more than twenty-five hundred pages on, about, and of pornography. This "discourse of pornography," which here immediately poses the problems of preposition and thus of stance and relation, can be taken as a discourse on the very nature of discursiveness, a discourse between the body and representation; yet it "reveals" nothing beyond textuality, only more discursiveness. For the referent of this "nothing," always deferred, is the ineffable and unspeakable referent of desire as it is socially structured. On the one hand, the examination of pornography cannot maintain a transcendent position. On the other, the discourse of pornography cannot establish a referent, cannot represent some "sex itself." Hence Michel Foucault's contention in *The History of Sexuality* that sex is "an imaginary point determined by the deployment of sexuality"[1] is of importance here; it outlines a strategy for managing the sexual, and social, practices of others. Thus we must pursue the discourse of pornography as a discourse designed to mobilize the inexplicable power of a "sex itself" behind a series of failed gestures of representation. This deployment of sexuality goes beyond a mere mystification of sexual practices; we must see such a mystification as being in the interest of ideology and the arrangement of social actors in social space. Thus pornography's move toward exposure has as its referent a marvelous, even magical *hiding*.

Ironically, the exposure that is the purpose of the Meese Commission *Report* can function only as a supplement to this same concealment in the interests of concealment. Such an irony was not lost on Sade as he constantly collapsed theory and practice, abstraction and experience. As Roland Barthes has contended, Sade achieved "that union of a work and its criticism which Mallarmé so clearly rendered for us."[2] For Sade to have done so is to have suspended the reader/viewer between complete absorption and complete transcendence, between a subjectivity unbearable in its sensual proximity and an objectivity unbearable in its monotonous distance. We are forced to collapse any distinction here between primary and secondary texts. Sade's taxonomy, his grammar, is constantly emergent at the levels of particularity; inversely, the Meese Commission *Report* cannot escape the necessity of content, a fate greatly evident in the fact that the *Report* itself has become a pornographic best seller.[3]

The Meese Commission *Report* can be seen as a seventeenth-century document, displaying all the contradictions between the Puritan and the baroque. *The 120 Days of Sodom* can be seen as an eighteenth-century document, poised between Enlightenment reason and Romantic striving: the libertine Curval, for example, wants to "dismember Nature and unhinge the Universe" in a gesture paying homage, despite itself, to nature.[4] Yet despite these multiple anachronisms, these two texts share a remarkable number of problems and functions in thematics, modes of production, and reception. It is clear that pornography (by definition a minor literature) compels, by moral force, an attempt at criticism in all its forms— from brute pragmatism (the Hite and Kinsey reports, marriage manuals, and so forth) to pure speculation (the chaste moves of semiotics). Here we see revealed the mixture of pragmatism and speculation implicit in the contaminating moves of criticism per se. It is the task of the Meese Commission *Report* to show a continuous emergence of pornography from Pompeii to the present, and to posit an epidemic for which the *Report* itself will somehow be the prescription, if not the cure. In claiming a continuous and marginalized history for pornography, the Meese Commission clearly posits a naturalized sexuality at pornography's unrepresentable center: the permutations and "perversions" of pornographic discourse are framed as testimony regarding the proper form and destination of a "natural" sexual practice. As the majority of the attorney general's commissioners make clear from their initial statements, such a proper sexuality belongs to married heterosexual couples engaging in sex for procreation.

But the appearance of continuity within pornographic discourse also tends toward a more sanguine view: that there is nothing new under the sun. When Leporello takes out his catalogue of Don Giovanni's 2,065 "conquests," we are neither surprised nor humiliated by sheer quantity. It is Sade's genius to see that the possibilities for sexual description (if not "sex itself") are a matter of degree and "style" as well as number. Each individual has a set of preferences, and such preferences are, for Sade as for Freud and Lacan, the sum total of one's very individuality. Corresponding to the experiences of the four duennas, Sade's four major divisions of "crimes" are compilations and hierarchizations of forms of extremity. In contrast, Meese's commissioners need to make claims, through numbers, for a crisis. Simultaneously, they need to proclaim their innocence of experience. The *Report* is characterized by what might be called an ornamental, or attached, historicism—the same kind of ornamental narrative found, in fact, in all pornographic discourse. Commissioner Diane D. Cusak includes these phrases in one paragraph of her opening statement: "Aristotle has taught us for years" and "one of those understandings held by society for thousands of years—that sex is private, to be cherished within the context of love, commitment, and fidelity."[5] Although the pressing and terrifying innovations in sexual scenes delineated by the *Report* have already appeared in *The 120 Days of Sodom*, the credibility of sincerity within the *Report* rests on the necessity of surprise or, more properly, *shock*. Thus the inevitability of history must be a matter of invention and erasure here.

Despite its diffuse and solipsistic intentions, the *Report* affords an examination of the sexual reasoning of the state at this particular historical moment, a reasoning constructed by particular social agents operating within a field construed by them as "public discourse." What are the methods of that reasoning? First, the notion of a "mandatory review." In a pornography where everything is visible, nothing hidden, figured, or imagined, the problem of this review becomes "What is the State to do?"—the problem of a doomed repetition.[6] Second, because of the impossibility of description, the *Report* gestures toward hierarchization, specification, and organization—gestures encompassing and thereby limiting the objectives of the *Report* itself. Third, an account—a measurement or sounding— is offered. And finally, the *Report* suggests a repression, and positions that repression within the discourse not of "freedom" but the law.

In fact, we find that some commissioners concluded that protecting pornography under the First Amendment would trivialize that amendment and lead the public to come to disrespect its powers!

Although the task of the Meese Commission *Report*, the task of remedying desire, may seem antithetical to the task of *The 120 Days of Sodom*, the task of mobilizing desire, we can witness through this comparison the homeopathy of reason. Sade is mannerly, even tender, toward the reader, always concerned with the reader's well-being or state of arousal. The ruthless "ethics" of the château of Silling become a contrapose to the authorly concern he displays. For Sade to please the reader, he must attempt to convince him or her that the discourse of *The 120 Days of Sodom* is realizable, that this schedule of narrations (for this is truly not yet a schedule of events and always marks the bifurcation of narrative and actualization quite clearly) is both complete and particular—the perfect experiential "tease." The duennas are constantly urged to leave nothing out of their narratives, yet Sade's account must simultaneously move as well to lists and tables as aids to comprehension. Specularity characterizes the realism of Sade's writing for the most obvious reason: such visualization simultaneously affords a sense of detail and a sense of overview. That is, it promises a totalized sexual consciousness. But this is a consciousness that always sees its limit, always sees *how* it is looking. The Sadian gaze, prototype of all pornographic gazes since, remains caught between movement and action, never quite satisfied and never engaged. Thus Sade describes the pornographic tease: "to allow voluptuousness to become irritated by the augmentation of a desire incessantly inflamed and never satisfied" (*ODS*, p. 241).[7] In sum, we find the same strategies in both of these "reports": the narrative survey, the formula, the account, and the articulation or positioning of the crime. In Sade these "outlines" of scenes (rather than the scene's "themselves") always preempt, always interrupt, the possibility of articulation; thus representation always preempts sexuality, just as the Meese Commission, in its search for a sexuality freed from representation, had feared.

We recall here an important aspect of Piranesi's project. Whereas we might be immediately struck by a set of common themes— enclosure, torture, language, and system—we must as readily note a common method, for, as Manfredo Tafuri asks, "does not Sade's counter generality of perversions, his 'total monstrousness,' perhaps help to clarify a question that in a way pertains as well to Piranesi, who was also tormented by the *difference* between the writing of an action and the concrete act? (Between *design* and architecture?)"[8] Once again what might be a shared dream seems to be the inevitable outcome of the structure of representation.

The binary comparative reasoning of pornographic writing constantly moves between the particular and the general. Such comparison is a matter of negotiating and maintaining a boundary between self and other, self and rule, self and nature that is part of the tension between act and limit, which is pornography's defining feature. For Sade and, we might contend, within all pornography, there is an intrinsic, even "natural" pleasure in comparison: the comparison of amounts, degrees, and intensities. The more private and restricted the domain, the more pleasure in comparison. The libertine Durcet explains:

> The inequality she has created in our persons proves that this discordance pleases Nature, since 'twas she established it, and since she wishes that it exist in fortunes as well as in bodies. . . . The universe would cease on the spot to subsist were there to be an exact similarity amongst all beings; 'tis of this disparity there is born the order which preserves, contains, directs everything. (*ODS*, p. 426)

Hence the centrality of what Durcet had earlier termed "the pleasure of comparison,"[9] the pleasure arising from difference, from the separation of pleasure from the domains of necessity, responsibility, pain, and all consequence. Here pleasure appears without limit because of its capacity to absorb all limits; to set into motion a differentiating machinery; to assume all positions, including those of pain and death. Such an unimaginable pleasure would in fact be the end of pornography—both its goal and its point of disappearance as a representation.

As in Sade's calendrical table of contents, problems of typology and enumeration appear in the *Report*'s headings: "The Problem of Multiple Causation"; "The Varieties of Evidence"; "The Need to Sub-divide" ("In many respects," commission chairman Henry E. Hudson writes, "we consider this one of our most important conclusions" [p. 321]), "Degradation, Domination, Subordination, or Humiliation"; "Witnesses Testifying Before the Commission"; "Witnesses Invited, but Unable to Appear Before the Commission";

"Persons Submitting Written Statements." Intensities, degrees, proximities, models, examples, categories. We can see that the work of pornographic discourse is the work of bureaucracy: the arrangement of bodies in and through social categories; the manipulation and reorganization of such categories themselves; the regulation of bodies in relation to technology and resources; the management of individuality through typification and assignment.

The Bureau of Ethnology

If we look for a scientific paradigm for a metadiscourse of pornography, we would no doubt find ethnology. Sade writes:

> The plan was to have described to them, in the greatest detail and in due order, every one of debauchery's extravagances, all its divagations, all its ramifications, all its contingencies, all of what is termed in libertine language its passions. There is simply no conceiving the degree to which man varies them when his imagination grows inflamed; excessive may be the differences between men that is created by all their other manias, by all their other tastes, but in this case it is even more so, and he who should succeed in isolating and categorizing and detailing these follies would perhaps perform one of the most splendid labors which might be undertaken in the study of manners, and perhaps one of the most interesting. It would thus be a question of finding some individuals capable of providing an account of all these excesses, then of analyzing them, of extending them, of itemizing them, of graduating them, and of running a story through it all, to provide coherence and amusement. (*ODS*, pp. 218–19)

The contents of the Sadian society have been closely analyzed by Barthes: "Once shut in, the libertines, their assistants, and their subjects form a total society, endowed with an economy, a morality, a language, and a time articulated into schedules, labors, and celebrations. Here, as elsewhere, the enclosure permits the system, i.e., the imagination" (*SFL*, p. 17). More reservation than prison, the Sadian world is an institution even more total than those we know from Erving Goffman's studies of asylums. For whereas such asylums have staffs in contact with "the outside world," Silling's closed sphere, all bridges destroyed behind the libertines and their entourage, is an ethnologist's paradise.[10] Once the field is limited,

all that need be done is to find "some individuals capable of providing an account . . . analyzing . . . extending . . . itemizing . . . grad-
uating . . . and . . . running a story through it all"—a story that, in
the critical move from ethnology to ethnography, tends toward the
drama of the closing of the field: the drama of integrity, identity,
and stability that thus will put the ethnography itself into the service
of comparison.

In considering the ethnological aspects of pornography, we might
concentrate on three constituents: the articulation of the space; the
positioning of actors within the space; the invention of the social.
In Sade, the enclosed site of pornography is the château or castle.
In the Meese Commission *Report,* the site of pornography is a net-
work of such enclosed spaces: the adult bookstore, with its peep-
show booths; the dark room; the motel room as film set; the private
home of the pornographer (where, horrifyingly enough, a man's
home *is* his castle). The site of the Sadian world is of course the
encircled power of the nobility in the age of Louis XV. The site of
the *Report* is a conspiratorial commodity system, an underground
defined by pockets of temporary sites, yet relying on the same modes
of production and consumption as any commodity system.

The conflicting characteristics of pornographic space are limit and,
inevitably, contamination. Sadian architecture is hellish—tableaus
of rooms, chambers, halls where complete penetration and surrender
might take place, where an *outside* might be abolished forever.[11]
This is the scene portrayed in Sadian discourse, and it is also the
scene of pornography's production—a prison writing in all senses,
written against a limit, its triumph destined to be its power of contamination, its dissemination beyond that limit. The minds of the
Meese commissioners also return constantly to imprisonment. A
prominent site for investigation is the prison, where the commissioners, writing in a side note, complain of inadequate censorship
of inmates' reading materials. The "crews" making pornographic
films are described as being "locked in"; the actors are "virtually
prisoners": "The Commission received testimony and other evidence from individuals who reported that they had been kidnapped
or held captive during the production of pornographic materials" (p.
794).

Who is positioned within this captive space? Pornography must
have a "captive" audience—enthralled, enraptured, forced, para-

lyzed. Like Sade's "solitaries" separated from the theatrical space of the storytelling hall,[12] the peep-show booth provides a perfect form for serving this need for privacy and accessibility, confinement and violation. The symbolics of the lock,[13] the "glory hole," and the "screen" work out the problematics of hiding and display, fantasy and realizability in a remarkable merging of pornographic form and function. For the commission members, these booths horrifyingly mime the contamination of bodily orifices: "The booths from which these videos or live performers are viewed become filthy beyond description as the day progresses. Police investigators testified before our Commission that the stench is unbearable and that the floor becomes sticky with semen, urine, and saliva" (p. 81). "The booths seem rarely to be cleaned, and the evidence of frequent sexual activity is apparent" (p. 290). "Some of the negative consequences [of adult bookstores in neighborhoods] arise from the style of the establishments themselves, which usually have garish lights and signs advertising the nature of what is to be found within in no uncertain terms" (pp. 385–86).

> Inside the booths, the floors and walls are often wet and sticky with liquid or viscous substances, including semen, urine, feces, used prophylactics, gels, saliva, or alcoholic beverages. The soles of a patron's shoes may stick to certain areas of the floor. The booths are also often littered with cigarette butts and tobacco. The trash and sewage and the application of disinfectants or ammonia on occasion create a particularly nauseating smell in the peep booths. (pp. 1476–77)

What is this repeated horror of viscosity, this horror of floors and walls, this horror of getting stuck? The suffocating stench and the scandalous hole—here, as always in the *Report*, is the terrifying possibility of a return to, and absorption in, the sexual orifices. In these passages, the possibility of action must be limited by the efflorescence of fantasy itself. Hence this architecture of pornography always emphasizes boundedness and contamination in such a way as to eroticize the boundary: the eroticization of bodily orifices and cavities; the eroticization of class and occupation; the eroticization of gender and race. These forces of eroticization have to do with transgression and, ultimately, reification. For the pleasures of comparison depend upon differences and separations articulated under the threat of identity. Identity and absorption emerge as the threat of "sex itself." Hence we find in pornography an eroticization of those positioned on the boundary, acting out the impossibility of fantasy realized. And we also discover the importance of the *pose* here; being poised, the pornographic actor waits on the cusp of the moment between representation and realization.

The social positions of Sadian space are the old whore/duenna/ storyteller, the public official/libertine, the priest/libertine, the wife/ daughter/mother, the "stud," and the child's body. But it is not accurate to define these positions as positions of subjectivity, for only the duennas possess a capacity for narration and the generation of topics; only the libertines possess a capacity for agency; and only the wives, daughters, mothers, studs, and children are the recipients of narrative and action. Subjects, verbs, predicates. Here we have a complex rhetoric: the grammatical system as the invention of the public officials; narrative, the invention of the duennas; predication, effected through the libertines; response and conversion, effected by the wives, mothers, and children. *The 120 Days of Sodom* is not a narrative, but a grammar of narratives. All the elements of the Sadian world—customs, rituals, dress, currencies, calendars, food-ways, and architecture—revolve around this grammar of positions and stories.[14]

Compare these Sadian positions with those of the (as the American Civil Liberties Union puts it in a recent mailing, fortuitously "handpicked") attorney general's commission. First, we find the commissioners themselves, all public officials, including (1) a "Commonwealth Attorney"; (2) a doctor and professor of medicine, with a specialty in the field of sex aggression; (3) a city council member, "active in scouting"; (4) a doctor and professor of law, medicine, and psychiatry; (5) a psychologist and radio-program ("Focus on the Family") host; (6) a U.S. District Court judge; (7) the editor of *Woman's Day* magazine; (8) a lawyer; (9) a priest; (10) a law professor; (11) a child-abuse specialist; and (12) another lawyer. And second, we find those who *appear* before the commission: more public officials, lawyers, and governmental administrators; a few "executives" of the pornography industry; and, most frequently, self-confessed victims of pornography—repentant female performers, wives, mothers, and victims of child abuse.

Twelve good m—— four of the commissioners seem to be women.

One of these four is the doctor and professor of medicine, and her "biography" at the opening of the report has the same structure as that of the other, seemingly male, commissioners. But the remaining three women are all described, at the close of these respective biographies, in a separate way: "Mrs. Cusack and her husband, Joseph, a Senior Engineer with Motorola, have three grown children and remain active members of their church and community" (p. 7). "Ellen Levine is a graduate of Wellesley College. . . . She lives with her husband, a physician, and two sons in Englewood, New Jersey" (p. 14). "[Ms. Tilton] is married to Child Psychiatrist Michael J. Durfee, M.D." (p. 20). Of course, we are never told the marital and/or procreative status of the eight male commissioners. Yet the banal sexism of these "biographies" is not so interesting in the abstract as it is in the specifics of a report on pornography. For just as *The 120 Days of Sodom* makes certain that we understand the overdetermined relations of the nuclear family in order to provoke our response to the travesty of those relations, so does the Meese Commission *Report* legitimate its female voices from the outset through their place in the patriarchal order. These wives and mothers about to listen to the testimony of whores, homosexuals, and abused children will acquire, as the *Report* unfolds, the dramatic potential of Sade's tender rebels, Adelaide and Sophie.

What is even more remarkable about the commission's scenario is that, in the consequent section presenting the commissioners' "Personal Statements," the male commissioners set the scene for complaint against pornography through outraged and effusive sexual metaphors and details, yet two of the women commissioners (Ellen Levine and the unattributed Dr. Judith Becker) write a somewhat dissenting opinion:

> After a year of forums and deliberations, it is tempting to join in offering simple solutions to complex problems, in the form of the Commission Recommendations. But we are not persuaded to do so. We believe it would be seriously misleading to read this report and see a green light for prosecuting all pornographers. We still know too little about why many men and women use and enjoy pornography; if and why women's and men's sexual arousal response patterns to pornography differ. We still have more questions than answers, and we stress the need for both non-governmental solutions and tolerance for the views of others. (pp. 211–12)[15]

Excepting a few scattered asides, the remaining two-thousand-odd pages of the *Report* never again take up this aspect of the debate.

The task of the Meese Commission is to define the forms of aberrant sexuality, to suggest means for the control of the field of representation, and to establish scenes of differentiation in the entire social and cultural field, scenes whose actuality and legitimacy are shaped in "the real," but ulterior, domain of those whom the commission refers to as "very normal people." Once again, therefore, the commission's task is the task of all pornography—to invent a realism that will convince us that our fantasies are inevitable and realizable. And of course this work of establishing a social scene or field for the aberration is doomed to normalize the aberration and to send one on a search for a more extreme form of aberration that will then go on to legitimate its own context of normality.

Where Sade drew careful distinctions based upon religion (saints, hypocrites, sinners), class (there are two: the aristocracy and the poor), and sexual preferences (bodies are not so much gendered as divided into fronts and backs, as the system of ribbons devised by the libertines explains), the Meese Commission draws distinctions based on race, occupation, and gender in a more abstract sense. For race, occupation, and gender are inviolable categories in the public culture of these public officials. The films and books described in the report by special agents of the Federal Bureau of Investigation (whose job descriptions specify that they are official "describers" of pornography) delineate the following pictorial categories: female/ male/clothed/unclothed/Caucasian/black/Asian. (The only exception here is the book *Tying Up Rebecca*, in which two characters are described as respectively "Puerto Rican" and "Irish" [pp. 1651, 1660].) Race, then, rather than class, is the category of domination here. The insistence on racial categories is even more emphasized when the special agents turn to examples of European pornography, which often delineate scenes between servants and mistresses (pp. 1632–37).

In a Hitchcockian move, the commission's *Report* and the pornographic texts themselves startle through propinquity: the uncanny is emergent in the neighborhood. Consider, for example, these passages from *Tying Up Rebecca* as described by Senior Investigator Joseph B. Haggerty: "When she had first been accepted to the team,

she mistakenly changed her clothes in the teacher's lockerroom."
Or:

> Patty Jones is described as a fifteen year old girl with dark hair,
> physically more mature than Becky. She calls Becky into the shower
> to look at something. She then shows Becky a hole in the wall through
> which she has been watching a boy, Judd Loomis, taking a shower.
> . . . As Patty watches Loomis she begins to masturbate herself but
> discovers she has her fingers in Becky's vagina. She stops immediately
> and leaves the shower soon after. (p. 1649)

This technique of sensationalist discourse—the textual internal-
ization of an amazement projected upon the reader—valorizes the
reader's naiveté as voyeur/virgin.[16] Hence the commissioners must
constantly assert their amazement at the amazing and their familiarity with the familiar. Such common-sense reasoning effects a social
world lying behind (and imagined before) the *Report* as a whole.
Here is Commissioner Cusack inventing the family:

> For 2500 years of western civilization, human sexuality and its expres-
> sion have been cherished as a private act between a loving couple
> committed to each other. This has created the strongest unit of so-
> ciety—the family. If our families become less wholesome, weaker,
> and less committed to the fidelity that is their core, our entire society
> will weaken as well. (p. 35)

Father Bruce Ritter commends a "sacred privacy" (p. 97) and "the
beauty of sexuality, and its role as the foundation of the family" (p.
107). And Chairman Hudson worries about promiscuity:

> A larger issue is the very question of promiscuity. Even to the extent
> that the behavior depicted is not inherently condemned by some or
> any of us, the manner of presentation almost necessarily suggests that
> the activities are taking place outside of the context of marriage, love,
> commitment, or even affection. . . . There are undoubtedly many
> causes for what used to be called the "sexual revolution," but it is
> absurd to suppose that depictions or descriptions of uncommitted
> sexuality were not among them. (p. 339)

Sex in the service of procreation and sex within the family are
universalized through time and space. Father Ritter cites Ford and
Beach's *Patterns of Sexual Behavior:* "In their still standard overview

of 191 human cultures, Ford and Beach found that 'There are no
peoples in our sample who generally allow women to expose their
genitals under any but the most restricted of circumstances' " (p.
120). Chairman Hudson proposes an analogously "common sense
anthropology": "Here the concern is with the preservation of sex
as an essentially private act, in conformity with the basic privateness
of sex long recognized by this and all other societies" (p. 340). Such
statements exemplify the commission's constant effort to produce
a consensual "sex itself," to ensure that whatever such a "sex itself"
might be is what they themselves have, albeit unimaginably, in
mind.

Pleasure and Waste: The Bureau of Labor

The invention of the social in the discourses of pornography, like
the architecture of such discourses, is thus a matter of positing a
limit and a direction, of maintaining a boundary against what is
outside it. It is not, as we can see, a matter of naming a common
referent. Yet as a material object, the discourses of pornography
must be produced—manufactured—and this production is at the
heart of one of pornography's most prominent contradictions: How
can pleasure be a labor? In a culture where labor must be framed
as a pleasure, this question, prominently posed by pornography,
must be answered by a separation effecting, and discrediting, a point
of pure pleasure.

Such a pure pleasure is conveyed in *The 120 Days of Sodom* through
Sade's tactic of isolation. A model of recycling, a society perfectly
merging waste and preservation, the world of the château is self-
contained, calendrical, and consuming. Coprophilia, incest, and cannibalism are the tautological practices perfecting this cyclical merging. Rule-governed, feudal, and despotic, Sadian pleasure is a matter
of a wholesale management of practices and behaviors. The inhabitants must obey large-scale taboos (such as the avoidance of the
female genitals) and small-scale manners (such as the shifting codes
of behavior at meals). The inevitability and arbitrariness of permutations and grammars characterize every aspect of the Sadian
world. Change is replaced by regulation. What "occurs" occurs according to plan. Therefore, the whole possibility of surprise is cir-

cumscribed; surprise is systematically replaced by titillation. The contingencies of history and nature, necessary to surprise, have been superseded by the discretionary powers of authority, and so desire is limited to the production of desire. The intense fear of the female reproductive organs is a fear of a reproduction of something outside the regulated cycle of activities at Silling. We know that the incestuously derived pregnancy of Constance will end in death, a negative production reserved for the *The 120 Days of Sodom*'s final scene of torture and death. The death of Constance—"Constance lay upon a kind of mausoleum, the four children decorated its corners" (*ODS*, p. 670)—completes the work's spatialization of pleasure. The tearing out of the child and the murder of the mother is here a death of past and future: death spreading in all directions except toward that of agency; pleasure reaching its limit and yet continuing, multiplying, catching fire. Thus it is logical that the death of Constance is the final tableau or scene of the book. Following this passage, the deaths are simply listed, a matter of linking time and numbers.

The tension in Sade's work between pleasure and the social is a late-eighteenth-century tension. The central problematic here is the relation of a fraying autocratic power to the inevitable dispersion, and consequent claims, of pleasure. By presenting a last idyll of the aristocracy, Sade imagines a domain of pure pleasure where even the forcing of pleasure is taken up into pleasure's rubric. Today, in fact, we can envision Silling as a kind of utopian gentrification, with all of gentrification's implications of despotism, invented authenticity, and abandoned context. The Meese Commission, however, has other problems, including the reconciliation of a work ethic to a commodity system veering toward unmitigated leisure. Even more significantly, the commission must pursue its ideological tasks by sorting through a spectrum of aberrations, a spectrum that, once it includes sex for sex's sake, threatens to erase the very grounds for inquiry by making the concept of sex disappear.

By means of this condemnation of pleasure for its own sake, the Meese Commission constantly covers over its disregard of the working conditions of the pornography industry: ten-hour days and other overtime infringements, occupational health and safety violations, discriminatory hiring practices, child labor, "home work," and other forms of labor exploitation. Commissioner Cusack says in her initial statement that "these materials, whose message is clearly that sexual pleasure and self-gratifications are paramount, have the ability to seriously undermine our social fabric" (pp. 35–36). And Commissioner Park Elliot Dietz writes:

> As a governmental body, we studiously avoided making judgments on behalf of the government about the morality of particular sexual acts between consenting adults or their depiction in pornography. This avoidance, however, should not be mistaken for the absence of moral sentiment among the Commissioners.
>
> I, for one, have no hesitation in condemning nearly every specimen of pornography that we have examined. . . . these materials are themselves immoral, and to the extent that they encourage immoral behavior they exert a corrupting influence on the family and on the moral fabric of Society. (p. 51)

Throughout the *Report*, a blindness to the existence of pleasure as a labor is accompanied by an insistence upon a morality of labor as preeminent pleasure. We see pornography "depicted" here as something unmediated, as a pure content and *literal* deviance. Thus the commissioners once more veer into the terms of a Sadian daydream of realization.

Yet the commission's gesture of masking pornography as an illegal labor practice with a generalized concern regarding the morality of sexuality is as well a pragmatic one. For a crime against labor does not at all pose the same threat to the social order as a crime against the idea of work. Georges Bataille has written that

> work endowed us with a clear and distinct consciousness of objects and science has always gone hand in hand with technology. Sexual exuberance, on the other hand, leads us away from awareness: it diminishes our perceptive powers, and anyway sexuality given free rein lessens our appetite for work, just as sustained work lessens our sexual appetite. An undeniably rigorous incompatibility, then, exists between awareness bound up with work and sexual activity.[17]

Bataille's point is that the objectivity of the social world of work necessarily struggles against the subjectivity of the private world of sexuality (hence his objection to the notion of "sexual research"). Yet it is the function of pornography to mediate this very struggle, to appear at this moment in a collapse from a "work" to a "leisure" model of the proper labor of pleasure. The work of pornography cannot remain objective; it must always collapse into the subjectivity of pleasure. From this contradiction derives the "problem of the cooks" in *The 120 Days of Sodom* (who cannot, but *must*, remain only cooks) and the correlative problem, which puts the Meese Commission into a veritable dither, regarding the industrial status of pornography.[18]

Pornography as a consumer good has a common logic with all consumer goods: a logic of capital, labor, production, distribution, and profit. But once this logic is reframed as an "underground," it develops all the qualities of an evil, if not an unconscious: excess; forced labor; secret, confused channels of production and distribution; contaminated, suspect profits. The underground of pornography as it appears in the commission's writings is linked up to other undergrounds—the Mafia, drug rings, prostitution networks—in such a way as to once again elide agency and intention. Particularly, the women employed in the pornography industry must be reframed: they are not employees; they are slaves, says the commission in a gesture borrowed from pornographic narrative as it translates the specificity of nurses, students, teachers, and housewives into the amorphousness of sexual objects. The commission's *Report* includes testimony denying the contention that pornographic models are generally coerced into performing in pornography, yet the commission ultimately decided to consider that "pornographic modeling is (1) a subset of prostitution; (2) a form of sex discrimination; and (3) an invasion of performers' personal rights" (p. 889). Each of these conclusions removes the locus of agency to the pornography system: these "sex workers" have no intentionality. To put into question the conditions of work under pornography as conditions of work would be to put into question all other forms of work exploitation within the general commodity system: abuses of power, whether overtly or covertly sexual; health and safety violations; and the whole panoply of labor abuses revealed thereby as abuses of "person." Economic exploitation must be framed here as a problem endemic to the underground, so that it is not put into the light of day and hence revealed in its full material consequences.

In the contradictions of pornography as a labor we see the tensions between desire as production and desire as representation. For the transformation of desire from experience to representation of experience is not worked by magic; it is worked by a specific labor responding to specific historical pressures. In other words, to attend to the ways in which pornography is a representation is to attend to it as something *made*. In *this* is the materiality of pornography and not in some unmediated relation between desire and reference. The denial of pornography as sublimation, a denial constantly made by the Meese Commission, is an attempt to magically "reanimate" this transformation, to make pornography appear as something given or natural, something like the imaginary gesture of a "sex itself." Chairman Hudson writes, for the committee, that "what emerges is that much of what this material involves is not so much a portrayal of sex, or discussion of sex, but simply sex itself" (p. 266). And in a review of obscenity laws, he concludes, "obscene materials lack cognitive content and are more closely akin to sexual conduct as opposed to the communicative process. The sole purpose of the material is to provide sexual gratification to the reader or viewer" (p. 1275). To say that pornography is sexuality itself is to deny the materiality of desire's production, to deny the gap between signifier and signified, to deny the gap between production and consumption. Hence the commission collapses all intentionality once more into a gesture miming the magical processes of commodification where objects seem to "spontaneously" appear in order to satisfy equally "spontaneous" desires.

Pornography's Image

These issues regarding the labor of pornography lead to certain questions about its form: What are the relations between desire and its representations? What theory of imitation underlies the presentation of pornography? How are animation and passivity negotiated as poles of the possible relations between the subject and his or her objects? The fantasy of literalization is of course the underlying fantasy of the Sadian universe. What would it mean to be without symbols?[19] How would sensation fare in such a utopia of realizability—total, immediate, stretching in all directions of time and space and thus the vivification of infinity and excess? This fantasy of the end of fantasy permeates the organization of all activity at the château of Silling. Hearing leads to cognition; visualization leads to action. This sequence of sensibility is enveloped by the voyeurism of the reader, who is called upon to visualize the narratives and the narratives of the narratives.[20] As Barthes writes, "practice follows speech, and is absolutely determined by it: what is done has been said" (*SFL*, p. 35).

Thus one must not merely pose; one must act. Or at least one must imagine acting. As we can see, all realization in Sade is immediately a matter of rhetoric. The maxims of *The 120 Days of Sodom* assert the standards of authenticity for the libertine: authenticity emerges from regularity, consistency, realizability. When Sade addresses the reader near the close of his introduction, he states regarding the forthcoming six hundred passions: "As for the diversity, it is authentic, you may be sure of it" (*ODS*, p. 254). And at the close of part 1, in a list of "Mistakes I Have Made," Sade writes, "I was wrong to have made Duclos react strongly to the death of her sister: that doesn't sort with the rest of her character: change it" (*ODS*, p. 570). Authenticity is a matter of continuous, fixed identity. And that identity is completely textual, in the service of a textual function. Thus Sade sheds a novel light on the notion of the stock character, providing a pun on the notion of positioned subjectivity: in the Sadian universe, all characters are stock characters, all identity is a matter of position within the sexual grammar. Silling is posed as a world without the world, an exemplary, even mathematical, rhetoric of permutations. Complexity in the world of Silling is not a matter of complex motivation. There is only one motivation—pleasure—and everything else, including of course pain, is a corollary of that motivation and of history. All contingency is sorted, either erased or assembled, in the text's introduction. Consequently, complexity is a matter of combination, degree, and multiplication. There is only one inevitable invention at Silling and that is death: all combinations, mixtures, derivations, possibilities pause before, and then plunge headlong into, death. Yet death cannot be totalized, as the cooks must have, with relief, realized, or there will be no possible articulation of death: something must live in order to preserve the grammar of death. Death: the stamp of failed originality, failed authenticity, waiting at the close of every sexual experiment here, yet unable to accommodate the death of Death.

Recurring to the moving statues in Plato's *Meno*,[21] the dream of animation always makes its dual move of setting the world into motion as it fixates the self. Just as the voyeur peeks in anticipation of an otherly gaze that will return and thereby transfix his or her subjectivity, so does the fetishist hope that acting upon the object will return an identification that stamps his or her subjectivity into place.[22] Simone de Beauvoir has written in her essay on Sade that "the world of the masochist is a magical one, and that is why he is almost always a fetishist. Objects such as shoes, furs, and whips, are charged with emanations which have the power to change him into a thing, and that is precisely what he wants" (*ODS*, pp. 26–27). Beauvoir argues that the masochistic and sadistic impulses are interchangeable and that "his [the masochist's] humiliating exhibitions and the tortures he undergoes humiliate and torture the other as well" (*ODS*, p. 27). Thus all elements of the Sadian tableau play into the systematic and inclusive play of differences: the animal organicism of leather; the technological allusions of chains, studs, and rivets; the dialogics of male, female, front, back, old, young, lower class, aristocrat. All reciprocations lead to an exchange from a position and hence legitimate the very possibility of positioning, emotion, and experience.[23]

We arrive again at the contradictions implicit in representing desire. Foucault has argued that mimetic theories both preserve and cut off the domain of representation: "There is a strict order governing the life of the libertine: every representation must be immediately endowed with life in the living body of desire, every desire must be expressed in the pure light of a representative discourse."[24] Of course, for Sade this was a fully lived contradiction. We have only to place his writing against his hatred of the Terror. Consider, for example, his reputation as a grand juror who constantly dismissed the charges against the accused.[25]

Today the reasoning of the state still wavers at the boundaries of the modern. In the Meese Commission *Report*, the tension between representation and contagion exerts an unbearable pressure, a pressure permitting the invention of a sexuality so powerful and pervasive that the state itself must analogously be invented in order to suppress and control it. In addition to Commissioner James C. Dobson's claim that pornography "involves sex itself," many other statements made by the commission display a problematic epistemology of the image: "a picture represents what it depicts" (p. 331); "definitionally, pornography requires a portrayal" (p. 249); "the weight of empirical evidence amassed in the last two decades by social psychologists, particularly in the area of media violence and aggressive behavior, hardly supports catharsis" (p. 40); "our most controversial category has been the category of sexually explicit materials that are not violent and are not degrading. . . . They are materials in which the participants appear to be fully willing participants" (p. 335).

The bewildered and bewildering tautology of these statements characterizes the commission's deepening crisis with regard to the real and its possible realisms. The dangerous forms of "knowledge" (sexual and otherwise) characterizing the production of pornographic drawings and writings are displaced, through the seemingly agentless magic of technology, to the dangerous forms of knowledge characterizing the consumption of pornographic photos, videos, films, and telephone and computer messages.[26] The same ambivalence is evidenced by the commission's debate regarding whether those photographed should be called "models" or "sex workers": "We adopt the term 'model' not only because it seems to have been the one most commonly used during our hearings, but also because it seems to be somewhat less loaded with positive and negative connotations" (p. 841). Keeping a lid on connotation becomes an increasingly difficult task. Meanwhile, we must note the virtual taboo upon the word *actor* here, as if the commission feared that once again what seems to be representation might slide into intention, and—perhaps even more frightening—that what seems to be intending might be as well representing.

The irreducible finality of "sex itself" precludes the possibility of "mere" representation. The commission wants to be able to say that this "sex itself" *takes place.* Yet the problematic of seeming "to be fully willing participants," the absolute frame of pornography as a representation (as in "the participants do not seem to be married") will not disappear. This problematic acquires its particular depth from the fact that a "sex itself" is unimaginable without visualization, scopic desire, anticipation, and projection. Commissioner Dobson finds himself in a quandary, for he contends that "until we are *certain* that the passion of fantasy does not destroy the passion of reality," we "dare not adorn" pornographic materials "with the crown of respectability" (p. 83). He earlier argued that "the totality of evidence supports the linkage between illustration and imitation" (p. 77). Yet there is no other possible relation that evidence can have to the real, so there goes the passion of reality. What we see here is pornography's symptomatic access to the general situation of representation in commodity culture. The sublimation of pornography is not the sublimation of its particular thematics, but a sublimation of a generalized desire to enter the commodity system and thus take on the conditions of that system's specificity and materiality for one's being. Pornography is the appropriately simulacral "sex itself" of consumer culture, just as the lived profligacy of Don Juanism appeared as the "sex itself" of Romantic self-expression and excess.

The power of the image here transcends the power of the real, even if we hypothetically, and rather unadventurously, limit the real to the realm of lived experience. Thus Justice Potter Stewart's famous definition of pornography—"I know it when I see it"—achieves an unacknowledged authority as an uncanny articulation of the uncanny. We realize that the Meese Commission's attempts to protect the virginity of sight have to do with the always present status of the primal scene.[27] The *Report* constantly juxtaposes the jadedness of recognition with a "habituation effect" (pp. 996–97) characterizing the accumulative force of addiction: "Those who are hooked on sex become obsessed by their need" (p. 77). To see the collapsing of sign and referent here, we need only imagine a "heroin addict" whose obsession is looking at pictures of farinaceous substances. Memory and addiction, the unforgettable and the repressed, become motifs that themselves play a role in suppressing the distinction between pornography's scenes of typification and the particular scenes of our experience. The commission constantly slips into a problematic of visualization and testimony. The commission witnesses, those subjects of the firsthand, must constantly, without exception, enter into language and visual representation in predictably pornographic ways. Hence we again arrive at the Sadian problem of authenticity and originality, the problem of reason as the problem of sexuality—the tragedy, or perhaps black comedy, of the comparable.

Pornography's Language

Nowhere is this matter of the relation between authenticity and originality more poignantly displayed than in the rhetorical situation of testimony. To testify is to claim being for one's own and, at the same time, to surrender being to the social. Testimony yokes the body irrevocably to narrative, and thus we see testimony as a supplement to fantasy, whose dream is always the deferred possibility of such a yoking of body and narrative, action and language. In the final instance, confession becomes the embracing category here, the point where all is spoken and exposed: the body's past, the imagination's totality—the realized and the hystericized, resplendent in their mutual, narrated glory.

In a statement on testimony, the commission reports:

> Some of the first-hand testimony has come from users of pornography, and a number of witnesses have told us how they became "addicted" to pornography, or how they were led to commit sex crimes as a result of exposure to pornographic materials. . . . As with more extensive studies based on self-reports of sex offenders, evidence relying on what an offender thought caused his problem is likely to so overstate the external and so understate the internal as to be of less value to us than other evidence.
>
> Most of the people who have testified about personal experiences, however, have not been at any point offenders, but rather have been women reporting on what men in their lives have done to them or to their children as a result of exposure to certain sexually explicit materials. (p. 313)

Why is the testimony of the victim of such interest? For Sade the victim's narration leads to the pleasures of pain. Women and children as the subjects of pornography allow the viewer to assume the positions of agency and passivity, male and female, aggressor and victim all at once. In the Meese Commission *Report*, pain leads to the pleasures of narration—catharsis, expulsion, an emptying out of experience validating the historical particularity of the speaking subject. Also, testimony always confirms the powerful gaze of the Other, the Social, represented by the commission itself. This statement, made by Chairman Hudson, is characteristic: "many of the stories these witnesses told were highly believable and extremely informative, leading us to think about possible harms of which some of us had previously been unaware" (p. 314). And, regarding the testimony of performers in sex industries: "the view of performers' lives which they provide is invaluable and grimly fascinating" (p. 862). The scenes of conversion in the *Report* are all scenes of light, records of the victory of rationality over the dark forces of sexuality. What is so interesting about these scenes is not their general thematic, but their particular quality of contagion. For an addiction to conversion seems to accompany an addiction to pornography. The commissioners found willing witnesses at every location of their convening ("all information at our disposal was presented to us voluntarily" [p. 852]), and the testimonial mode of narration required such scenic reenactments of humiliation as the following: "I have experienced and continue to experience . . . humiliation"; "It was the same shame and humiliation as in the other experiences"; "I felt humiliated and hollow"; "The chilling horror I felt in my kitchen after my first encounter with Dial-A-Porn lingers with me today. After my initial reaction of disbelief subsided, I was overcome with grief. I cried uncontrollably for myself, my son" (pp. 805–6).[28]

This is a rather sublime statement of emotion consequent to what might have been a wrong number (although "my first encounter" makes this echo a repetition compulsion): what power of language! In recent government hearings, from farm aid (Jane Fonda, Sissy Spacek, Jessica Lange, and others) to tobacco abuse (the Reynolds heir and Hollywood aspirant), the notion of a governmental "star witness" has become suggestively entangled, à la the Reagancy, with show business. One of the stars of the Meese Commission hearings was Linda Marchiano, who performed in pornographic films under the name Linda Lovelace. Her testimony begins: "I have a son who will be ten in April. My daughter Lindsay will be six on the 4th of July. . . . I have no rights as a victim. The only right I have is to be able to tell my story and hope that someone listens" (p. 809). The specificity of the daughter in this narrative (and her providential birth date) is typical of commission testimony. But Marchiano's appearance was not viewed as typical. Of all the testimony in this section of the *Report,* hers is particularly characterized by the "victim's" name, by the press's attention to it as representative testimony, and by the simultaneous appearance of her autobiography on the market. Marchiano's conversion to the antipornography movement thus neatly replays and inverts the conversion to insatiable sexuality that she enacted in her most famous film, *Deep Throat.*[29]

The structure of conversion, as was the case with taxonomy and repetition, characterizes the narrative of pornography in all its discourses. We thereby are able to conclude that the tension between the private and the public generates certain rhetorical moves, regardless of the specific content or focus of the discourse. In fact, this process of generation is rather elegantly parodied by pornography's own underlying emphasis on sublimation. For pornography emphasizes that, regardless of the rhetorical move made, the viewer, in a "despite himself" that confirms himself, is looking for "the good parts."

Someone was listening to these narratives, just as public officials listened to the narratives at Silling; the proper audience was the commissioners themselves, positioned on their high chairs behind a broad dais, with the American eagle behind them, a flag at their collective side.[30] The discourse of the *Report* is full of reciprocal conversions. The testimony of Commissioner Dobson regarding his exposure to a picture of a murdered and molested child is as dramatic as that of any witness:

> I served for 14 years as a member of a medical school faculty and thought I had seen it all. But my knees buckled and tears came to my eyes as these and hundreds of other photographs of children were presented. . . . Speaking personally, I now passionately support the control of sexually explicit material that is legally obscene, whether it relates to children or adults. (pp. 75–76)

It is worth noting, if not surprising, that the dominant poetic devices of pornographic discourse are symptomatic of contamination and convey, in language, a sense of spatiality or visuality through coincidence or overlapping: puns, parody, and parallelism are the foreplay of pornographic discourse in contrast to the conversion narrative's more brutely climactic spatiality. On page 1354 of the *Report* the word *pubic* has been typed for *public* and this seepage is characteristic of the typographical "error" that is the *Report* itself: a kind of eruption of the unconscious amid the discourse of the state. Every aspect of the *Report* reveals the way its discursiveness must simply be a matter of adding, supplementing, and decorating the "itself" of sexual practices. In an effort at "stripping away," the *Report* keeps arriving at ornament and multiplication. The commissioners' statements opening the *Report* (but, as prefaces, dating of course to its conclusion) are striking in their use of sexual imagery. Commissioner Dobson's is typical:

> I now understand how mountain climbers must feel when they finally stand atop the highest peak. They overcome insurmountable obstacles to reach the rim of the world and announce proudly to one

another, "we made it"! In a similar context, I feel a sense of accomplishment as the Commission releases its final report. (p. 71)

"Hit squads"; "poppycock"; "if the deck were stacked"; "fling it about"; "skyrocketed"; "rivers of obscenity which have inundated the American landscape"; "obscenity flowing freely through the veins of society"; "obscenity cannot be permitted to flow freely through the veins of society"; "the rising tide of obscenity" (pp. 72–83)—these seemingly unintended double entendres appear within just a few pages. By the time one finishes reading the *Report*, it is difficult to imagine obscenity in anything but liquid form.

The argument that viewing pornography is corrupting is in fact quite substantiated by the language of the commissioners and of others arguing against pornography after exposure to it. Commissioner Dietz begins a litany that he seems unable to close, citing

> sex with one's children, stepchildren, parents, stepparents, siblings, cousins, nephews, nieces, aunts, uncles, and pets, and with neighbors, milkmen, plumbers, salesmen, burglars and peepers, who had learned that people take off their clothes and have sex within the first five minutes of meeting one another, who had learned to misjudge the percentage of women who prepare for sex by shaving their pubic hair, having their breasts, buttocks, or legs tattooed. (p. 43)

(This list of "deviant sexual practices" goes on in detail for two pages.) But Dietz's lyric parallelism is hardly as elegant as that of Andrea Dworkin, whose "eloquent testimony" (as the commissioners often refer to it) is generated along oral-formulaic principles of composition:

> My name is Andrea Dworkin. I am a citizen of the United States, and in this country where I live, every year millions of pictures are being made of women with our legs spread. We are called beaver, we are called pussy, our genitals are tied up, they are pasted. . . . In this country where I live as a citizen, women are penetrated by animals and objects for public entertainment, women are urinated on and defecated on. (p. 769)

The "excerpts" from Dworkin's testimony included in the *Report* extend to four single-spaced pages. In order to make their point, they use litotes and hyperbole in juxtaposition, serialism, parallelism, arrangement and display of detail, irony, parody, rhetorical climax, and resolution—that is, all the traditional rhetorical devices of pornographic discourse. It is not surprising that this testimony generated much excitement and is frequently referred to in other sections of the *Report*, for even though it does not at all meet standards of evidence or even seem to be framed as "personal experience," it generates in full force the rhetorical structure of the testimonial. Dworkin's remarks form a kind of sermon, or metaconversion, for the smaller conversions of the other witnesses.

The seepages of puns, the waves and climaxes of lyric parallelism, all the overlapping and contagious rhetorics of pornographic discourse, tend toward parody. Pornography relies upon its capacity for reinscription; it is in this sense, not in its poverty-stricken plots, that it is novelistic. What pornography specifically parodies are the forms of rationality: learning, culture, and control. The effort of the commission's *Report* to make sex be about other things (marriage and procreation) results of course in the eroticization of all things. Once morbid interest becomes "candid" interest, all candid interest turns morbid. Just as the *Report* itself is a best-selling piece of pornography, so do antipornography films such as *Not a Love Story* or displays exhibited by Women Organized Against Pornography help disseminate pornographic images. The parody of learning presented traditionally by forms such as "marriage manuals," "medical textbooks," or "the Tijuana Bible" is echoed in the puns on "authority, instruction, and knowledge" revealed in the commission's claim that pornography presents the "theory" or "instruction manual" for sexual aberrations and crimes. Finally, pornography continually parodies the very idea of culture by taking sublimation to the point of the ridiculous. Some movie titles from the *Report*: *On Golden Blonde*, *Romancing the Bone*, *The Wizard of Ahas*. Or a selection from pornography advertising: "Gourmet Treats Escort Agency Menu (Take Out) Entrées: Each Dish Available Individually or in any Combination." We are reminded of Commissioner Dietz imagining sex with the plumber. No aspect of the culture is immune to the contagion of eroticization or the contagion of parody. We thus arrive at the inevitable possibility of pornography parodying pornography, as in films such as *The Devil in Miss Jones*[31] or the videotape *Foot Torture*: "A pretty jogger is taken to a man's apartment. . . . After smelling her socks he licks her bare feet, ties them up and places them over a Hibachi. Then he tickles them and . . . " (p. 1620). The ultimate pun of pornography is the literalization of fantasy—just as the impossibility of that literalization in its totality is pornography's own self-parodying shadow.

The Bureau of Anonymity

"Who would speak publicly in favor of pornography?" ask the dissenting women commissioners at the beginning of the *Report*. Pornography inserts itself as a particular mode of pleasure for a society characterized by anonymity. Here every aspect of pornography as a private practice stands in contradiction to every aspect of pornography as a public form. Witnesses must step into the pornographic mode by the very fact of "exposing themselves."

Once we face the unbearable realization that the realization of fantasy would be unbearable, the concept of anonymity arises as a solution. For what is this concept other than a solution to the disjunctions between fantasy and action under pressure from the social? Anonymity preserves the public face of the subject by privatizing it and allows the private to be put on display without risk or consequence. The abstract language of anonymity releases the body from its proper name and thus sustains the illusion of a "basic" subjectivity beyond (both outside of and prior to) language—a subjectivity limited by neither the body nor the social.

From the Good Samaritan to the product tamperer, the anonymous agent stands poised between causality and responsibility, subjectivity and objectivity. Beauvoir argues, in fact, that such an erotics of "apartness" is central to Sade: "a combination of passionate sexual appetites with a basic emotional 'apartness' which seems to me to be the key to his eroticism" (*ODS*, p. 21). The key to this apartness is its reliance upon a mechanization and objectification of the body as a body. For the body freed from its proper name is not released into a natural state; it is released into a pure objectivity allowing it to take place within the sexual system as a bodily location: anonymity and detachment are accompanied by an insatiable physical desire. The libertines of the most extreme degree invent veritable machines for sexual practices.

Thus it is not a random attachment that anonymity bears to technology. Each new technology of communication has generated its own sexual field, merging the promised, but perpetually deferred, intimacies of consumerism with the abstractions of serial reproduction. Writing, printing, lithography, photography, film, video technology, telephone sex and Dial-A-Porn, peep-show apparatuses, computer sex networks—the technological dissemination of sexual fantasy mystifies a "sex itself" just as the spread of the Gospels mystifies the face of God. "Any enjoyment is weakened when shared," writes Sade (*ODS*, p. 22). Contrary to the fears of the antipornography movement, technology has allowed pornography to shrink farther and farther from a common public view. Adult theaters and "skin" magazines have decreased in favor of home video and home computer pornography: the anonymity of the public field of technology can thereby augment the intimacy of the private field of technology. Here the technology has simply developed along the lines of the mores of those who can afford it. The middle-class sanctification of the sexuality of the parents' bedroom and the concomitant denigration of the public sexuality of prostitution and homosexuality are well served by these technological developments.

The horror of the Meese Commission members in finding themselves in peep-show booths—the particular terror with which these booths are described, including the shoes sticking to the floor, the filth, and stench noted earlier—points to the ways in which these forms of anonymous sexuality are particularly threatening to the bourgeoisie's standards of sexual conduct. For the "glory hole" permits a particular form of anonymity—an anonymity of the body in pieces. Sex is detached from the whole or organic body, from gender, from race, class, age, and all accouterments of the proper name. "The anonymity provided by the 'glory holes' allows the participants to fantasize about the gender and other characteristics of their partners," states the *Report* (p. 1475). But the point is that such a sexuality removes the necessity of fantasy: fantasy is a moot issue, for sex here has no concrete form, no literalization of the Other against which fantasy can articulate itself. The commission's noteworthy solution to this problem of an aberrant relation to representation appears on page 457: "INDIVIDUAL BOOTHS . . . SHOULD NOT BE EQUIPPED WITH DOORS. THE OCCUPANT OF THE BOOTH SHOULD BE CLEARLY VISIBLE." It does not occur to the commissioners (and one must not discount the possibility that certain portions of the *Report* are precisely designed to attest to the commissioners' naiveté and hence qualifications) that the removal of doors—as is the case with the removal of doors from high school toilets—results in its own voyeuristic, and thereby pleasurable, possibilities.

Finally, it must be noted that although pornography is often characterized by its "explicitness" (the commission considers the depiction of "individuals with clearly visible pubic hairs" [p. 1355] as an index to explicitness, for example), such detail is shown in the light of anonymity and other technological processes as a matter of increasing abstraction. Pornography film stars choose allegorical names; telephone sex is delivered by taped messages; child pornography is disseminated over personal computers. The *Report* itself criticizes the productions of pornography for being unattributed: "These books generally do not provide specific information about the authors of the books. Many books do not even include the name of the author. And, when the author's name is given, many times this name is fictitious" (pp. 1453–54). Analogously, pornography is accused of not having a "plot"—an accusation that should be read in light of the valorization of conversion and individuality within the *Report*'s own politics. The unattributed dissemination of pornography throughout the culture is no more remarkable than the unattributed dissemination of cornflakes or roller bearings; what is remarkable, and threatening, is the capacity of pornographic discourse to approach a dismantling of sublimation. Not only is the merely ornamental status of narrative foregrounded, but the ornamental status of all of culture is foregrounded to a point where *everything* is sublimation. But of course once everything is revealed as a pun or parody of sexuality, everything gets reinscribed as being of interest in its own right, and mere description emerges as a possibility of critique.

The Suppression of the Female Gaze

This outline of the relations common to pornographic discourse in all its forms thus enables us to reinscribe, in a similar gesture, some aspects of the feminine problematized by pornography. For a critique of pornography must be a critique of those forms of rationality employed within and against it as well as a critique of pornography's thematics alone. My aim has been to point to the impossibility of mounting a critique of pornography within those forms of rationality, to assert thereby the identity of the Meese Commission *Report* with the tradition of the Sadian project, and to broadly position the pornographic gesture within the state and the rationality of the state.

Clearly, the *Report* is designed to reify a certain form of sexuality, a procreative sexuality within the context of bourgeois family structure. Yet it is also clear that the *Report* has a broader ideological program in linking pornography and the underworld of crime and illegality with threatening developments within the middle classes themselves. Father Ritter offers a set of chilling correlations (and within his discourse, correlation always suffices as causality) between "women's lib" and rape.[32] Commissioner Dobson argues that "latchkey kids by the millions are watching porn on Cable TV and reading their parents' adult magazines. . . . they can hear shocking vulgarities for free on their heavy metal radio stations." He also links pornography with "unwed pregnancy and abortion" (p. 79).[33]

It is a commonplace of Sade criticism to note Sade's virulent hatred of the mother,[34] his fear of the female genitalia, and the consequent hiding and "perverse" eroticizing of the woman's body in his work. Yet the logic of the oppression of the feminine in the pornographic tradition cannot be addressed simply by focusing on the thematics of pornography. For pornography is merely a symptom of oppression and one that, like all forms of representation, reveals (by means of features such as its tendency toward self-parody) contradictions in the logic of this oppression. Even on the surface, it is clear that endeavors such as the Meese Commission *Report* draw attention away from the material existence of rape, murder, assault, labor abuses, public health and safety violations, child molestation, and other clearly illegal acts by displacing their import, and their remedy, to the domain of this "underground" form of representation. It is as if we could rid ourselves of social evils by lobotomizing some social unconscious.

Thus it is imperative that we consider the function of all forms of pornography's discourses in preserving the power of a hidden sexuality. It is clear that obscenity definitions, for example, are designed to protect the ineffable, inarticulatable power of this sexuality.[35] But we must equally consider the function of pornography's discourses in suppressing the articulation of a female gaze. This

suppression appears in the Meese Commission *Report* on a remarkable variety of levels: the positioning of the female commissioners
within the patriarchal structure; the correlative fear, expressed in
comments like those of Ritter and Dobson, of the social mobilization
of women in the workplace and the demands made by women for
bodily autonomy; the anonymity and typification of the female witness (see, for example, the testimony of "Miss F," "Miss I," and
"Miss P" on pages 791–92, and the pictures of shrouded anonymous
witnesses closing the *Report* [figure 12]); and, consequently, the
occlusion of a female "voluntary" desire and a female voluntary
gaze. The only voluntary impulse allotted to a woman here is the
narrative or confessional impulse of "emptying out" her sexuality.

The sexual problematic of the commission echoes a political problematic as deep as the term *pornography* itself. The pleasures of
sexual testimony, of which the women here are the vehicles, are
present in the very etymology of pornography as the writing of
whores. Here the whore, whose sexuality has been objectified and
dispersed from her body, makes the final gesture of disclosure in
the outpourings of her writing. Yet the actuality of her lack of access
to writing (even if writing is only in some conventional sense a good,
and not naturally so), the exposure of this etymology as a lie and a
"cover-up," and the totalitarian daydream of the Sadian taxonomy
(where complete access to the knowledge of four whores will suffice
to account for all the sexual possibilities of the world) reframe the
very concept of pornography within a binary (both castrating and
restorative) articulation of necessarily "masculine" mastery.[36]

The suppression of a female gaze acquires the status of a structural
principle of such implicitness as to give evidence to its importance
as a cultural rule. For example, the commission constantly relies
upon a science of "experimentation" within a "controlled environment." Thus we can see that the return of the repressed Sadian
scenario at every location of curiosity here begins to acquire slapstick
proportions. A witness, Professor Edward Donnerstein, testifies:
"Let me point out one thing. We use in our research very normal
people" (p. 168). Although Donnerstein's work "now" involves fe-
males, virtually all the experimental evidence relied on by the commissioners comes from the reactions of male college students to
pornography. In looking for evidence of contamination by pornography, what more likely spot than earlier versions of the commis-

sioners themselves? The point of such research, and of its function for the commission, is the light it sheds upon the genesis of the perversion—a genesis that would explain away the very notion of sexual identity by naturalizing it into an equally naturalized biology.

Among the very normal people exposed to pornography, we therefore do not find women. Women are constantly framed by the *Report* as "unwilling viewers" or "forced viewers" of pornography. The pornographic films, books, and videos included as examples in the *Report* are described by "trained [male] professionals." The commission declares: "we obviously cannot here explore fully all of the forms in which women are discriminated against in contemporary society. Nor can we explore all the causes of that discrimination" (p. 334). Thus—and here the link to aspects of "feminism" is strained but nevertheless accomplished—the censorship of pornography will attack a "pornography industry" within which "the most powerless citizens in society are singled out on the basis of their gender . . . for deprivations of liberty, property, labor, bodily and psychic security and integrity, privacy, reputation, and even life" (p. 755). Presumably, women's powerlessness can then be fully exercised in other, more passionately real, domains.

In his initial statement, Chairman Hudson explains his objection to Class III materials (materials that are not by definition obscene): "Therefore, in the final analysis, Class III material appears to impact adversely on the family concept and its value to society. . . . Those items which tend to distort the moral sensitivity of women and undermine the values underlying the family unit are socially harmful" (p. 29). Here is a resounding echo of the earlier "anthropology" of the *Report*—the contention that the display of female genitals is universally tabooed. Pornography's bandaging of the female gaze is "only" a recapitulation of a larger bandaging of female sexuality that finds its binary logic in the erect and at-ease postures of masculine power.

In her incisive essay on masochism and subjectivity, Kaja Silverman argues that a female voluntary desire, a female gaze finding pleasure beyond the identifications of the situational, would result in jeopardizing the illusion of masculine activity:

> Voluntary exhibitionism makes overt the disquieting fact that the female spectacle is defined not by any actual male gaze, but by the

> Gaze of the Other. . . . It poses a much more profound castration threat
> than Freud was willing to acknowledge, for by making overt the
> distance between the gaze and the Gaze, and by revealing the fatal
> attractiveness of the feminine/masochistic position, it quite literally
> cuts off the masculine sadistic position.[37]

In other words, the female gaze reminds us of the *situation* of comparison, of the impossibility of fixity, and of the materiality of representation.

To look on pornography is to be caught in pornography's binary logic, but it is also to begin to imagine, beyond the sutures of imagining, those taboos that pornography cannot accommodate: the taboos of the female body in its nonspecificity, nonfixity as an identity. We have only to notice the Sadian railings against the breast and disgust at the (unnamable) female genitalia, the "undermining" perversion of milk and pregnancy in the Meese Commission *Report*, and the generalized anxiety of pornography's repression of menstruation. We find ourselves in the situated heterogeneity of the preposition once again: the *without* of castration; the *within, of*, and *about* of pregnancy; "*behind* every man"; *before* there was a proper name, there was another proper name. It is clear that liberation from identity is constituted by the liberation of the gaze from identity, a mobilization and confiscation of the gaze that would put into question elements of subjectivity and assert the heterogeneity of pleasure. Of this wish (Freud would no doubt call it a matter of "preaching to the winds"), we can only say that we are defined by our doing without it, and yet, that we will most certainly know it when we see it.

Notes

1. Michel Foucault, *The History of Sexuality*, vol. 1: *An Introduction*, trans. Robert Hurley (New York: Vintage Books, 1980), p. 155.
2. Roland Barthes, *Sade, Fourier, Loyola*, trans. Richard Miller (New York: Hill and Wang, 1976), p. 36; hereafter abbreviated *SFL*.
3. According to the Philadelphia Government Bookstore, the Government Printing Office is, by this writing, completely sold out of the *Report*. Like all classics of pornography, the *Report* has now been "pirated" by secondary publishers. My own university's government documents librarian keeps the library's copy of the *Report* locked in a drawer lest it be "stolen by students."
4. Marquis de Sade, *The 120 Days of Sodom and Other Writings*, ed. and trans.

Austryn Wainhouse and Richard Seaver (New York: Grove Press, 1966), p. 538; hereafter abbreviated *ODS*.

5. The Attorney General's Commission on Pornography, *Final Report* (Washington, D.C.: Government Printing Office, 1986), vol. 1, p. 36; hereafter cited by page number alone.

6. Jean Baudrillard, "What Are You Doing After the Orgy?" *Artforum* 22 (October 1983): "Our obscenity, our pornography does not stem from sexual lust, it stems from the paralyzed frenzy of the image" (p. 43).

7. This phrase appears at the conclusion of a description of the schedule of deflorations "at which times the respective seals shall be broken," and thereby illustrates the ways in which a rhetoric of seals, clasps, chains, and covers links desire's domains of writing and orifices. Furthermore, the decisive play between readability and unreadability, the very impossibility of Sade's text as text, is symptomatic of Sade's perfected technique: the reader's pleasure is as well a matter of unbearable waiting juxtaposed with unbearable excess. Simone de Beauvoir makes this point in her essay "Must We Burn Sade?": "Even his admirers will readily admit that his work is, for the most part, unreadable" (quoted in *ODS*, p. 4).

8. Manfredo Tafuri, *The Sphere and the Labyrinth: Avant-Gardes and Architecture from Piranesi to the 1970s*, trans. Pelligrino d'Acierno and Robert Connolly (Cambridge, Mass.: MIT Press), p. 47.

9. "The pleasure of comparison" is "a pleasure which can only be born of the sight of wretched persons, and here one sees none at all. It is from the sight of him who does not in the least enjoy what I enjoy, and who suffers, that comes the charm of being able to say to one's self: 'I am therefore happier than he.' Wherever men may be found equal, and where these differences do not exist, happiness shall never exist either" (*ODS*, p. 362).

10. Erving Goffman, "On the Characteristics of Total Institutions," in *Asylums: Essays on the Social Situation of Mental Patients and Other Inmates* (Garden City, N.Y.: Anchor Books, 1961), pp. 1–124.

11. Mikhail Bakhtin in *Speech Genres and Other Late Essays*, trans. Vern W. McGee, ed. Caryl Emerson and Michael Holquist (Austin: University of Texas Press, 1986) has described hell as a place where there is no third person, no listener: "Cf. the understanding of the Fascist torture chamber or hell in Thomas Mann as absolute *lack of being heard*, as the absolute absence of a *third party*" (p. 126). Thus we have a further gloss on the aurality of Piranesi's vast spaces and the impression they give of a cry on the horizon of language—a cry heard only by a viewer/"listener" caught on the other side of a horizon of representation. And, of course, while such a binary "dialogue" is the purported aim of the Sadian scenario (where the masochistic/sadistic, acted-on/acting equation is a matter of a simple splitting of the subject), Sade continually and humorously reminds us of the intervention of contingency in this pure dialogue of power: inconsistency in the rules of the château's society, inconsistencies in the plot itself, premature ejaculations, outbursts of "feeling." Control always receives, reluctantly, its own limit.

12. See the drawing of the storytelling arena in *SFL*, p. 147.

13. "The booth is sometimes equipped with a lock on the door. Many patrons intentionally leave the door unlocked. Some patrons look inside the booths in an attempt to find one already occupied" (p. 1476).

14. But this grammar of stories remains a grammar; subjectivity is only positioning

within the grammar. As we shall consider later in this essay, there are no completed narratives in *The 120 Days of Sodom,* for there can be no plot, no peripeteia, no teleology. There is only the narrative situation, halted by the unbearable prospect of its realizability: stopped, frozen, perpetually erect.

15. The full statement by Becker and Levine is on pp. 195–212.

16. See, for example, D. A. Miller's argument in *"Cage aux folles:* Sensation and Gender in Wilkie Collins's *The Woman in White,"* *Representations* 14 (Spring 1986): 107–36. Walter Kendrick's recent study of pornography, *The Secret Museum: Pornography in Modern Culture* (New York: Viking, Press, 1987), provides a useful summary of the shifting historical content of this figure of the naive viewer. See the chapter "Adventures of the Young Person," pp. 67–94.

17. Georges Bataille, *Erotism, Death and Sensuality,* trans. Mary Dalwood (San Francisco: City Lights Books, 1986), p. 161.

18. See, for example, *ODS,* p. 634: "The cooks complain and say that the service will not be able to continue any longer if Messieurs go on fussing about with the help, and the society agrees to a truce extending until March."

19. Other than to be dead, of course, the final collapse of the physiological and the symbolic.

20. "The recital continues, leaving the spectators convinced of a truth wherewith, I believe, they have already been penetrated for a long time: that the idea of crime is able always to ignite the senses and lead us to lubricity" (*ODS,* p. 296). Dalia Judovitz has provided an important discussion of Sade's technique in relation to his novelistic aesthetics here in her essay " 'Sex,' Or, the Misfortunes of Literature," in *Sade Without Measure,* ed. D. Allison, M. Roberts, and A. Weiss (New York: Cambridge University Press, 1991): "Sade's description of the novelist as the true man of nature [in his *Reflections on the Novel*] involves the fundamental task of representing nature. However, this relation of depiction (*peindre*), or representation, is interpreted by Sade according to the logic of parody or simulation, as an incestuous relationship, a relation of crime and complicity. As nature's lover and son, Sade situates the novelistic project in the cultural space, where the imitation of nature through cultural acts is perverted through the deployment of a scandalous filiation. The task of the author according to Sade, is not simply to replicate nature, but to imitate its sublime excesses, and, consequently, to engage in a complicitous and criminal relation. The act of writing is tied fundamentally to the production of excess in the domain of representation, which because of its parodic nature disrupts irrevocably the conventional formulation of novelistic mimesis. The attempt to mimic nature, by being truly faithful to her designs, leads to the complicitous identification of the hand of nature with that of the author." For another helpful gloss on Sade's theory of the novel in relation to the theory of reason posed in the Justine–Juliette sequence, see Josué Harari, "Staging the Libertine Imaginary II: Personal and Fictional Scenarios," in *Scenarios of the Imaginary: Theorizing the French Enlightenment* (Ithaca, N.Y.: Cornell University Press, 1987), pp. 161–93.

21. Plato, *Meno: The Immortality of the Soul,* in *The Works of Plato,* trans. Benjamin Jowett (New York: Tudor, n.d.), vol. 3, pp. 3–55.

22. See Jacques Lacan, *The Four Fundamental Concepts of Psycho-Analysis,* trans. Alan Sheridan, ed. Jacques-Alain Miller (New York: Norton, 1981): "What the voyeur is looking for and finds is merely a shadow, a shadow behind the curtain. There he will phantasize any magic of presence, the most graceful of girls, for example, even

if on the other side there is only a hairy athlete. What he is looking for is not, as one says, the phallus—but precisely its absence, hence the pre-eminence of certain forms as objects of his search" (p. 182).

23. This argument finds a complementary elaboration in Leo Bersani, *A Future for Astyanax: Character and Desire in Literature* (New York: Columbia University Press, 1984), pp. 286–315.

24. Michel Foucault, *The Order of Things: An Archaeology of the Human Sciences* (New York: Pantheon Books, 1973), p. 209.

25. See *ODS*, pp. 15–16.

26. For discussion of the relations between "the real" and photography, see pp. 383, 405, 597, 839.

27. Consider Justice William Brennan's comment in *Paris Adult Theatre I* v. *Slaton:* "While the material may have varying degrees of social importance, it is hardly a source of edification to the members of this Court who are compelled to view it before passing on its obscenity" (quoted on pp. 222–23).

28. Although one woman testified that "victims are a curiosity. People come to see us talk about our genitals as if we are some form of entertainment" (p. 821), she did testify.

29. For a discussion regarding the credibility of Marchiano's testimony and the credibility of her accounts of her experiences in her autobiography, *Ordeal*, see p. 866n.

30. See photograph on p. 1941.

31. Described on pp. 1701–15.

32. See p. 144, n. 11.

33. Dobson suggests that "at an age when elementary school children should be reading *Tom Sawyer* and viewing traditional entertainment in the spirit of Walt Disney, they are learning perverted facts" (p. 79).

34. Indeed, many of the pleasures of the libertine—measuring, collating, washing, feeding, handling excrement—are duties of the mother. And the labor/pain/pleasure configuration leading to death pursued here has an evident inverse analogue in childbirth, as the death of Constance makes clear. For further discussion of Sade's relation to the maternal and the feminine, see Beauvoir, "Must We Burn Sade?" in *ODS*, pp. 3–64, and Pierre Klossowski, "Nature as Destructive Principle," in *ODS*, pp. 65–86, as well as Barthes, "Hiding the Woman," *SFL*, pp. 123–24.

35. See pp. 1277–88.

36. In a number of recent theoretical works, the parameters of pornography's presentation of sexuality are suggestively formulated. Jean Laplanche's investigations of the relations of nonsexual aggression to sexual violence and of the relations of representations of aggression to representations of the Sadian scenario lead to an understanding of why what gets repressed is the fantasy and not the "actual memory" of sexual pleasure in violence (*Life and Death in Psychoanalysis*, trans. Jeffrey Mehlman [Baltimore: Johns Hopkins University Press, 1976], p. 102). We can thus see the Meese Commission attack on fantasy within the context of a frustrated relation to "sex itself"—a frustration, of course, mobilizing and articulating all sexual desire. Laplanche's work and Juliet Mitchell's readings of Freud and Lacan further outline the necessity of perversion in the realization of sexuality, sexuality being emergent in the necessary perversion of desire away from biology/need. Psychoanalysis thereby offers a powerful model of sexuality's ability to take its point of departure from

"absolutely anything" (Laplanche, *Life and Death in Psychoanalysis*, p. 101; Juliet Mitchell, "Introduction—I," in Jacques Lacan, *Feminine Sexuality*, ed. Juliet Mitchell and Jacqueline Rose, trans. Jacqueline Rose [New York: Norton, 1982], pp. 10–11). And finally, works by Dennis Giles and Kaja Silverman on the specific relations between masochism and scopic desire in pornographic film have explored the ways pornographic images situate the male viewer within an inclusive scenario where a variety of roles and attributes (predominantly, of course, his "masculinity" in relation to his "femininity") can be set in sequence (Giles), and the ways pornographic images allow the male viewer to compulsively repeat "an elaborate denial of passivity and masochism" (Silverman) (Giles, "Pornographic Space: The Other Place," in *Film: Historical–Theoretical Speculations*, 1977 Film Studies Annual, part 2 [Pleasantville, N.Y.: Redgrave, 1977], pp. 52–66; Kaja Silverman, "Masochism and Subjectivity," *Framework* 12 [1980]: 2–9).

    37. Silverman, "Masochism and Subjectivity," p. 6.

9

Coda: Reverse Trompe L'Oeil\ The Eruption of the Real

This time, I remembered I was lying in the oak closet, and I heard distinctly the gusty wind, and the driving of the snow; I heard, also, the fir-bough repeat its teasing sound, and ascribed it to the right cause; but it annoyed me so much, that I resolved to silence it, if possible; and, I thought, I rose and endeavoured to unhasp the casement. The hook was soldered into the staple, a circumstance observed by me when awake, but forgotten.

"I must stop it, nevertheless!" I muttered, knocking my knuckles through the glass, and stretching an arm out to seize the importunate branch; instead of which, my fingers closed on the fingers of a little, ice-cold hand! . . .

"Let me in—let me in!"

"Who are you?" I asked, struggling, meanwhile, to disengage myself.

"Catherine Linton," it replied shiveringly . . .

As it spoke, I discerned, obscurely, a child's face looking through the window—terror made me cruel; and, finding it useless to attempt shaking the creature off, I pulled its wrist on to the broken pane, and rubbed it to and fro till the blood ran down and soaked the bedclothes: still it wailed, "Let me in!" and maintained its tenacious grip, almost maddening me with fear.

"How can I!" I said at length. "Let me go, if you want me to let you in!"

The fingers relaxed, I snatched mine through the hole, hurriedly piled the books up in a pyramid against it, and stopped my ears to exclude the lamentable prayer.

Emily Brontë, *Wuthering Heights*[1]

You notice that the metaphor of surface begins to break down. The metaphor of surface becomes the surface of metaphor; the relation among signifiers, posited as a material and historical relation, nevertheless continues to be haunted by the deferred ontology that is its point of origin. What has been suppressed is the alterity that will erupt as nature and death—the alterity of the Real. As in the figuration/disfiguration of Piranesi, what seems to be noise turns into a cry, what seems to be nature becomes a matter of history. Mr. Lockwood, who wants to enter the house, is the perpetrator of the most violent crime in all of *Wuthering Heights*, staunching the wound/wind with a pyramid of books. The bough turned into a child's icy hand: the trauma. The child's icy hand turned into a dream: the fantasy. The dream turned into the wish of the other: the ontology of the subject. The wish of the other bound about by pain: the ontology of recognition.

The "retro mode," in its eighteenth-century and later forms, is accomplished as the superimposition of surface upon a site of discontinuity and temporal loss. All representations of the past foreground their representational aspects in these cases; thus allusion is emphasized over particularity. Consider then the retro mode as a form of trompe l'oeil, a triumph of surface over materiality and time, as in Horace Walpole's Strawberry Hill:

> He seems never to have realized that Gothic was an art of construction, and not simply decoration, and his interpretation of the form was peculiarly limited to surfaces and visibilities. He could not afford groining or fretwork for the stairways, but he felt they were necessary. According to his practice he might have made them out of plaster and lath; he might have made them out of carved cardboard; but what he actually did was simply paste up wallpaper with groining painted on it. For battlements he nailed cardboard on the framework of the cottage. One of the quips of the day was that Horrie had outlived four sets of battlements.[2]

But then, in a dream Walpole finds his imaginary architecture taking shape, as though the absconding of agency were the key to securing a relation to history: "on the uppermost bannister of a great staircase I saw a gigantic hand in armour. In the evening I sat down and began to write, without knowing in the least what I intended to say or relate. The work grew on my hands, and I grew fond of it."[3] How can language absolve itself of agency and consequence? The triumph of trompe l'oeil is not that it seems to be what it is not, but that it presents the illusion of not being at all—that is, the illusion of having no author, no history, and hence no capacity for decay or death. This is not a matter of a hyperrealism, which always celebrates the triumph of art and artifice over constraint; instead, trompe l'oeil attempts to bypass the limits of representation and hence to make all appearances representative. From the trompe l'oeil of Walpole's battlements to that of the punished graffiti writer's flowerpots and windowsills, a surface of signs papers the founding disjunctions of the trompe l'oeil's own occasion.

Language attempting artifactuality, transcendence over particularity and over a context of origin: this is language coming forward in a dream, in automatic writing, or in its most desperate attempt, the forgeries made possible by a belief in ghosts. Picture Chatterton reading the opening of *The Castle of Otranto*:

> The following work was found in the library of an ancient Catholic family in the north of England. It was printed at Naples, in the black letter, in the year 1529. How much sooner it was written does not appear. The principal incidents are such as were believed in the darkest ages of christianity. . . . There is no other circumstance in the work, that can lead us to guess at the period in which the scene is laid.[4]

After all, Percy had found the manuscript under the bureau. When the work then erupts—storms and geological upheavals miming the Lisbon earthquake of 1755, ancestral portraits sighing and moaning, the giant crashing in pieces through the roof or stretching through the courtyard before ascending straight to heaven—we see a representation suppressing the Real in an attempt to represent its relation to the Real. This eruption is the reverse trompe l'oeil delayed by the play of representation.

Yet immediately, we encounter the problem of the representation of nature and death—those end points of representation itself. Death, deferred by the play of representation, necessarily signals the death of representation. What is the representation of violence here other than an abandonment of agency? Thus in closing, I want to consider the interrelated problems of the eruption of the Real, the death of representation, and the representation of this eruption. Consequently, I want to consider the failed theories of agency and

causality illustrated in the impossibility of the representation of the
Real. The formal qualities of the representation that simulate this
eruption—the second person, the copy, the attack on nature—appear as the secondariness of all ontological figures.

First the tuché, which we have borrowed . . . from Aristotle,
who uses it in his search for cause. We have translated it as
the encounter with the real. The real is beyond the automaton,
the return, the coming-back, the insistence of the signs, by
which we see ourselves governed by the pleasure principle.
The real is that which always lies behind the automaton, and
it is quite obvious, throughout Freud's research, that it is this
that is the object of his concern. . . . What is repeated, in fact,
is always something that occurs—the expression tells us quite
a lot about its relation to the tuché—as if by chance. This is
something that we analysts never allow ourselves to be taken
in by, on principle. . . . The function of the tuché, of the real
as encounter—the encounter in so far as it may be missed, in
so far as it is essentially the missed encounter—first presented
itself in the history of psycho-analysis in a form that was in
itself already enough to arouse our attention, that of the trauma.
. . . The place of the real, which stretches from the trauma to
the phantasy—in so far as the phantasy is never anything more
than the screen that conceals something quite primary, something determinant in the function of repetition—this is what
we must now examine. This, indeed, is what, for us, explains
both the ambiguity of the function of awakening and the function of the real in this awakening. The real may be represented
by the accident, the noise, the small element of reality, which
is evidence that we are not dreaming. . . . How can we fail to
see that awakening works in two directions—and that the awakening that re-situates us in a constituted and represented reality
carries out two tasks? The real has to be sought beyond the
dream—in what the dream has enveloped, hidden from us, behind the lack of representation of which there is only one representative. This is the Real that governs our activities more than
any other and it is psycho-analysis that designates it for us.

Lacan, *The Four Fundamental Concepts of Psycho-Analysis*[5]

According to Lacan, the Real cannot be articulated, for it is the
inarticulatable aspect of experience—that which comes from out of

bounds, upon which the Symbolic stumbles and the Imaginary is rescued from automation and repetition. Yet we must analyze the Real not as that which resists language (because such a possibility is already weakly reinscribed within the possibilities of language itself, just as concepts of nature and death arise in the Symbolic as stays against the inevitable appearance of an irreducible nature and death outside it), but, as Aristotle has set forth the problem, as a problem of causality. And in this sense, as an issue regarding causality, the history of Freud's relation to the concept of trauma becomes of much importance for us. In their textbook *The Language of Psycho-Analysis*, Jean Laplanche and J.-B. Pontalis outline a history of this relation that begins to critique the function of the concept of trauma itself.

Freud took the term *trauma* from medicine and specifically surgery, where the Greek origins of the word connected it to the effect of a wound. Hence for Freud, the trauma came from the world outside the ego and had the effect of a surplus, an overload of excitation that the system of the psyche was unable to manage. Laplanche and Pontalis explain that psychoanalysis carried over three aspects of the physical trauma to the notion of a psychical trauma: "the idea of a violent shock, the idea of a wound, and the idea of consequences affecting the whole organism."[6] As Freud pursues the concept, especially between 1895 and 1897, he moves from this physical model to one hypothesizing the trauma as being of an "essentially sexual nature,"[7] and eventually returns to the physical model in his interest in "accident" or "war" neuroses. But in the course of this development, he increasingly notices a doubled form of the trauma whereby the ego sets up a "pathological defence," a repression or repetition of the traumatic event that then, by means of further repetition, enables the excitations to be bound in such a way that the ego seems to dominate it. Obviously, Freud thereby enables the economy of the ego to continue to accommodate the ruptures of an alterity that threatens the very notion of such an economy.[8]

In the accommodations Freud makes as his theory proceeds, we see a repetition of the eruption of the Real in the interest of its containment. In other words, the trauma gives evidence of the limits of a topographical model, the projection of a surface that is in the interest of the ego both in its functioning and in the theoretical terms of Freud's argument. The trauma appears in the break between ego and world, and *is* the break between ego and world. It generates the repetition, the representation as a containment, yet it resists containment at this point of originating effect. Thus in theory and in practice, the rupture threatens the integrity of the subject, which is as well the integrity of psychoanalytic theory regarding the subject.

In his discovery of the repetition compulsion, Freud finds a threat to the pleasure principle, a threat that admits the possibility of a system gone haywire, a system no longer a system—not because it has experienced the shock of alterity so much as because it has internalized the effects of alterity, has turned the eruption upon itself. Laplanche and Pontalis succinctly explain this development:

> It may thus be seen how psycho-analytic investigation throws the concept of traumatic neurosis into question: it contests the decisive function of the traumatic event—first by stressing its relativity vis-à-vis the subject's tolerance and secondly, by inserting the traumatic experience into the context of the subject's particular history and organisation. Seen in this light, the notion of traumatic neurosis appears as nothing more than an initial, purely descriptive approximation which cannot survive any deeper analysis of the factors in question.[9]

Thus the trauma is a product of its repetition. And, as well, theory asserts its need to displace the trauma threatening its allegory and its ability to claim a capacity for repetition. In this sense, the development of the psychoanalytic concept of trauma vividly displays the inevitable reincorporation of the eruption of the Real back into the realm of the Symbolic. But in the *Outline of Psycho-Analysis* (1940) Freud wrote: "It is possible that what are known as traumatic neuroses (due to excessive fright or severe somatic shocks, such as railway collisions, burials under falls of earth, and so on) are an exception to this: their relations to determinants in childhood have hitherto eluded investigation."[10]

Once again, the theory illustrates a problem of ontology and causality exemplified by the phenomenon itself. If the trauma can only be inferred from its repetition, its status as a causal agent is continually held in abeyance.[11] To repeat in a somewhat different way, then, the Real is not the ineffable here, but the unattributable. When theories have an interest in displacing the Real, they have

no choice, for any attempt to establish the Real's location, and
certainly any attempt to restore it, will result in the sentimental
reinscription of historically articulated concepts of nature and death
back into the Symbolic. We see a dramatic example of this sentimentality in theories of postmodernism that diagnose a proliferation
of signs and surfaces as the cultural dominant. Consider these two
passages from well-known essays on postmodernism, the first from
Fredric Jameson's "Postmodernism and Consumer Society," the
second from Jean Baudrillard's "The Ecstasy of Communication":

> I believe that the emergence of postmodernism is closely related to
> the emergence of this new moment of late, consumer or multinational
> capitalism. I believe also that its formal features in many ways express
> the deeper logic of that particular social system. I will only be able,
> however, to show this for one major theme: namely the disappearance
> of a sense of history, the way in which our entire contemporary social
> system has little by little begun to lose its capacity to retain its own
> past, has begun to live in a perpetual present and in a perpetual
> change that obliterates traditions of the kind which all earlier social
> formations have had in one way or another to preserve.[12]

> ... today the scene [of domestic life, as opposed to the scene of
> history] and the mirror no longer exist; instead there is a screen and
> network. In place of the reflexive transcendence of mirror and scene,
> there is a nonreflecting surface, an immanent surface where operations
> unfold—the smooth operational surface of communication.[13]

Elsewhere Jameson has criticized postmodernism's "exhilaration
of the gleaming surface" and the way in which "objects fall into the
world and become decoration again; visual depth and systems of
interpretation fade away, and something peculiar happens to historical time."[14]

What both Jameson and Baudrillard mourn here is a loss of profundity and a slackening of tension, a tension that Jameson finds in
modernism and Baudrillard in earlier forms of commodity culture
or, in an extension of his argument, in primitive forms of "use
value." But neither can escape the reifying function of the theory
of postmodernism itself; neither can ignore the retro mode of the
argument here, whereby a surface is projected so that a profundity
can be lost—or perhaps more aptly, so that a profundity can be
restored in a utopian and futuristic politics of deferral. But this
problem of surface, trompe l'oeil, and the displacement of the Real

is not a historical problem per se. To claim so is to ignore the logic of representation itself, a logic emergent in the historical particularity and uses of its appearance. Any vertigo to be experienced here is not the result of a loss of a previously intimate relation to historical tradition, as Jameson proposes. Instead it is the vertigo of the re-alization of the ontological difference between alterity and the founding of representation, including the representation necessary for any theoretical allegory to "forget" its particular grounds. And the fear of a loss of profundity here is a fear regarding the end of thought, the death of representation as a moment of stasis, ennui, the unthinking that would characterize the abeyance of language itself.

But be careful! We have not yet said what this *Trieb* is—and if, for lack of representation, it is not there, what is this *Trieb?* We have to consider it as being only *Trieb* to come. How can we fail to see that awakening works in two directions—and that the awakening that re-situates us in a constituted and repre-sented reality carries out two tasks? The real has to be sought beyond the dream—in what the dream has enveloped, hidden from us, behind the lack of representation of which there is only one representative. This is the real that governs our ac-tivities more than any other.
    Lacan, *The Four Fundamental Concepts of Psycho-Analysis*[15]

You notice that the metaphor of surface begins to break down. The metaphor of surface is metaphor forgetting its metonymical ground. We thus return to the problem of return—the problem of the concept of language as artifact, as an illusion produced at the expense of a concept of language as action. As in a variety of eighteenth-century forms—consider the dark martial satire of John-son's *The Vanity of Human Wishes*, the allegorical eruptions alluding to the Book of Revelation and the fall of Rome in Benjamin West's *Death on a Pale Horse*, and those Gothic moments of breaking and transformation discussed earlier—postmodern art has an interest in probing the wound and exploring the effects of the repetition of the trauma. In one sense, this "work" is a continuation of the attack on nature that Sade represents. I am thinking here of cultural devel-opments ranging from the diabolical reality of the "snuff film" to the repetition compulsion evidenced in the popularity of postsurgery videotapes of one's surgery designed for viewing by the recuperating patient. Here the reality of the trauma is affirmed only by its containment in representation. The staging of pain follows, yet thereby comes to precede, the experience of pain.

What we witness in this process is once again an attempt at the containment of death of the kind we find in Gray's "Elegy," in Sade's taxonomies, and in the trompe l'oeil of distressed genres. And yet the proliferation of the representation only the more exemplifies the alterity of the rupture brought about by the "act of God," the out-of-the-blue alterity of the Real's appearance. Thus in these phenomena attempting the staging of pain or the probing of a wound, we find two techniques—intensification, and coincidence or accident—that mime the experience of the eruption of the Real, yet inevitably condemn the representation to the limits of the Symbolic.

We should remember that the very first defining trait of the trauma is its "intensity," the degree to which it resists incorporation into the economy of the subject and so incapacitates that subject. The abasement of the subject is thus a consequence of intensity, but as we witnessed in the case of the impostor and suicide, the subject's abasement also defines an articulation that counterbalances the unstable projections of the self-aggrandizing ego of the daydreamer. When a narrative seeks to represent the trauma, it is forced to intensify the stakes of narrative convention—to continue to seek new formal means of representing pain, accident, disruption. As with the language of wishes, the hope is that what is uttered might somehow come true. Thus we are within the realm of the animation and the breach—the aesthetic equivalents of traumatic eruptions.

One of the most rigorous meditations on these issues is Georges Bataille's 1928 work, *Story of the Eye*.[16] This "partly imaginary tale" is literally an exercise in obscenity, that is, an exercise in the formation of utterances "out of place," while metaphors both proliferate and disappear as "mere" metaphors, since any language can take effect. Two brief passages might serve as examples here:

> At any rate, the swampy regions of the cunt (nothing resembles them more than the days of flood and storm or even the suffocating gaseous

eruptions of volcanoes, and they never turn active except like storms or volcanoes, with something of catastrophe or disaster)—those heart-breaking regions . . . [17]

Upon my asking what the word *urinate* reminded her of, she replied: *terminate*, the eyes, with a razor, something red, the sun. And *egg?* A calf's eye because of the colour of the head (the calf's head) and also because the white of the egg was the white of the eye and the yolk the eyeball. The eye, she said, was egg-shaped.[18]

Bataille himself described the process of the work's construction: "I began writing with no precise goal, animated chiefly by a desire to forget, at least for the time being, the things I can be or do personally."[19] The "story" proceeds by accounting for actions that multiply symmetrically and increase algebraically. There is a min-imum of mediation: thoughts come true; all nature is sympathetic; characters communicate by gesture and by reciprocal actions of vi-olence and rupture. "Thus a love life started between the girl and myself and it was so intimate and so intense that we could hardly let a week go by without meeting. And yet we virtually never talked about it."[20] "By a sort of shared modesty, Simone and I had always avoided talking about the most important objects of our obses-sions."[21] This world of gestures and magical sympathies is a world of metaphor by definition, but only by definition. Since metaphor no longer is constrained by "likeness," it generates an infinite set of likenesses. Association and correspondences will come to char-acterize, and eventually dominate, even the seeming directness of acts of violence. Here is the first "collision" of plot and metaphor:

I remember that one day, when we were in a car tooling along at top speed, we crashed into a cyclist, an apparently very young and very pretty girl. Her head was almost totally ripped off by the wheels. . . . The horror and despair at so much bloody flesh, nauseating in part, and in part very beautiful, was fairly equivalent to our usual impres-sion upon seeing one another.[22]

Thus the intensification of sexual violence (and of course, as in Sade, sexuality and violence are always linked) only serves to reify the connections such acts bear to a structure of language. Whereas the accumulation of coincidences—coincidences of thoughts, coin-cidences of symmetry, coincidences of metaphor and analogy, co-incidences of seeing, coincidences of truth and story—comes to represent the rupture of a nonintentional causality or, more simply, the effect of the unconscious in the design of the work, Bataille is compelled to write an explanation of his practice (called, appropriately enough, "Coincidences") in which such coincidences are "described" and thereby ascribed to causal/autobiographical events.[23] We thereby see the complete structure of the trauma—action, fantasy, compulsion to repeat—worked out in Bataille's practice. But we also see that writing is unable to write its own grounds, that we have, regardless of the intensification of the description of the trauma, "merely" an intensification of description. Desire and fear are shown to be themselves coincidental here, as they are in the spontaneous realm of the Real's eruption, where all wishes are commands.

In his visual pun (the pun as a violent coincidence brought forward as a symptom of the unconscious is of course to be emphasized here) on the relation between "eyes" and "eggs," whereby seeing is a kind of action and visualizing a kind of breaking or violence, Bataille anticipates the meditations upon the separating function of the gaze found in such works as Andy Warhol's *Disaster* silk-screen series, Barbara Kruger's poster/assemblages captioning forms of visual "collision" and appropriation, and David Lynch's *Blue Velvet*, with its formal apparatus of eruption. But Bataille's narrative technique is also echoed in those post-modern novels working out the relation between intensification and coincidence. Here Kathy Acker's *Don Quixote* (1986) and J. G. Ballard's *Crash* (1973) provide a repertory of techniques, and their limitations, regarding the narrative presentation of the eruption of the Real.

In his 1974 introduction to the French edition of *Crash*, Ballard asks:

> Has the writer still the moral authority to invent a self-sufficient and self-enclosed world, to preside over his characters like an examiner, knowing all the questions in advance? . . . I feel that, in a sense, the writer knows nothing any longer. He has no moral stance. He offers the reader the contents of his own head, he offers a set of options and imaginative alternatives. His role is that of the scientist, whether on safari or in his laboratory, faced with a completely unknown terrain or subject. All he can do is devise hypotheses and test them against the facts.[24]

In fact, *Crash*, which he describes as "the first pornographic novel based on technology," continually takes as its theme and method the merger of accident and intentionality. Of course, this can hardly be the first pornographic novel based on technology, since pornography is by definition a technology of desire, an assemblage of techniques. But Ballard's contribution is to attempt to represent the construction of this representation: the merger of intentional acts and designs with retrospective techniques of causal interpretation. If we are reminded of the narrative technology of Sade, we are reminded as well of Victor Frankenstein's experiment in galvanization in which a birth awakens a death and intentions and effects continually are in flight from each other—the murderous merging of author and creation marking each contingency of plot.

The narrator of *Crash*, "Ballard" (whom we are nevertheless startled to hear addressed by his first name, "James," at the opening to chapter 6) has as his task the making of analogies: the articulation of a series of differences and resemblances marking the coincidence of sex and technology or successive disasters and collisions, and the ultimate analogy—that between one death and another. In telling the life of "Vaughan," the protagonist has dedicated himself to a practice of sexual/vehicular collisions that, being truly "practices," are designed to lead to a kind of ultimate performance piece—an orchestrated crash between his car and the limousine of Elizabeth Taylor. But the intended death is not the real death; the planned accident is defeated by the eruption of a true accident, as the opening to the novel claims:

> Vaughan died yesterday in his last car-crash. During our friendship he had rehearsed his death in many crashes, but this was his only true accident. Driven on a collision course towards the limousine of the film actress, his car jumped the rails of the London Airport flyover and plunged through the roof of a bus filled with airline passengers.[25]

Vaughan's rehearsals of his death are as well repetitions of the traumatic crash that transformed his destiny from a life as a scientist to a life pursuing, documenting, and intervening in the pain of other crash victims. Here is the breakdown of the system that Freud had described: repetition does not in this case lead to mastery and expulsion, but to a domination of the entire ego by the trajectory of the trauma.

As in *Frankenstein*, the narrator comes to suffer from his invention. Vaughan's recognition is the condition of Ballard's emergent identity. Ballard becomes Vaughan's narrator, collaborator, lover, and accomplice. Vaughan "drives" first Ballard's wife and then his car, the car he drives in the final crash. The pun on the drive becomes almost sentimental here, as the trajectories of "individuals" offer the only retrospective glimpse of "identities." And technology, as a system of effects, is a technology of sexual devices: the manipulation of orifices, handles, parts. Yet the book is rescued from an underlying humanism and incipient comedy by its relentless allegory. "Ballard," like Ballard, is unable to author his fate, yet must attempt to represent the relation between his intentions and the contingency that will erupt in his collision with death. Just as Vaughan has died in Ballard's car, so does Ballard, after Vaughan's death, return with his wife, Catherine, to Vaughan's Lincoln (presenting a rather unbearable pun, in that the narrator notes it is an exact copy of the car in which Kennedy was shot) and make "brief, ritual love." Afterward, he carries his semen in his hands to the "dismembered remains" of the car in which Vaughan died, and

> with the semen in my hands I marked the crushed controls and instrument dials, defining for the last time the contours of Vaughan's presence on the seats. The imprint of his buttocks seemed to hover among the creases of these deformed seats. I spread my semen over the seat, and then marked the sharp barb of the steering column, a bloodied lance rising from the deformed instrument panel. . . . Already I knew that I was designing the elements of my own car-crash.[26]

The last sentences of the book continue this claim to ritual: "Meanwhile, the traffic moves in an unceasing flow along the flyover. The aircraft rise from the runways of the airport, carrying the remnants of Vaughan's semen to the instrument panels and radiator grilles of a thousand crashing cars, the leg stances of a million passengers."[27] Yet looked at more closely, this sentence makes no "sense" at all: it is as gratuitously enigmatic as the smearing/figuring of semen produced in one crashed vehicle upon the instrument panel of another, as gratuitously enigmatic as the sexuality in the rest of the novel. Thus it is the perfect exemplum of the problem of the gap between intentions and effects—and the eruption of death in that gap—that the novel as nightmare takes as its theme and method. Ballard the "writer/scientist" and "Ballard" the invention have no claim to meaning because Ballard's claim is that the old world of replete meaning and human emotion is gone. We thereby have only the proliferation of metaphor and analogy, a desire for likeness forced by a violent and unattributable process of disfiguration.

Kathy Acker's *Don Quixote* is also "motivated" by the activities of metaphor severed from temporal and spatial constraints, from history, and from any "integrated" subjectivity of authorship. Subtitled *which was a dream,* the book is nevertheless structured in three sections: "The First Part of Don Quixote: The Beginning of Night"; "The Second Part of Don Quixote: Other Texts"; and "The Third Part of Don Quixote: The End of the Night." And so, from the table of contents on, there is an emptying out, and overdetermination, of content: the book will write Cervantes, Celine, and Borges's "Pierre Menard," and so "plagiarize" and forge whatever "identity" it might arrive at. Here it is important not to consider this a matter of rewriting or revision, for there is no attempt to translate, update, or improve upon the fabric of history other than to parody such a gesture of renovation. Indeed, the book opens with the heroine wrapped in "pale or puke green paper," about to have an abortion. Her goal will be "to love." And this goal will proceed as an attack on nature as nature has been articulated by the Symbolic:

> She decided that since she was setting out on the greatest adventure any person can take, that of the Holy Grail, she ought to have a name (identity). She had to name herself. . . . She needed a new life. She had to be named. . . . her wheeling bed's name was "Hack-kneed" or "Hackneyed," meaning "once a hack" or "always a hack" or "a writer" or "an attempt to have an identity that always fails." Just as "Hackneyed" is the glorification or change from non-existence into existence of "Hack-kneed," so, she decided, "catheter" is the glorification of "Kathy." By taking on such a name which, being long, is male, she would be able to become a female–male or a night–knight.[28]

Coincidences of aurality and visuality prop the actions of the text throughout. Association is causality; every change is a material, a "hackneyed" change. Pronouns and modes of characterization shift as discourses critiquing gender and property. For example, Thomas Hobbes's appellation is "The Angel of Death," and Quixote's sidekick, St. Simeon, becomes a dog (that is, an underdog) and, when combined with a history of the United States and the last days of the Nixon administration, an elaborate pun on "Virginia/Woof": "the only language you hear and can hear is 'Woof.' " Textual allusions from Catullus, Lampedusa, Biely's "Peterburg" (and so, of course, *Crime and Punishment*), and Wedekind's Lulu plays, and a writing over the classical and Christian pantheons following Goya's *The Fates*, overlap in an attack on originality and imagination. Devices of contradiction and repetition foreground the materiality of the writing itself. (See, for example, the "Intrusion of a Badly Written Section": "If I can't escape from the room by kiling [*sic*] myself, I must be able to escape, if I can, by being happy. By embracing and believing myself, just appearances, the night. By embracing, and believing, my deepest being which is not knowing. Therefore my vision has ended.")[29] Shifts in register and diction, explosions of tabooed phrases, and descriptions of tabooed acts attack the threshold of the representation, which poses not as an artifact but as an unfolding of effects of writing.[30]

The epigraph to "The Second Part of Don Quixote: Other Texts" is: "BEING DEAD, DON QUIXOTE COULD NO LONGER SPEAK, BEING BORN INTO AND PART OF A MALE WORLD, SHE HAD NO SPEECH OF HER OWN. ALL SHE COULD DO WAS READ MALE TEXTS WHICH WEREN'T HERS."[31] Like Sade, Acker thereby erases the distinction between a book and its criticism; but unlike Sade, Acker erases the distinction between sincere and parodying forms of theory. The gloss seems as plagiarized as any "text itself," so we are compelled to continually shift positions, much as we are by the "art of copying" found in the paintings and photographs of Acker's contemporaries Sherril Levine and Cindy Sherman. What is at stake here is any distinction between acting and being, which the historicized "nature" of language—that is, our relation to the Symbolic—compels us continually, if tragically, to put into question.

Here Don Quixote, Celine's Bardamu, and "Kathy" (Catherine Linton) are conflated as "pirates," adventurers questing in the interstices of war and other human evils. Acker's "Texts of Wars for Those Who Live in Silence," Text 3 of the book's middle section, brackets a discourse on nuclear holocaust with soliloquies by Kathy/Cathy:

> :I need you. :Because you had to be out of my life, I closed myself off to all other men. I didn't want. :Now, I'm very scared. Every other living being is a nuisance to me. My being alone is my only absolute pleasure. :I won't accept the norms I've been given. (Explaining to others): We've decided to rebel: If I can't get Heathcliff into my arms because we're too poor, I'll go off adventuring: :Wars are raging everywhere. Males dumber than nonhuman animals're

running the economic and political world. I want. what do I want? Is it wrong to want life? . . . :The perception of wartime. :A dog sticks its head over a barricade. You can't tell what the barricade is. The only event you see and you can see is the dog's head. :"Woof." The only language you hear and can hear is "Woof." :I thought I was at home. I thought I was lying in my bedroom by the moors. Because I'm weak, my brain becomes confused, and I unwillingly unconsciously screamed. Don't say anything. I've got to have someone. So stay with me. I don't need someone: I'm alone. I hate solitude. I need—so I can be in paradise. I dread to go to sleep now: my dreams shock me: I don't sleep anymore. Oh, if I were only but in my old bed in my old house! And the wind sounding through the gables sounding in the firs by the lattice. Do let me feel—the moors, the solitude come straight down to my heart—let me be alive! I am no better than a wailing child.[32]

As the preliminary colons imply, the sentence here and the thought itself are not produced by a spontaneous and original consciousness, but in response to an utterance already made, a previous sentence erased or fragmented, or what could be called the lost cause of some prior causality. The dog, we know, is Francisco Goya's *Perro* (1820–23), while the passage "A dog sticks its head over a barricade. You can't tell what the barricade is. . . . 'Woof' " comes as an act of self-plagiarism from Acker's 1984 essay "Realism for the Cause of Future Revolution."[33] All the relations between attribution, authority, theory and practice, primary and secondary texts, intention, repetition, and effects become exaggerated here, as if postmodernism could achieve an intensity beyond novelty.

You begin to see the surface in the metaphor of breakdown. You begin to see the breakdown in the surface of metaphor. You begin to see the metaphor in the breakdown of surface. :You can't see what the barricade is.

Notes

1. Emily Brontë, *Wuthering Heights*, ed. David Daiches (Harmondsworth: Penguin Books, 1965), p. 67.

2. E. F. Bleiler, "Horace Walpole and *The Castle of Otranto*," in *Three Gothic Novels*, ed. E. F. Bleiler (New York: Dover, 1966), pp. viii–ix.

3. Horace Walpole to William Cole, 9 March 1765, *Horace Walpole's Correspondence with the Reverend William Cole, 1762–1775*, ed. W. S. Lewis and A. Dayle Wallace (New Haven, Conn.: Yale University Press, 1937), p. 88.

4. Bleiler, "Horace Walpole and *The Castle of Otranto*," p. 17.

5. Jacques Lacan, *The Four Fundamental Concepts of Psycho-Analysis*, trans. Alan Sheridan, ed. Jacques-Alain Miller (New York: Norton, 1981), p. 60.

6. Jean Laplanche and J.-B. Pontalis, "Trauma," in *The Language of Psychoanalysis*, trans. Donald Nicholson-Smith (London: Hogarth Press, 1973), p. 466.

7. Ibid., p. 467.

8. Here, of course, we have another instance of the problem of a restricted economy. See the critique of restricted economy in Hegel in Georges Bataille, *Visions of Excess: Selected Writings, 1927–1939*, trans. A. Stoekl (Minneapolis: University of Minnesota Press, 1985), and in Jacques Derrida, "From Restricted to General Economy; A Hegelianism Without Reserve," in *Writing and Difference*, trans. Alan Bass (Chicago: University of Chicago Press, 1978), pp. 251–78, and "Difference," in *Margins of Philosophy*, trans. Alan Bass (Chicago: University of Chicago Press, 1982), pp. 1–27.

9. Laplanche and Pontalis, "Traumatic Neurosis," p. 472.

10. Quoted in ibid.

11. This is, then, the source of Lacan's "serious pun" on *souffrance* as "in suspense," "in abeyance," "awaiting attention," and pain. "Reality is in abeyance there, awaiting attention," he writes in *Four Fundamental Concepts of Psycho-Analysis*, p. 56.

12. Fredric Jameson, "Postmodernism and Consumer Society," in *The Anti-Aesthetic: Essays on Postmodern Culture*, ed. Hal Foster (Port Townsend, Wash.: Bay Press, 1983), p. 125. See also Anders Stephanson, "Regarding Postmodernism—A Conversation with Fredric Jameson," in *Universal Abandon: The Politics of Postmodernism*, ed. Andrew Ross (Minneapolis: University of Minnesota Press, 1988), pp. 3–30.

13. Jean Baudrillard, "The Ecstasy of Communication," in Foster, ed., *Anti-Aesthetic*, pp. 126–27.

14. Stephanson "Regarding Postmodernism," pp. 4–5.

15. Lacan, *Four Fundamental Concepts of Psycho Analysis*, p. 56.

16. Georges Bataille, *Story of the Eye*, trans. Joachim Neugroschel (1928; reprint, New York: Urizen Books, 1977).

17. Ibid., p. 22.

18. Ibid., p. 37.

19. Ibid., p. 69.

20. Ibid., p. 10.

21. Ibid., p. 37.

22. Ibid., p. 10.

23. Bataille recounts how three of the scenes in the story rely on biographical details he had suppressed or refused to connect: being scared by his brother, dressed as a ghost, at the foot of a castle wall; seeing a bull's horn tear out a matador's eye; being told by a doctor that he was making a "true" association that he claimed to be unaware of: the testicles of a bull as looking like eggs and eyes (p. 69). Of course, such "disclaimers" of knowledge result in a suspicion regarding the authenticity of the subject's language. Bataille writes in another supplementary text to *Story of the Eye*—its "Preface," entitled "W. C.": "A few people, reading *Coincidences*, wondered whether it did not have the fictional character of the tale itself" (p. 76).

24. J. G. Ballard, *Crash* (New York: Vintage Books, 1985), pp. 5–6.

25. Ibid., p. 7.

26. Ibid., p. 224.

27. Ibid.

28. Kathy Acker, *Don Quixote: which was a dream* (New York: Grove Press, 1986), p. 10.

29. Ibid., pp. 190–91.

30. Like the graffiti writer, Acker has an interest in the proximity of "taboo" and "tattoo." *Empire of the Senseless* (New York: Grove Press, 1988) is dedicated to her tattooist and explains: "The tattoo is primal parent to the visual arts. Beginning as abstract maps of spiritual visions, records of the 'other' world, tattoos were originally icons of power and mystery designating realms beyond normal land-dweller's experience. The extra-ordinary qualities of the tattoo's magic–religious origin remain constant even today, transferring to the bearer some sense of existing outside the conventions of normal society" (p. 140). This theme of the inscribed body—both self-inscribed and so an expression of the agency of the subject, and other-inscribed and so an expression of the logic of the Symbolic and its capacity to position the subject—becomes an important theme in her plagiarism of Hawthorne's *Scarlet Letter* in *Blood and Guts in High School* (New York: Grove Press, 1984).

31. Acker, *Don Quixote*, p. 39.

32. Ibid., pp. 76–77.

33. Kathy Acker, "Realism for the Cause of Future Revolution," in *Art After Modernism: Rethinking Representation*, ed. Marcia Tucker and Brian Wallis (Boston: Godine, for the New Museum of Contemporary Art, 1984), p. 34.

Works Cited

Abrahams, Roger. "Patterns of Structure and Role Relationships in the Child Ballad in the United States." *Journal of American Folklore* 79 (July–September, 1966): 448–62.

Abrahams, Roger, and George Foss. *Anglo-American Folk Song Style*. Englewood Cliffs, N.J.: Prentice-Hall, 1968.

Acker, Kathy. *Blood and Guts in High School*. New York: Grove Press, 1984.

———. *Don Quixote: which was a dream*. New York: Grove Press, 1986.

———. *Empire of the Senseless*. New York: Grove Press, 1988.

———. "Realism for the Cause of Future Revolution." In *Art After Modernism: Rethinking Representation*, edited by Marcia Tucker and Brian Wallis. Boston: Godine, for the New Museum of Contemporary Art, 1984.

Ackroyd, Peter. *Chatterton*. New York: Grove Press, 1987.

Adams, Percy. *Travel Literature and the Evolution of the Novel*. Lexington: University Press of Kentucky, 1983.

Addison, Joseph, and Richard Steele. *The Spectator*. 5 vols. Edited by Donald F. Bond. Oxford: Clarendon Press, 1965.

Adorno, Theodor. *Aesthetic Theory*. Translated by C. Lenhardt, edited by Gretel Adorno and Rolf Tiedemann. London: Routledge & Kegan Paul, 1970.

Alloula, Malek. *The Colonial Harem*. Translated by Myrna Godzich and Wlad Godzich. Minneapolis: University of Minnesota Press, 1986.

Altick, Richard. *The Scholar Adventurers*. New York: Macmillan, 1950.

Ames, Daniel T. *Ames on Forgery: Its Detection and Illustration*. San Francisco: Bancroft-Whitney, 1899.

Ancient Scottish Poems: Published from the Manuscript of George Bannatyne. MDLXVIII. Edinburgh: A. Murray and J. Cochran, 1770.

Anthony, Piers. *Kirlian Quest.* New York: Avon Books, 1978.

Appleton, William. *A Cycle of Cathay: The Chinese Vogue in England During the Seventeenth and Eighteenth Centuries.* New York: Columbia University Press, 1951.

Ariès, Philippe. "At the Point of Origin." In *The Child's Part,* edited by Peter Brooks. Boston: Beacon Press, 1969.

Aristotle. *Rhetoric.* In *The Basic Works of Aristotle,* edited by Richard McKeon, translated by W. D. Ross. New York: Random House, 1941.

Attorney General's Commission on Pornography. *Final Report.* 2 vols. Washington, D.C.: Government Printing Office, 1986.

Auerbach, Jonathan. "Executing the Model: Painting, Sculpture, and Romance-writing in Hawthorne's *The Marble Faun.*" *ELH* 47 (1980): 103–20.

Saint Augustine. *Confessions.* Translated by R. S. Pine-Coffin. Harmondsworth: Penguin Books, 1961.

Austin, J. L. *How to Do Things with Words.* Edited by J. O. Urmson. New York: Oxford University Press, 1962.

Bagnani, Gilbert. "On Fakes and Forgeries." *The Phoenix* 14 (1960): 228–44.

Baird, Theodore. "The Time-Scheme of *Tristram Shandy* and a Source." *PMLA* 51 (1936): 803–20.

Bakhtin, Mikhail. *The Dialogic Imagination.* Edited by Michael Holquist, translated by Michael Holquist and Caryl Emerson. Austin: University of Texas Press, 1981.

———. *Speech Genres and Other Late Essays.* Translated by Vern W. McGee, edited by Caryl Emerson and Michael Holquist. Austin: University of Texas Press, 1986.

Ballard, J. G. *Crash.* New York: Vintage Books, 1985.

Barchilon, Jacques, and Peter Flinders. *Charles Perrault.* Boston: Twayne, 1981.

Barthes, Roland. *Sade, Fourier, Loyola.* Translated by Richard Miller. New York: Hill and Wang, 1976.

Bataille, Georges. *Erotism, Death and Sensuality.* Translated by Mary Dalwood. San Francisco: City Lights Books, 1986.

———. *Story of the Eye.* Translated by Joachim Neugroschel. 1928. Reprint. New York: Urizen Books, 1977.

———. *Visions of Excess: Selected Writings, 1927–1939.* Translated by A. Stoekl. Minneapolis: University of Minnesota Press, 1985.

Batten, Charles. *Pleasurable Instruction: Form and Convention in Eighteenth-Century Travel Literature.* Berkeley: University of California Press, 1978.

Baudrillard, Jean. "The Ecstasy of Communication." In *The Anti-Aesthetic:*

Essays on Postmodern Culture, edited by Hal Foster. Port Townsend, Wash.: Bay Press, 1983.

———. "Gesture and Signature: Semiurgy in Contemporary Art." In *For a Critique of the Political Economy of the Sign,* translated by Charles Levin. St. Louis: Telos Press, 1981.

———. *Le Système des objets.* Paris: Gallimard, 1968.

———. "What Are You Doing After the Orgy?" *Artforum* 22 (October 1983): 43–46.

Beckford, William. *Dreams, Waking Thoughts and Incidents.* Edited by Robert J. Gemmett. Rutherford, N.J.: Fairleigh Dickinson University Press, 1971.

Ben-Amos, Dan, ed. *Folklore Genres.* Austin: University of Texas Press, 1976.

Bernheimer, Charles, and Claire Kahane, eds. *In Dora's Case: Freud— Hysteria—Feminism.* New York: Columbia University Press, 1985.

Bersani, Leo. *A Future for Astynax: Character and Desire in Literature.* New York: Columbia University Press, 1984.

Birrell, Augustine. *Seven Lectures on the Law and History of Copyright in Books.* London: Cassell, 1899.

Blagden, Cyprian. *The Stationers' Company: A History, 1403–1959.* Cambridge, Mass.: Harvard University Press, 1960.

Bleiler, E. F., ed. *Three Gothic Novels.* New York: Dover, 1966.

Boas, George. *Vox Populi: Essays in the History of an Idea.* Baltimore: Johns Hopkins University Press, 1969.

Bold, Alan. *The Ballad.* London: Methuen, 1979.

Boswell, James. *Boswell's Life of Johnson.* 6 vols. Edited by George Birbeck Hill and L. F. Powell. Oxford: Clarendon Press, 1934. Appendix A, "George Psalmanazar" (vol. 3, pp. 443–49), by G. B. Hill.

———. *The Life of Samuel Johnson.* 4 vols. New York: John W. Lovell, 1884.

Bourdieu, Pierre. *Distinction: A Social Critique of the Judgement of Taste.* Translated by Richard Nice. Cambridge, Mass.: Harvard University Press, 1984.

Bowra, C. M. *From Virgil to Milton.* London: Macmillan, 1948.

Boys, Richard C. *Sir Richard Blackmore and the Wits.* New York: Octagon Books, 1969.

Brodtkorb, Paul. "Art Allegory in *The Marble Faun.*" *PMLA* 77 (June 1962): 254–67.

Bronson, Bertrand. *Facets of the Enlightenment: Studies in English Literature and Its Contexts.* Berkeley: University of California Press, 1968.

———. "The Writer." In *Man Versus Society in 18th Century Britain,* edited by James L. Clifford. Cambridge: Cambridge University Press, 1968.

Bruford, Alan. " 'Deirdire' and Alexander Carmichael's Treatment of Oral Sources." *Scottish Gaelic Studies* 14, part 1 (1983): 1–24.

Brumbaugh, Thomas. "Concerning Nathaniel Hawthorne and Art as Magic." *American Imago* 11 (1954): 399–405.

Bunn, James H. "The Aesthetics of British Mercantilism." *New Literary History* 11 (1980): 303–21.

Bunyan, John. *A Book for Boys and Girls; or Country Rhymes for Children.* Edited by E. S. Buchanan. 1686. Reprint. New York: American Tract Society, 1928. (After 1701, recast as *Divine Emblems for Children*)

———. *Holy War.* Philadelphia: Presbyterian Board of Publication, 1803.

Butor, Michael. "Travel and Writing." *Mosaic* 8 (1974): 1–16.

Castleman, Craig. *Getting Up: Subway Graffiti in New York.* Cambridge, Mass.: MIT Press, 1982.

Chambers, Edmund K. *The History and Motives of Literary Forgeries.* 1891. Reprint. New York: Burt Franklin, 1970.

Chambers, Robert. *The Popular Rhymes of Scotland, Chiefly Collected from Oral Sources.* Edinburgh: William Hunter, 1826.

———. *The Romantic Scottish Ballads: Their Epoch and Authorship.* 1849. Reprint. Folcroft, Pa.: Folcroft Press, 1969.

Chatterton, Thomas. *The Complete Works of Thomas Chatterton.* 2 vols. Edited by Donald S. Taylor with Benjamin B. Hoover. Oxford: Clarendon Press, 1971.

Clifford, James. "On Ethnographic Authority." *Representations* 1 (Spring 1983): 118–46.

Clifford, James L. *Young Sam Johnson.* New York: McGraw-Hill, 1955.

Clyne, Norval. *The Romantic Scottish Ballads and the Lady Wardlaw Heresy.* Aberdeen: A. Brown, 1859.

Cohen, Ralph. "On the Interrelations of Eighteenth-Century Literary Forms." In *New Approaches to Eighteenth-Century Literature*, edited by Phillip Harth. New York: Columbia University Press, 1974.

Colie, Rosalie. *The Resources of Kind: Genre Theory in the Renaissance.* Edited by Barbara Lewalski. Berkeley: University of California Press, 1973.

Colimore, Edward. "Vandals Fire Back in Graffiti War." *Philadelphia Inquirer*, 25 January 1984, p. B-2.

Collin, Rita K. "Hawthorne and the Anxiety of Aesthetic Response." *The Centennial Review* 4 (Fall 1984): 28–29, 94–104.

Collins, A. S. *Authorship in the Days of Johnson: Being a Study of the Relations Between Author, Patron, Publisher and Public, 1726–1780.* 1927. Reprint. Clifton, N.J.: Augustus M. Kelley Publishers, 1973.

Constable, Giles. "Forgery and Plagiarism in the Middle Ages." *Archiv für Diplomatik, Schriftgeschichte, Siegel-und Wappenkunde* 29 (1983): 1–41.

Cooper, James Fenimore. *Excursions in Italy*. 2 vols. London: Richard Bentley, 1838.

———. *Gleanings in Europe, Italy*. Edited by John Conron and Constance Ayers Denne. Albany: State University of New York Press, 1981.

Cooper, Martha, and Henry Chalfant. *Subway Art*. New York: Holt, Rinehart and Winston, 1984.

Cottom, Daniel. *The Civilized Imagination: A Study of Ann Radcliffe, Jane Austen, and Sir Walter Scott*. Cambridge: Cambridge University Press, 1985.

Crews, Frederick. *The Sins of the Fathers*. London: Oxford University Press, 1966.

Cummings, Edith. "The Literary Development of the Romantic Fairy Tale in France." Ph.D. diss., Bryn Mawr College, 1934.

Curley, Thomas M. *Samuel Johnson and the Age of Travel*. Athens: University of Georgia Press, 1976.

D'Aulnoy, Madame [Marie-Catherine J. De Barneville]. *Histoire d'Hippolyte*. Paris: Sevestre, 1690.

Davies, Edward. *The Claims of Ossian, Examined and Appreciated*. London: Longman, 1825.

Davis, Bertram. *Thomas Percy: A Scholar-Cleric in the Age of Johnson*. Philadelphia: University of Pennsylvania Press, 1989.

De Certeau, Michel. *Heterologies: Discourse on the Other*. Translated by Brian Massumi. Minneapolis: University of Minnesota Press, 1986.

DeJean, Joan. *Literary Fortifications*. Princeton, N.J.: Princeton University Press, 1984.

De Man, Paul. "The Rhetoric of Temporality." In *Interpretation: Theory and Practice*, edited by Charles Singleton. Baltimore: Johns Hopkins University Press, 1969.

De Quincey, Thomas. *A Selection of the Best Works*. 2 vols. Edited by W. H. Bennett. London: David Stott, 1890.

Derrida, Jacques. *Edmund Husserl's Origin of Geometry: An Introduction*. Translated by John P. Leavey, edited by David B. Allison. Stony Brook, N.Y.: Nicolas Hays, 1978.

———. *Glas*. Paris: Editions Galilée, 1974.

———. *Of Grammatology*. Translated by Gayatri Chakravorty Spivak. Baltimore: Johns Hopkins University Press, 1976.

———. "The Pit and the Pyramid: Introduction to Hegel's Semiology." In *Margins of Philosophy*, translated by Alan Bass. Chicago: University of Chicago Press, 1982.

———. *Writing and Difference*. Translated by Alan Bass. Chicago: University of Chicago Press, 1978.

de Ventós, Xavier Rubert. *Heresies of Modern Art*. Translated by J. S. Bernstein. New York: Columbia University Press, 1980.

Dickerson, Reed. *The Fundamentals of Legal Drafting*. Boston: Little, Brown, 1965.

D'Israeli, [Isaac]. *Curiosities of Literature*. 3 vols. Paris: Baudry's European Library, 1835.

Dolis, John. "Hawthorne's Metonymic Gaze: Image and Object." *American Literature* 56 (October 1984): 362–78.

Dorr, David F. *A Coloured Man Around the World: By a Quadroon*. Cleveland: the author, 1858.

Dorson, Richard M. *Folklore and Fakelore*. Cambridge, Mass.: Harvard University Press, 1976.

Douglas, Mary. *Purity and Danger*. London: Routledge & Kegan Paul, 1966.

Dundes, Alan. *Folklore Matters*. Knoxville: University of Tennessee Press, 1989.

Durkheim, Emile. *Incest, the Nature and Origin of the Taboo*. Translated by Edward Sagarin. New York: Lyle Stuart, 1963.

———. *Montesquieu and Rousseau: Forerunners of Sociology*. Translated by Ralph Manheim, foreword by Henri Peyre. Ann Arbor: University of Michigan Press, 1965.

Eagleton, Terry. *The Function of Criticism: From "The Spectator" to Post-Structuralism*. London: Verso, 1984.

Edinburgh. Painted by John Fulleylove. Described by Rosalind Masson. London: Adam and Charles Black, 1907.

Eisenstein, Elizabeth. *The Printing Press as an Agent of Change: Communications and Cultural Transformation in Early-Modern Europe*. 2 vols. Cambridge: Cambridge University Press, 1979.

Ellinger, Esther Park. *Thomas Chatterton, The Marvelous Boy to which is added The Exhibition, a Personal Satire*. Philadelphia: University of Pennsylvania Press, 1930.

Empson, William. *Some Versions of Pastoral*. New York: New Directions, 1974.

Erlich, Gloria C. *Family Themes and Hawthorne's Fiction: The Tenacious Web*. New Brunswick, N.J.: Rutgers University Press, 1984.

Even-Zohar, Itamar. *Papers in Historical Poetics*. Tel Aviv: Porter Institute for Poetics and Semiotics, 1978.

Farrer, J. A. *Literary Forgeries*. 1907. Reprint. Detroit: Gale Research, 1969.

Field, Henry. *Camel Brands and Graffiti from Iraq, Syria, Jordan, Iran, and Arabia*. Baltimore: American Oriental Society, 1952.

Fish, Stanley. "Critical Legal Studies, Unger, and Milton." *Raritan* (Fall 1988): 1–20.

———. "Critical Legal Studies (II), Roberto Unger's 'Transformative Politics.' " *Raritan* 7 (Winter 1988): 1–24.

———. *Doing What Comes Naturally: Change, Rhetoric, and the Practice of Theory in Literary and Legal Studies*. Durham, N.C.: Duke University Press, 1989.

Flexner, James Thomas. *The Light of Distant Skies: History of American Painting, 1760–1835*. New York: Dover, 1954.

Forsythe, R. S. "Modern Imitations of the Popular Ballad." *Journal of English and Germanic Philology* 13 (1914): 88–97.

Fortescue, J. W. *A History of the British Army*. 13 vols. London: Macmillan, 1879.

Foss, Michael. *The Age of Patronage: The Arts in England, 1660–1750*. Ithaca, N.Y.: Cornell University Press, 1971.

Foucault, Michel. *Discipline and Punish: The Birth of the Prison*. Translated by Alan Sheridan. New York: Vintage Books, 1979.

———. *The History of Sexuality*. Vol. 1: *An Introduction*. Translated by Robert Hurley. New York: Vintage Books, 1980.

———. *The Order of Things: An Archaeology of the Human Sciences*. New York: Pantheon Books, 1970.

———. "What Is an Author?" In *Textual Strategies*, edited by Josué Harari. Ithaca, N.Y.: Cornell University Press, 1979.

Fox, William S. "Folklore and Fakelore: Some Sociological Considerations." *Journal of the Folklore Institute* 17 (1980): 244–61.

Freud, Sigmund. "Hysterical Phantasies and Their Relation to Bisexuality" (1908). In *Dora: An Analysis of a Case of Hysteria*, translated by Douglas Bryan, edited by Philip Rieff. New York: Collier Books, 1963.

———. *Inhibitions, Symptoms and Anxiety* (1926). Translated by Alix Strachey, edited by James Strachey. New York: Norton, 1959.

———. "Notes upon a Case of Obsessional Neurosis" (1909). In *Standard Edition of the Complete Psychological Works of Sigmund Freud*, translated and edited by James Strachey. Vol. 10. 1955. Reprint. London: Hogarth Press, 1975.

———. "The Paths to Symptom Formation" (1917). In *Introductory Lectures in Psychoanalysis*, translated and edited by James Strachey. New York: Norton, 1977.

———. "The Relation of the Poet to Day-dreaming" (1908). In *Character and Culture*, translated by I. F. Grant Duff, edited by Philip Rieff. New York: Collier Books, 1963.

Fried, Michael. *Realism, Writing, Disfiguration: On Thomas Eakins and Stephen Crane*. Chicago: University of Chicago Press, 1987.

Gallop, Jane. *The Daughter's Seduction: Feminism and Psychoanalysis*. Ithaca, N.Y.: Cornell University Press, 1982.

Gardiner, S. R., ed. *The Constitutional Documents of the Puritan Revolution*. 2nd ed. Oxford: Clarendon Press, 1899.

Geddie, John. *The Balladists*. Edinburgh: Oliphant, Anderson and Ferrier, 1896.

Giamatti, A. Bartlett. *The Play of Double Senses: Spenser's Faerie Queen*. Englewood Cliffs, N.J.: Prentice-Hall, 1975.

Gibbon, Edward. *Memoirs of My Life*. Edited by Georges A. Bonnard. London: Thomas Nelson, 1966.

Giles, Dennis. "Pornographic Space: The Other Place." In *Film: Historical–Theoretical Speculations*. The 1977 Film Studies Annual, part 2. Pleasantville, N.Y.: Redgrave, 1977.

Gilpin, William. "On Picturesque Travel" (1792). In *Eighteenth Century Critical Essays*, edited by Scott Elledge. 2 vols. Ithaca, N.Y.: Cornell University Press, 1961.

Glover, Richard. *Leonidas*. 1814. Reprint. Baltimore: Neal, Wills and Coles, n.d.

Goethe, Johann Wolfgang von. *Italian Journey*. Translated by W. H. Auden and Elizabeth Mayer. 1962. Reprint. San Francisco: North Point Press, 1982.

Goetz, William. "Genealogy and Incest in *Wuthering Heights*." *Studies in the Novel* 14 (Winter 1982): 359–76.

Goffman, Erving. "On the Characteristics of Total Institutions." In *Asylums: Essays on the Social Situation of Mental Patients and Other Inmates*. Garden City, N.Y.: Anchor Books, 1961.

Goldstein, Laurence. *Ruins and Empire: The Evolution of a Theme in Augustan and Romantic Literature*. Pittsburgh: University of Pittsburgh Press, 1977.

Goodrich, Lloyd. *Thomas Eakins*. Cambridge, Mass.: Harvard University Press, for the National Gallery of Art, 1982.

Goody, Jack. "A Comparative Approach to Incest and Adultery." In *Marriage, Family and Residence*, edited by Paul Bohannan and John Middleton. Garden City, N.Y.: Natural History Press, 1968.

Gossen, Gary. "Chamula Genres of Verbal Behavior." *Journal of American Folklore* 84 (1971): 145–67.

Grafton, Anthony. *Forgers and Critics: Creativity and Duplicity in Western Scholarship*. Princeton, N.J.: Princeton University Press, 1990.

Greenacre, Phyllis. "The Impostor." *Psychoanalytic Quarterly* 27 (1958): 359–82.

Grider, Sylvia Ann. "Con Safos: Mexican-Americans, Names and Graffiti." In *Readings in American Folklore*, edited by Jan Harold Brunvand. New York: Norton, 1979.

Guerazzi, Francesco. *Beatrice Cenci*. Translated by Luigi Monti. London: National Alumni, 1906.

Hagin, Peter. *The Epic Hero and the Decline of Heroic Poetry: A Study of the*

Neoclassical English Epic with Special Reference to Milton's "Paradise Lost." Bern: Francke Verlag, 1964. New York: Folcroft Press, 1970.

Harari, Josué. *Scenarios of the Imaginary: Theorizing the French Enlightenment.* Ithaca, N.Y.: Cornell University Press, 1987.

Hart, Walter Morris. *Ballad and Epic: A Study in the Development of the Narrative Art.* 1907. Reprint. New York: Russell and Russell, 1967.

Hawkins, Sir John. *The Life of Samuel Johnson, LL.D.* Edited by Bertram Davis. New York: Macmillan, 1961.

Hawthorne, Nathaniel. Centenary Edition of the Works of Nathaniel Hawthorne. Vol. 14: *The French and Italian Notebooks.* Edited by Thomas Woodson. Columbus: Ohio State University Press, 1980.

———. *Hawthorne's Short Stories.* Edited by Newton Arvin. New York: Knopf, 1961.

———. *The Marble Faun, or The Romance of Monte Beni.* New York: Penguin Books, 1961.

Haywood, Ian. *Faking It: Art and the Politics of Forgery.* New York: St. Martin's Press, 1987.

———. *The Making of History: A Study of the Literary Forgeries of James Macpherson and Thomas Chatterton in Relation to Eighteenth-Century Ideas of History and Fiction.* Rutherford, N.J.: Fairleigh Dickinson University Press, 1986.

Hegel, G. W. F. *Phenomenology of Spirit.* Translated by A. V. Miller. Oxford: Clarendon Press, 1977.

———. *The Philosophy of Fine Art.* 4 vols. Translated by F. P. B. Osmaston. London: Bell, 1920.

Hertz, Neil. *The End of the Line: Essays on Psychoanalysis and the Sublime.* New York: Columbia University Press, 1985.

———. "The Notion of Blockage in the Literature of the Sublime." In *Psychoanalysis and the Question of the Text: Selected Papers from the English Institute, 1976–1977,* edited by Geoffrey Hartman. Baltimore: Johns Hopkins University Press, 1978.

Hill, Christopher. *The Century of Revolution, 1603–1714.* London: Sphere, 1969.

Hind, Arthur M. *Giovanni Battista Piranesi: A Critical Study.* 1922. Reprint. London: Holland Press, 1978.

Hobbes, Thomas. *Leviathan.* Buffalo, N.Y.: Prometheus Books, 1988.

Hobsbawm, Eric, and Terence Ranger, eds. *The Invention of Tradition.* Cambridge: Cambridge University Press, 1983.

Hoeveler, Diane Long. "La Cenci: The Incest Motif in Hawthorne and Melville." *American Transcendental Quarterly* 44 (1979): 247–59.

Hogg, James. *Domestic Manners of Sir Walter Scott.* Stirling: Eneas Mackay, 1909.

Howe, Susan. *A Bibliography of the King's Book or, Eikon Basilike*. Providence: Paradigm Press, 1989.

Hugo, Victor. *Notre-Dame de Paris*. 2 vols. Paris: Librairie de L. Hachette, 1869.

Husserl, Edmund. "The Origin of Geometry." In Jacques Derrida, *Edmund Husserl's Origin of Geometry: An Introduction*, translated by John P. Leavey, edited by David B. Allison. Stony Brook, N.Y.: Nicolas Hays, 1978.

Hustvedt, Sigurd B. *Ballad Books and Ballad Men*. Cambridge, Mass.: Harvard University Press, 1930.

———. *Ballad Criticism in Scandinavia and Great Britain During the 18th Century*. New York: American-Scandinavian Foundation, 1916.

Huxley, Aldous. "Variations on *The Prisons*." In *Themes and Variations*. London: Chatto and Windus, 1954.

Irving, Washington [Geoffrey Crayon, pseud.]. *Tales of a Traveller*. Philadelphia: Carey and Lea, 1837.

Irwin, John T. *Doubling and Incest/Repetition and Revenge: A Speculative Reading of Faulkner*. Baltimore: Johns Hopkins University Press, 1975.

James, Alice. *The Diary of Alice James*. Edited by Leon Edel. New York: Dodd, Mead, 1964.

Jameson, Fredric. "Postmodernism and Consumer Society." In *The Anti-Aesthetic: Essays on Postmodern Culture*, edited by Hal Foster. Port Townsend, Wash.: Bay Press, 1983.

———. "Postmodernism, or the Cultural Logic of Late Capitalism." *New Left Review* 146 (1984): 53–92.

Johnson, Samuel. "Fable of the Vultures." *The Idler*, no. 22, September 1758.

Jones, Mark, ed. *Fake? The Art of Deception*. Berkeley: University of California Press, 1990.

Judovitz, Dalia. " 'Sex,' Or, the Misfortunes of Literature." In *Sade Without Measure*, edited by D. Allison, M. Roberts, and A. Weiss. New York: Cambridge University Press, 1991.

Kaplan, Benjamin. *An Unhurried View of Copyright*. New York: Columbia University Press, 1967.

Kaplan, Louise. *The Family Romance of the Impostor-Poet Thomas Chatterton*. Berkeley: University of California Press, 1987.

Kendrick, Walter. *The Secret Museum: Pornography in Modern Culture*. New York: Viking Press, 1987.

Kenyon, Nicholas, ed. *Authenticity and Early Music*. New York: Oxford University Press, 1990.

Kernan, Alvin. *Printing Technology, Letters and Samuel Johnson*. Princeton, N.J.: Princeton University Press, 1987.

Kierkegaard, Søren. *The Concept of Anxiety: A Simple Psychologically Orienting Deliberation on the Dogmatic Issue of Hereditary Sin.* Edited and translated by Reidar Thomte with Albert Anderson. Princeton, N.J.: Princeton University Press, 1980.

Kleiner, Juliusz. "The Role of Time in Literary Genres." *Zagadienia rodzajow literackich (Les Problèmes des genres littéraires)* 2 (1959): 5–12.

Kolson, Ann. "Subways Were Her Canvases, a Spray Can Her Brush." *Philadelphia Inquirer,* 13 April 1984, p. E-1.

Korshin, Paul. "Types of Eighteenth-Century Patronage." *Eighteenth-Century Studies* 7 (1973–74): 453–73.

Kready, Laura F. *A Study of Fairy Tales.* Boston: Houghton Mifflin, 1916.

Kurlansky, Mervyn, and Jon Naar. *The Faith of Graffiti.* Essay by Norman Mailer. New York: Praeger, 1973.

Kurz, Otto. *Fakes: A Handbook for Collectors and Students.* New York: Dover, 1967.

Lacan, Jacques. *The Four Fundamental Concepts of Psycho-Analysis.* Translated by Alan Sheridan, edited by Jacques-Alain Miller. New York: Norton, 1981.

Lach, Donald. *Asia in the Making of Europe.* Vol. 2, book 1: *The Visual Arts.* Chicago: University of Chicago Press, 1970.

———. *Asia in the Making of Europe.* Vol. 2, book 2: *The Literary Arts.* Chicago: University of Chicago Press, 1977.

Lacoue-Labarthe, Philippe, and Jean-Luc Nancy. *The Literary Absolute: The Theory of Literature in German Romanticism.* Translated by Philip Barnard and Cheryl Lester. Albany: State University of New York Press, 1988.

Laplanche, Jean. *Life and Death in Psychoanalysis.* Translated by Jeffrey Mehlman. Baltimore: Johns Hopkins University Press, 1976.

Laplanche, Jean, and J.-B. Pontalis. *The Language of Psycho-analysis.* Translated by Donald Nicholson-Smith. London: Hogarth Press, 1973.

Leach, Edmund. "Anthropological Aspects of Language: Animal Categories and Verbal Abuse." In *Reader in Comparative Religion,* edited by William Lessa and Evon Vogt. New York: Harper & Row, 1972.

Leach, MacEdward. *The Ballad Book.* New York: Barnes, 1955.

Leach, MacEdward, and Tristram P. Coffin, eds. *The Critic and the Ballad.* Carbondale: Southern Illinois University Press, 1961.

Lee, Sidney. "George Psalmanazar." *Dictionary of National Biography.* Vol. 16. London: Oxford University Press, 1917.

Lefebvre, Henri. *The Survival of Capitalism: Reproduction of the Relations of Production.* Translated by Frank Bryant. New York: St. Martin's Press, 1976.

Lerner, Max, and Edwin Mims, Jr. "Literature." *Encyclopedia of the Social Sciences*. Vol. 9. New York: Macmillan, 1933.

Levinson, Marjorie. *Keats's Life of Allegory: The Origins of a Style*. Oxford: Basil Blackwell, 1988.

——. *The Romantic Fragment Poem: A Critique of a Form*. Chapel Hill: University of North Carolina Press, 1986.

Lévi-Strauss, Claude. *The Elementary Structures of Kinship*. Translated by James Harle Bell, John Richard von Struner, and Rodney Needham. Boston: Beacon Press, 1969.

Lindey, Alexander. *Plagiarism and Originality*. New York: Harper, 1952.

Lloyd, A. L. *Folk Song in England*. New York: International Publishers, 1967.

Locke, John. *An Essay Concerning Human Understanding*. 2 vols. New York: Dover, 1959.

——. *Two Treatises of Government*. Edited by Peter Laslett. Cambridge: Cambridge University Press, 1960.

Lockwood, Allison. *Passionate Pilgrims: The American Traveler in Great Britain, 1800–1914*. Rutherford, N.J.: Fairleigh Dickinson University Press, 1981.

McCaffrey, Anne. *Dragonsinger*. New York: Bantam Books, 1977.

MacDonald, William L. *Piranesi's "Carceri": Sources of Invention*. Katherine Asher Engel Lectures of 1978. Northampton, Mass.: Smith College, 1979.

Mackay, Agnes E. *La Fontaine and His Friends: A Biography*. New York: Braziller, 1973.

Mackey, Carol Hanberry. "Hawthorne, Sophia, and Hilda as Copyists: Duplication and Transformation in *The Marble Faun*." *Browning Institute Studies* 12 (1984): 93–120.

Macpherson, James. *The Poems of Ossian. With an Essay in which they are Authenticated, Illustrated and Explained by Hugh Campbell*. 2 vols. London: Sir Richard Phillips, 1822.

Mallon, Thomas. *Stolen Words: Forays into the Origins and Ravages of Plagiarism*. New York: Ticknor and Fields, 1989.

Manwaring, Elizabeth Wheeler. *Italian Landscape in Eighteenth Century England: A Study Chiefly of the Influence of Claude Lorrain and Salvator Rosa on English Taste, 1700–1800*. New York: Russell and Russell, 1965.

Marmer, Nancy. "Pop Art in California." In *Pop Art*, edited by Lucy Lippard. New York: Praeger, 1966.

Marx, Karl. *The German Ideology*. In *Marx, Engels, on Literature and Art*, edited by Lee Baxandall and Stefan Morawski. New York: International General, 1977.

Masson, David. "Lady Wardlaw and the Baroness Nairne." In *Edinburgh Sketches and Memoirs*. London: A. and C. Black, 1892.

Mawdsley, Ralph D. *Legal Aspects of Plagiarism.* Topeka, Kans.: National Organization on Legal Problems in Education, 1985.

Merchant, Paul. *The Epic.* London: Methuen, 1971.

Meyerstein, E. H. W. *A Life of Thomas Chatterton.* New York: Scribner, 1930.

Miller, D. A. *"Cage aux folles:* Sensation and Gender in Wilkie Collins's *The Woman in White." Representations* 14 (Spring 1986): 107–36.

Mitchell, Juliet. "Introduction—I." In Jacques Lacan, *Feminine Sexuality,* edited by Juliet Mitchell and Jacqueline Rose, translated by Jacqueline Rose. New York: Norton, 1982.

Monro, Isabel Stevenson, and Kate M. Monro. *Index to Reproductions of European Paintings.* New York: Wilson, 1956.

Moore, Edward. *Fables for the Female Sex.* 3rd ed. London: J. Listee, 1766.

Nairne, Lady [Carolina Oliphant]. Lady Nairne Collection. National Library of Scotland #980–986 (Nairne correspondence, 1763–1873).

Needham, Rodney. *Exemplars.* Berkeley: University of California Press, 1985.

Noel, Thomas. *Theories of the Fable in the Eighteenth Century.* New York: Columbia University Press, 1975.

Osborn, Albert S. *Questioned Documents.* Rochester, N.Y.: Lawyer's Cooperative Publishing Co., 1916.

Pagden, Anthony. *The Fall of Natural Man: The American Indian and the Origins of Comparative Ethnology.* Cambridge: Cambridge University Press, 1982.

Palmer, Robert. "Street Smart Rapping Is Innovative Art Form." *New York Times,* 4 February 1985, p. C-13.

Parks, George B. *The English Traveler to Italy.* Vol. 1: *The Middle Ages to 1525.* Stanford, Calif.: Stanford University Press, 1954.

Patterson, Lyman Ray. *Copyright in Historical Perspective.* Nashville, Tenn.: Vanderbilt University Press, 1968.

Peale, Rembrandt. *Graphics: A Manual of Drawing and Writing for the Use of Schools and Families.* New York: J. P. Peaslee, 1835.

———. *Notes on Italy, Written During a Tour in the Years 1829–1830.* Philadelphia: Carey and Lea, 1831.

Pepper, Simon, and Nicholas Adams. *Firearms and Fortifications: Military Architecture and Siege Warfare in Sixteenth-Century Siena.* Chicago: University of Chicago Press, 1986.

Percy, Thomas. *Bishop Percy's Folio Ms. Ballads and Romances.* 3 vols. Edited by John W. Hales and Frederick Furnivall. London: N. Trubner, 1868.

———. "An Essay on the Ancient Minstrels in England." In *Reliques of Ancient English Poetry.* With memoir and critical dissertation by

G. Gilfillan. 3 vols. Edited by Charles Cowden Clarke. 1794. Reprint. Edinburgh: William P. Nimmo, 1869.

———. *Reliques of Ancient English Poetry.* Edited by Edward Walford. 1794. Reprint. London: Frederick Warne, 1880.

Percy–Hailes Correspondence. British Library #32,331 (1762–83).

Percy Literary Correspondence. British Library #32,329 (1762–80).

Percy–Warton Correspondence. British Library #42560 (1761–70).

Perry, B. E. "Fable." *Stadium Generale* 12 (1959): 17–37.

Piozzi, Hester Lynch. *Dr. Johnson by Mrs. Thrale: The "Anecdotes" of Mrs. Piozzi in Their Original Form.* Edited by R. Ingrams. London: Chatto and Windus, the Hogarth Press, 1984.

Piranesi, Giovanni Battista. *Le carceri: Giovan Battista Piranesi.* Edited by Mario Praz. Milan: Bilioteca Universals Rizzoli, 1975.

———. *Piranesi: Drawings and Etchings at the Avery Architectural Library, Columbia University.* New York: Arthur M. Sackler Foundation, 1975.

———. *Piranesi: Etchings and Drawings.* Introduction by Roseline Bacon. Boston: New York Graphic Society, 1975.

———. *Piranesi: The Imaginary Views.* Edited by Miranda Harvey. New York: Crown, 1979.

———. *The Prisons (Le Carceri) by Giovanni Battista Piranesi: The Complete First and Second States.* Introduction by Philip Hofer. New York: Dover, 1973.

Pitkin, Hanna. *The Concept of Representation.* Berkeley: University of California Press, 1972.

Plato. *Memo: The Immortality of the Soul.* In *The Works of Plato,* translated by Benjamin Jowett. 4 vols. New York: Tudor, n.d.

———. *Phaedrus.* In *The Works of Plato,* translated by B. Jowett. 4 vols. New York: Tudor, n.d.

Posner, Richard. *Law and Literature: A Misunderstood Relation.* Cambridge, Mass.: Harvard University Press, 1988.

Post-Graffiti. New York: Sidney Janis Gallery, 1983.

Pound, Roscoe. *An Introduction to the Philosophy of Law.* New Haven, Conn.: Yale University Press, 1961.

Prager, F. D. "The Early Growth and Influence of Intellectual Property." *Journal of the Patent Office Society* 34 (February 1952): 106–40.

———. "A History of Intellectual Property from 1545 to 1787." *Journal of the Patent Office Society* 26 (November 1944): 711–60.

Pratt, Mary Louise. "Fieldwork in Common Places." In *Writing Culture: The Poetics and Politics of Ethnography,* edited by James Clifford and George E. Marcus. Berkeley: University of California Press, 1986.

Preziosi, Donald. *Architecture, Language, and Meaning.* The Hague: Mouton, 1979.

Prince, Dinah. "The New Chic in Decorating? Graffiti in the Home." *Philadelphia Inquirer*, 23 December 1982, p. 3-D.

Pritchard, Earl. *Anglo-Chinese Relations During the Seventeenth and Eighteenth Centuries*. New York: Octagon Books, 1970.

Pritchard, Violet. *English Medieval Graffiti*. Cambridge: Cambridge University Press, 1967.

Psalmanazar, George [pseud.]. *An Historical and Geographical Description of Formosa, an Island Subject to the Emperor of Japan. Giving an Account of the Religion, Customs, Manners &c. of the Inhabitants. Together with a Relation of what happen'd to the Author in his Travels; particularly his Conferences with the Jesuits, and others, in several parts of Europe. Also the History and Reasons of his Conversion to Christianity, with his Objections against it (in defense of Paganism) and their Answers. To which is prefix'd, A Preface in vindication of himself from the Reflections of a Jesuit lately come from China. With an account of what passed between them.* London: Printed for Dan. Brown, at the Black Swan without Temple Bar; G. Strahan, and W. Davis, in Cornhill; and Fran. Coggan, in the Inner-Temple Lane, 1704.

———. *The Second Edition corrected, with many large and useful Additions, particularly a new Preface clearly answering every thing that has been objected against the Author and the Book. Illustrated with several cuts To which are added, A Map, and the Figure of an Idol not in the former Edition.* London: Mat. Wotten, Abel Roper, and B. Lintott in Fleetstreet; Fr. Coggan in the Inner-Temple Lane; G. Strahan and W. Davis in Cornhill, 1705.

———. "The History of the Jews." In *An Universal History, from the Earliest Account of Time to the Present: Compiled from Original Authors; and Illustrated with Maps, Cuts, Notes, Chronological and Other Tables.* 2nd ed. 7 vols. London: S. Richardson, T. Osborne, J. Osborn, A. Millar, and J. Hinton, 1738–44.

———. *Memoirs of ****, Commonly Known by the Name of George Psalmanazar; A Reputed Native of Formosa. Written by himself. In order to be published after his Death: Containing An Account of His Education, Travels, Adventures, Connections, Literary Productions, and pretended Conversion from Heathenism to Christianity; which last proved the Occasion of his being brought over into this Kingdom, and passing for a Proselyte and a Member of the Church of England.* 2nd ed. London: R. Davis, 1765.

Putnam, George Haven. *The Question of Copyright*. New York: Putnam, 1891.

Rabinow, Paul. "Representations Are Social Facts." In *Writing Culture: The Poetics and Politics of Ethnography*, edited by James Clifford and George E. Marcus. Berkeley: University of California Press, 1986.

Ralph, James. *The Case of Authors by Profession or Trade (1758) together with*

The Champion (1739–1740). Introduction by Philip Stevick. Gainesville, Fla.: Scholars' Facsimiles and Reprints, 1966.

Ramsay, Allan, ed. *The Ever Green: A Collection of Scots Poems. Wrote by the
Ingenious before 1600.* 2 vols. 1724. Reprint. Glasgow: Robert Forrester, 1876.

————, ed. *Tea-Table Miscellany: A Collection of Choice Song Scots and English.*
2 vols. Reprinted from the 14th ed. Glasgow: Robert Forrester, 1876.

Ranzal, Edward. "Ronan Backs Lindsay Anti-Graffiti Plan." *New York
Times,* 29 August 1972, p. 66.

Ricci, Corrado. *Beatrice Cenci.* Translated by Morris Bishop and Henry Longan Stuart. New York: Boni and Liveright, 1925.

Richter, David. *Fable's End: Completeness and Closure in Rhetorical Fiction.*
Chicago: University of Chicago Press, 1974.

Rivière, Pierre. *I, Pierre Rivière, having slaughtered my mother, my sister, and
my brother . . . A Case of Parricide in the 19th Century.* Edited by Michel
Foucault, translated by Frank Jellinek. New York: Pantheon Books,
1975.

Rölleke, Heinz. "The 'Utterly Hessian' Fairy Tales by 'Old Marie': The
End of a Myth." Translated by Ruth Bottigheimer. In *Fairy Tales
and Society: Illusion, Allusion and Paradigm,* edited by Ruth Bottigheimer. Philadelphia: University of Pennsylvania Press, 1986.

Rose, Mark. "The Author as Proprietor: *Donaldson v. Becket* [*sic*] and the
Genealogy of Modern Authorship." *Representations* 23 (Summer
1988): 51–85.

Rosen, Charles. "The Shock of the Old." Review of *Authenticity and Early
Music. New York Review of Books,* 19 July 1990, pp. 46–52.

Rousseau, Jean-Jacques. *Confessions of Jean-Jacques Rousseau.* New York:
Modern Library, n.d.

Roy, John Flint. *A Guide to Barsoom.* New York: Ballantine Books, 1976.

Sade, Marquis de [Donatien Alphonse Francois Xavier]. *The 120 Days of
Sodom and Other Writings.* Edited and translated by Austryn Wainhouse and Richard Seaver. New York: Grove Press, 1966.

Salas, Floyd. *Tattoo the Wicked Cross.* New York: Grove Press, 1967.

Sambrook, James. *The Eighteenth Century: The Intellectual and Cultural Context
of English Literature, 1700–1789.* London: Longman, 1986.

Sampson, George, ed. *The Concise Cambridge History of English Literature.*
3rd ed. Cambridge: Cambridge University Press, 1970.

Sandell, Sandra. "A Very Poetic Circumstance": Incest and the English
Literary Imagination, 1770–1830." Ph.D. diss., University of Minnesota, 1981.

Saunders, Bailey. *The Life and Letters of James Macpherson.* London: Swan
Sonnenschein, 1894.

Scott, Sir Walter. *The Lay of the Last Minstrel.* New ed. New York: C. S. Francis, 1854.

———. *Minstrelsy of the Scottish Border.* 4 vols. Revised and edited by T. F. Henderson. Edinburgh: Oliver and Boyd, 1932.

Seznec, Jean. *The Survival of the Pagan Gods: The Mythological Tradition and Its Place in Renaissance Humanism and Art.* The Bollingen Foundation. Translated by Barbara F. Sessions. New York: Pantheon Books, 1953.

Shavit, Zohar. *Poetics of Children's Literature.* Athens: University of Georgia Press, 1986.

Shaw, Peter. "Plagiary." *American Scholar* 51 (1982): 325–37.

Silverman, Kaja. "Masochism and Subjectivity." *Framework* 12 (1980): 2–9.

Smith, Barbara Herrnstein. "Contingencies of Value." *Critical Inquiry* 10 (September 1983): 1–35.

———. *Contingencies of Value: Alternative Perspectives for Critical Theory.* Cambridge, Mass.: Harvard University Press, 1988.

Smith, Harold E. *American Travellers Abroad: A Bibliography of Accounts Published Before 1900.* Carbondale: Southern Illinois University Press, 1969.

Smith, William Jay. *The Spectra Hoax.* Middletown, Conn.: Wesleyan University Press, 1961.

Soriano, Marc. *Les Contes de Perrault: culture savante et traditions populaires.* Paris: Gallimard, 1968.

———. *Le Dossier Perrault.* Paris: Hachette, 1972.

Southey, Robert. *The Lives and Works of the Uneducated Poets.* Edited by J. S. Childers. London: Humphrey Milford, 1925.

Spacks, Patricia Meyer, ed. *Eighteenth-Century Poetry.* Englewood Cliffs, N.J.: Prentice-Hall, 1964.

Stafford, Fiona J. *The Sublime Savage: A Study of James Macpherson and the Poems of Ossian.* Edinburgh: Edinburgh University Press, 1988.

Stekert, Ellen. "Cents and Nonsense in the Urban Folksong Movement: 1930–1966." In *Folklore and Society: Essays in Honor of Benjamin Botkin,* edited by Bruce Jackson. Hatboro, Pa.: Folklore Associates, 1966.

Stendahl [Henri Beyle]. *Rome, Naples and Florence.* Translated by Richard N. Coe. New York: Braziller, 1959.

Stephanson, Anders. "Regarding Postmodernism—A Conversation with Fredric Jameson." In *Universal Abandon: The Politics of Postmodernism,* edited by Andrew Ross. Minneapolis: University of Minnesota Press, 1988.

Sterne, Laurence. *Tristram Shandy.* Edited by Howard Anderson. New York: Norton, 1980.

Sussman, Henry. *The Hegelian Aftermath: Readings in Hegel, Kierkegaard, Freud, Proust, and James.* Baltimore: Johns Hopkins University Press, 1982.

———. *High Resolution.* New York: Oxford University Press, 1989.

Swift, Jonathan. *The Drapier's Letters and Other Works, 1724–1725.* Edited by Herbert Davis. Oxford: Basil Blackwell, 1941.

———. *A Modest Proposal for preventing the children of poor people from being a burthen to their parents, or the country, and for making them beneficial to the publick.* Dublin: S. Harding, 1729.

Sypher, Wylie. "Chatterton's African Eclogues and the Deluge." *PMLA* 54 (1939): 246–60.

Tafuri, Manfredo. *The Sphere and the Labyrinth: Avant-Gardes and Architecture from Piranesi to the 1970s.* Translated by Pelligrino d'Acierno and Robert Connolly. Cambridge, Mass.: MIT Press, 1987.

Tanner, J. R. *English Constitutional Conflicts of the Seventeenth Century, 1603–1689.* Cambridge: Cambridge University Press, 1962.

Tanzer, Helen H. *The Common People of Pompeii: A Study of the Graffiti.* Baltimore: Johns Hopkins University Press, 1939.

———. *Graffiti in the Athenian Agora.* Princeton, N.J.: American School of Classical Studies in Athens, 1974.

Taruskin, Richard. "The Spin Doctors of Early Music." *New York Times,* 29 July 1990 sec. 2, p. 1.

Taylor, A. J. W. "Tattooing Among Male and Female Offenders of Different Ages in Different Types of Institutions." *Genetic Psychology Monographs* 81 (1970): 81–119.

Taylor, Archer. *The Literary Riddle Before 1600.* Berkeley: University of California Press, 1948.

———. *The Proverb.* Cambridge, Mass.: Harvard University Press, 1931.

Taylor, Donald. *Thomas Chatterton's Art: Experiments in Imagined History.* Princeton, N.J.: Princeton University Press, 1978.

Thayer, Frank. *Legal Control of the Press.* New York: Foundation Press, 1962.

Thomas, Jean. *Ballad Makin' in the Mountains of Kentucky.* New York: Holt, 1939.

Thompson, Michael. *Rubbish Theory: The Creation and Destruction of Value.* Oxford: Oxford University Press, 1979.

Thomson, Derick S. *The Gaelic Sources of Macpherson's "Ossian."* Edinburgh: Oliver and Boyd, 1952.

Tompkins, Calvin. "The Art World: Up from the I.R.T." *New Yorker,* 26 March 1984, p. 101.

Tuckerman, Henry Theodore. *Isabel: or Sicily, a Pilgrimage.* Philadelphia: Lea and Blanchard, 1839.

Tylor, E. B. "On a Method of Investigating the Development of Institutions, Applied to Laws of Marriage and Descent." *Journal of the Royal Anthropological Institute* 18 (1888): 245–72.

———. *Researches into the Early History of Mankind and the Development of Civilization.* London: T. Murray, 1870.

Unger, Roberto Mangabeira. *The Critical Legal Studies Movement.* Cambridge, Mass.: Harvard University Press, 1983.

Varnedoe, Kirk, and Adam Gopnik. *High and Low: Modern Art and Popular Culture.* New York: Museum of Modern Art, 1990.

Vauban, Marquis de [Sébastien le Prestre]. *Véritable Manière de Fortifier. Où l'on voit de quelle méthode on se sert aujourd'hui en France, pour la fortification des places.* 2 vols. Amsterdam: Jannsons à Waesberge, 1718.

Wales, Nym. *Fables and Parables for Mid-Century.* New York: Philosophical Library, 1952.

Walpole, Horace. *Anecdotes of Painting in England.* 4 vols. 1765. Reprint. New York: Arno Press, 1969. (Reprinted from an 1876 edition at Wesleyan University Library)

———. *The Yale Edition of Horace Walpole's Correspondence.* Vol. 1: *Horace Walpole's Correspondence with the Reverend William Cole, 1762–1775.* Edited by W. S. Lewis and A. Dayle Wallace. New Haven, Conn.: Yale University Press, 1937.

———. *The Yale Edition of Horace Walpole's Correspondence.* Vol. 28: *Horace Walpole's Correspondence with William Mason, 1756–1779.* Edited by W. S. Lewis, Grober Cronin, and Charles Bennett. New Haven, Conn.: Yale University Press, 1955.

Walters, Gwyn. "The Booksellers in 1759 and 1774: The Battle for Literary Property." *Library* 29 (1974): 287–311.

Ward, James, and Robert Kuntz. *Advanced Dungeons and Dragons: Special Reference Work, Deities and Demigods Cyclopedia.* Lake Geneva, Wis.: TSR Games, 1980.

Wardlaw, Lady [Elizabeth Halkett of Pitreavie]. *Lady Wardlaw Papers.* Pitfirrane Collection. National Library of Scotland #6503.

Watkin-Jones, A. "Bishop Percy, Thomas Warton, and Chatterton's Rowley Poems, 1773–1790." *PMLA* 50 (1935): 769–84.

Watt, Ian. *The Rise of the Novel: Studies in Defoe, Richardson, and Fielding.* Berkeley: University of California Press, 1957.

Weber, Samuel. *The Legend of Freud.* Minneapolis: University of Minnesota Press, 1982.

Wesley, Samuel. "Essay on Heroic Poetry." In *Series Two: Essays on Poetry,* no. 2, edited by Edward N. Hooker. Los Angeles: Augustan Reprint Society, 1947.

West, Benjamin. *A Discourse delivered to the Students of the Royal Academy on the Distribution of Prizes, December 10, 1792, by the President.* London: Thomas Podell, 1793.

Wharton, Edith. *Roman Fever and Other Stories.* New York: Scribner, 1964.

Whisnant, David E. *Folk Festival Issue: Report from a Seminar.* JEMF Special Series, no. 12. Los Angeles: John Edwards Memorial Foundation, University of California at Los Angeles, 1977.

White, Harold Ogden. *Plagiarism and Imitation During the English Renaissance. A Study of Critical Distinctions.* Cambridge, Mass.: Harvard University Press, 1935.

Williams, Raymond. "Taste." In *Keywords.* New York: Oxford University Press, 1976.

Wilson, W. Daniel. "Science, Natural Law, and Unwitting Sibling Incest in Eighteenth-Century Literature." *Studies in Eighteenth-Century Culture* 13 (1984): 249–70.

Wilton-Ely, John. *The Mind and Art of Giovanni Battista Piranesi.* London: Thames and Hudson, 1978.

Wincor, Richard. *Literary Property.* New York: Clarkson Potter, 1967.

Winnet, A. R. "George Psalmanazar." *The New Rambler* 110 (Spring 1971): 6–18.

Wittgenstein, Ludwig. *Lectures and Conversations on Aesthetics, Psychology and Religious Belief* [compiled from notes taken by Yorick Smythies, Rush Rhees, and James Taylor]. Edited by Cyril Barrett. Berkeley: University of California Press, 1972.

Woodmansee, Martha. "The Genius and the Copyright: Economic and Legal Conditions of the Emergence of the Author." *Eighteenth-Century Studies* 17 (1984): 425–48.

Young, Edward. "Conjectures on Original Composition." In *A Letter to the Author of Sir Charles Grandison.* 1759. Reprint. Leeds: Scolar Press, 1966.

Young, Philip. *Hawthorne's Secret: An Un-Told Tale.* Boston: Godine, 1984.

Yourcenar, Marguerite. *The Dark Brain of Piranesi and Other Essays.* Translated by Richard Howard. New York: Farrar, Straus & Giroux, 1984.

Zipes, Jack. *Breaking the Magic Spell: Radical Theories of Folk and Fairy Tales.* London: Heinemann, 1979.

———. *Victorian Fairy Tales: The Revolt of the Fairies and Elves.* New York: Methuen, 1987.

Index